AF594029

abstract **art**

THE NEW MEXICO
ARTIST SERIES

STUART ASHMAN
CURATOR

SUZANNE DEATS
ARTIST PROFILES

DEDICATED IN LOVING AND GRATEFUL MEMORY TO ARLENE LEWALLEN, WHOSE CONTRIBUTIONS TO NEW MEXICO'S ART COMMUNITY WERE PROFOUND AND ALL-ENCOMPASSING.

Fresco Fine Art Publications, llc
9812 Nimitz NE, Suite 100
Albuquerque, NM 87111
505 822-0062
fresco@newmexico.com

Stuart Ashman, Curator, Essay
Suzanne Deats, Editor, Artist Profiles
Robert Ewing, Foreword
Design: Nancy Stem

Printed by Sfera International
Milan, Italy

ISBN 0-9741023-1-8
Library of Congress Catalog Card Number: 2003104665

FOREWORD

6 ROBERT EWING

NEW MEXICO ABSTRACT ARTISTS

7 STUART ASHMAN, CURATOR

THE ARTISTS

26 SUZANNE DEATS, PROFILES

26 EUGENE NEWMANN
32 EARL STROH
38 FREDERICK HAMMERSLEY
44 SETH ANDERSON
50 GARO Z. ANTREASIAN
56 RICHARD C SMITH
62 JANET LIPPINCOTT
68 KEN PRICE
74 SAM SCOTT
80 LARRY BELL
86 KEVIN TOLMAN
92 EMMI WHITEHORSE
98 ZACARIAH RIEKE
104 HELMUT LÖHR
110 MICHAEL WRIGHT
116 SALLY ANDERSON
122 BILL BARRETT
128 RICHARD HOGAN
134 JOHNNIE WINONA ROSS
140 FLORENCE PIERCE
146 KAREN YANK
152 ALAN PAINE RADEBAUGH
158 VALDEZ ABEYTA Y VALDEZ
164 CONNIE MISSISSIPPI
170 NANCY KOZIKOWSKI
176 MERCEDES LITTLE CROW VELARDE
182 PASCAL
188 ERNEST WILMETH
194 NANCY ORTENSTONE
200 FRANK ETTENBERG
206 ROBERT KELLY
212 RICARDO MAZAL
218 LINDA J GING
224 TIM KLABUNDE
230 STAN BERNING
236 STEPHANIE DRAGON
242 DERUSHA
248 PETER SARKISIAN

254 INDEX

FOREWORD

The word 'abstract' has two meanings in the art of our time. Originally it meant the simplification of subject matter to its essence as in the work of Picasso and Braque, who created Cubism from sources as varied as the work of Cézanne and what was then called "primitive art." Today "abstract" has come to mean that which is purely non-objective with no reference to realistic sources. Abstraction, as we know it, is the truly innovative art form of the last century, and has become an important style for artists working in New Mexico from the early part of the century.

As with any innovation in the arts it has taken some time for the general public to understand and appreciate the new style. New Mexico has, from the early days of the Taos and Santa Fe art colonies, been in the forefront of American art, and it is inevitable that a style as powerful as abstraction would have many gifted adherents in the state. The artists who originally moved to New Mexico were attracted by the extraordinary subject matter in the land and its people. But many artists who currently work in the state chose to live here out of love for the environment and for the strongly supportive audience for the arts; these find the inspiration for their work from purely introspective sources.

Artists such as Georgia O'Keeffe and Agnes Martin, whose recognition extends far beyond New Mexico, chose to live and work in the state rather than in such urban centers as New York, Chicago and Los Angeles, where abstraction first found its audience. O'Keeffe, who is arguably the most important artist to have lived and worked in New Mexico, utilized abstraction in her work from her earliest charcoal drawings in which she began to develop very unique vision through her "designed realism" responses to the New Mexican landscape. She often did paintings in series, and in a particularly famous one, based on the plant called "Jack in the Pulpit," the paintings progressed from a very realistic rendition to a lyrical abstraction of the element of the plant. The work of many artists now recognized for their abstraction began with a form of realism which then became increasingly abstract. Other artists, such as Agnes Martin, have worked in an abstract style from the beginning. Her earlier works combined abstract shapes in compositions enlivened by her extraordinary color sense. For some years she has investigated a format of stripes with her signature pencil lines containing color-areas painted with her unique technical expertise. Now in her nineties, she pursues her vision of abstraction in an ever surprising body of work.

It has been said that abstraction is the most difficult style in which to make a personal statement, and indeed many would-be artists simply copy the work of the true innovators. However, there will always be unique and gifted artists who find in abstraction the style in which to express their true originality. In New Mexico today there are a number of artists who are exploring new ways to work with realism, even as others are committed to the investigation of the abstract as evidenced by the may examples in this book. We know that the gifted young artists among us will create innovative work which we cannot imagine now, and it is certain that abstraction will remain a major style in the art of this century.

Robert Ewing

NEW MEXICO ABSTRACT ARTISTS

New Mexico has been a rich contributor to modern art in America for over a century. The recent attention directed toward Taos, Santa Fe, and Albuquerque points up the area's long history of abstract art production, as well as its remarkable multicultural legacy. In the current era, perhaps even more than in previous times, it has defined itself as an important art center. Today's robust activity ranges from important public institutions to flourishing art galleries to the artists themselves. Their numbers, variety, and sheer quality have caused their influence to exceed what might be expected from an isolated Southwestern state, yet a closer look at their antecedents reveals a unique and coherent foundation.

For many centuries, New Mexico has been a center of artistic activity and production. In prehistoric times, the Anasazi, ancestors of the Pueblo Indians, created timeless pottery, weavings and crafts. Examples of these objects have survived and are on display in museums and galleries in the area, providing a look at the way their traditions have evolved through the years. The first famous native American artist was Nampeyo, a Hopi potter who revived the ancient, highly geometric Sikyatki patterns of her people and reestablished the link between contemporary work and its cultural ancestry. In more recent years potters like Maria Martinez, Blue Corn and Lonnie Vigil have expanded the horizons of classic Pueblo design. Whole families of Pueblo potters are celebrated for their consistent innovation within their heritage.

In the late 16th century, the Spanish came to New Mexico with their own artistic traditions and culture that have survived and evolved like that of the Indians. The Hispanic art forms include functional objects, weaving, tinwork, straw appliqué, and devotional images sculpted in wood or painted on wood.

Although there was some sharing of materials and even imagery between the Indians and the Spaniards, the traditions have remained pure. They continue to this day through a large community of artists devoted to maintaining their legacy. The interactions and mutual influences of these two groups created a stylistic and cultural basis for contemporary art in New Mexico.

In the 19th century, with the advent of the railroad and the Santa Fe Trail, an influx of newcomers from the eastern United States and Western Europe arrived in New Mexico. For the lack of a better classification, they were known as the Anglos. This group included many artists who were very taken with the purity of the artistic traditions in New Mexico.

Many of these artists were already well recognized landscape painters and portraitists. Those who could best depict the region's natural beauty and unique cultures were encouraged to come out west and then, through their work, influence others to do the same, thus helping with the efforts of development and commercialization.

Two of the best known of these early painters were Ernest Blumenschein and Bert Phillips, who, along with artist Joseph Sharp, are credited with founding the Taos art colony. The year was 1898 as the two headed for Mexico from Chicago in a covered wagon filled with everything they would need for their trip to paint a little-known world. Outside of Taos, one of the wheels of their wagon broke. As the pair pondered their fate, they decided that Blumenschein would take the wheel to nearby Taos, while Philips would stay with the wagon, protecting the horses and their load. By the time the wheel was repaired, they were so enchanted by the beauty of the region that they decided to go no further. At the coaxing of fellow painter Joseph Sharp, they settled in Taos.

There the three formed the Taos Society of Artists, which flourished and became known as the seat of modernist art in New Mexico. At its height, the Society boasted 17 members who met regularly to discuss art and philosophy, and to maintain a social circle in this remote outpost.

These artists of the Taos Society produced an important legacy that is just now receiving its deserved recognition through exhibitions and publications. The Harwood Museum in Taos and David Witt, Senior Curator, presenting numerous exhibitions and publications, have been in the forefront of establishing the importance of this group to the development of modern artistic activity throughout the region.

Santa Fe, 65 miles south of Taos, was founded in the early 17th century by Spanish settlers as the seat of the Territorial government. New Mexico did not become a state until 1912. In the late 19th century, the Santa Fe Railroad came to the area with a spur to the city from nearby Lamy. By now, the mystique of the West, and particularly the Rio Grande corridor between Taos and Albuquerque had become a destination for travelers, business people, and artists.

Forming an artistic parallel to the activity begun in Taos by the Taos Society of Artists two decades earlier, a group of Santa Fe artists known as the Cinco Pintores (the five painters) settled on the east side of Santa Fe and excitedly built adobe houses on what is now the picturesque Camino del Monte Sol. Having come from the eastern United States and from as far away as Hungary, in the case of Jozef Bakos, they embraced the architecture and the lifestyle of the region and soon became knowledgeable about many aspects of the indigenous and the Hispano communities.

The Cinco Pintores, like many of their predecessors, were very taken with the uniqueness of the landscape and the cultures of the region. These became the subjects of their works. A local artist, Eliseo Rodriguez, developed a friendship with the Pintores, particularly with Bakos. Rodriguez, who lived in the nearby Santander and San Acacio area, became a genuine link between the Hispano community and the painters, thereby contributing to their understanding of the people and their traditions.

By the second decade of the 20th century in Santa Fe, artistic activity and the demand for exhibition space were growing. Through the efforts of the art community, which included such notables as John Sloane and Robert Henri, and the generosity of a rancher named Frank Springer, who donated $30,000 and convinced the State Legislature that an equal amount should be allocated, the Museum of New Mexico Fine Arts Gallery (now the Museum of Fine Arts) was built and opened in November of 1917. This institution quickly became the center of activity for the artists of the region, many of whom were exploring areas other than traditional landscape painting and portraiture. The Fine Arts Gallery not only served as an exhibition venue and a gathering place for artists and art lovers, but it also provided studio space on a rotating basis for many of the artists in the region.

The founding of the Museum of New Mexico Fine Art Gallery coincided with Georgia O'Keeffe's first visit to New Mexico in 1917. When O'Keeffe visited Santa Fe, a town of 6,000 residents, she became enamored with the "adobe village," as she called it, and was certain that she would return. And indeed, she did return many times before settling permanently in Abiquiu in 1949.

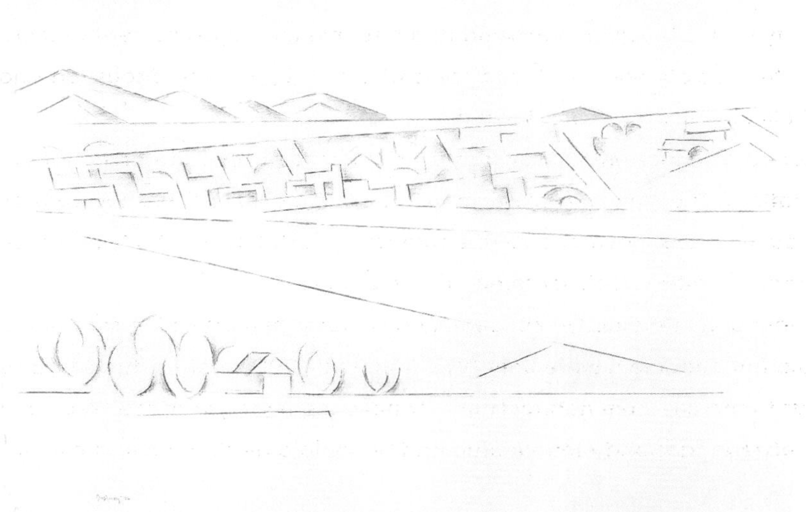

ANDREW DASBURG (1887-1979)
Ranchos Valley Lines and Curves
Graphite on paper 17½ x 24½ inches
Courtesy Owings Dewey Fine Art
and Cline Fine Art, Santa Fe

As Santa Fe established itself as an art center, Taos continued to verify its mportance as a center for the visual arts through the previously mentioned Taos Society of Artists and with the arrival of Andrew Dasburg in 1918. Dasburg quickly established himself as an artist who recognized the contributions of his predecessors but was more interested in developing his singular vision. He befriended the artists John Marin and Marsden Hartley, both of whom had been working in Taos. Marin's work provided Dasburg with the kind of artistic license he was seeking. He integrated this newfound freedom into his landscape paintings, which then became more Cubist. Later, he further reduced the landscape to a series of exquisite geometric lines, often in black and white, and established himself as the first "modern" artist in Taos.

Much has been written about Dasburg and his contributions, and about his contemporaries in Taos who participated in the Taos Society of Artists. David Witt, in his book Taos Moderns, newly released by Red Crane Books, makes strong points about the importance of Dasburg to the development of Taos as a center for modern art. His influence continued until his death in 1979. Many parallels to his style are evident in the work of artists of the current era.

In 1939, Thomas Benrimo arrived in Taos to find a welcoming community with many kindred spirits. Dasburg was a key figure for him and the other moderns who decided to make Taos their home. Benrimo had enjoyed a successful career as an illustrator and set designer in the East, but after curing himself of tuberculosis and marrying his second wife, Dorothy, they relocated to Taos for a fresh start. Benrimo brought with him from San Francisco a well-rounded education and an artistic style formed by diverse influences. An avid interest in astronomy, an interest in mysticism and the occult, and early influences drawn from his Chinese artist friends in San Francisco contributed to the creation of his unique artistic style. With elements of surrealism not unlike the work of Yves Tanguy, Benrimo introduced a new influence to the region. His participation in the 1913

Armory Show in New York was a defining moment in his career, after which he continued to pursue his vision and to develop his artistic persona.

J. Ward Lockwood had been coming to Taos since the 1920s. There he found a supportive environment and inspirational atmosphere which led to his settling there in 1962. Elements of Lockwood's work paralleled some of Dasburg's geometric treatment of the landscape, and although he preferred to maintain a closer connection to the landscape he was depicting, their kinship was clearly established.

Earl Stroh, who arrived in Taos in 1947 and is still working today, also reaped the benefits of the early Taos Modernists. Stroh is widely recognized as one of Taos' own. He has studied in depth the artistic development of Taos, and has become an authority on the artists of the area. His personal contact with many of the artists provides a clear sense of the lines of heredity in the development of Taos as an important art center. Stroh's atmospheric landscapes reference the work of Dasburg, using geometric elements to reduce form to elegant lines and fields of color while bringing his own sensibilities to the images. In his paintings he consistently places the emphasis on the sky to highlight its colors and heavenly qualities while diminishing the rest of the landscape. When viewing a painting by Earl Stroh, one can imagine the breadth of the landscape that surrounds him.

In 1944 Beatrice Mandelman and her artist husband Louis Ribak came to Taos and quickly established themselves as part of this progressive artistic community. They brought with them an awareness of the most current trends in New York and were great contributors to the social and cultural life of Taos. Beatrice Mandelman was a prolific painter and has in recent years become more widely recognized for her explorations in form and color. Her use of bright reds and yellows, colors that are not seen in the landscape in the way she depicted them, demonstrate her commitment to her internal vision. Like many of the Taos Moderns, Mandelman had studied the work of Cézanne.

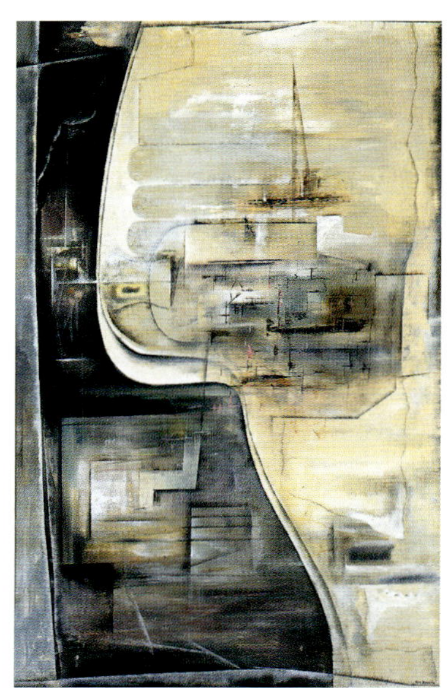

THOMAS BENRIMO (1887-1958)
Aquatic Image
Oil on gesso panel 47 5/8 x 31 3/8 inches
Courtesy Canfield Gallery, Santa Fe

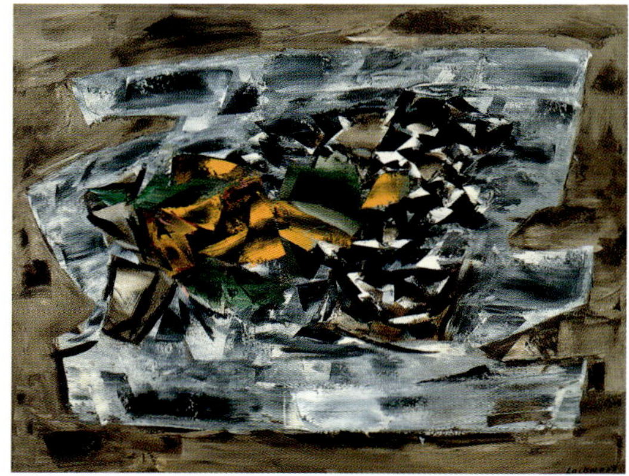

J. WARD LOCKWOOD (1894-1963)
Autumn Apparition, 1961
Acrylic on canvas 50 x 65 inches
Courtesy Canfield Gallery, Santa Fe

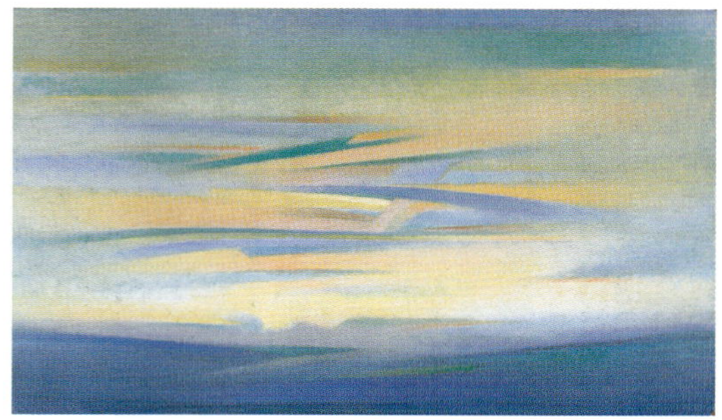

EARL STROH
Sea of Skys
Oil on gessoed panel 26 x 41 inches
Courtesy Bidstrup Collection

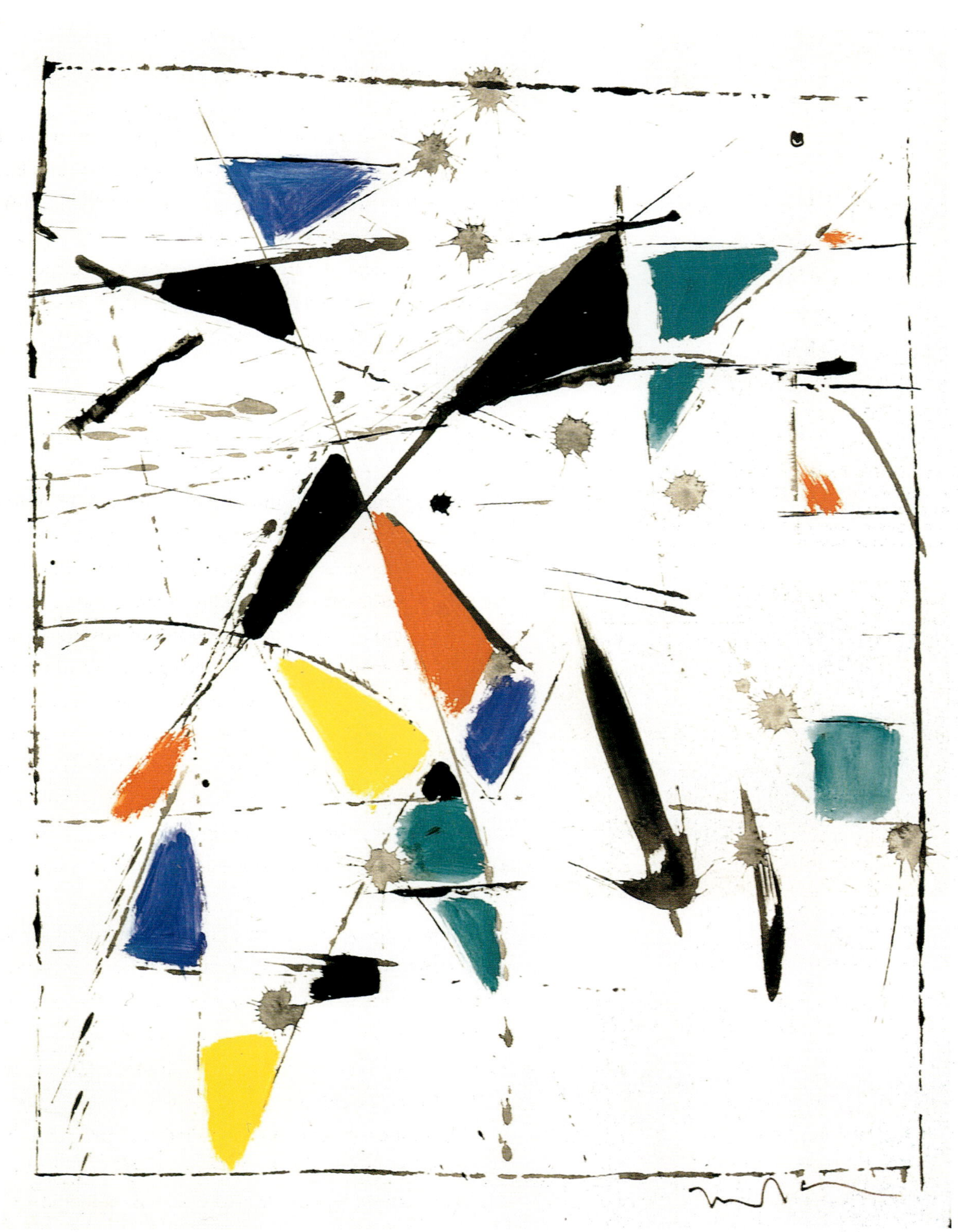

BEATRICE MANDELMAN (1912-1998)
Untitled, Circus series, 1992
Acrylic on paper 17 5/16 x 14 inches
Courtesy Mandelman Foundation, Taos

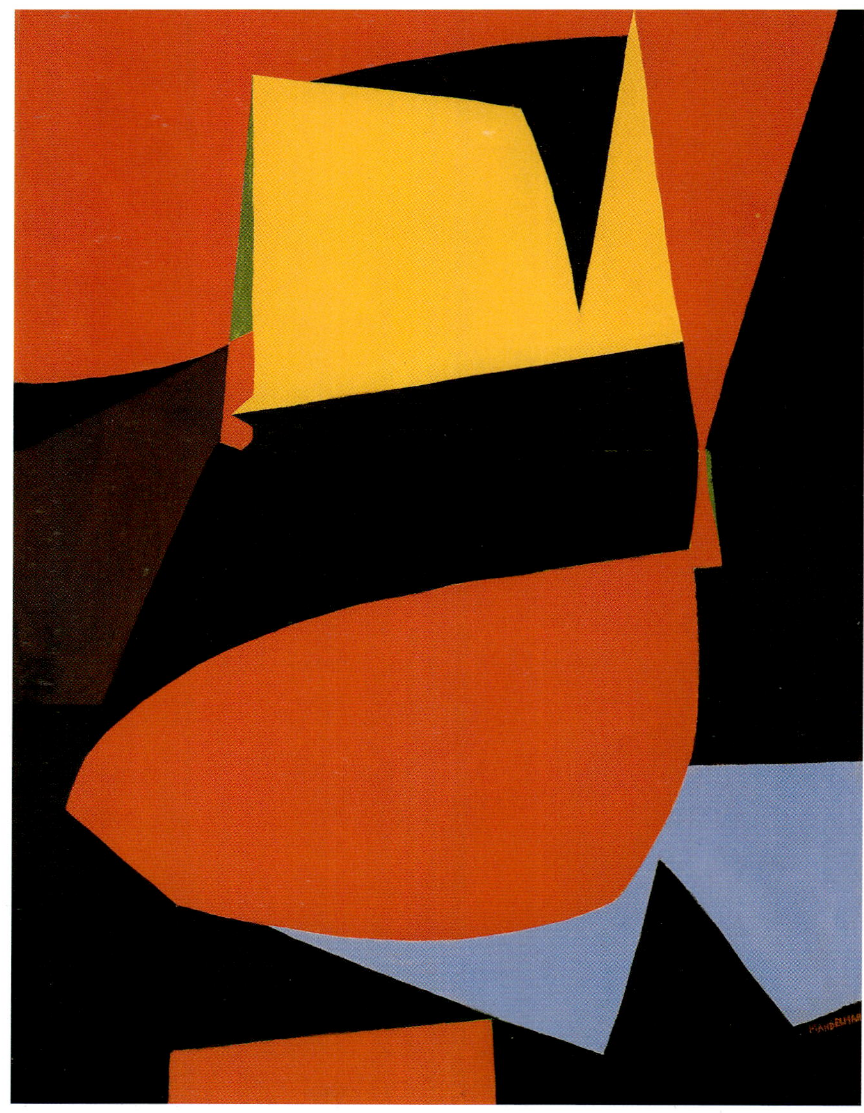

BEATRICE MANDELMAN
Red and the Black
ca. 1960s
Oil on canvas 65 x 50 inches
Courtesy Mandelman Foundation, Taos

An early body of her work interpreted Cézanne's forms and then translated them into areas of color and light. This exercise was a formative moment in Mandlelman's artistic style. As a young woman she was enthralled with the New York art scene and made every effort to interact with the important artists of the era. She met Gorky and deKooning, and although she found her own style, their influence remained a strong element in her work

In subsequent decades, the artist Lawrence Calcagno began to visit Taos and became a part of its community. He was a New York artist who had exhibited widely, beginning in 1955, but who maintained a studio in Taos and considered it to be his artistic home. A series of his paintings was donated to the Museum of Fine Arts, which created a significant document of this important artist's work. Calcagno painted in a variety

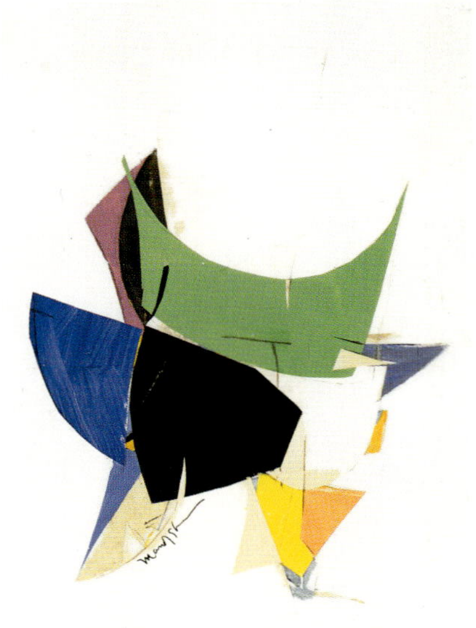

BEATRICE MANDELMAN
Birds, 1957
Mixed media on canvas
$23\frac{1}{2}$ x $15\frac{11}{16}$ inches
Courtesy Mandelman Foundation, Taos

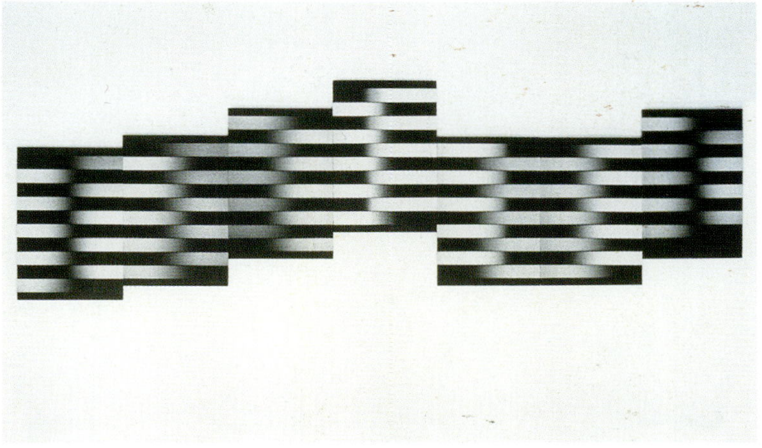

LARRY BELL
Moving Ways, 1979
Aluminum coated vapor drawings
7 panels: 42 x 28 inches each
Courtesy Larry Bell

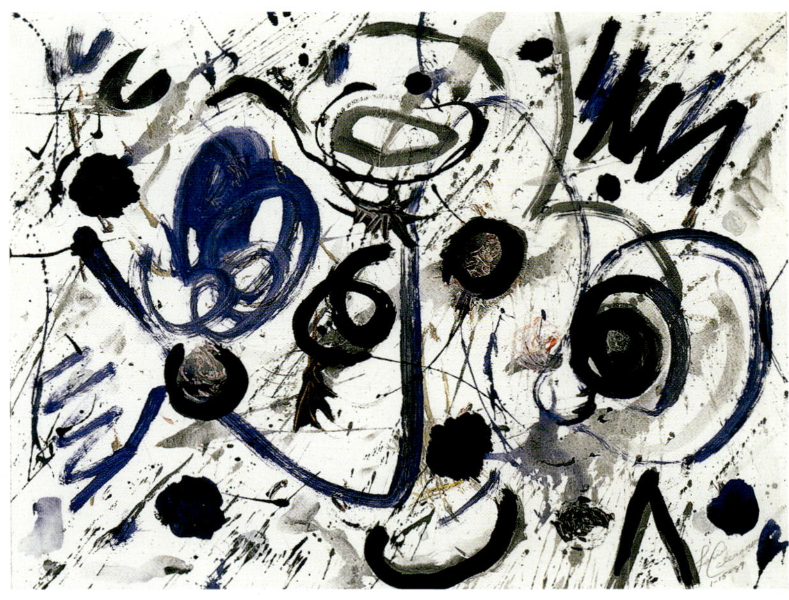

LAWRENCE CALCAGNO (1913-1993)
Untitled, 1989
Acrylic on paper 22 x 30 inches
Courtesy Canfield Gallery, Santa Fe

of abstract styles, at times emphasizing fields of color and at others focusing on the line. It is always clear when viewing his work that he revered the work of the Taos Moderns.

Larry Bell, whose early influences included deKooning, Pollock, and Franz Kline, established a studio in Taos in the 1960s. Bell had already earned an international reputation at a young age. Much like his predecessors, he found in Taos a fertile and supportive environment for his explorations. Bell is a self-admitted dreamer who creates complex works using reflection, both figuratively and literally, in his work. He has broken through many barriers of perception, both in how his work is perceived by others and

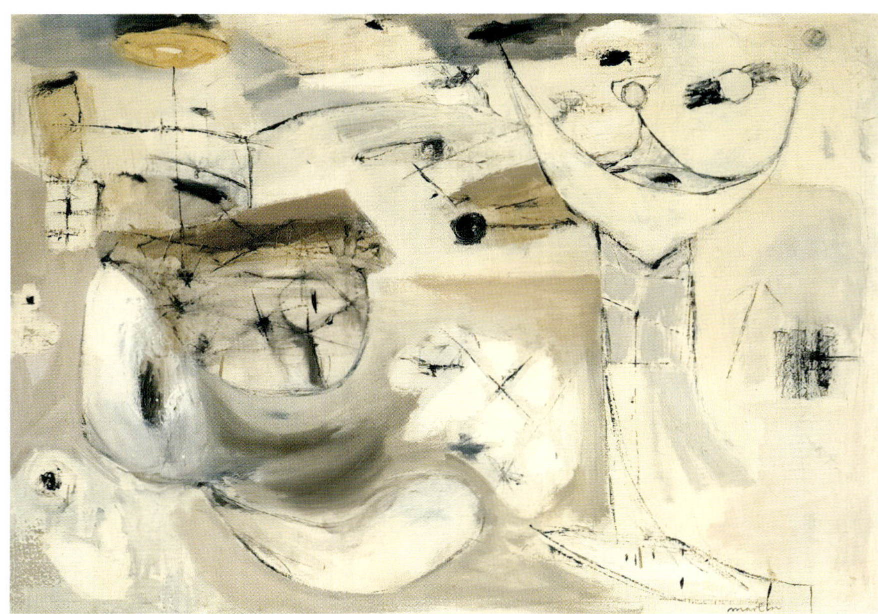

AGNES MARTIN
Two People In Moonlight, 1954
Oil on canvas 28 x 40 inches
Courtesy Canfield Gallery, Santa Fe

in how he allows his own perception of an object to form the central core of his work. Bell's work has been characterized as "applications of technical phenomena and of the physical properties of light and surface". His response is that his art comes from his fantasies about what he is doing and about being very serious during the process, though he admits those qualities have a lot to do with being a kid. In his Taos studio, Bell produces many bodies of work using unconventional technologies. His famous vapor drawings, which are akin to his large scale glass sculptures, deal with the atmospheric qualities of the sky, and concrete and abstract space. His work evolves with his artistic vision, which is in a continuous state of metamorphosis. One never knows what to expect next from Bell except that his work will be innovative and groundbreaking.

The distinguished career of Agnes Martin spans over six decades. She is recognized globally as an instigator of Minimalism. Martin came to New Mexico in 1946, establishing studios first in Cuba, New Mexico, and then in Galisteo, outside of Santa Fe. Finally, she settled in Taos. Her well known grid paintings have much to do with the size and breadth of the universe as an external body as well as an expression of inner space. Perhaps in Martin's meditative vision they are one and the same. Although she is primarily interested in continuing to work daily in her studio, at age 91 she is still very much a part of the Taos art scene. Her newly inaugurated Agnes Martin Gallery at the Harwood Museum has become a destination for art pilgrims from all parts of the world.

I had the privilege of spending several afternoons with Agnes, as she likes to be called. On one occasion we were having a discussion about the meaning of art. She told me that people often ask her what her work is about. She said, "My paintings are not about anything," and then added, "but they are not about nothing." This is, perhaps, the most concise statement that can be made about this complex artist and monumental

AGNES MARTIN
Untitled #6, 1980
Acrylic and graphite on canvas
Courtesy Museum of New Mexico
Museum of Fine Arts
Gift of American Art Foundation
Photo by Blair Clark

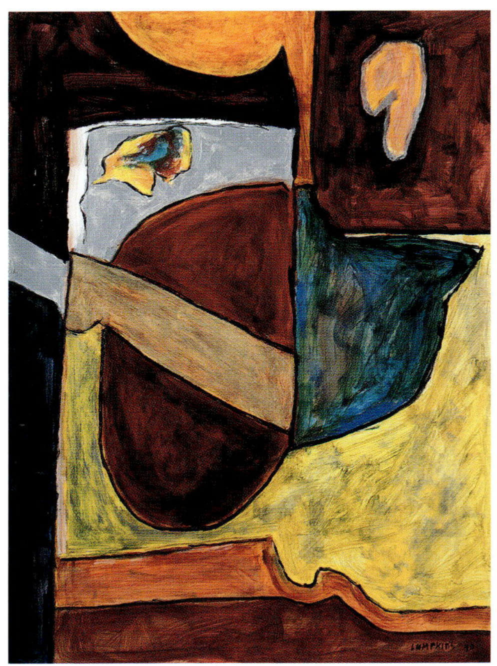
WILLIAM LUMPKINS (1909-2000)
Untitled #43, 1990
Acrylic on paper 40 x 30 inches
Estate of William Lumpkins
Courtesy Cline Fine Art, Santa Fe

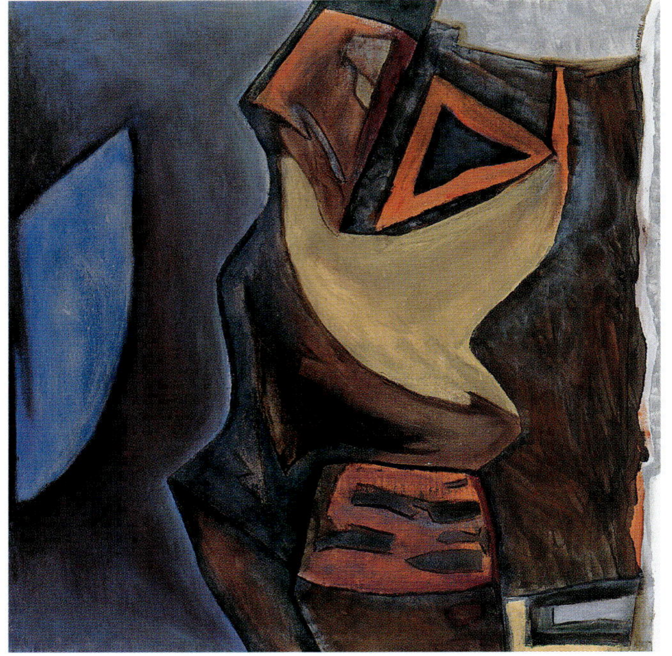
WILLIAM LUMPKINS
Untitled #38, 1986
Acrylic on paper 45 x 45 inches
Estate of William Lumpkins
Courtesy Cline Fine Art, Santa Fe

artist who has added tremendously to the artistic mix of New Mexico.

In the late 1920s, with the economy in the United States suffering and moving relentlessly toward the fateful crash of the Stock Market in 1929, President Franklin Delano Roosevelt, in his successful efforts to revive the economy, created the New Deal. This included many public works programs such as the Farm Security Administration, which was a boon for many photographers around the country and particularly in New Mexico. Artists such as Russell Lee, John Collier, Jack Delano, and Walker Evans created important artistic records of the region. The Works Progress Administration was another such program initiated by the Roosevelt administration. In the New Mexico version of the program, artists were contracted to paint murals, teach, or just work in their studios to create visual artistic records of the era. In Santa Fe, Gustave Baumann, an exceptional artist from Chicago who had settled in New Mexico, was charged with the project. He quickly put the word out that funds were available for artists who qualified and then began to review portfolios.

Artists came from all over the state and were commissioned by Baumann to pursue their individual passions. He hired many local artists including Esquipula Esquipula de Romero and Emil Bisttram, as well as an important contemporary of theirs who was to become a key figure in the development of abstract art in the region. William Lumpkins, affectionately known by all as Bill, was born and raised on a ranch in Roswell, New Mexico. He had trained as an architect and was an accomplished landscape painter as well, but his sense of design and his interest in "the spirit of a thing" made him want to pursue abstract painting.

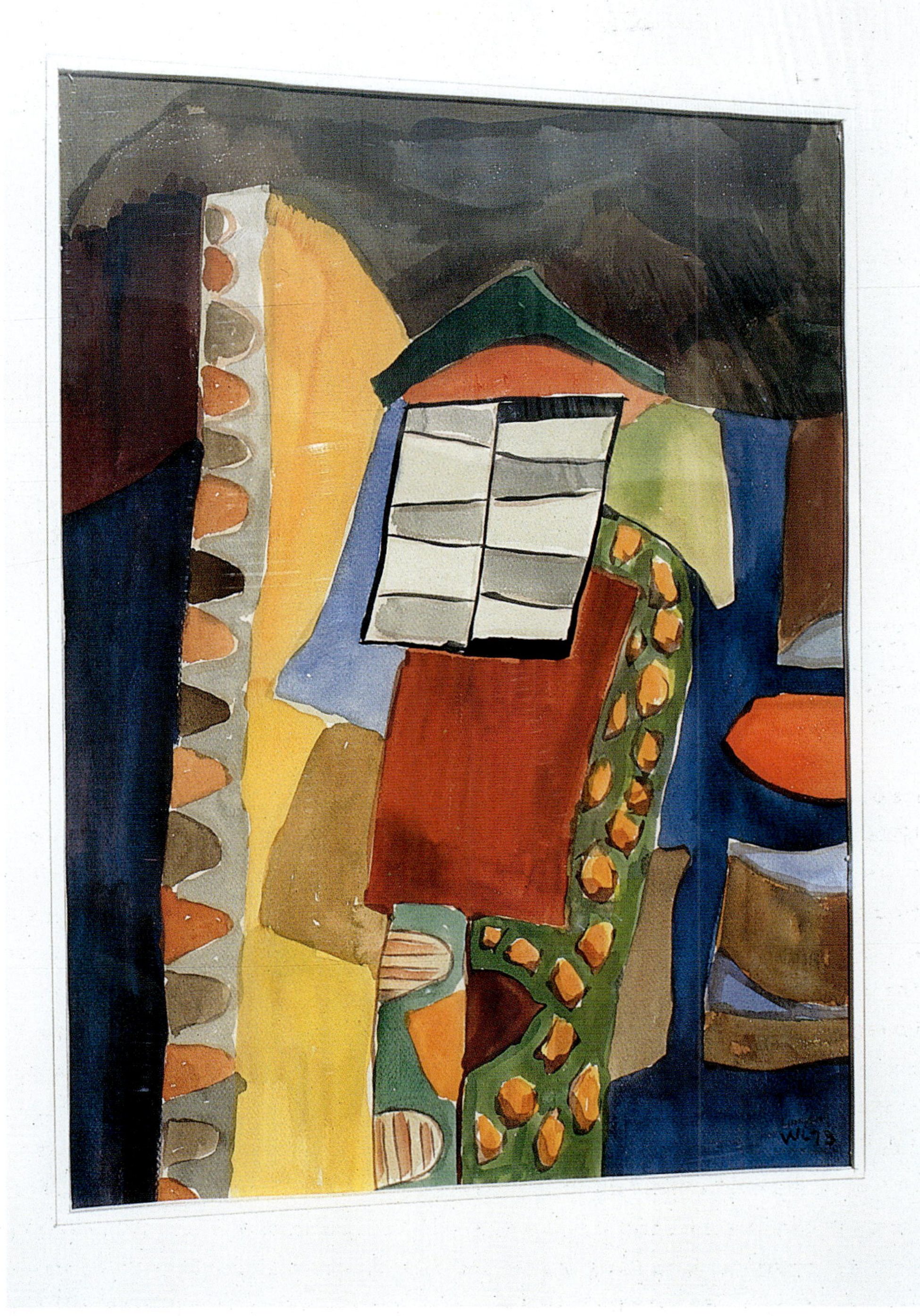

WILLIAM LUMPKINS
Untitled (The Playhouse), 1978
Mixed media
22 x 30 inches
Courtesy Cline Fine Art, Santa Fe

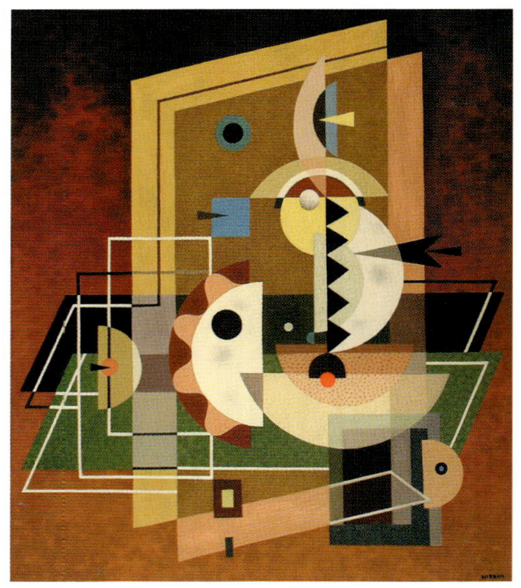

EMIL BISTTRAM (1895-1976)
Inter or, 1938
Courtesy Jonson Gallery
University of New Mexico

Lumpkins made the long trek to Santa Fe to meet Baumann and to see if he qualified for the WPA contract. Baumann was very encouraging of Lumpkins' work and was very interested in his abstract watercolors. When he later settled in Santa Fe with his wife Norma, he continued to pursue his interests in both architecture and abstract painting, receiving numerous awards for both, including the Governors Award for Excellence In the Arts.

Bill Lumpkins was the quintessential Santa Fe artist. A debonair gentleman with cowboy manners and a flat brimmed Stetson, he was often seen on the Santa Fe Plaza involved in discussions of his continued advocacy for the acceptance of abstraction as a legitimate and even superior form of artistic expression. Lumpkins' work clearly demonstrates his evolution from a landscape painter to an abstract painter, a step taken by many artists who felt freed when they came to New Mexico. His fields of color and arrangement of space reference the landscape and often architecture, but in a more complex and profound way than a landscape painter's depictions. Lumpkins achieved his goal of taking abstraction a step further.

The city of Albuqerque is another area that has been of great importance to the development of New Mexico as a center for abstract painting and sculpture. Although its art community began somewhat later than Taos and Santa Fe, some very important artists have been generated by the city and especially by the University of New Mexico, the most important arts educational institution in the state.

The list begins with Emil Bisttram. Bisttram founded a school in Taos and, along with Albuquerque painter Raymond Jonson, founded the Transcendental Painting Group. These painters wanted to create an intellectual genre that would contextualize their work and provide a point of reference for their audiences. Bisttram had worked in the WPA program and created numerous murals around the state, but like many of his contemporaries, was intrigued by the possibilities found in abstract painting. Jonson, who taught at the University of New Mexico, created on campus the Jonson Gallery, a small museum dedicated to the work of modernists and the Transcendentalists. The Gallery still serves as an important venue for the study, appreciation and understanding of the work of these pioneers.

The University also established a world class printmaking center, the Tamarind Institute, which has supported the work of many artists of national and international stature. Garo Antreasian and Clinton Adams were the Tamarind's co-directors who solidified its reputation. Antreasian taught at the University and has, over several decades, helped to continue the abstract traditions in New Mexico. Richard Diebenkorn's presence in New Mexico is also noteworthy. Diebenkorn maintained a studio in Albuquerque in the 1950's and was a tremendous, long lasting influence on the art of the region. It could be said that his artistic development followed a path similar to some of the Taos Moderns. In the 1940's, his paintings were figurative and bore some stylistic

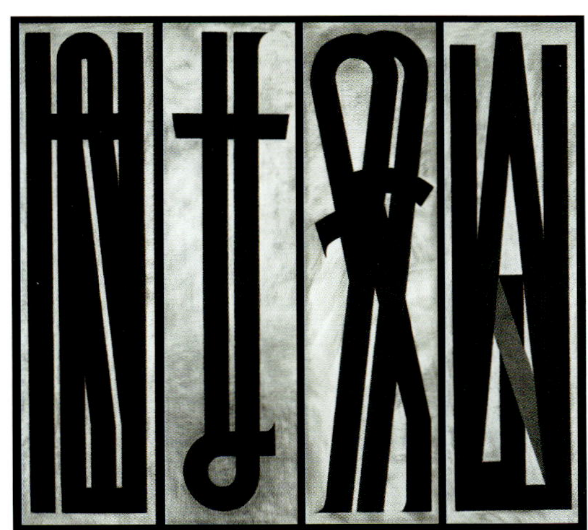

GARO ANTREASIAN
Geometers I-IV, 1998
Charcoal on paper
4 panels: 85 x 24 inches each
Courtesy Cline Fine Art, Santa Fe

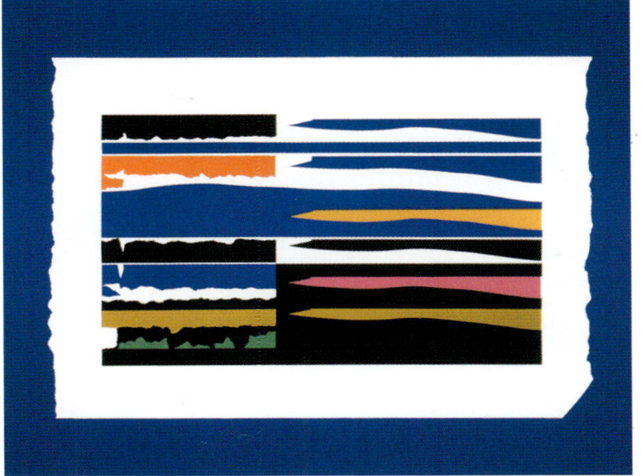

CLINTON ADAMS (1918-2002)
Coda, 1991
Lithograph
Courtesy University of New Mexico Museum

resemblance to the work of Edward Hopper, an artist whom he greatly admired. By the mid 1940's Diebenkorn had evolved a more abstract style, incorporating stylized and abstracted figures. He was also very interested in Cézanne, a book of whose work accompanied Diebenkorn when he left for active duty in the Marine Corps. After his military service, he and his wife decided to move to Albuquerque so that Diebenkorn could study at the University of New Mexico. Through the GI Bill, he enrolled at UNM in 1950. He came into his own as a painter while in Albuquerque, finding it a receptive environment that supported the development of his vision. "Things really started to come together for me there," he said. "It was a very good situation for me because there was none of this fear of painting." While at UNM he established lifetime work patterns that included long hours in the studio. He also had contact with important artistic mentors, one of whom was Raymond Jonson who served on Diebenkorn's thesis committee. He was awarded a Master of Arts degree in 1951. One element that characterized Diebenkorn's work was his ability to accept the "accidents" or painterly images in his canvases, elaborating on them and finding new images as he worked.

Diebenkorn was yet another artist who thrived in the atmosphere of the freedom and expansiveness that he found in New Mexico. Though he was apprehensive at first about moving away from the sea, he found that "the sky took the place of the ocean."

Whereas Albuquerque was considered a remote outpost in the 1950s, Santa Fe is even today a town of a scant 60,000 residents. It boasts, however, 12 museums and over 120 art galleries. Ripe with artistic life, the City Different has now become an important center for modern and contemporary art. In the 1960s and 70s, artists like Eugene Newmann, Sam Scott, and Frank Ettenberg settled in Santa Fe and brought with them their unique brand of abstract expressionism. Newmann, whose mysterious paintings evolved from abstracted figures to enigmatic moments, helped to further establish the abstract traditions in Santa Fe. Scott, a prolific painter, teacher and speaker on issues of world peace (he spoke to the UN General Assembly on the role of

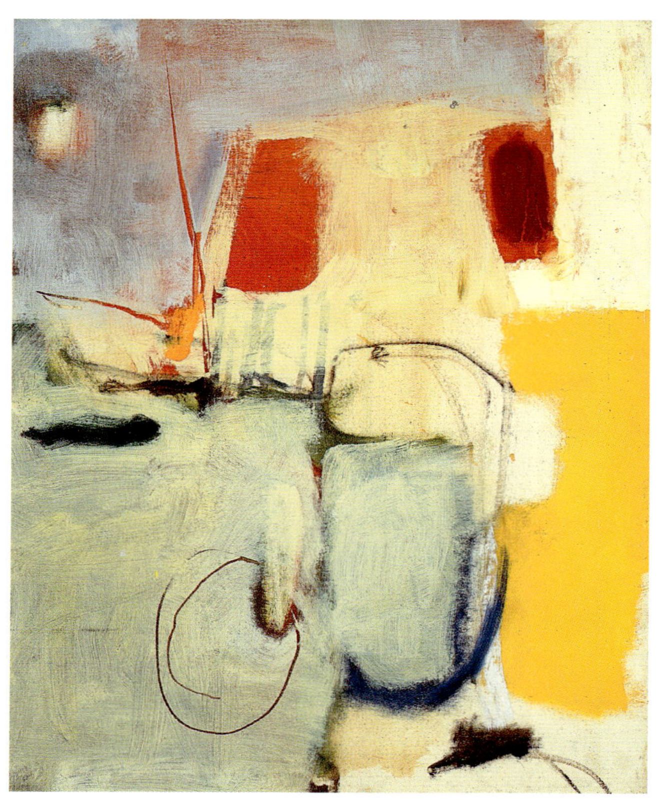

RICHARD DIEBENKORN (1922-1993)
Untitled, 1950
Oil on board 25½ x 21½ inches
Courtesy Jonson Gallery, University of New Mexico

the artist in creating world peace), creates paintings and monotypes that reference nature and its mystery. His seemingly freehanded gestural paintings celebrate the earth and all its creatures and pay homage to natural deities that govern our existence.

Ettenberg is a mystical painter. His abstract paintings are about inward spaces, and he uses the metaphor of a room's interior to explore his internal space. He paints with beautiful translucent washes that invite the viewer to look further into the paintings, and perhaps their own inner space.

Several artists of international stature have settled in New Mexico and continue their work with the same sensibilities as their predecessors. Bruce Nauman, who is perhaps the best known American artist of this age, maintains a studio outside of Santa Fe where he creates his massive conceptual works alongside Susan Rothenberg, who has continued her important career there. Nauman and Rothenberg add an element to the art community that is similar to the excitement that Louis Ribak and Bea Mandlemann added to Taos when they arrived there. Nauman's presence in New Mexico is further testimony of the area's power to attract visionary artists. In Nauman's case, it is perhaps the solitude and vast open spaces that provide him with the kind of intellectual stimulation and inspiration that he brings to his expression. A pioneer in removing his work from the realm of "formal" art, he began his conceptual art using the body to create molds for casting in many different materials. He later developed a series of work using his now well known word-plays.

Nauman stopped painting in 1965 to make objects. His work has been amazingly original in concept, in his use of diverse media, and in the apparent lack of relationship to other work. In contrast to an artist like Pablo Picasso who deliberately drew from other artists, it has been said that Nauman's work is "underivative" of other art. Although one could not cite his residence in New Mexico as the catalyst for his extraordinary work, as he was already formed as an artist when he relocated here, it is clearly evident that Nauman's studio outside of Santa Fe has provided him with an inspiring venue for his thought provoking works. It also points up the fact that New Mexico continues to attract artists of national and international stature to its midst.

Rothenberg, who has simplified natural forms to their essence, clearly benefits from the meditative qualities of the mountains and open spaces in the state. Though one could draw connections to earlier New Mexico artists, her vision is clearly singular and formed by the complex influences of her distinguished artistic life. Writers and

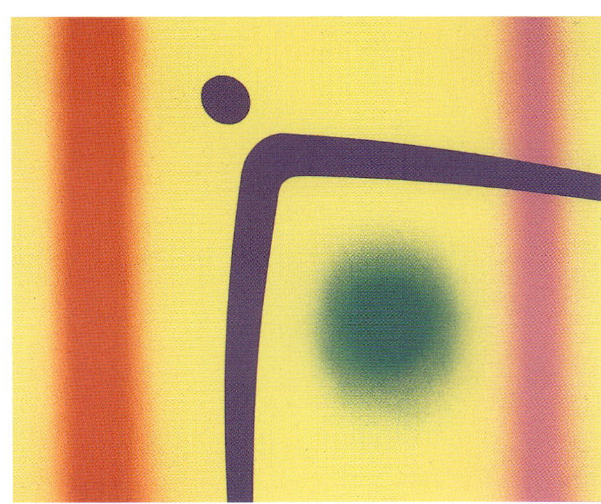

RAYMOND JONSON (1891-1982)
Polymer #23, 1974
Polymer 39 x 48 inches
Courtesy Jonson Gallery, University of New Mexico

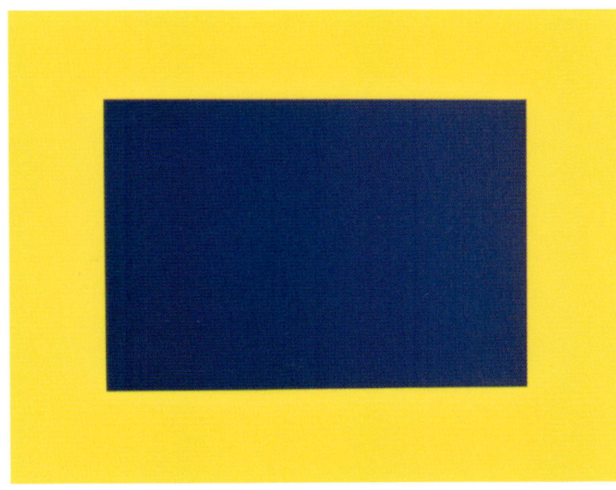

RICHARD TUTTLE
Colors, 1997
Waterless lithograph on silk tissue
$15^{1}/_{4}$ x 19 inches Edition of 40
Published by 21 Steps Editions
Courtesy Richard Levy Gallery, Albuquerque

critics have characterized her work in many different genres, but in many ways Susan Rothenberg exemplifies the abstract artist. Rothenberg's recent works continue to demonstrate her development and maturity as an artist. Her experience, the appreciation of her work, and her stature as one of America's premier woman artists, are a source of pride in the New Mexico's art world.

The late Don Fabricant, an artist who came to Santa Fe in the 1960s from the East coast, painted in a very graphic abstract style. He once said that the realist painter begins with an image, while the abstract artist starts with an idea or a concept, or with no pre-conception, and then searches for the image in the canvas, accepting it as it develops. This is the approach that Diebenkorn used and is, in some measure perhaps, how Rothenberg reaches her complex visual compositions. Her compelling paintings, drawings and works on paper are obviously the result of deep meditative moments, and although many of her works include the suggestion of a form, they arise from an abstract premise.

Another artist who should be mentioned is Richard Tuttle. Tuttle, who creates sculpture, drawings, and constructions, has been shown internationally, and was given a solo exhibition at the Museum of Fine Arts in Santa Fe. Tuttle sees the beautiful in the mundane. His ability to create art from what is apparently nothing is testimony to his understanding of abstraction, as he uses remnants of everyday materials to create complex visual statements. Herbert Vogel, one of Tuttle's earliest and most important patrons, collaborated with him in the creation of an important collection of his works. He wrote: "Richard Tuttle is poetical, spiritual and intellectual. Much of his work is like contemporary manuscripts – and gem-like."

Like life itself, Tuttle's work is full of contradiction. Very often, his work is of an extremely delicate nature. How can an object made so simply and from such fragile materials offer so much beauty and introspection? His work looks very simple, but it is mysteriously and beautifully complex, a fleeting moment in an eternal continuum. Perhaps these characteristics of his work were a part of his attraction to New Mexico, a place of great beauty, mystery, spirit, and fragility.

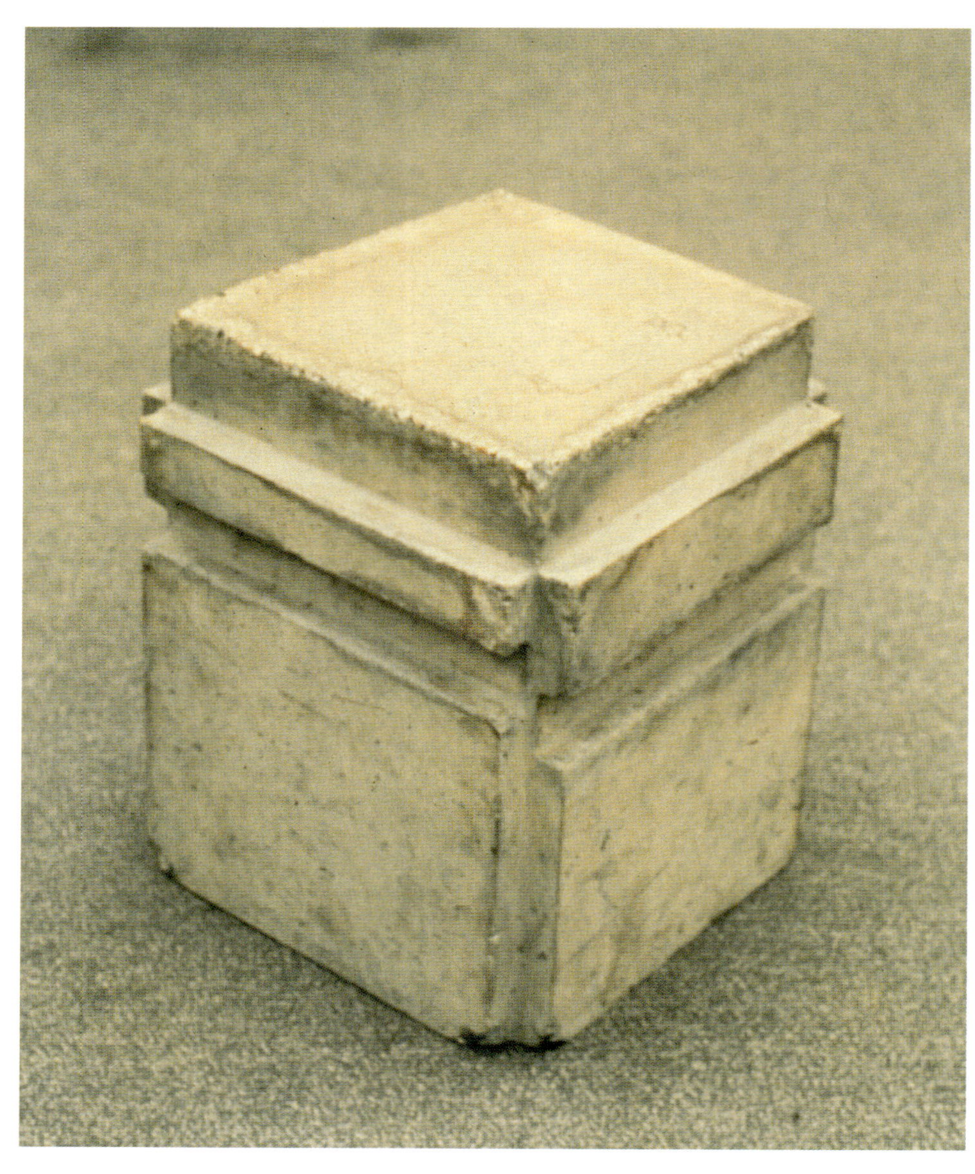

BRUCE NAUMAN
A Cast of the Space under My Chair, 1965-68
Concrete
$17^{1}/_{2}$ x $15^{3}/_{8}$ x $14^{5}/_{8}$ inches
Private Collection
Courtesy Sperone Westwater, New York

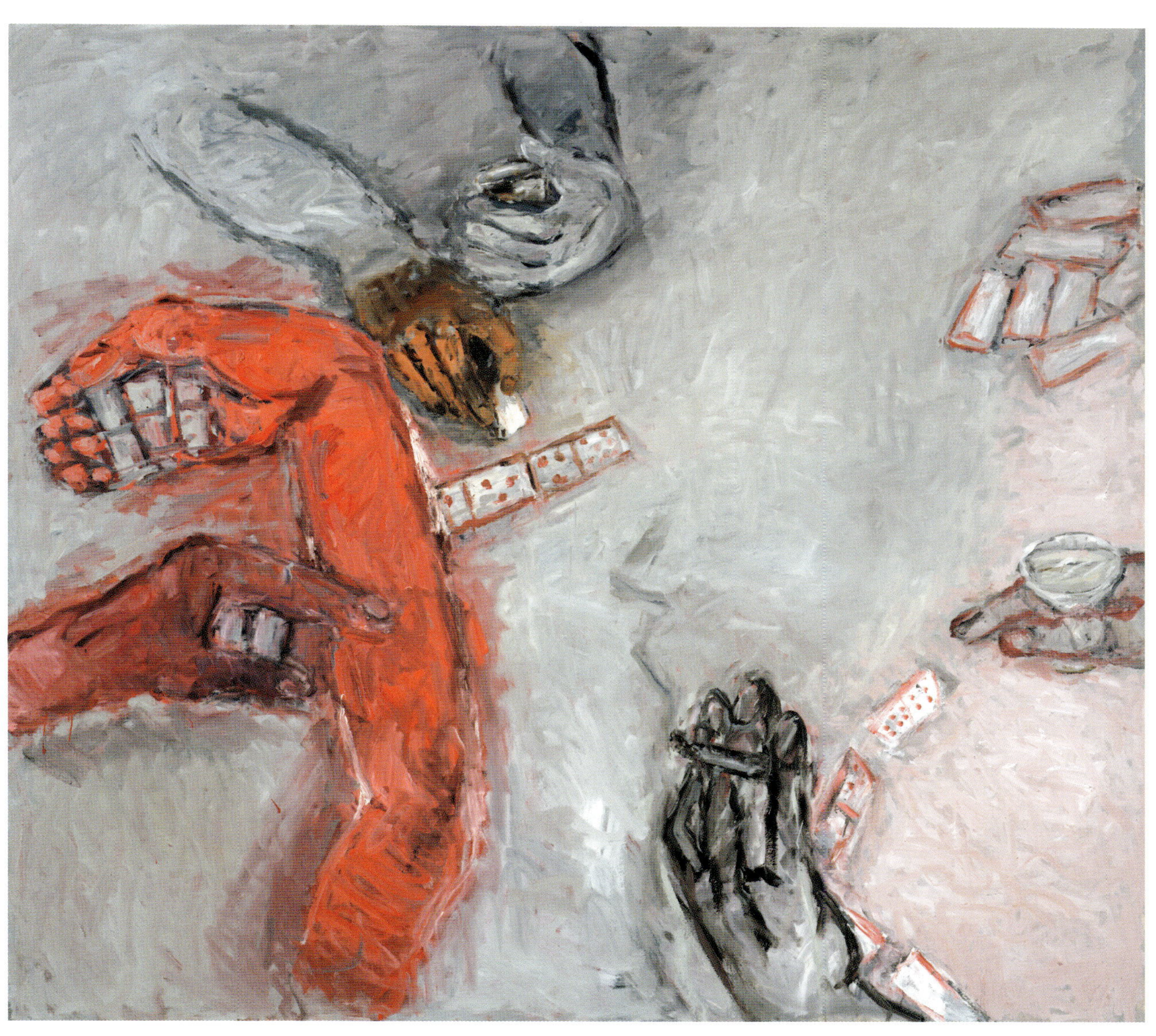

SUSAN ROTHENBERG
With Martini, 2002
Oil on canvas
76 x 87 inches
Courtesy Sperone Westwater, New York

In 1995, a group of people that included art dealer Laura Carpenter and was led by philanthropists Anne and John Marion recognized the importance and the potential of the region as an expanding center for the contemporary arts. A first and important step was the creation of SITE Santa Fe, a contemporary museum in the style of a European Kunsthaus. SITE Santa Fe, as host to a biennial exhibition of international artists as well as numerous exhibitions of the most relevant contemporary expressions, has made a significant mark in demonstrating New Mexico's continued viability as an important artistic center. Peter Sarkisian, whose art is illustrated later in this volume, is one of the many artists who has launched his career through an exhibition at this important new institution. Sarkisian works in video, creating compelling visual statements using fragments of the human body in continuous motion.

In 1997, the long awaited Georgia O'Keeffe Museum opened to great fanfare and a warm welcome from Santa Fe and the world art community. This museum, dedicated to the legacy of America's best known woman artist, is educating a vast public about the contributions of O'Keeffe and her contemporaries. Under the guidance of its director, George King, and the scholarship of its curator, Barbara Buhler Lynes, the Georgia O'Keeffe Museum is dramatically demonstrating New Mexico's contributions to modernist art.

The O'Keeffe has included the works of Mardsen Hartley, Andrew Dasburg, and Arthur Dove in exhibitions that place O'Keeffe and these other artists, who either lived in New Mexico or spent a great deal of time here, within the context of New Mexico as the stage for their inspiration and artistic production.

The question is always asked, what is it that attracts artists to New Mexico?

The answer, in all its complexity, must be the light, the dazzling landscape, and the diversity of the community. It is the Native American, who had existed here since the prehistoric period, who provides those with artistic sensibilities a sense that this place is different, rich and unexplored. It is the Hispano culture of New Mexico, which remains quite pure and which continues to be a source of tremendous pride for the people of New Mexico, as evidenced by the newly opened Museum of Spanish Colonial Art in Santa Fe and the National Hispanic Cultural Center in Albuquerque. It is the East Coast and European influence reflected in the museums and educational institutions. It is the natural, awe-inspiring environment of high mesas, snow covered peaks and architectural styles that date back many centuries. And there is the presence of the spirit of this ancient land, making New Mexico fertile ground for artistic expression.

The traditions that established themselves in New Mexico in the beginning of the 20th century have continued to evolve. Many volumes could be written and illustrated about abstract artistic traditions in New Mexico. I would be remiss if I didn't note that there are many omissions owed to the brevity of a single text. Although only a sampling of the abstract artists in the region, the artists included in this text present the tradition of abstract art and its evolution in New Mexico.

Stuart Ashman

EUGENE NEWMANN

History never repeats itself. It just resurfaces occasionally as a projection screen upon which the present can hurl its fantasies. An image from the past is different, however. Preserved in museums and in the collective memory, it becomes raw material for the demolition and reconstruction of consciousness.

In the hard hat zone of art history, abstract artists go to work on the images of the past, remodeling old ideas and putting up new ones to create the intellectual structures of their own time. Unexpected elements appear in their work, exist for a moment, and change into stronger but still unidentifiable elements. Any concept that does not belong to the process is summarily eradicated and replaced with new imagery, new information, new revelations, all directed toward an unimaginable resolution. The pace changes exponentially. All the world's a phase.

Eugene Newmann's art addresses the process by which, for instance, Vermeer has morphed into Francis Bacon and then into the fifteen-minutes-of-fame crowd. It faithfully mirrors the technological phenomenon of planned obsolescence run amok. As the days of using grandfather's adding machine or owning the same telephone for ten years have ended, so have the conventions of reference and succession in art history. Now change happens all at once.

Newmann is known for the contradictory dynamics at work in the production of each of his paintings, and for his ability to mediate them. He draws upon a vast reservoir of art history and theory, turning it into something brand new that is, nevertheless, built on bedrock. His process is profoundly interactive as he sets down images, paints over them, and moves certain forms around the canvas. He covers up the literal in order to allow the abstract to emerge. "Cézanne showed us the shifting ground of what is real," Newmann says. "I've always been in that brokered territory between narrative and abstract art. There are certain polarities, and one can be criticized for not taking a position at either pole. But I don't stay put. I'm always in flux."

Eugene Newmann is a world citizen who settled in Santa Fe more than thirty years ago. He has become known as an intellectual moderator, a generous teacher, and a central figure in New Mexico's abstract art world. In countless conversations and works of art, he addresses large ideas such as missed chances, the nature of memory, or the accountability of a culture. Ranging across the expanse of canvas that is the litmus for his ideas, he sets down whole forms and then obscures or truncates them, leaving only the essential fragments, the visual poetry, the elusive hint of the reality behind reality that keeps on changing at warp speed.

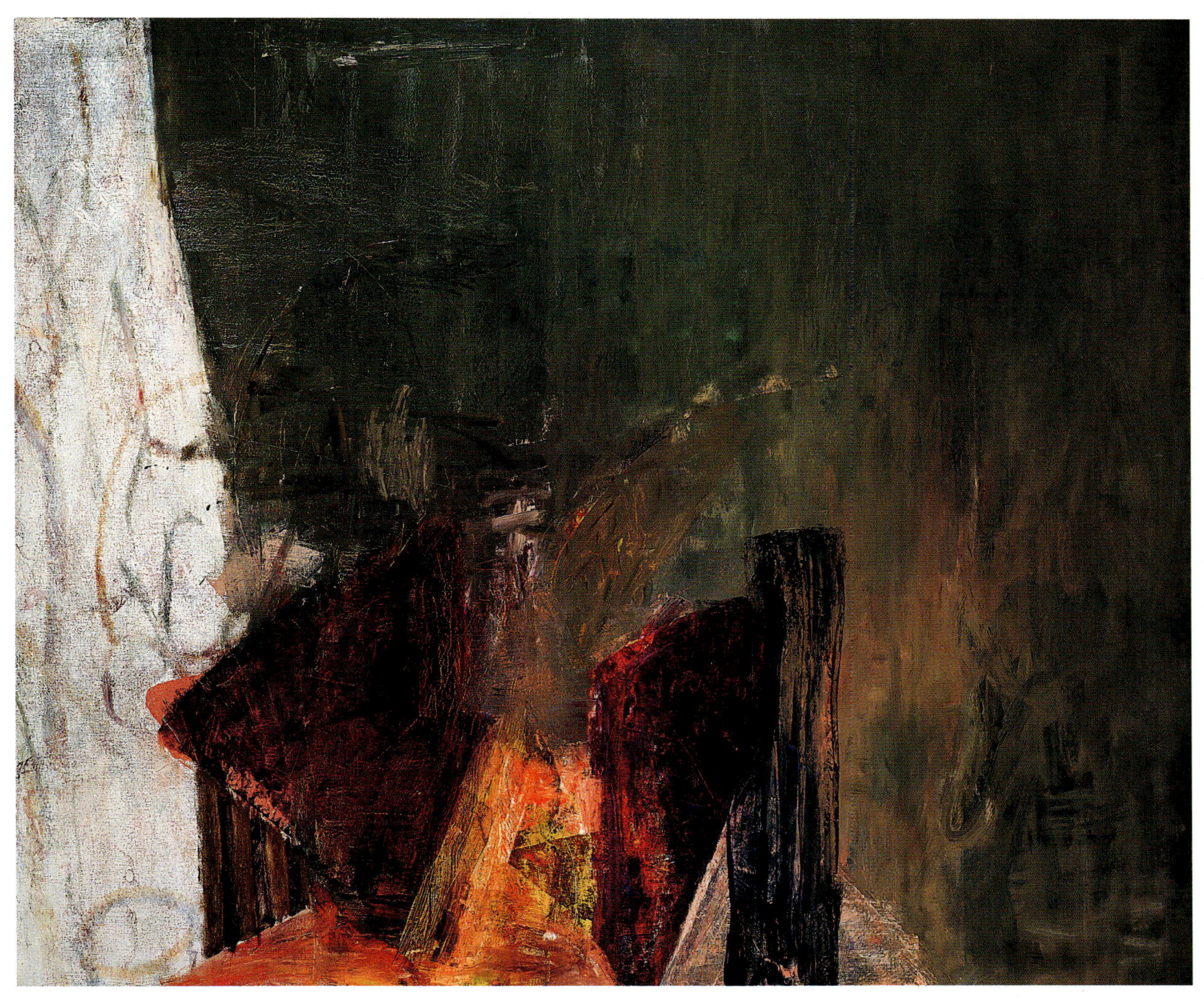

UNTITLED, 1983
OIL ON CANVAS
48 X 58 INCHES

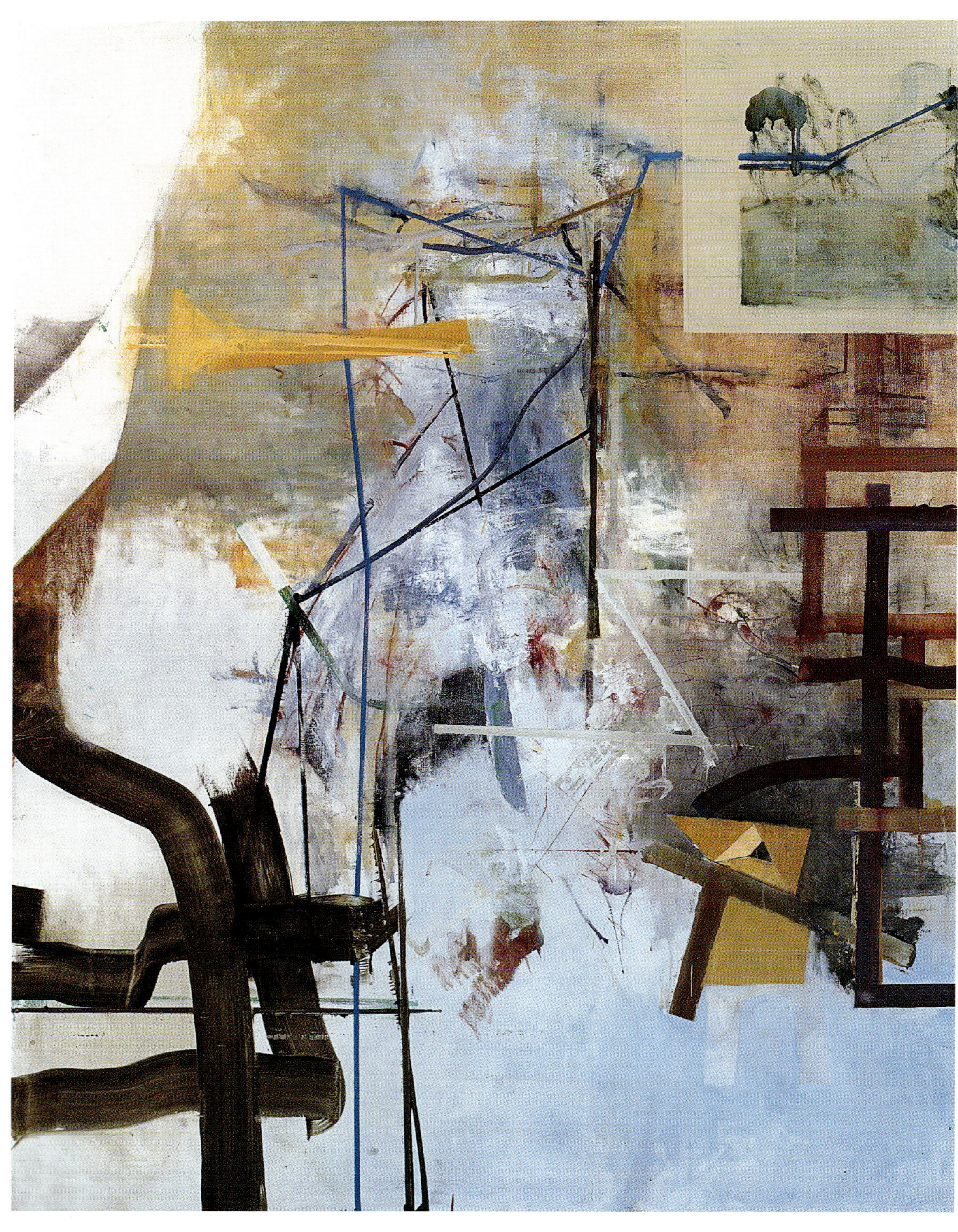

VARIATIONS ON A THEME BY VERMEER:
FAN FARE VARIATION, 1979
OIL ON CANVAS
60 X 48 INCHES
Collection of David and Susan Hill

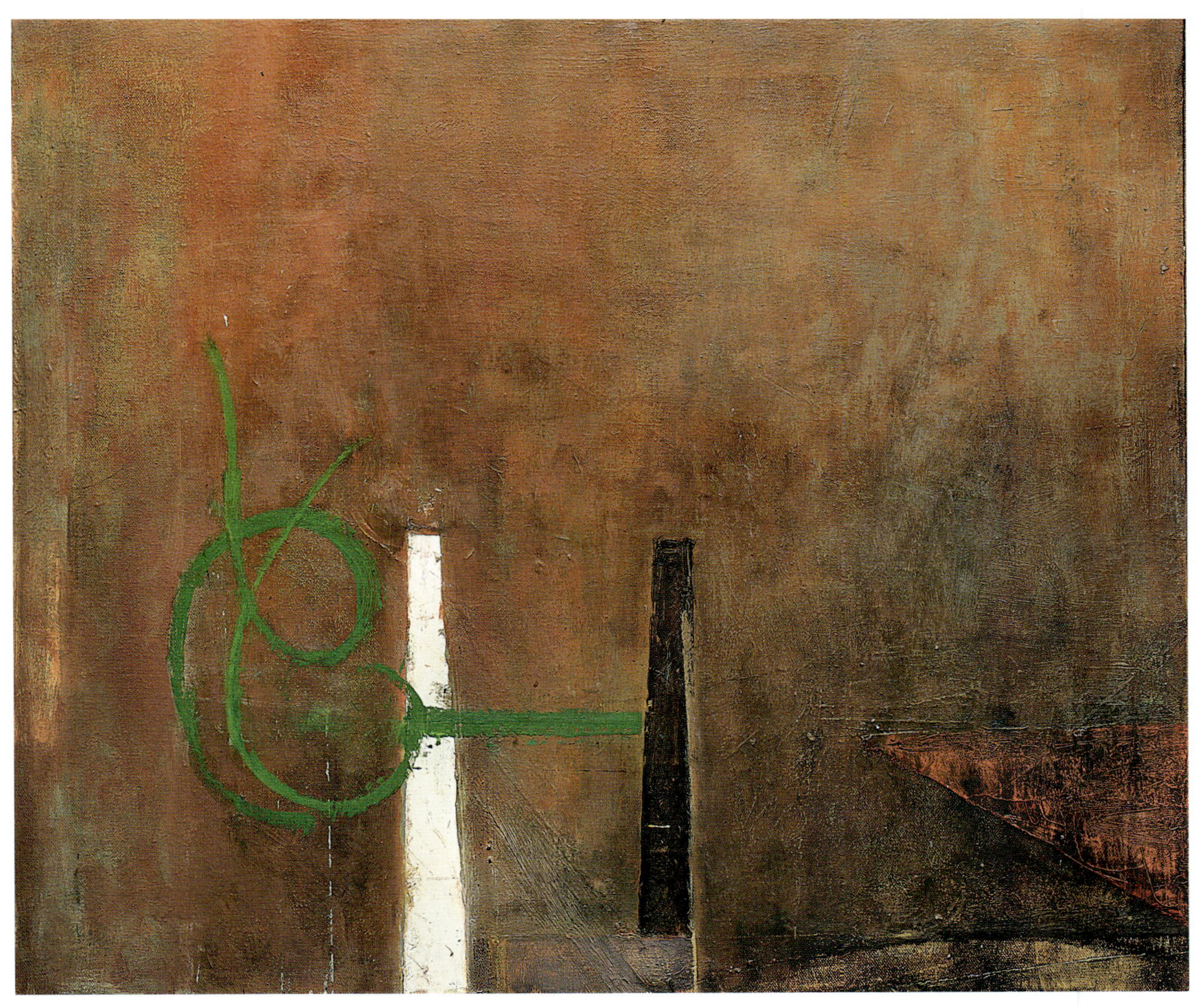

SMALL BODIES #5, 1981
OIL ON CANVAS
20 X 24 INCHES

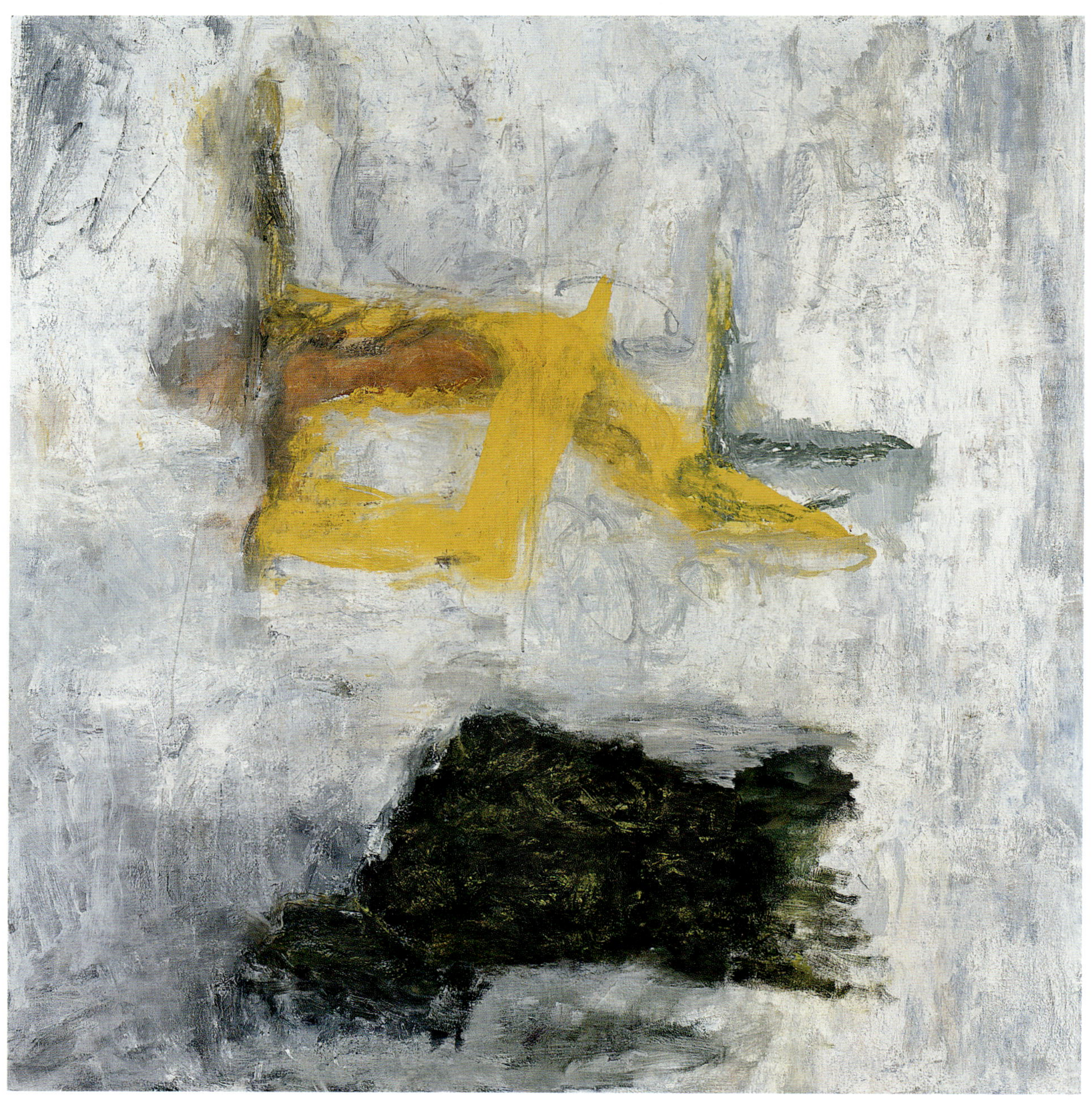

COUNTRY EXERCISES (YELLOW), 2001
OIL ON CANVAS
44 X 44 INCHES
Collection Dr. Jonathan Abrams

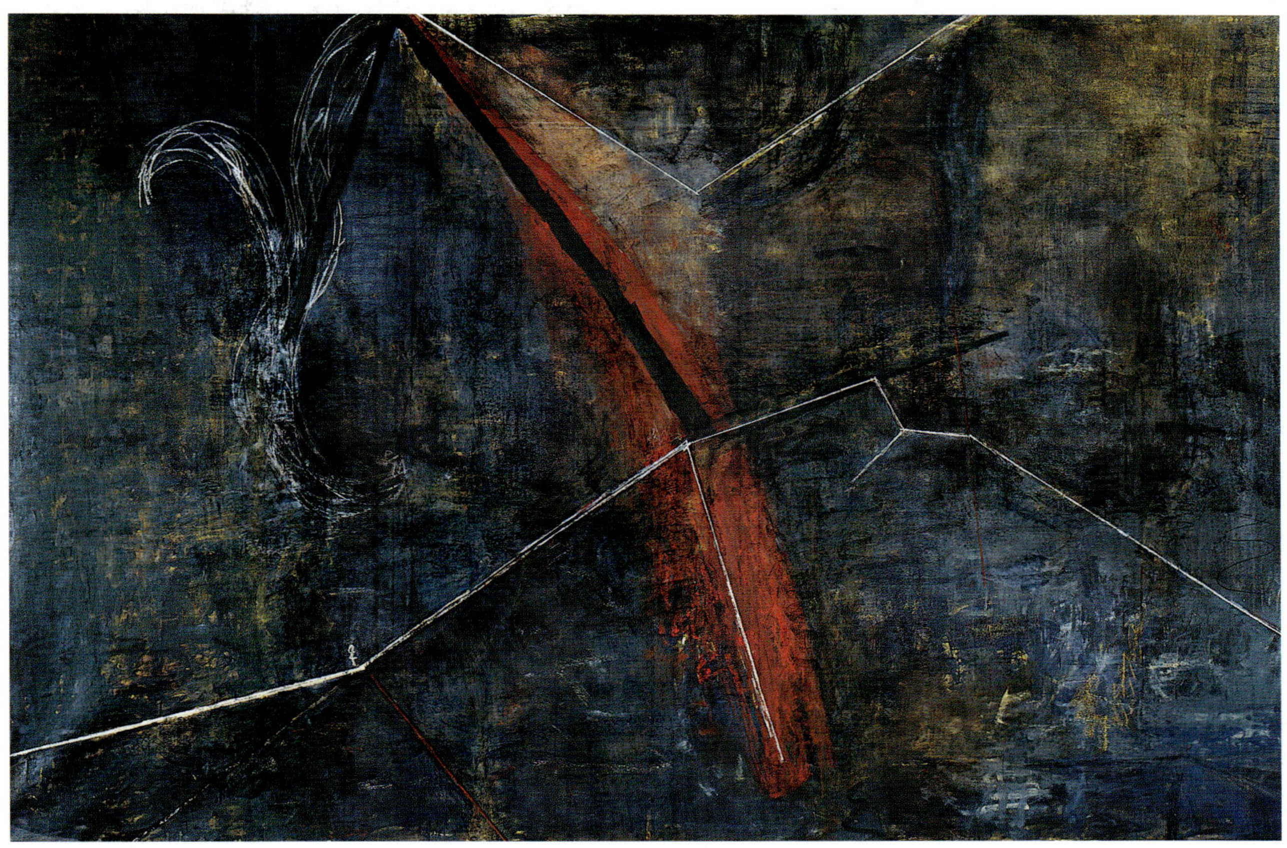

EUGENE NEWMANN b. 1936 Bratislava, Czechoslovakia. Ed. Univ. Chicago. Coll. Museum of New Mexico, Museum of Albuquerque, Roswell Museum NM; Monterey Peninsula Museum of Art CA; McNay Art Museum, San Antonio TX; etal. Representation: Linda Durham Contemporary Art, Galisteo NM and New York.

THE 22ND HOUR, 1991
OIL ON CANVAS
110 X 169 INCHES

EARL STROH

The reason stars and distant city lights twinkle is that they are filtered through atmospheric particles before they reach the eye. The light bends and refracts, scatters and dances, bounces off mountaintops and nestles in valleys. Light is never static. It lives and breathes, and gives life and breath to all it touches.

When Earl Stroh arrived in Taos in 1947, he fell in love with the unique quality of the northern New Mexico light. In the intervening years, he made it his own. Stroh's abstract work is important not only for the intellectual rigor of its composition but for the movement and nuances of its vibrant, light-saturated atmosphere.

Stroh was immediately at home with the intellectual environment of Taos, even then a small but mighty art colony. Several important modernists had recently arrived, and Stroh studied privately with two of them. From Andrew Dasburg, he learned a Cézannesque approach to the landscape. Tom Benrimo's elegant textures, in vastly different form, found their way into Stroh's mature, strongly individual style, which is characterized by his great respect for the medium and the surface. Subject is incidental to him; what matters is intent, ethics, integrity.

Even as he became a vital part of the Taos community, Stroh continued to travel in Europe and South America, studying in Paris, honing his eye in great museums, and maintaining his place in the larger world of art. By thus keeping abreast of world trends, he has made one of his most valuable contributions: an unflinching criticism of the history of New Mexico art as he has witnessed it.

His knowledge is encyclopedic. Like a modern Socrates, he takes aim at the extraneous, the inauthentic, and the presumptuous. He reserves a special satiric approach for those he deems "modernoid," yet observes that certain figurative painting in the twentieth century succeeded because it was somehow modern. "There are no absolute rules," he points out, "but the general tendency had to be toward the more abstract."

Critical though he may be, he has established a strong personal community of artist friends throughout the years. He was closely involved in the Taos Artists Association and the Stables Gallery when it was a true cooperative, and he has wonderful tales to tell of their differences as well as their progress. Through it all, he has supported that which elevates challenging, creative art.

In the fifty-plus years since he arrived in New Mexico, Earl Stroh has taken his place as one of the most important Taos artists from the last half of the twentieth century. He continues into the twenty-first with undiminished skill and passion, expanding his vision and refining his technique, giving life and breath to his subjects through rigorous abstraction.

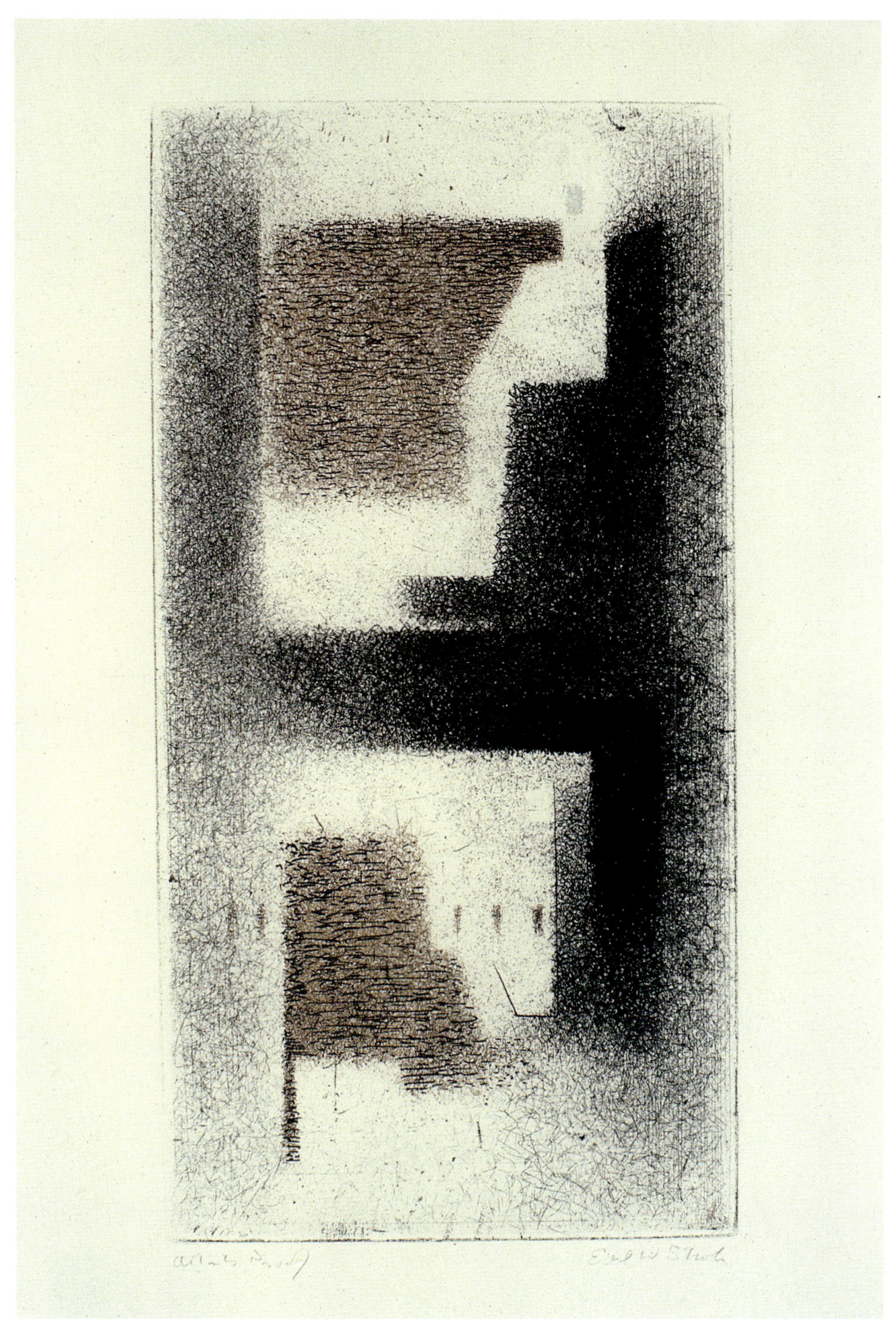

DUET, 1959
ETCHING
21 X 14 INCHES
Collection J. Kendall, Fenix Gallery

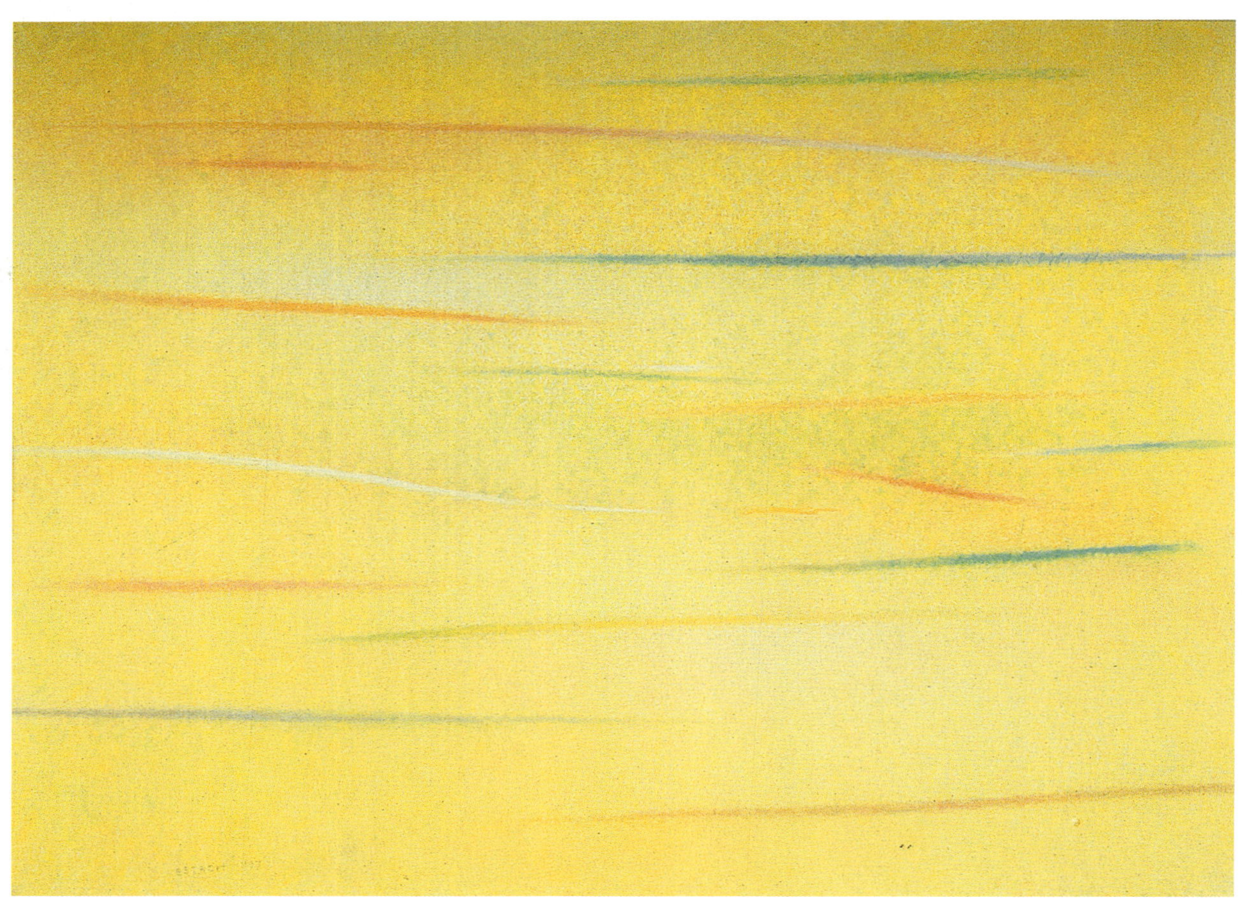

HELIOS, 1995
PASTEL
37 X 48 INCHES
Collection J. Kendall, Fenix Gallery

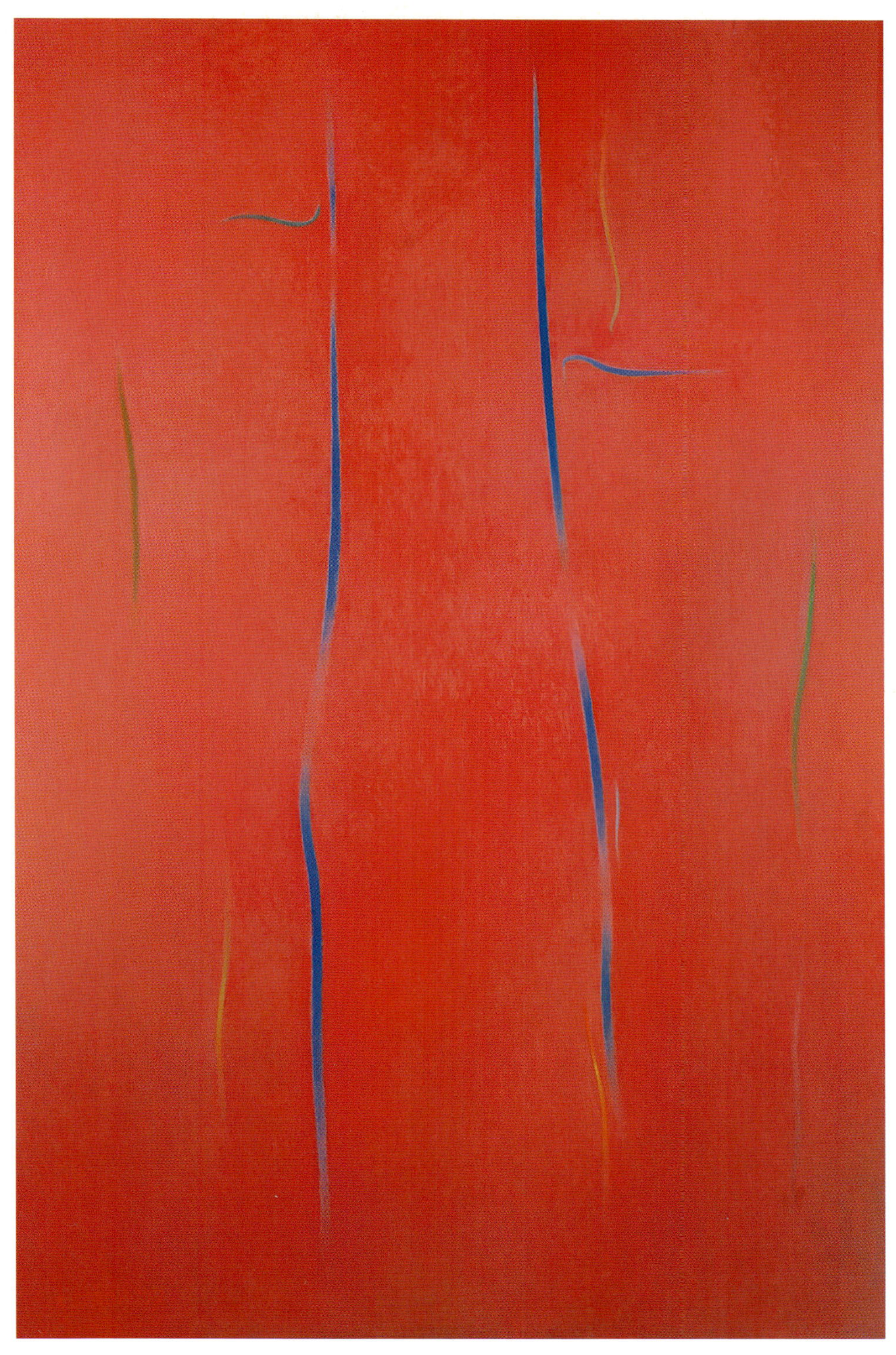

HEPHAESTUS
OIL ON CANVAS
72 X 48 INCHES
Private Collection

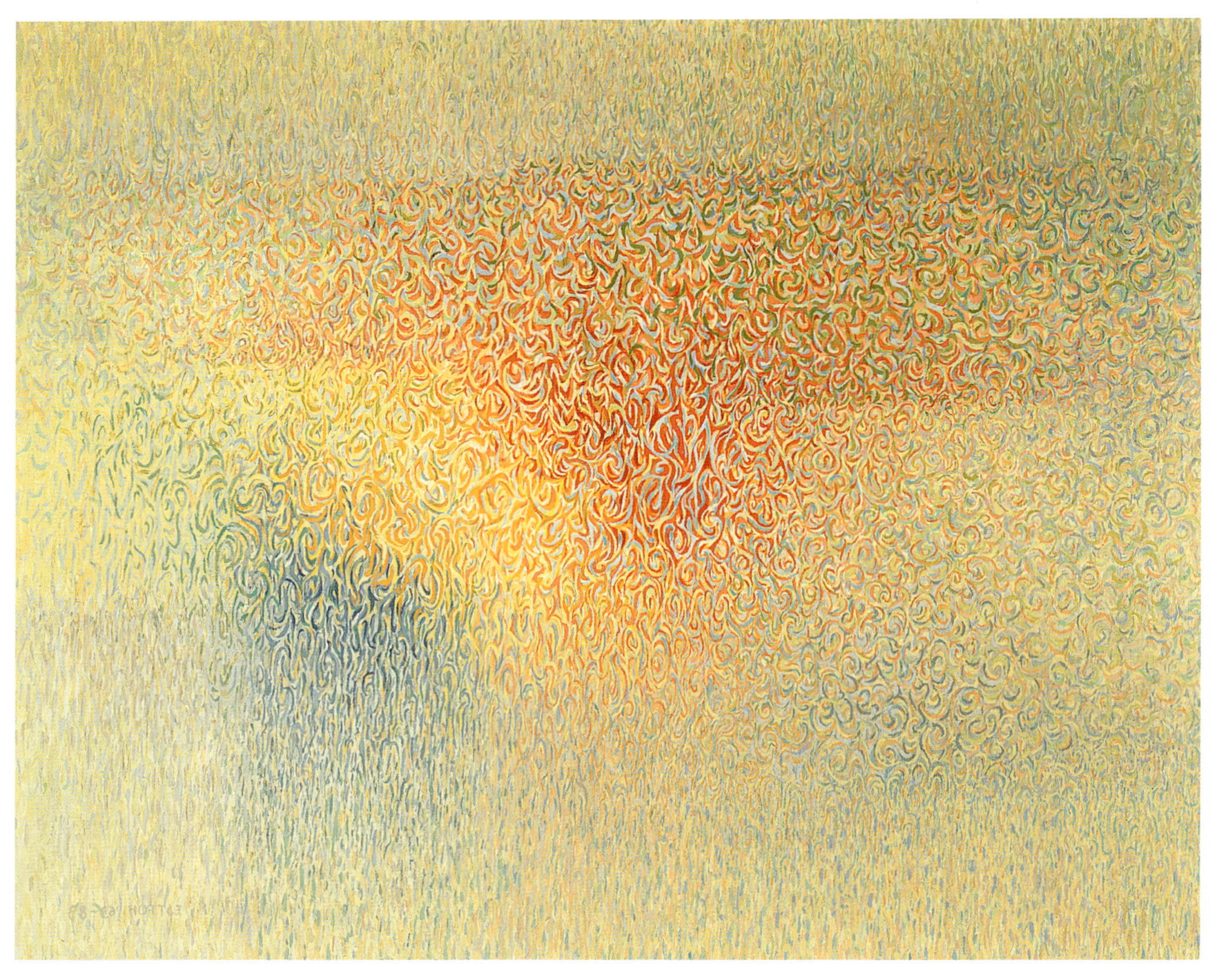

WINDS, 1963-1993
OIL ON CANVAS
47 X 57 INCHES
Courtesy Bidstrup Collection

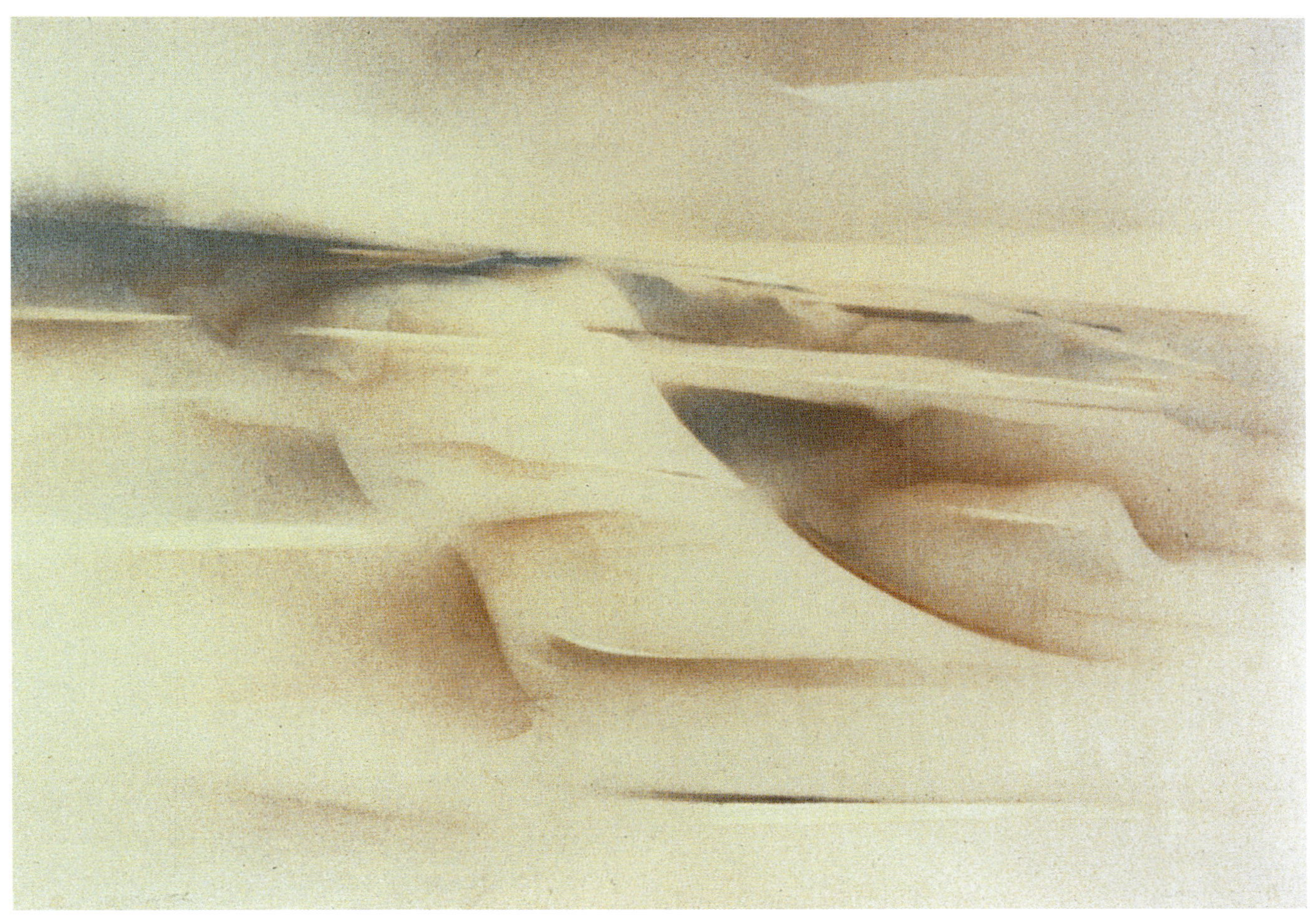

EARL STROH b. 1924 Buffalo NY. Ed: Buffalo Art Institute; Art Students League, NYC; Univ. New Mexico. Atelier Friedlander, Paris; Tamarind Institute NM. Coll: Metropolitan Museum; Chicago Art Institute; Denver Museum of Art; Fort Worth Modern; Museum of Fine Arts NM; etal. Representation: Fenix Gallery, Taos.

THRACIAN MODE, 1979
LITHOGRAPH
20 X 29 INCHES
Collection J. Kendall, Fenix Gallery

FREDERICK HAMMERSLEY

When one big shape comes up against another big shape, energy is generated. When a strong color meets black and white, chemistry happens. When one important part of life fits closely against another, the most amazing patterns occur.

Questions are generated: how, exactly, does one's philosophy fit into one's environment? Where does an individual psyche leave off and a marriage begin? According to Frederick Hammersley, the answer is painting. Hammersley, who has been called one of the living treasures of New Mexico, has been quietly working in Albuquerque for many years – but his fame preceded him and has transcended his New Mexico sojourn. He has been widely recognized and appreciated since the mid-twentieth century, when he and a handful of other Californians departed radically from the norms of the day and ushered in the era of hard-edge painting. He was also a pioneer of Minimalism.

Hammersley remembers looking at his work from that long-ago time in Los Angeles. "I was doing a marriage of opposites," he says. "There is a peculiar pleasure in seeing opposites that work. It's not intentional. I rely on gut feeling, intuition, and first impulse. If it feels right to me, then it might promote a smile of understanding in the observer."

He also spends a great deal of time on titles. "Sometimes the title takes longer than the painting," he says. "I keep on working with words and free associations, then let them age. The painting and I age, too. Words are fascinating. I like the marriage of opposites in words as well as images." For example, there are two paintings that do this. One is called Next is Now, the other, Sacred and Pro Fame. The reason titles are important is that he wants the words to do what the painting does – thereby providing a logical and easy entrance into the visual world, the painting. Jokes, too, are like paintings, like poems: they do two things at once.

Hammersley once described his work method as proceeding by "hunch." Nothing was done unless it felt right. "I'd wait until color would come, then paint," he says. "I think what I've been doing all this while is talking about the center of me, about being alive. When I get there I know it. And, when I get there I like to think it has something in common with the one who looks at it. You see something of yourself."

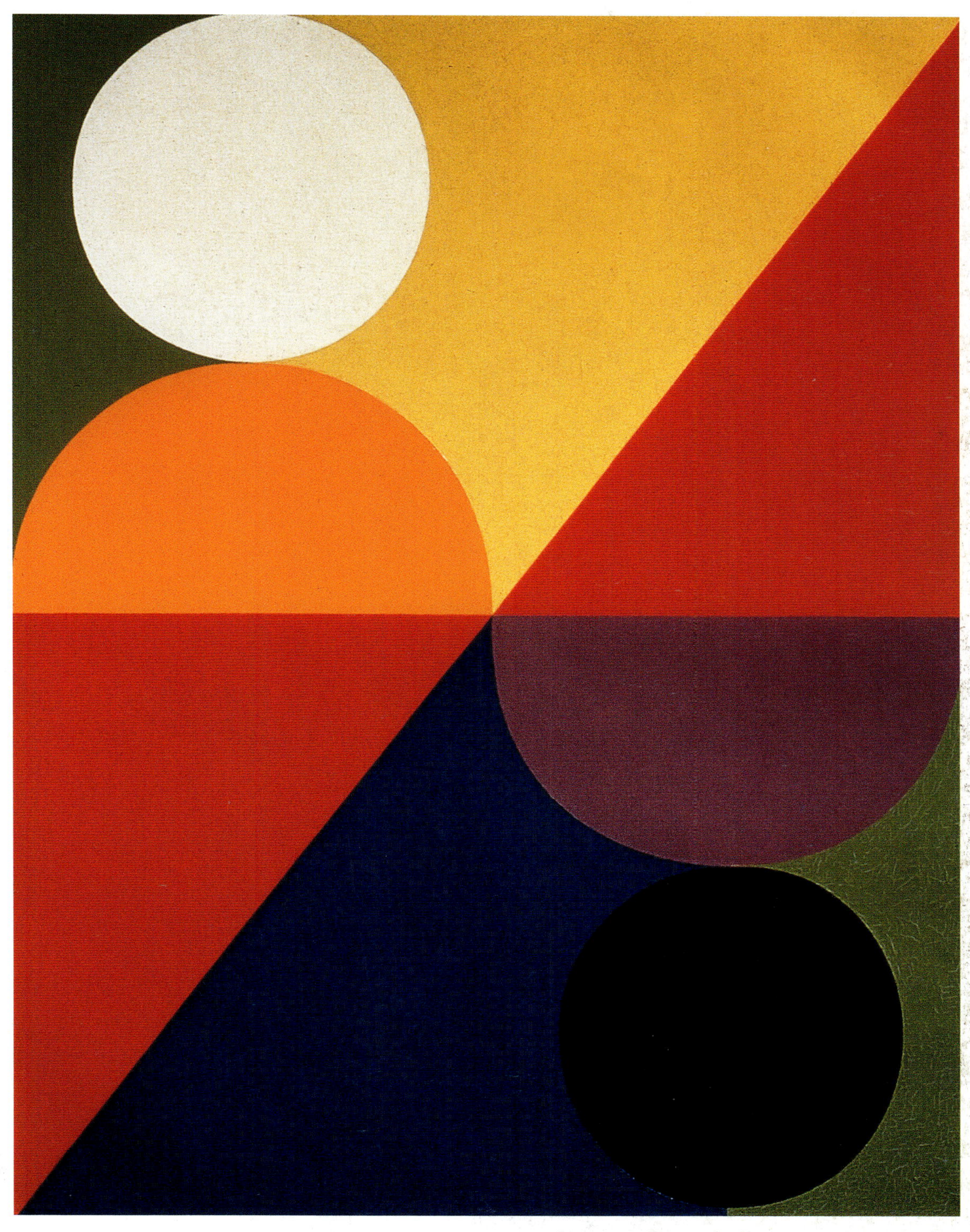

HALF WHOLE #16, 1959
OIL ON LINEN
50 X 40 INCHES
Private Collector, New York City
Courtesy Snyder Fine Art

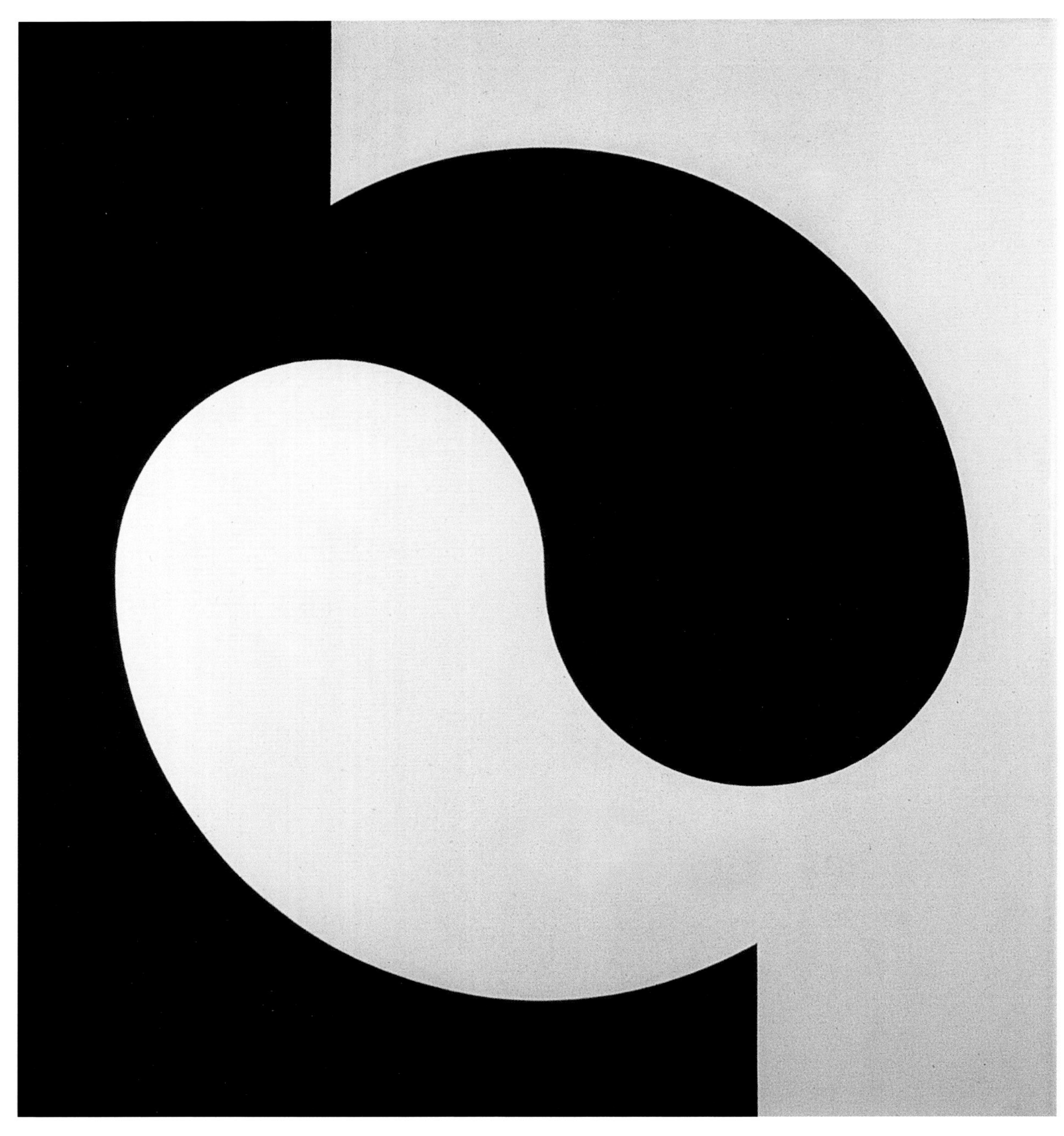

NEXT IS NOW #18, 1965
OIL ON LINEN
48 X 44 INCHES
Collection Howard Ahmanson
Los Angeles CA

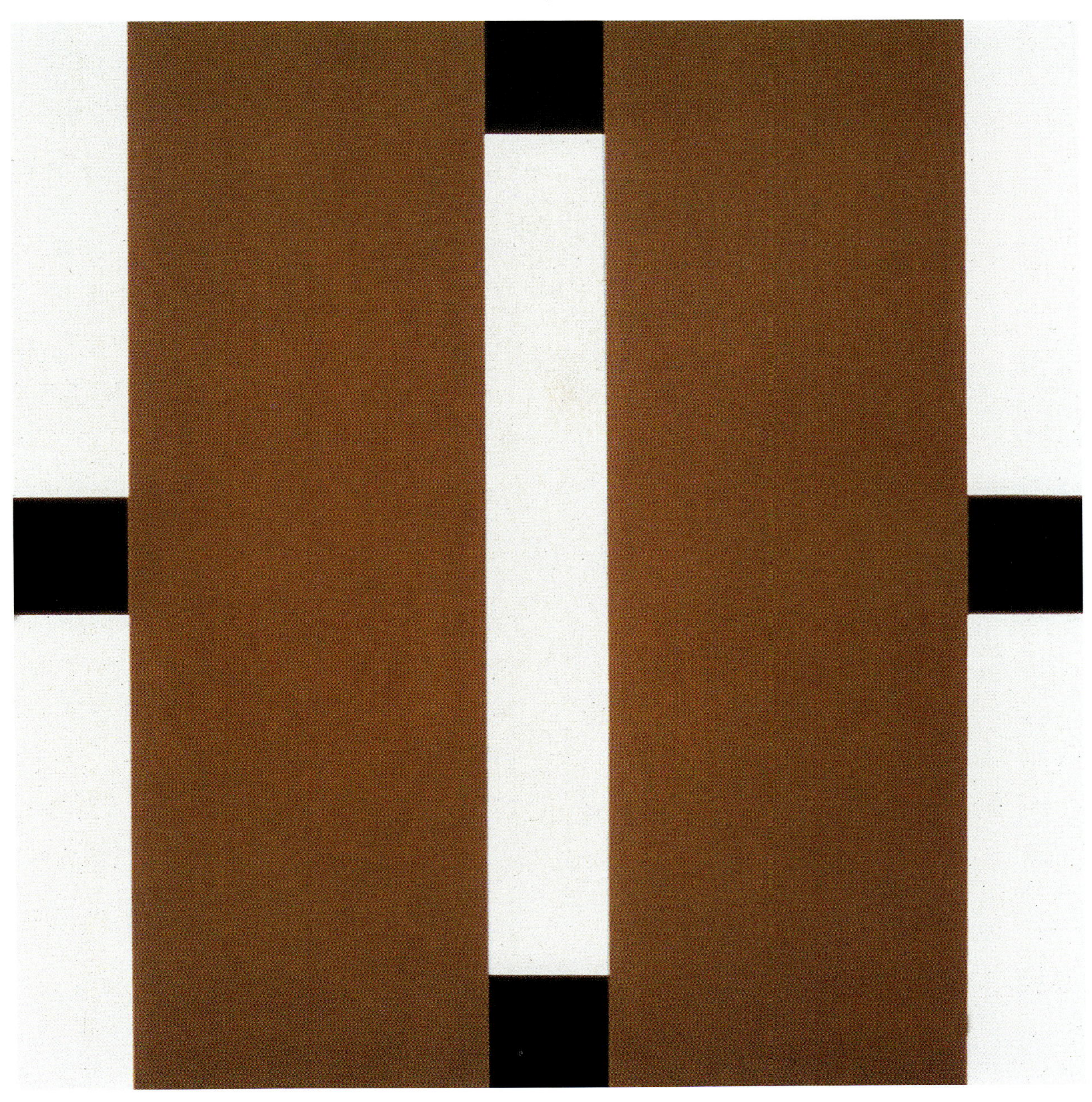

REFER TWO #8, 1973
OIL ON LINEN
42 X 42 INCHES
Collection Corcoran Gallery of Art
1977 Biennial, Washington DC

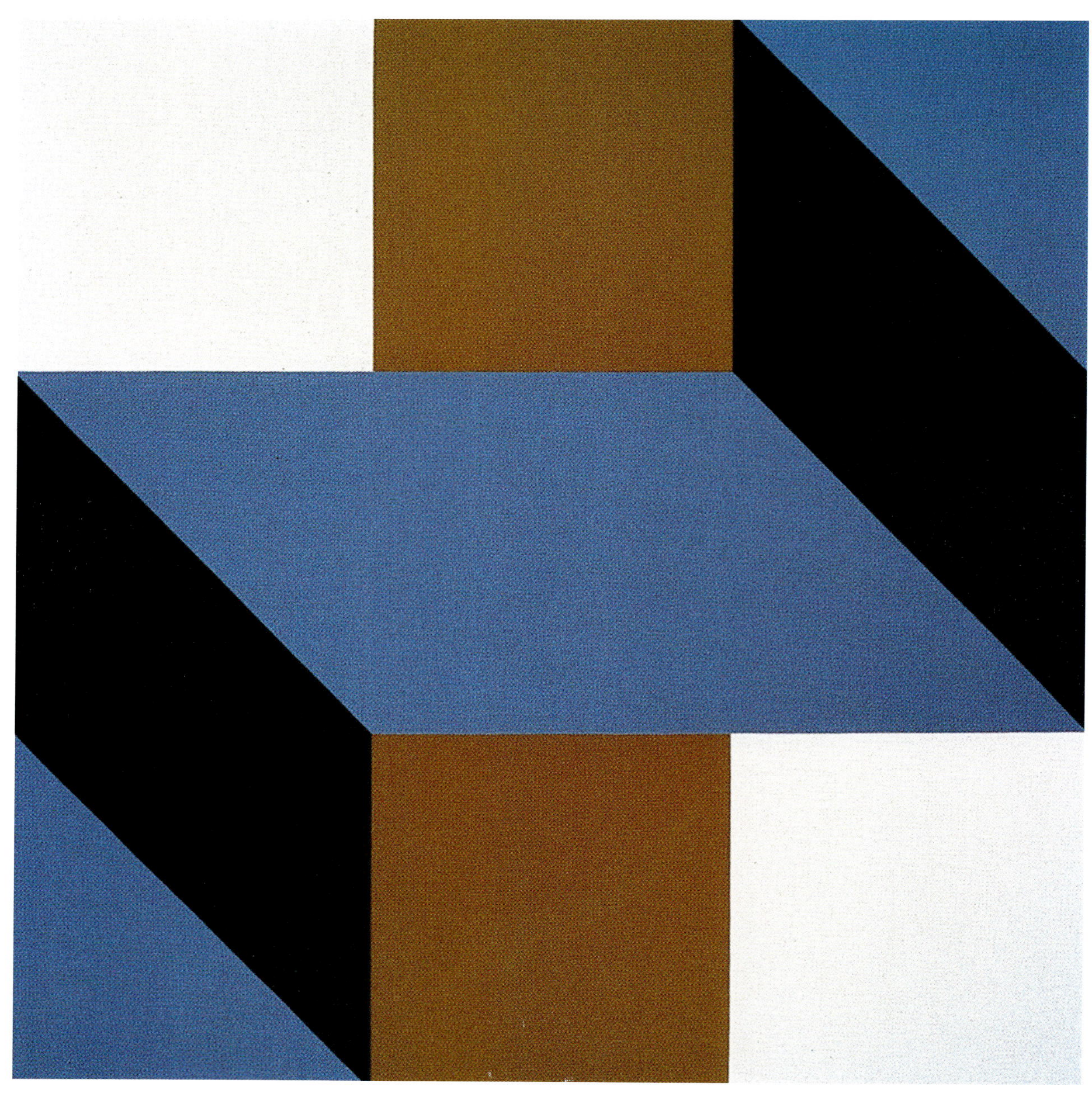

WILL POWER #6, 1980
OIL ON LINEN
48 X 48 INCHES
Collection Roswell Museum & Art Center
Roswell NM

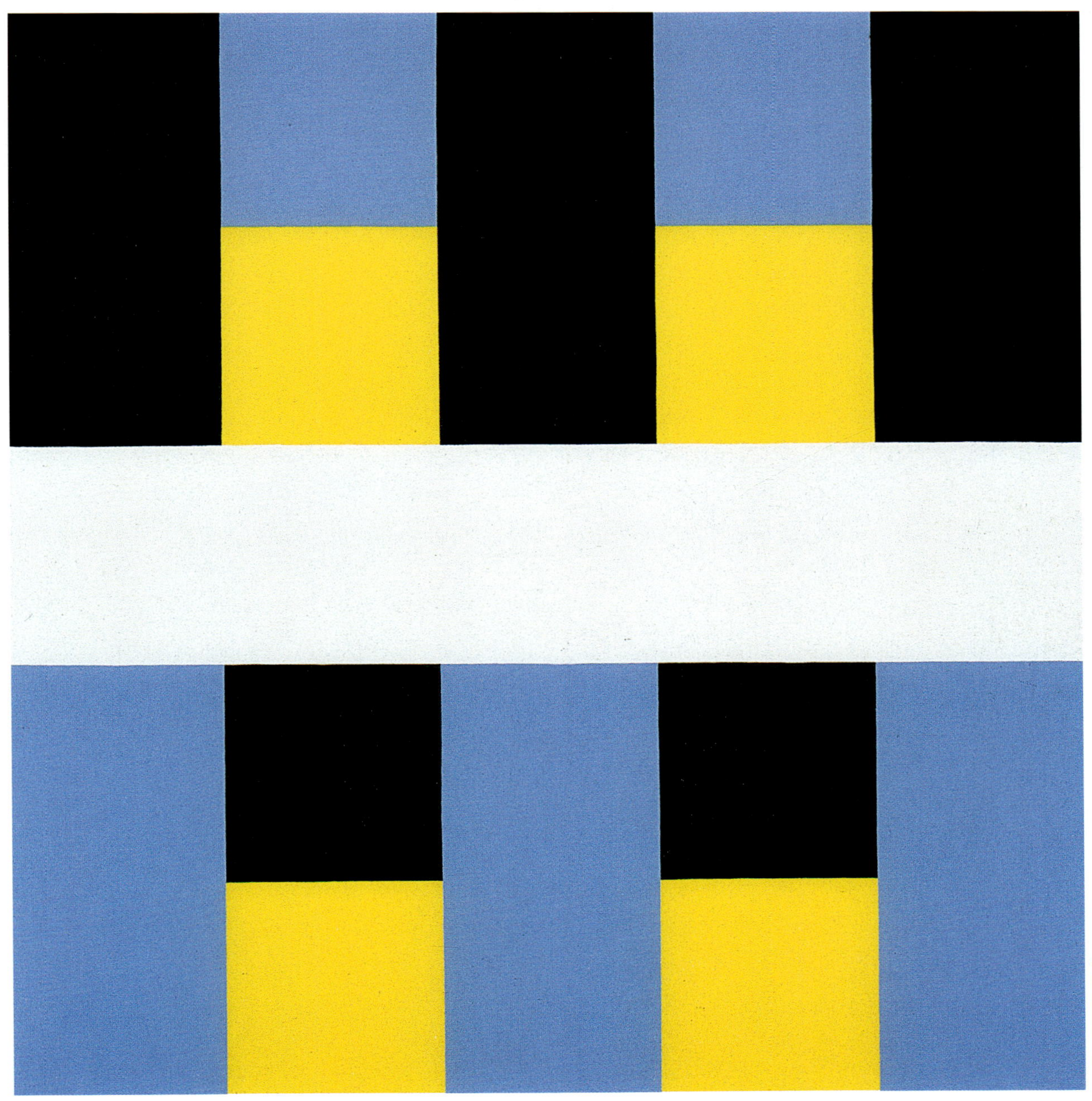

FREDERICK HAMMERSLEY b. 1919 Salt Lake City. Ed: Jepson Art School and Chouinard, Los Angeles; École des Beaux Arts, Paris, France. Coll: Corcoran Gallery DC; San Francisco Museum of Modern Art CA; Vincent Price; etal. Representation: Richard Levy Gallery, Albuquerque; Charlotte Jackson Fine Art, Santa Fe.

DOUBLE DIP #1, 1996
OIL ON LINEN
40 X 40 INCHES
Collection of the Artist
Courtesy L.A. Louver, Venice CA

SETH ANDERSON

Follow an impulse down a neural pathway and it will detour through a dizzying configuration of cells on its way to its destination. Follow a life down time and it will inhabit many different rooms in the course of its journey. Follow a line of thought as it crosses other lines, and it will alter its direction. More importantly perhaps, it will change the line it is crossing.

Seth Anderson incorporates all this linear intelligence into works of art that stand alone as elegant esthetic objects. In his imagery, line becomes texture becomes map becomes puzzle. It dances, explores, and runs around exuberantly. It leaves one plane and vaults to the next. It circles back upon itself and gathers pools of color and light. It becomes a tapestry, an exalted circus, an indelible heartprint.

Anderson utilizes uncommon materials in his carefully developed and highly personal painting technique, which incorporates collage, construction, painting, and drawing. For his classic pieces, he begins with the application of acrylic paints, inks, and acrylic inks on paper. He sometimes cuts up the paper and reassembles it, creating texture with hand-rubbed oils and stains. The individual fragments are affixed to a wood or Plexiglas™ base. Finally, he applies a coat of beeswax, both for protection and for giving the work its lovely tactile quality.

Together with these works, for which he is best known, is a concurrent series involving digital imagery. These images are deconstructed and reassembled in a more random order. His line, that lyrical and elegant line, takes on an edgier and more conflicted quality as it is summarily halted at the edge of one plane and then arbitrarily takes up again on another unrelated one. Compartmentalization is a fact of contemporary life, says the chaotic grid. And yet, says the stubbornly joyous line, the life of the mind is not compromised by even the most severe strictures unless the individual acquiesces to them.

Anderson frames these latter works in thick glass and aluminum which underscores their thought-provoking interplay between freedom and containment. "To me," he says, "these pieces suggest a free-flowing line of subconscious thought that is restricted in some way. What I believe it involves is the process of thinking through everyday realities, of dealing with responsibilities, balancing practical considerations with creativity and of trying to be truly free."

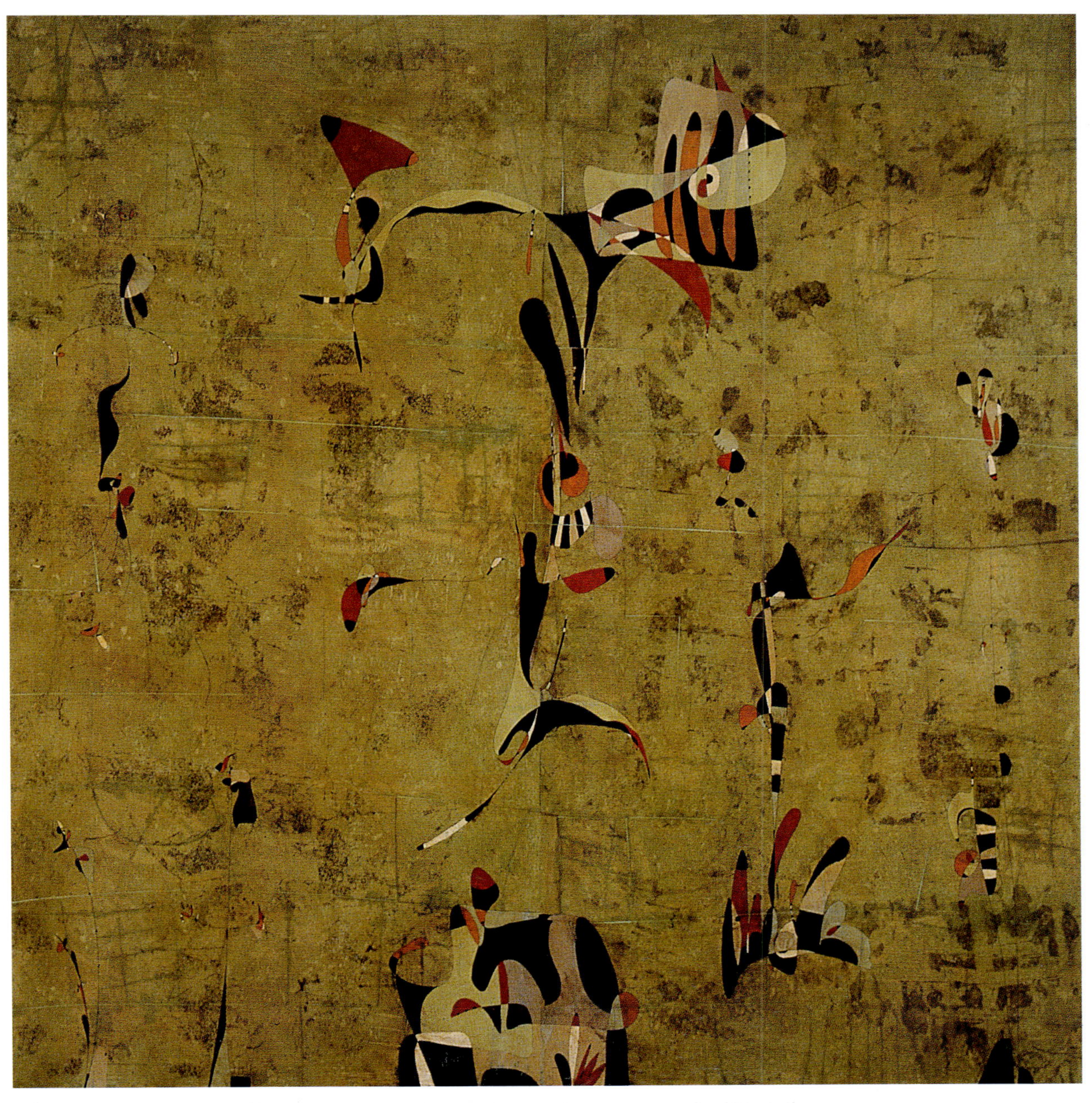

IN A SINGLE BOUND
MIXED MEDIA ON WOOD
60 X 60 X 3 INCHES

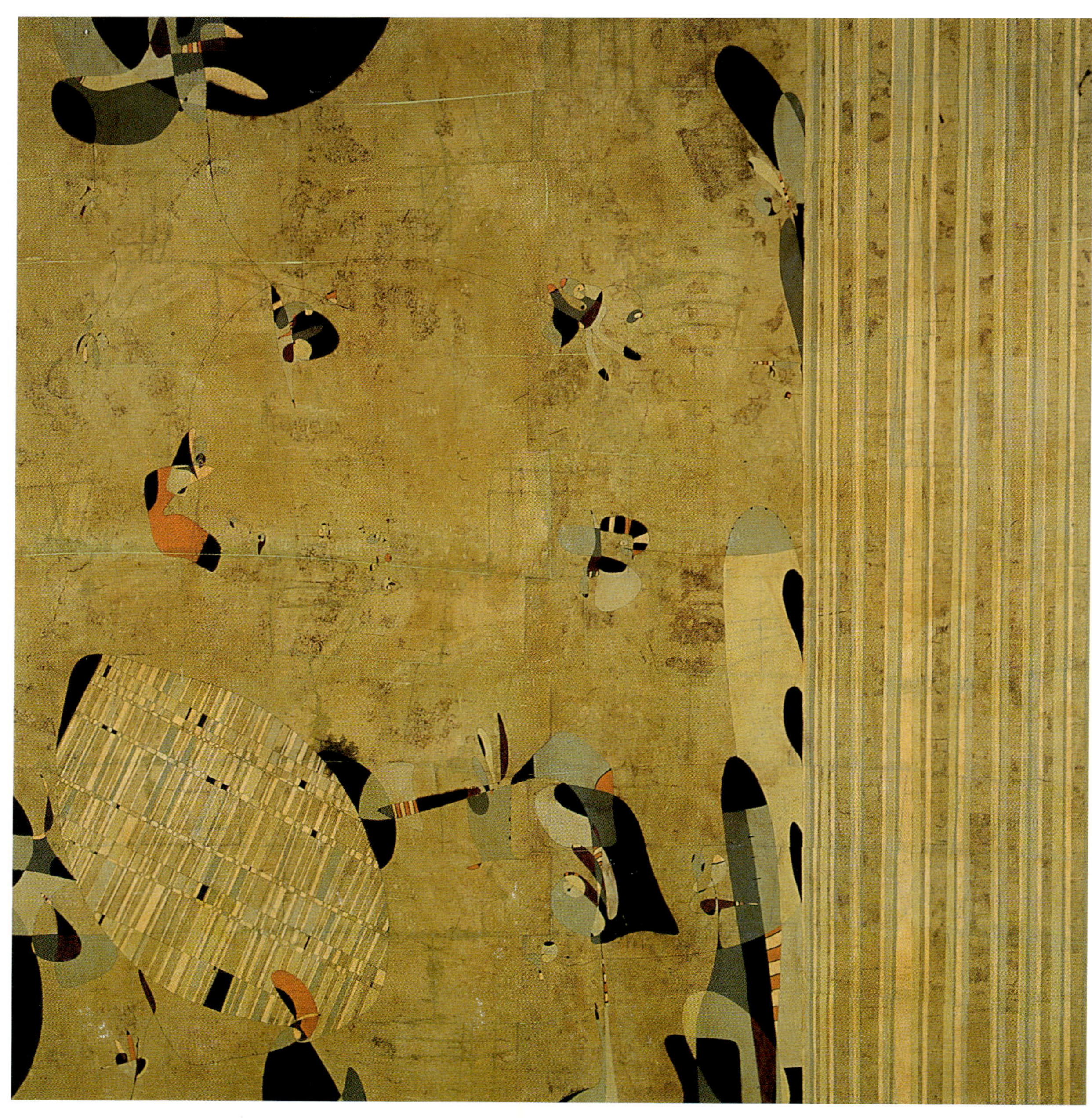

MOVING THE EGG
MIXED MEDIA ON WOOD
60 X 60 X 3 INCHES

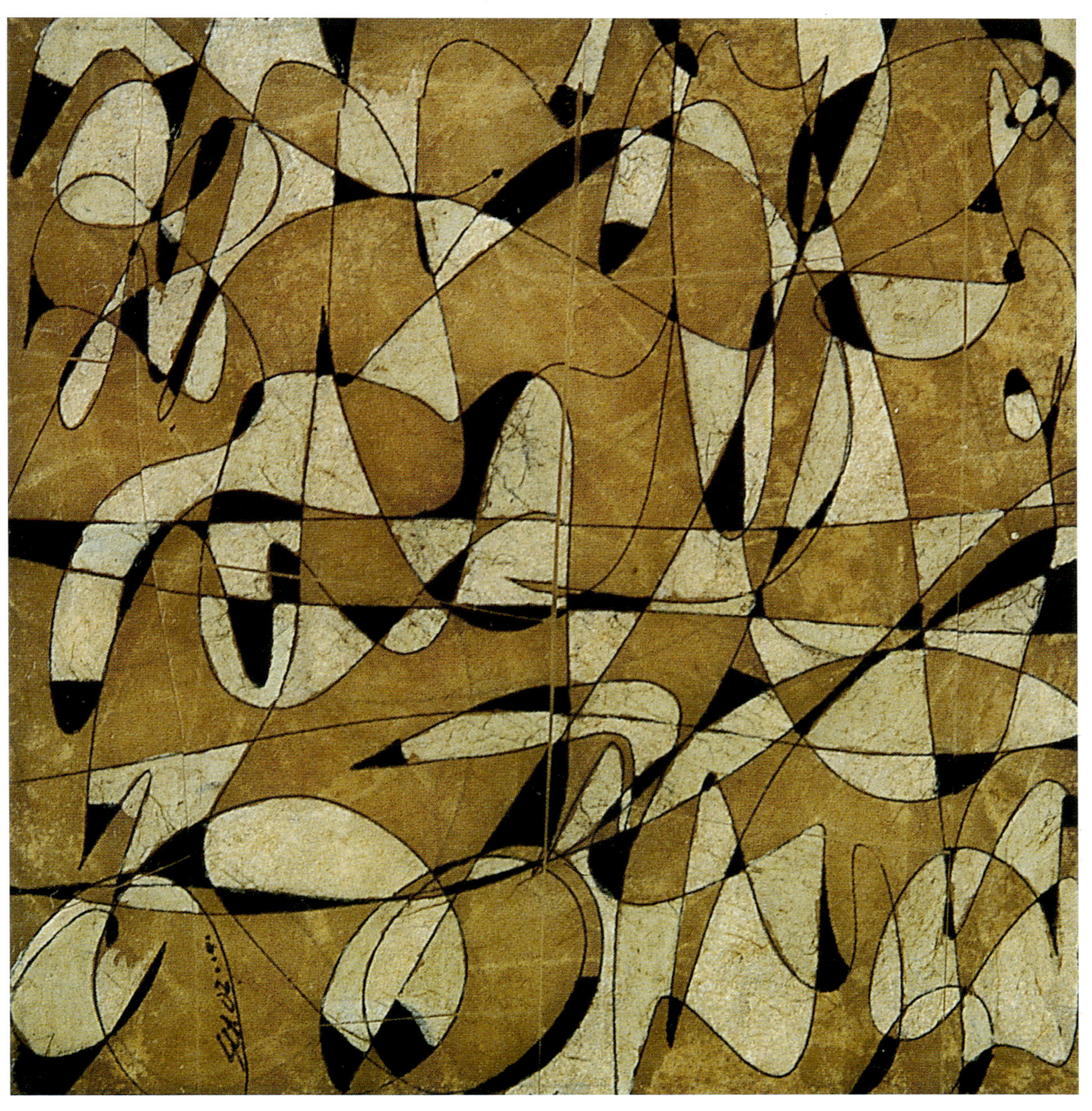

SMALL BLK/WHITE #2
MIXED MEDIA ON PLEXIGLAS
10 X 10 INCHES

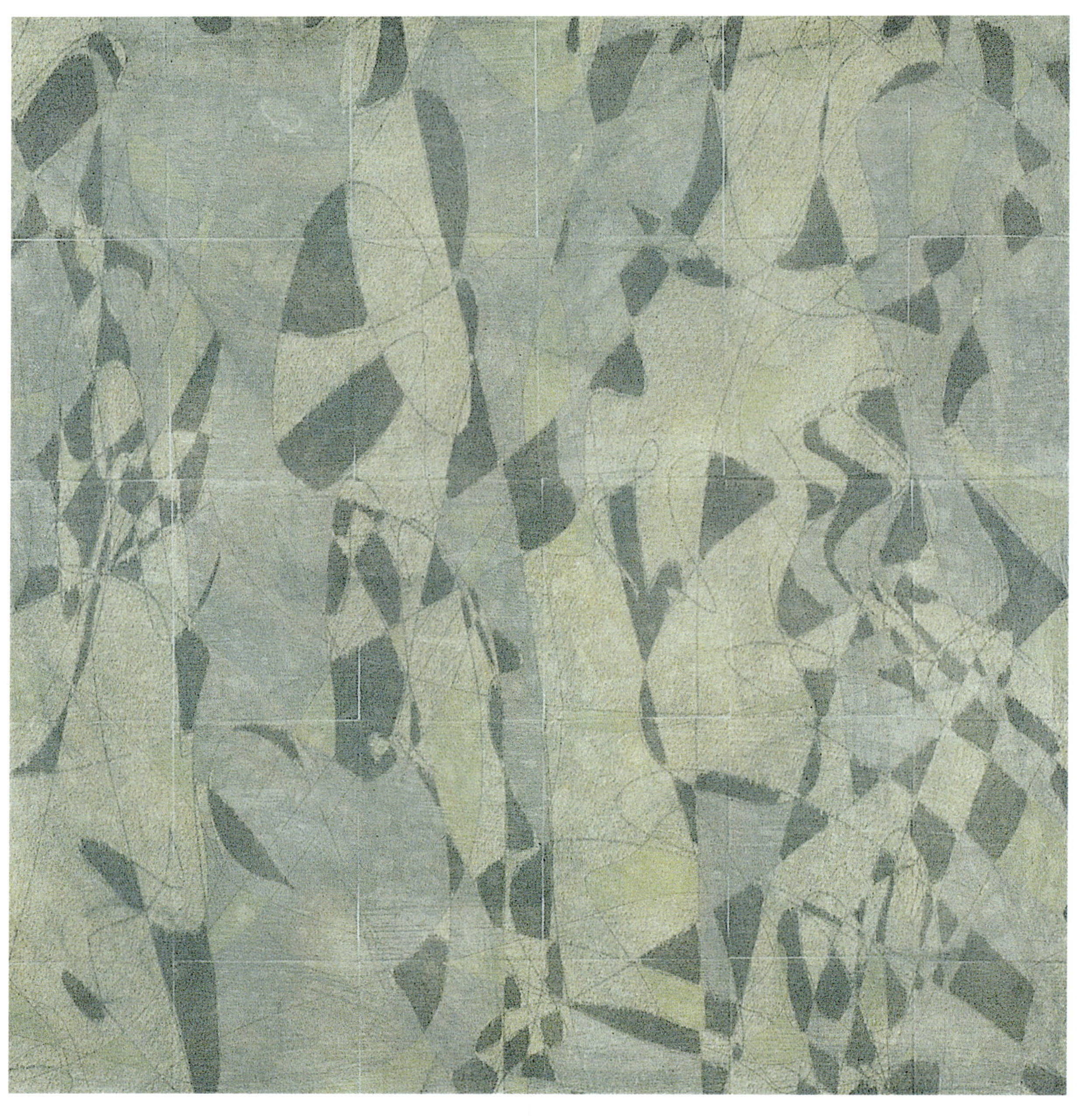

A LINE SERIES #44
MIXED MEDIA ON WOOD
48 X 48 INCHES

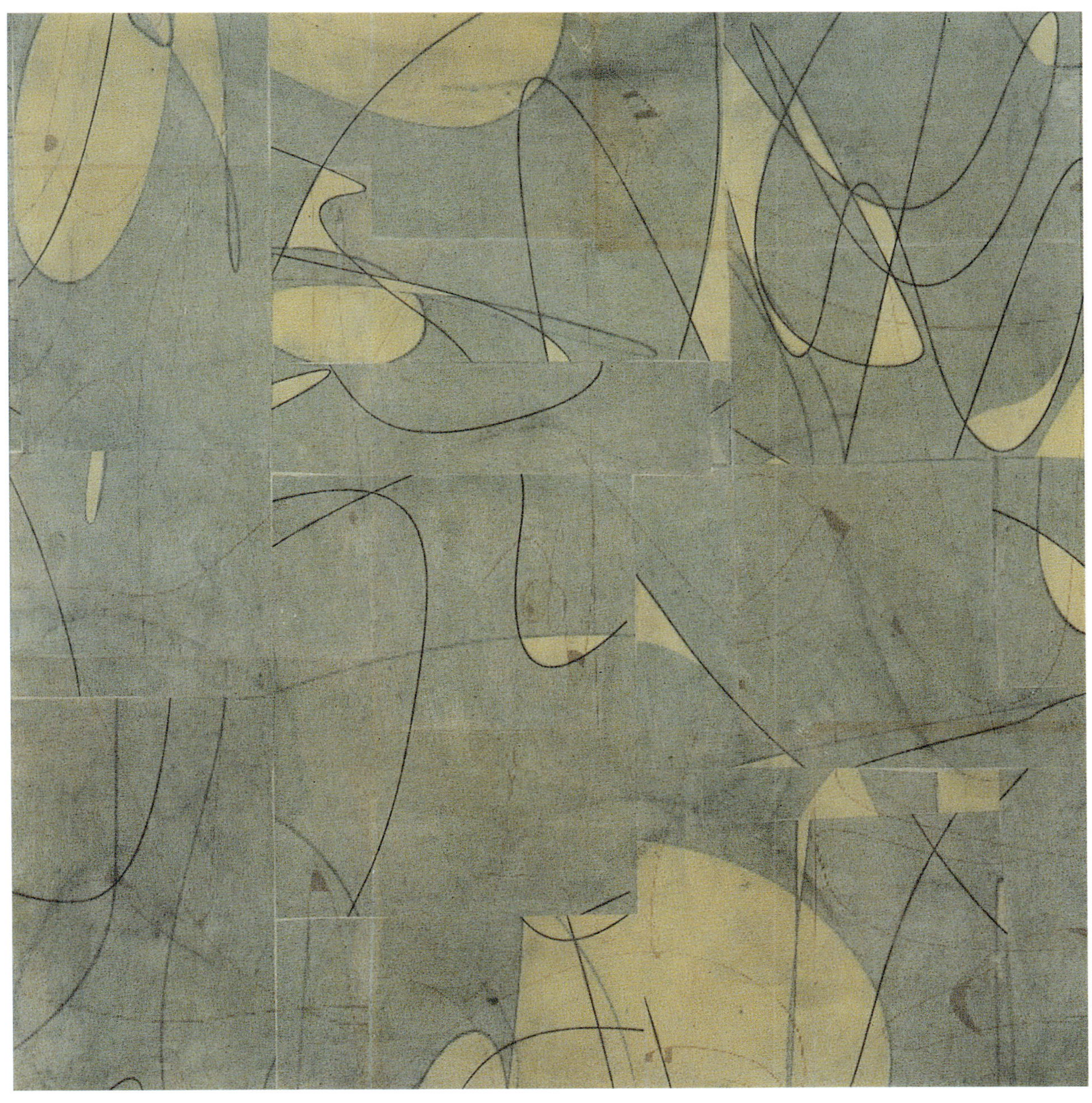

SETH ANDERSON b. 1972 Washington DC. Ed: Univ. Colorado; fellow, Glasgow School of Art, Scotland. Exhib/Coll: Contemporary Art Society of NM. Invitational: Houston's Restaurant Collection NYC; Capitol Art Collection NM. Representation: Anderson Contemporary Art, Santa Fe.

A LINE SERIES #31
MIXED MEDIA ON WOOD
24 X 24 INCHES

GARO Z. ANTREASIAN

The paradox of the Renaissance was that it set art free yet simultaneously established certain restrictive conventions, among them the primacy of one medium over another. Oil paint was superior to watercolor and drawing, so the thinking went, and a stone sculpture was somehow loftier than a bronze one. This conceit lasted until the twentieth century, when Picasso and Duchamp opened the floodgates for experimentation with any and every conceivable material and technique.

Not until the last quarter of the twentieth century, however, did certain mediums come into their own. This was due largely to a few individuals who created outstanding art by pushing the limitations of their chosen field past all previous conceptions. Clay, fiber, and glass left the factory and went willingly with artists who could teach them to dance and sing. Fine printmaking, languishing in the propwash of mechanized reproduction, found its footing again as an expressive method with unique capabilities.

Garo Antreasian is widely recognized to be among a handful of artists responsible for this revival of lithographic printmaking in America. A prodigious artist in his own right, he pioneered the advancement of modern lithography as a generative painterly medium. He laid down many layers of translucent ink to produce a depth and density not unlike that of oil paint. Ever the innovator, Antreasian developed ways to print outsize pieces that permitted bold statements. "Because my development was far from a classical one," he says, "totally unorthodox procedures and materials would many times produce new and uniquely exciting results."

As a painter, he worked on the same bold scale, producing monumental canvases in his signature style of architectural, geometric vitality that focused on formal relationships but projected a subtly emotional undertone of memory. Over the years, as he balanced painting with printmaking, a basic shift occurred. "Whereas previously the images of my prints derived from my efforts in painting," he recalled, "thereafter the concepts of my paintings were to derive from my prints."

Antreasian has been fully as creative in his various administrative roles and his lifelong community involvement as he has been in his own art. He was founding Technical Director of the Tamarind Lithography Workshop in Los Angeles. He was Chairman of the Department of Art and Art History at the University of New Mexico, where his tenure was dynamic rather than custodial. With fellow printmaker Clinton Adams he was originally the Co-Director of Tamarind Institute, University of New Mexico, as well as the principal author of the *Tamarind Book of Lithography: Art and Techniques*, a definitive reference for the medium. He was a Trustee of the Albuquerque Museum for nine years helping to shape its current policies and development. Today, at the top of his form, Garo Z. Antreasian can survey his lifetime achievements and know that he has made lasting contributions to the creative heritage of New Mexico.

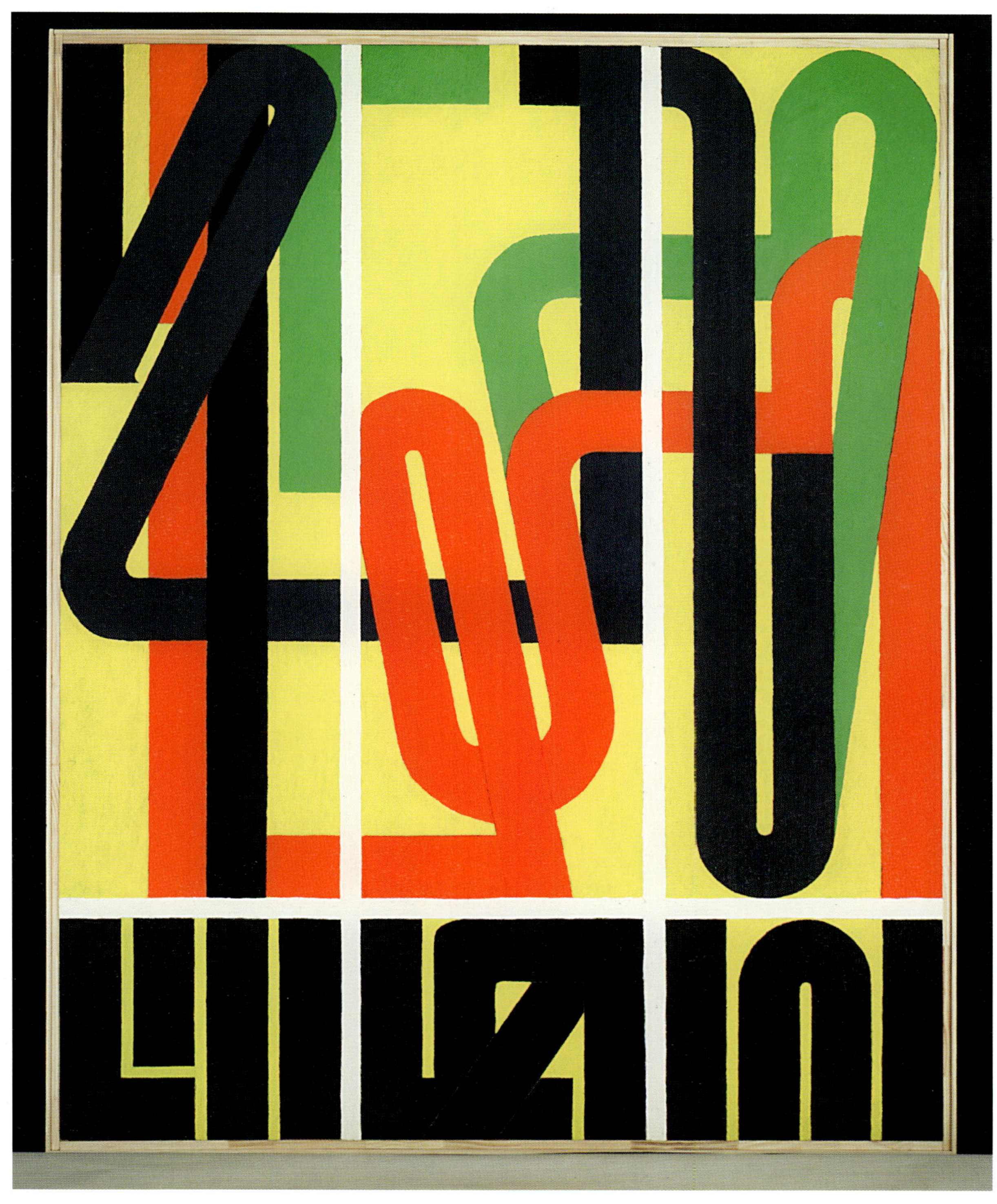

DAZZLE RAZZLE, 2003
ACRYLIC/WOOD
80½ X 65

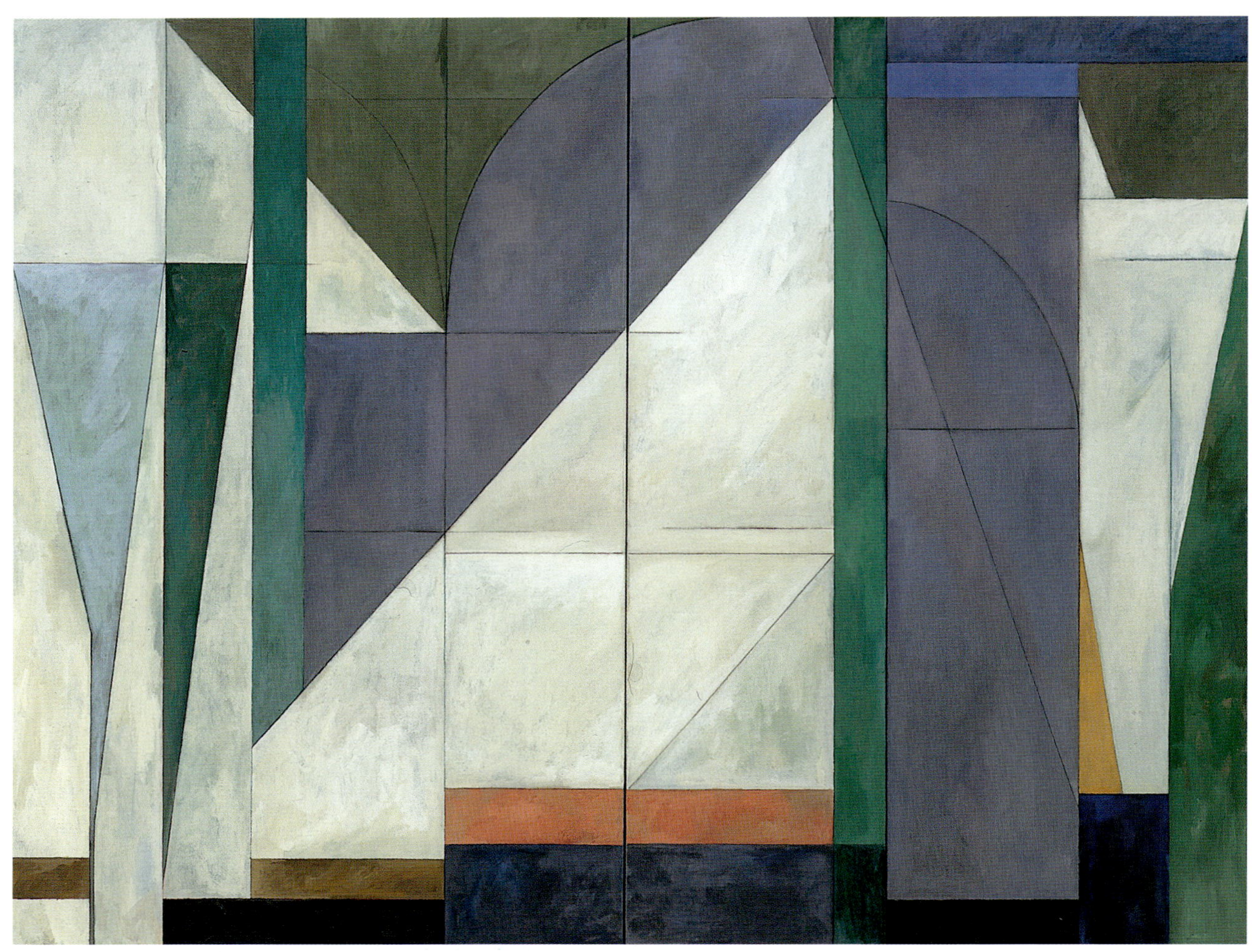

ADANA, 1986
ACRYLIC/CANVAS, DIPTYCH
72 X 96 INCHES
Private Collection

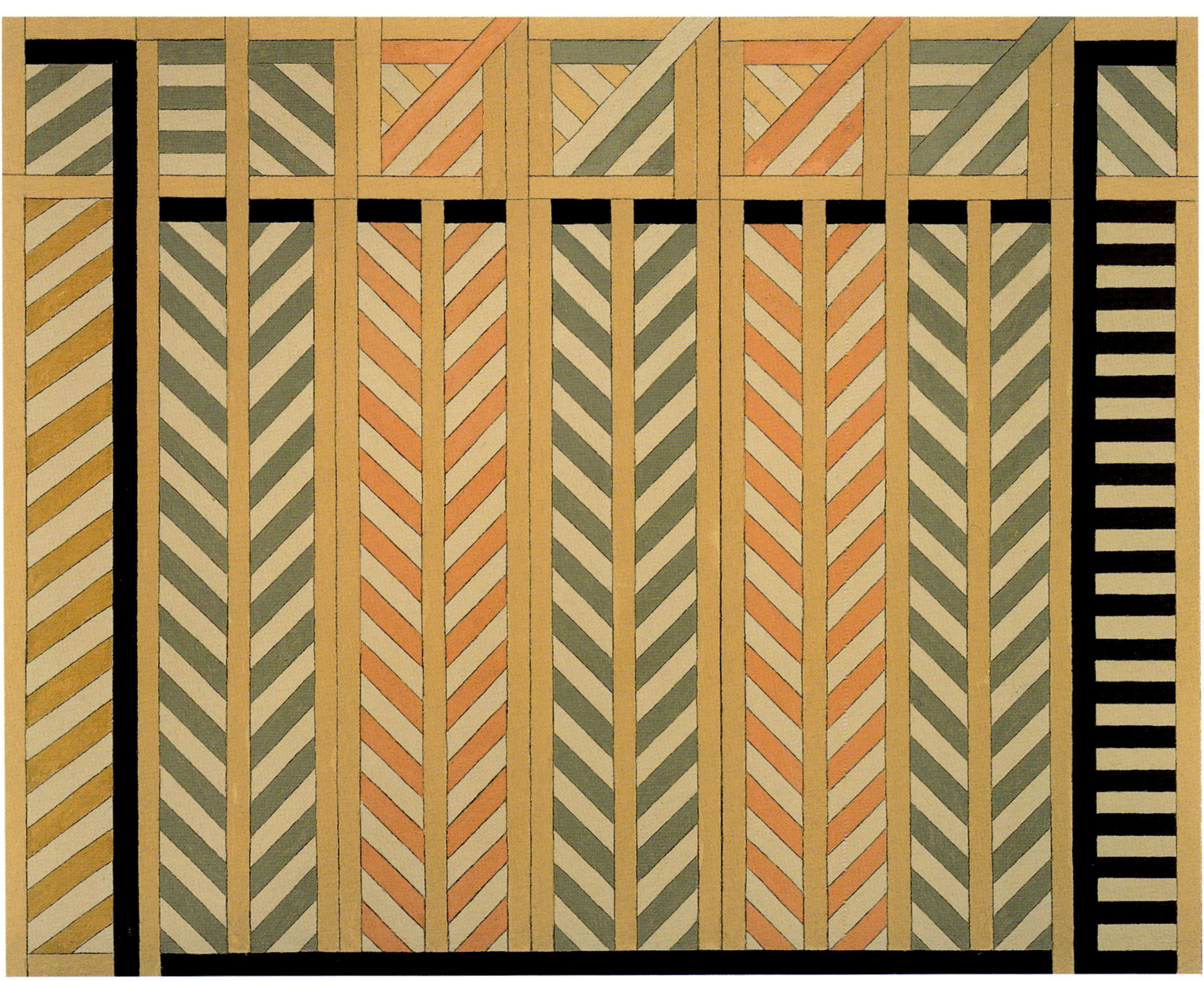

ANATOLIA, 1994
ACRYLIC/CANVAS, DIPTYCH
80 X 108 INCHES
Collection Roswell Museum & Art Center

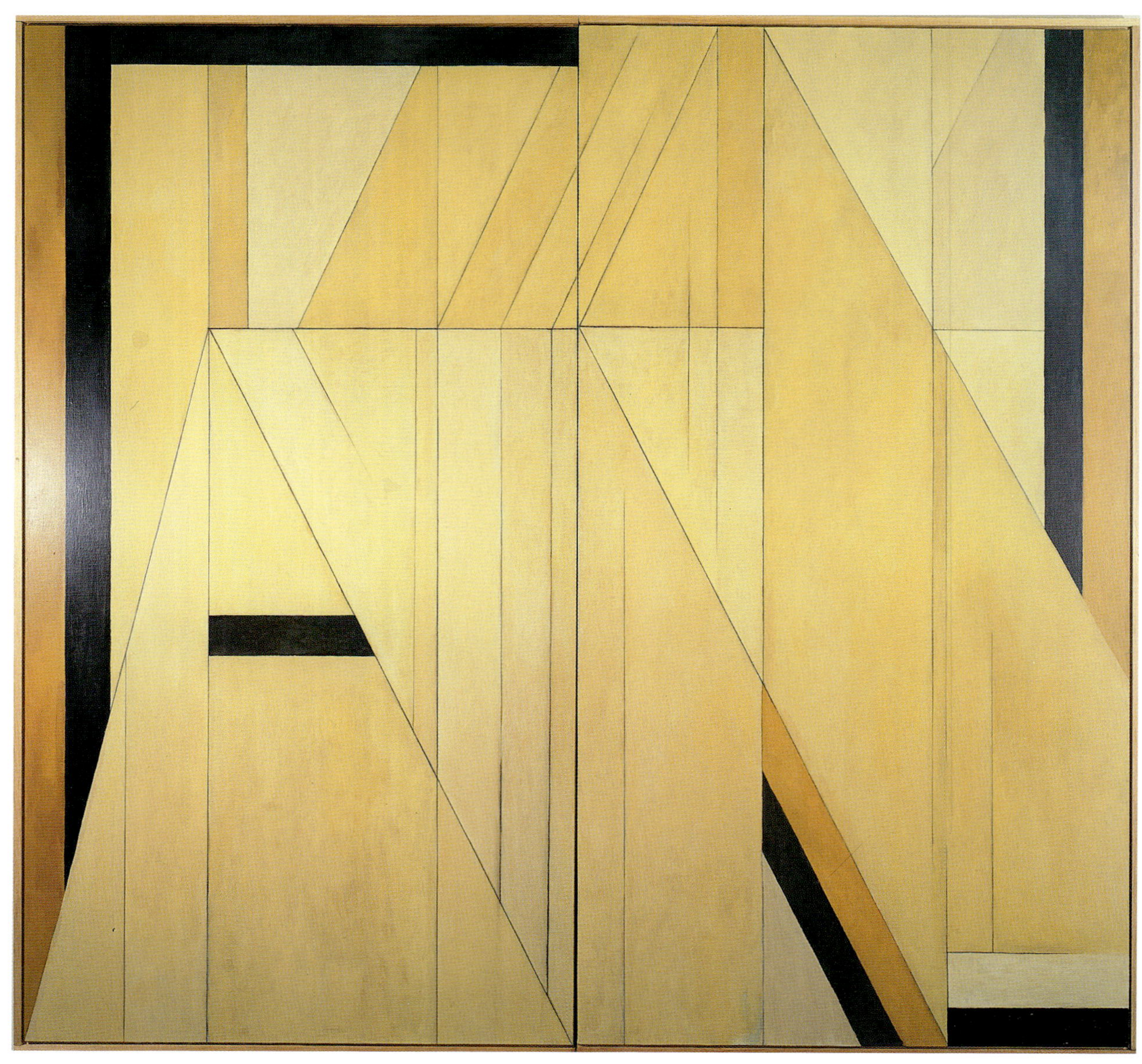

ALEPPO, 1985
ACRYLIC/CANVAS, DIPTYCH
80 X 70 INCHES
Collection Museum of New Mexico

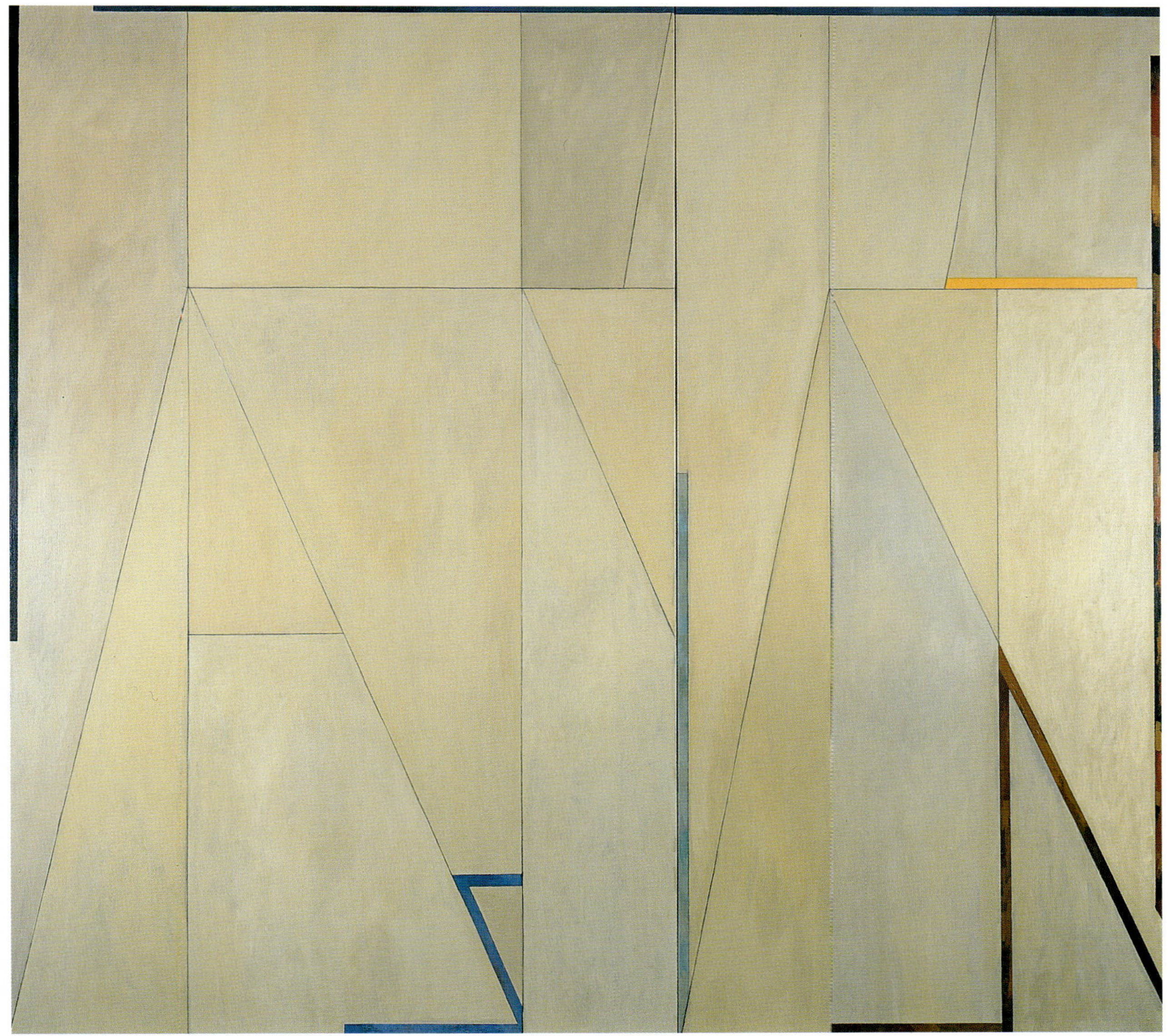

GARO Z. ANTREASIAN b. 1922 Indianapolis IN. Ed: BFA Herron School of Art, Indianapolis. Exhib: The White House, Library of Congress DC; retrospectives, Albuquerque Museum, Univ. New Mexico; Indianapolis Museum of Art. Coll: Chicago Art Institute; Boston Museum; Brooklyn Museum; Metropolitan Museum, MOMA NY; Smithsonian Institution DC; etal. Representation: Cline Fine Art, Santa Fe; Fenix Gallery, Taos.

SANJAK, 1985
ACRYLIC/CANVAS, DIPTYCH
80 X 90 INCHES
Private Collection

RICHARD C SMITH

Compartmentalization is an inescapable fact of modern life. Our rooms are boxes, our vehicles are boxes, our electronic servants are boxes. We live on the grid, in boxes that contain other grids. Our brains are becoming microchips.

Because we are human, however, we never quite manage to fit into the mechanical mode. Our hearts remain free. They beat unsteadily and change color at will beneath the sleek conceits of contemporary life. Despite the uniform appearance of our postmodern lives, there will always be a contrary streak of individuality, a sense of self that manifests in subtle irregularity and displacement.

Richard C Smith's California background has given him the tools and the mindset to posit these realities as bold, enigmatic works of art. Like the car culture and the celluloid lifestyle, his paintings present the smoothest of surfaces, without a trace of the artist's hand. He creates meticulous finishes with varnish, wax, and polishing machines similar to those used on auto bodies.

It is beneath those surfaces, however, that the wisdom lies. Just as an elegant and seamless public persona may conceal the most complex mind and personality, so do Smith's paintings yield up unexpected depths. He remembers the crumbling billboards he observed when he lived by the sea, and how each panel would peel off at different wear rates. In a similar fashion, he builds layers of information into his paintings, only to take some of it off at carefully chosen intervals. Sometimes he places the topmost coat at the bottom and works backward. "It takes a lot of layers underneath to add up to what I want," says Smith. "I always know how they're going to turn out. Of course, there are surprises in the juxtaposition of information, and sometimes they will change the subsequent layers."

Smith came of age in the hot Los Angeles art scene of the sixties. After attending school and working in an art gallery there, he took an extended tour of Europe. Then he settled in Venice, California for another six years. Returning to Europe, he lived in England for eighteen years, leading the life of a gentleman farmer and working with the Rare Breeds Survival Trust to keep certain livestock bloodlines intact. Smith's penchant for exactitude was the Trust's most valuable asset.

He had turned his back on his art for a time, but not on his passion for order. Like a portion of one of his grids, he had simply compartmentalized his life. When he returned to the States, it was with a renewed zest for painting. He chose to relocate to Santa Fe, where he has spent the past decade.

"My work may look symmetrical," he says, "but some of it is distinctly not. Some of it looks three dimensional, too, but it is completely flat. The geometry, for me, is a way of dealing with the concept of chaos versus order."

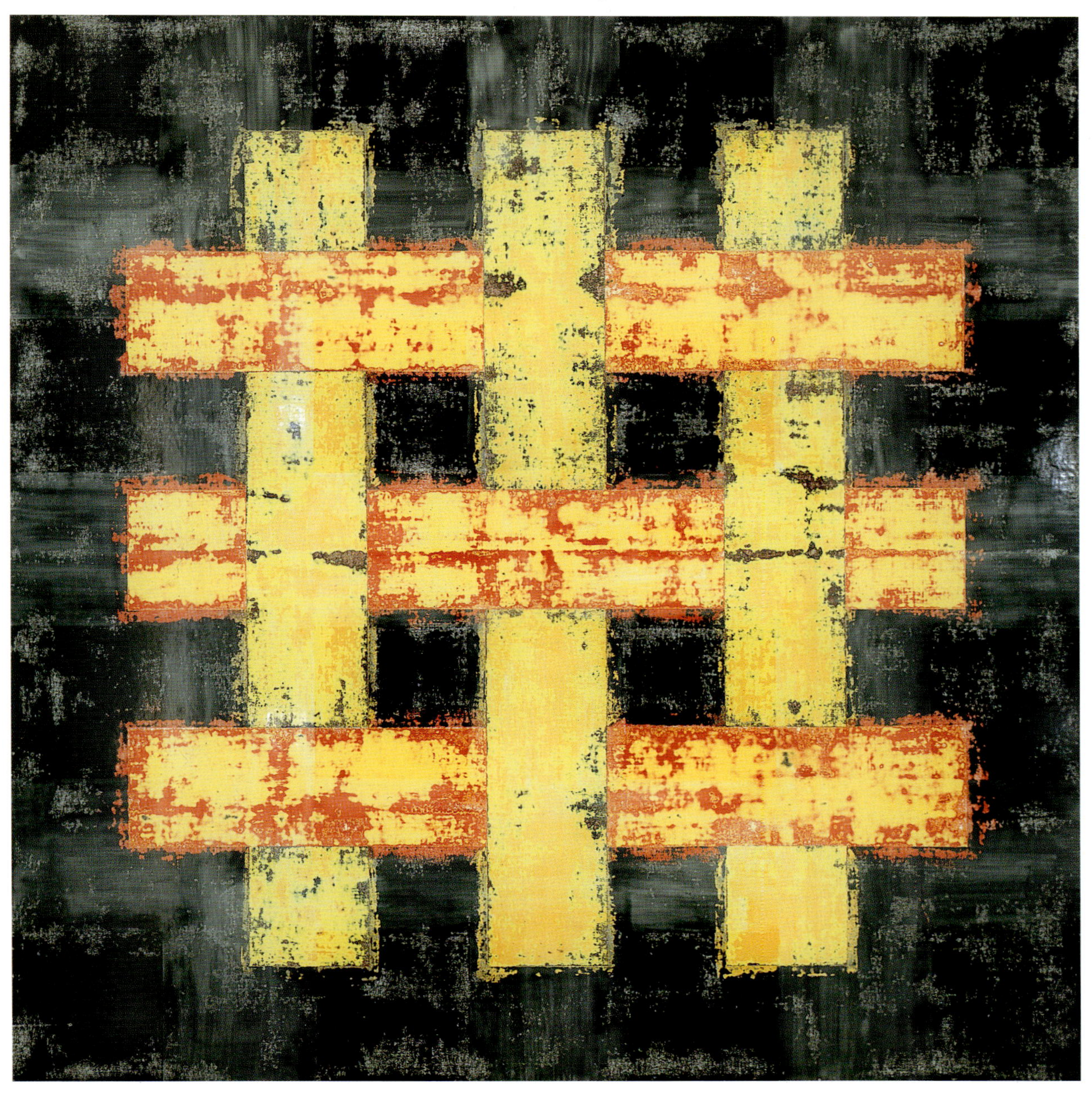

LATTICE #11, 1998
ENAMEL ON CANVAS
72 X 72 INCHES

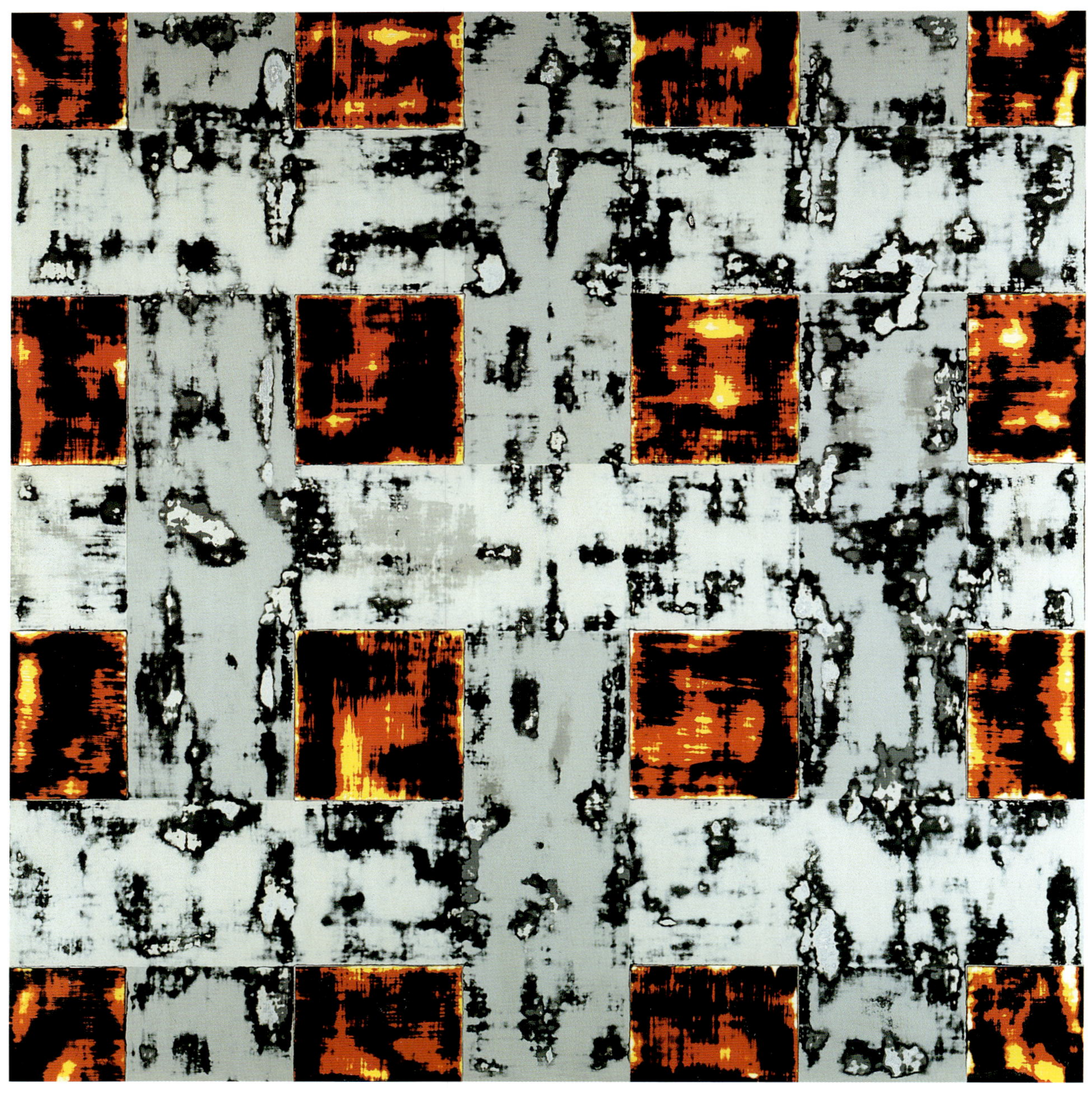

LATTICE #12, 1998
ENAMEL ON CANVAS
72 X 72 INCHES

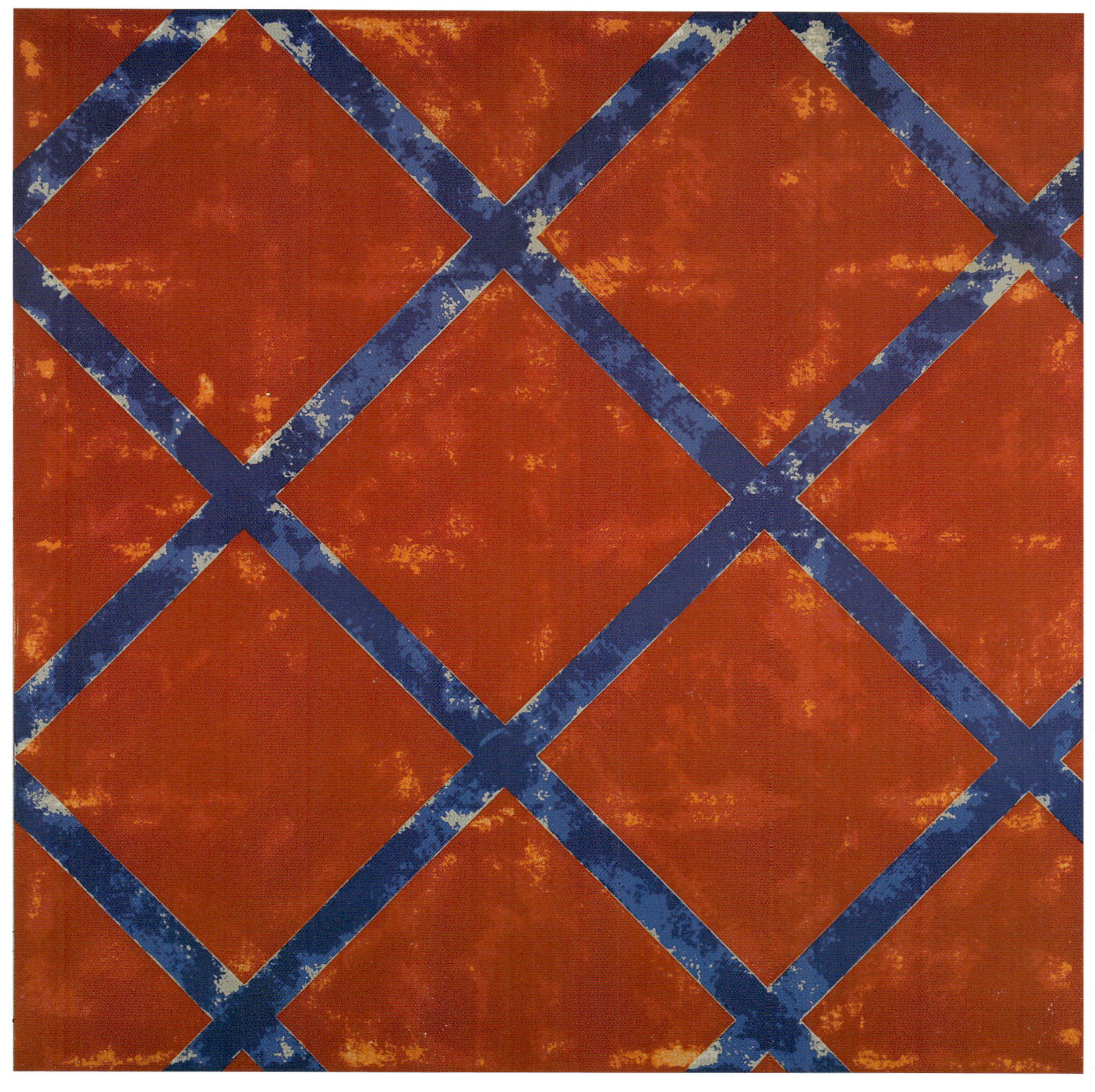

LATTICE #18, 2000
ENAMEL ON CANVAS
72 X 72 INCHES

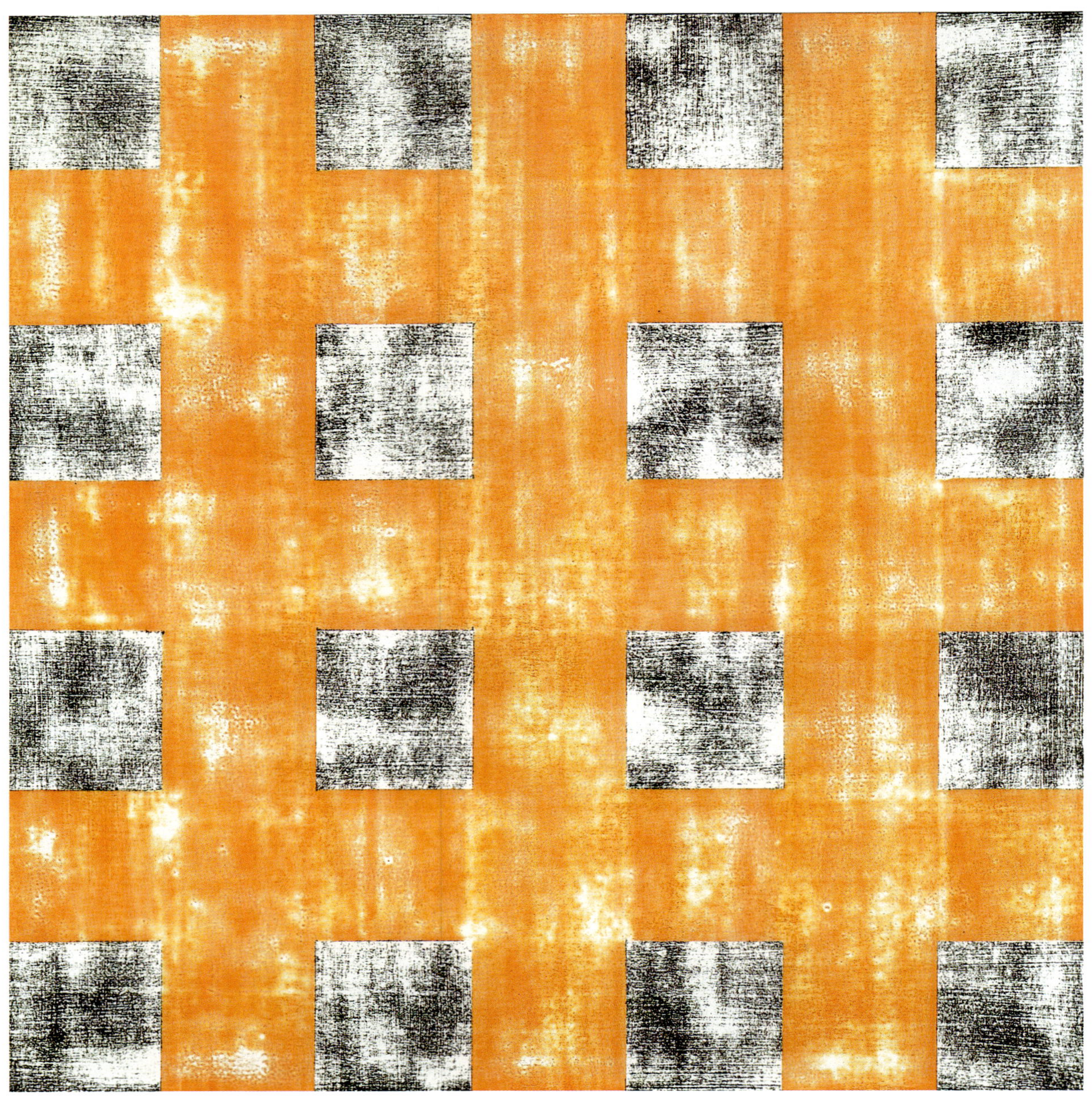

LATTICE #15, 2000
ENAMEL ON CANVAS
72 X 72 INCHES

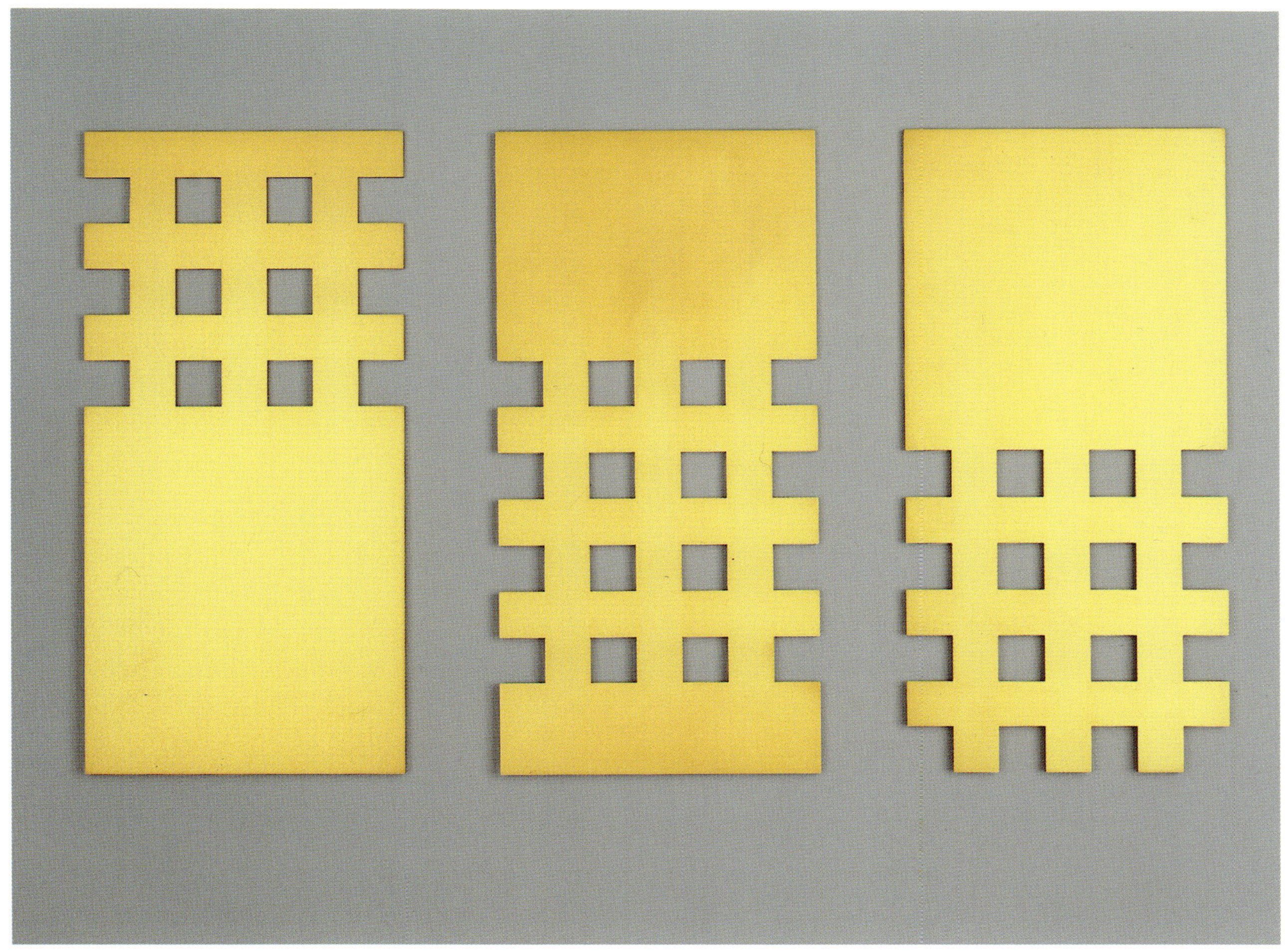

RICHARD C SMITH b. 1949 Burbank CA. Ed: Chouinard (now Cal Arts) CA. Exhib: Friends of Contemporary Art, Santa Fe NM. Coll: Duke of Wellington Estate, Spain; Museum of Fine Arts, Santa Fe, Santa Fe Community College NM. Representation: Linda Durham Contemporary Art, Galisteo NM and New York.

FALLING LATTICE #41; 7,9,15; 2002
ANODIZED ALUMINUM
22⅝ X 11¾ X ⅜ INCHES

JANET LIPPINCOTT

The simple task of an abstract artist is to delineate the indefinable. Once that is accomplished, it is then a matter of getting down into the depths, nuances, and relationships within the image, of finding the edges, of bridging the gaps. The artist thus becomes a kind of human neuron, leaping across the chasm of unknowing and throwing back a lifeline.

Janet Lippincott, a major New Mexico artist who has kept the traditions of artists like Robert Motherwell and Louise Nevelson alive through her painting, personifies this particular energy. Lippincott was exposed to great art while growing up in New York City and Paris, and even painted at the Art Students League as a teenager. However, instead of becoming an artist straight away, she decided to join the Women's Army Corps as a young woman. She served under Eisenhower, was injured in a London bombing and was present in Paris when DeGaulle celebrated the liberation of the city. When she completed her military service in 1945 she was looking for a way to use her G. I. Bill educational benefits. In 1949 she discovered the Emil Bisttram Art School in Taos, New Mexico – and found her vocation.

Recognition came slowly at first. Lippincott's early exposure to Picasso and Matisse in the museums of New York and Paris, as well as her war experiences, had given her a modern sensibility that was foreign to the American Southwest. She persisted in her work, built a studio on Canyon Road in Santa Fe, and became a solid and notable force in the art world. She also acted as a wise mentor to younger artists on their way up. "You have to give them something tangible to hold onto," she said. "They need all the reinforcement they can get. Some become very discouraged but they must not give up no matter what comes."

Lippincott took her own advice to heart and stuck to a career that has spanned more than five decades. She has exhibited in France, Mexico, and Canada, as well as the length and breadth of the United States. Her work has remained strong, clear, complex, and forceful. Her former teacher, Emil Bisttram, once said, "It has been my opportunity to observe her development in the field of contemporary art wherein her paintings span the gamut of earth themes to imaginative design in pure esthetics." The respect accorded her by her peers and the press in the ensuing decades bore him out.

"Abstract painting is an intellectual process," Janet Lippincott says. "To be a modern painter and to make a truthful statement is the sum total of all I am and what I am continually striving to create. I am a painter and my paintings are all I can contribute to the world."

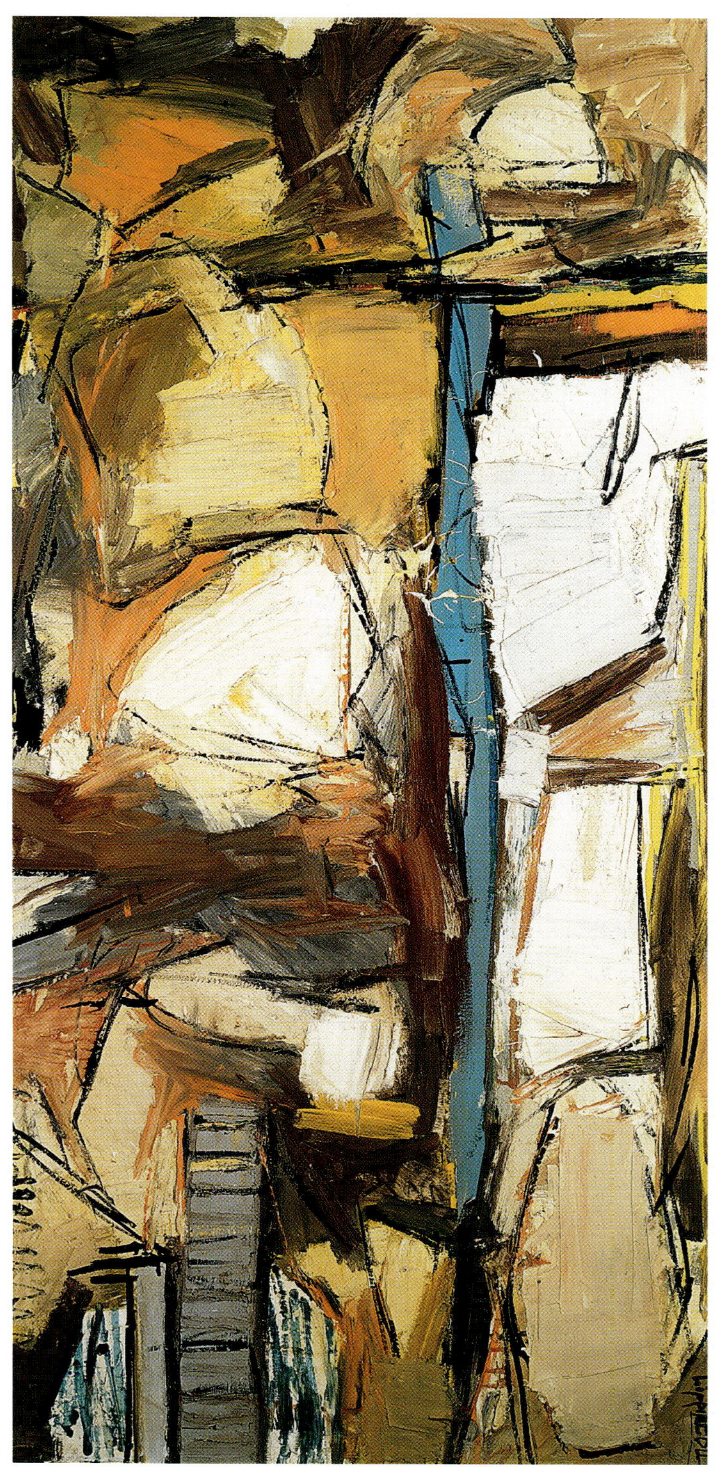

THE POND, 1957
OIL ON WOOD PANEL
60 X 30 INCHES

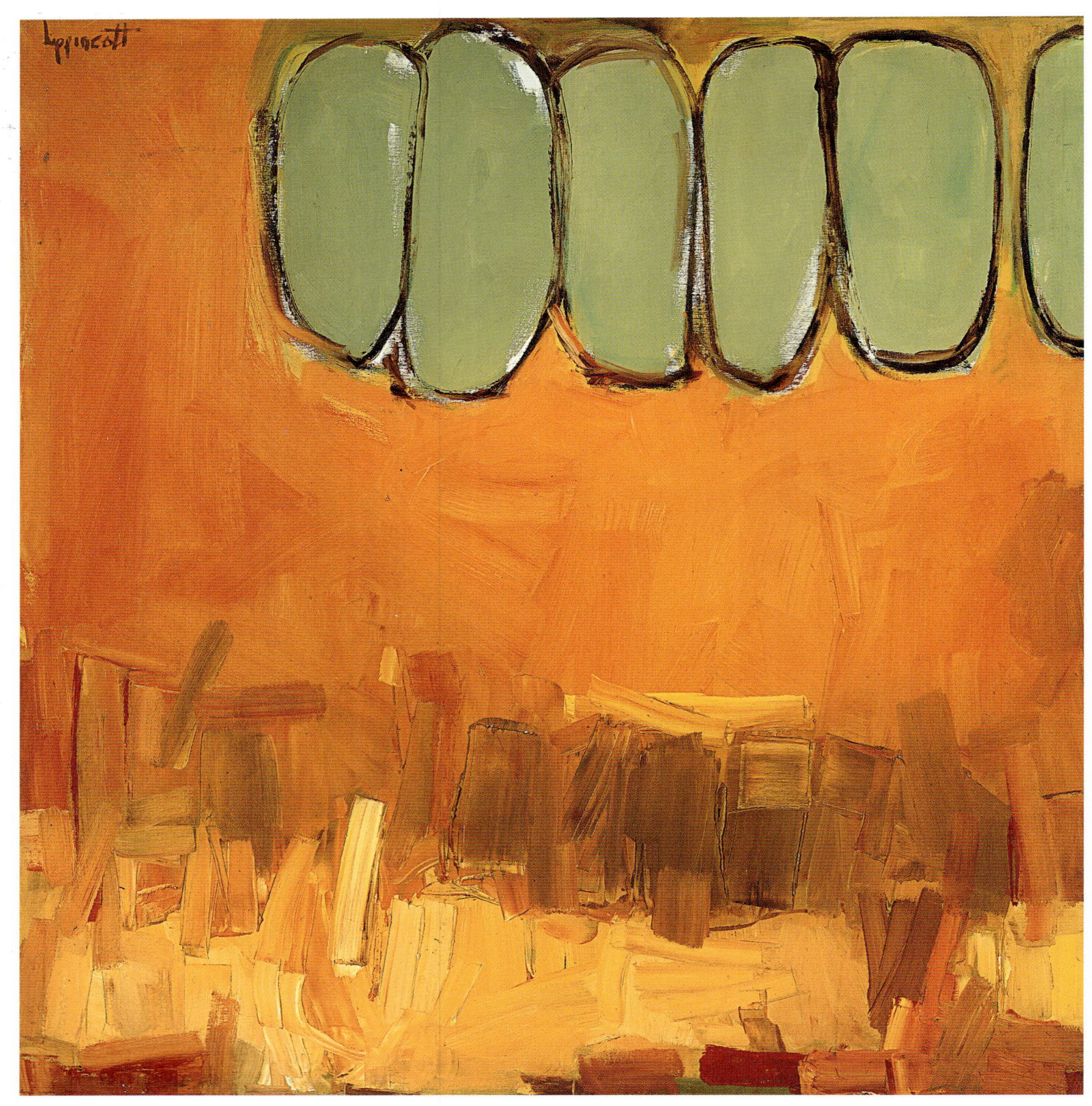

ACOMA, 1963
OIL ON CANVAS
50 X 50 INCHES

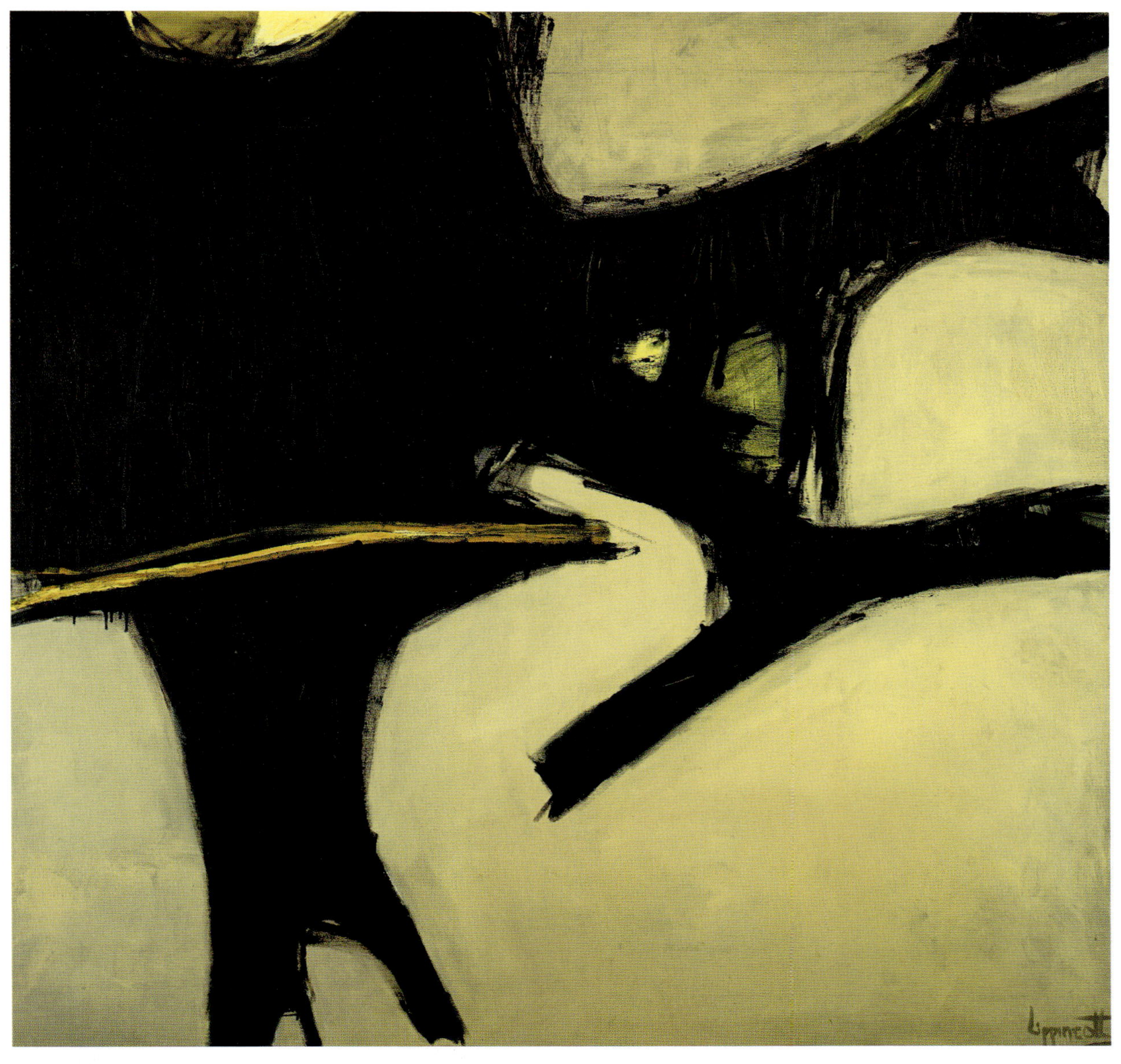

UNTITLED 1961
OIL ON CANVAS
64 X 68 INCHES

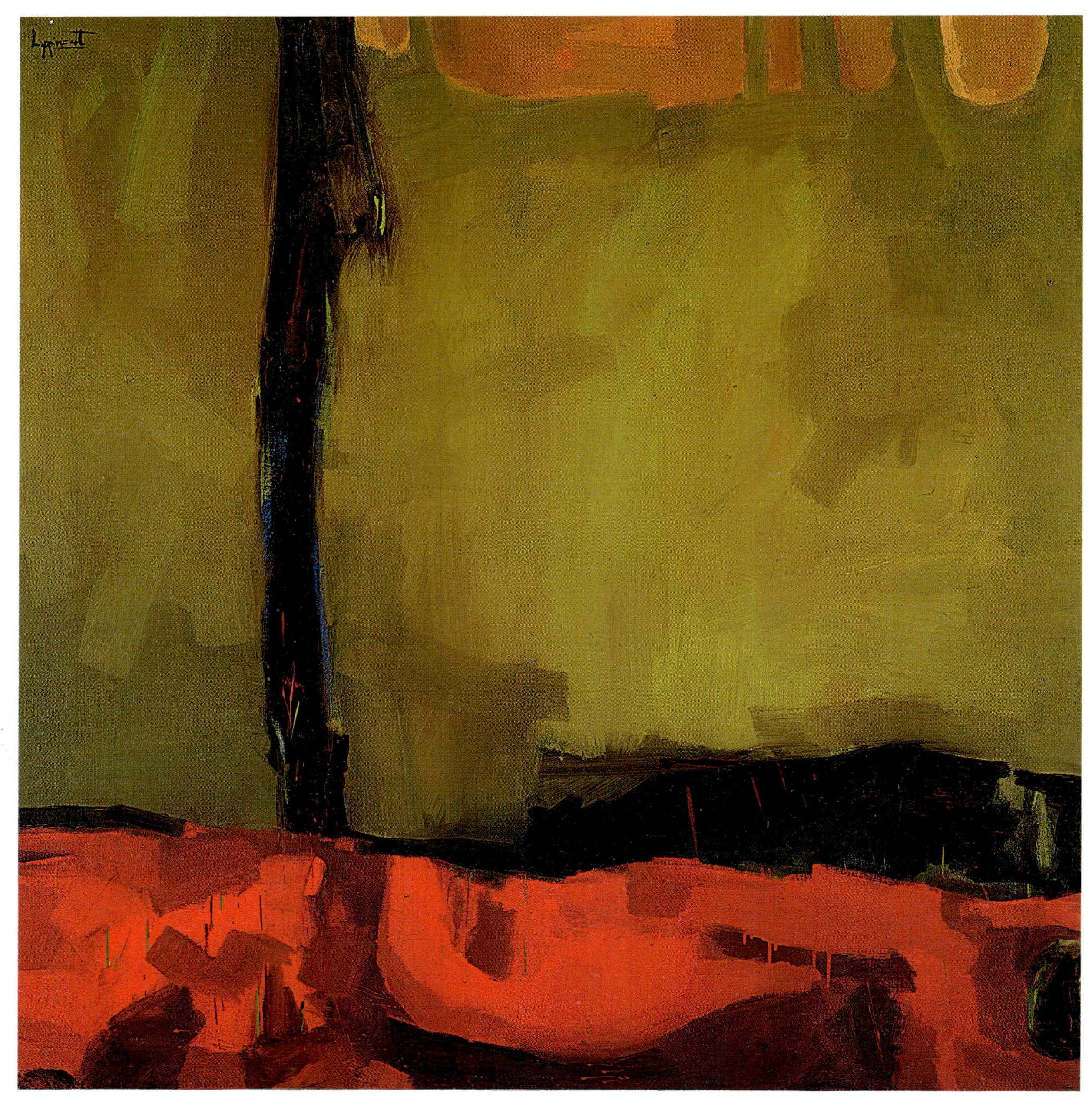

LANDSCAPE REVISITED, 1963
OIL ON CANVAS
60 X 60 INCHES

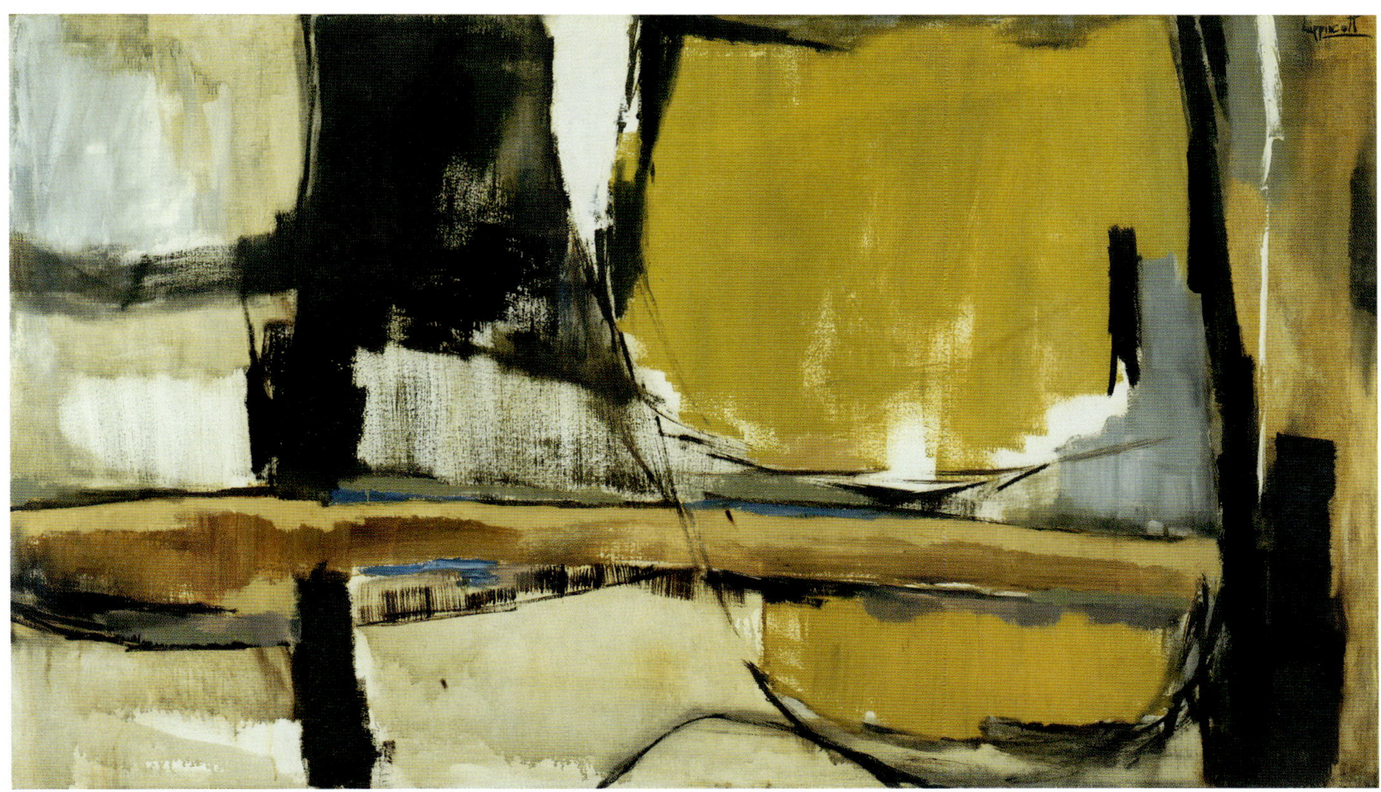

JANET LIPPINCOTT b. 1918 New York NY. Ed: Emil Bisttram Art School, Taos NM; Colorado Springs Fine Art Center; Art Students League NYC; San Francisco Art Institute. Honors: Governors Award for Excellence In the Arts NM; Guest Artist, Tamarind Institute NM; Achievement Award, National Museum of Women in the Arts DC. Coll: Museum of Fine Art, Santa Fe NM; Capitol Art Collection NM; Denver Museum of Fine Art; etal. Representation: Karan Ruhlen Gallery, Santa Fe.

BYE BYE BLACKBIRD, 1959
OIL ON CANVAS
42 X 60 INCHES

KEN PRICE

The beta version of reality, as presented by the media, is a hard, bright, convoluted mass. There are no sharp edges that would make it difficult to swallow. On the contrary, the pervasive atmosphere of sexuality makes it very attractive. The movie and TV screens and the glossy magazine pages exert a come-hither allure, yet they are slick and unyielding to the touch.

This über-reality dictates that everything we see on television or read in print or view on the Internet must be brand new, flashy, in your face. War, fashion, comedy, and crime have equal drama; the same urgency applies to commercials and breaking news. There is scant perceptible difference between the artificial and the genuine. Everything levels out to fit a predetermined package of viewing minutes or paragraph inches.

In this sense, Ken Price is a consummate realist. He gives strict representational form to the experience of living in this culture at this time in history. He applies the medium of ceramics to painterly concerns, and vice versa, to create riveting sculptures with a strange, perverse undertone. His California roots are evident in each gritty texture, each burgeoning form, each sharply focused meditation on directionlessness and sensuous pleasure that comes out of his studio.

Price grew up in Los Angeles. He had the supreme good fortune to study with Peter Voulkos at the Los Angeles Art Institute, later known as the Otis Art Institute. Price and his fellow students, along with Voulkos, became the core of the Abstract Expressionist Ceramics movement, an awkward term intended to recognize the serious content of fine art created in a traditional craft medium.

Price became a part of the progressive L. A. art scene, and then began to exhibit in the United States and abroad. He took ceramics in new directions, sometimes riffing on conventional forms and sometimes turning the clay and the glazes to the service of ideas that stretch the medium to the outer limits of painting and sculpture.

By the time Price moved to Taos, New Mexico, along with several other prominent L. A. artists, his international reputation was secure. Today he divides his time between the high-energy art scene of southern California and the hard, bright, convoluted desert earth of northern New Mexico.

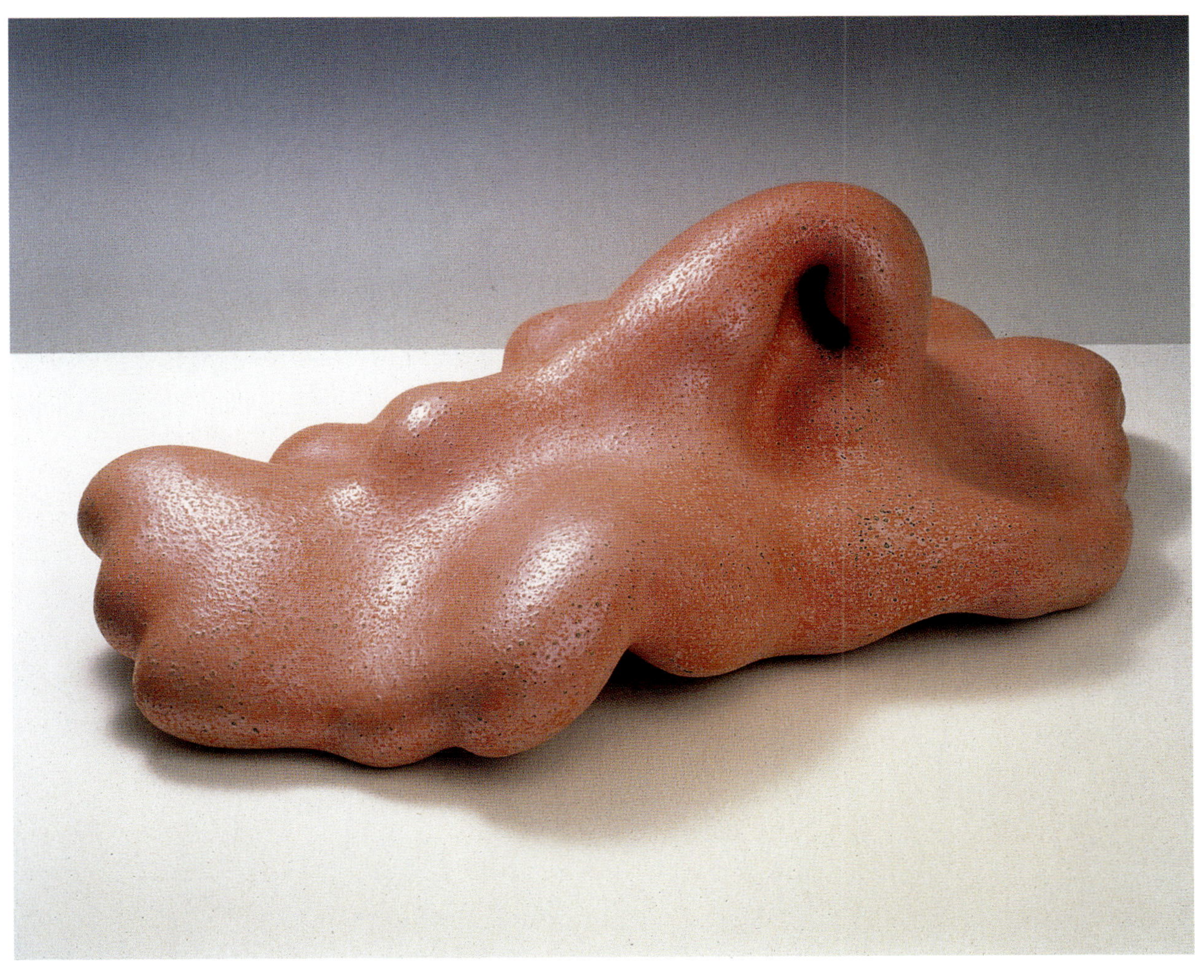

PRONE, 1997
FIRED AND PAINTED CLAY
6¼ X 28½ X 18¾ INCHES

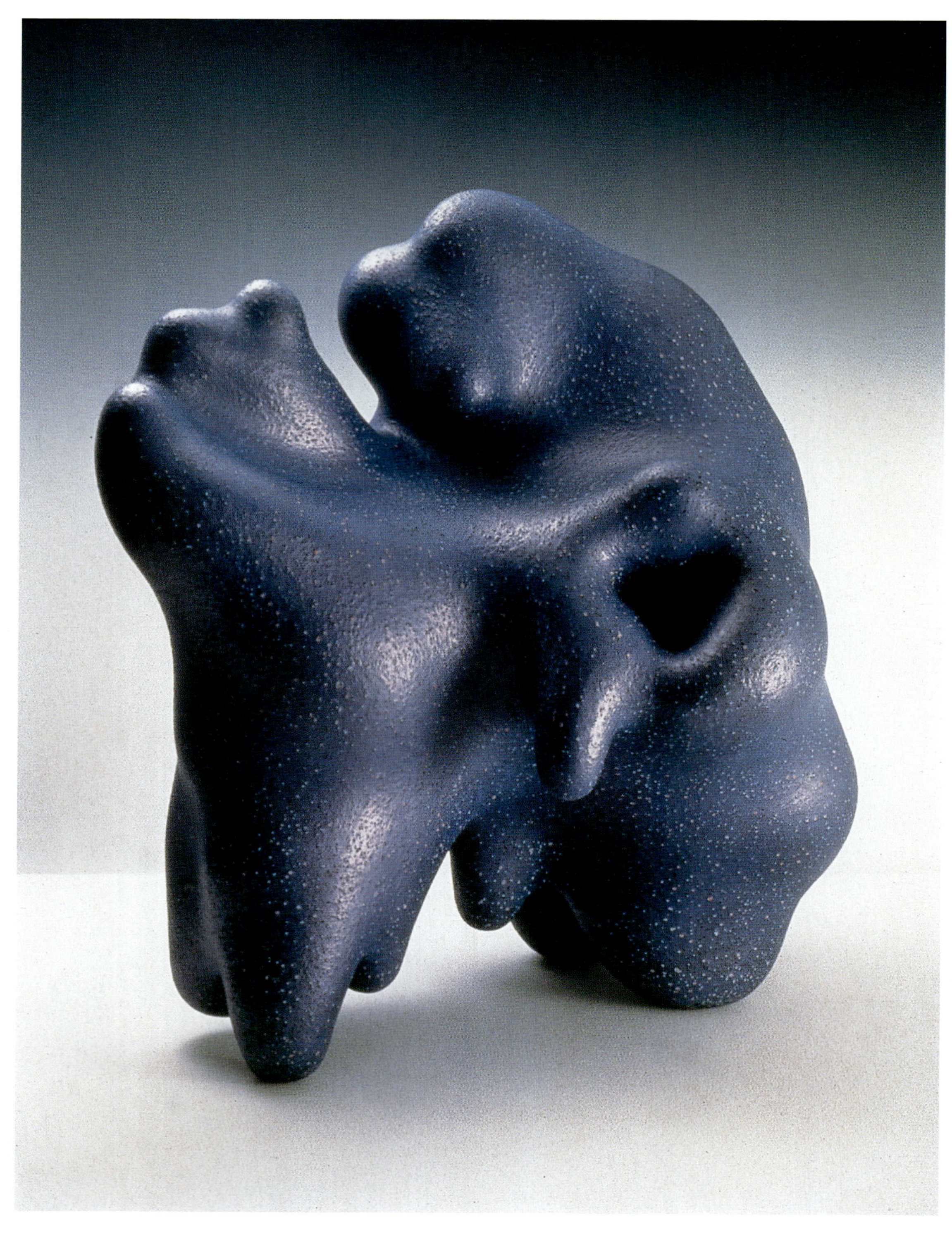

UNDERHUNG, 1997
FIRED AND PAINTED CLAY
23½ X 21½ X 16 INCHES

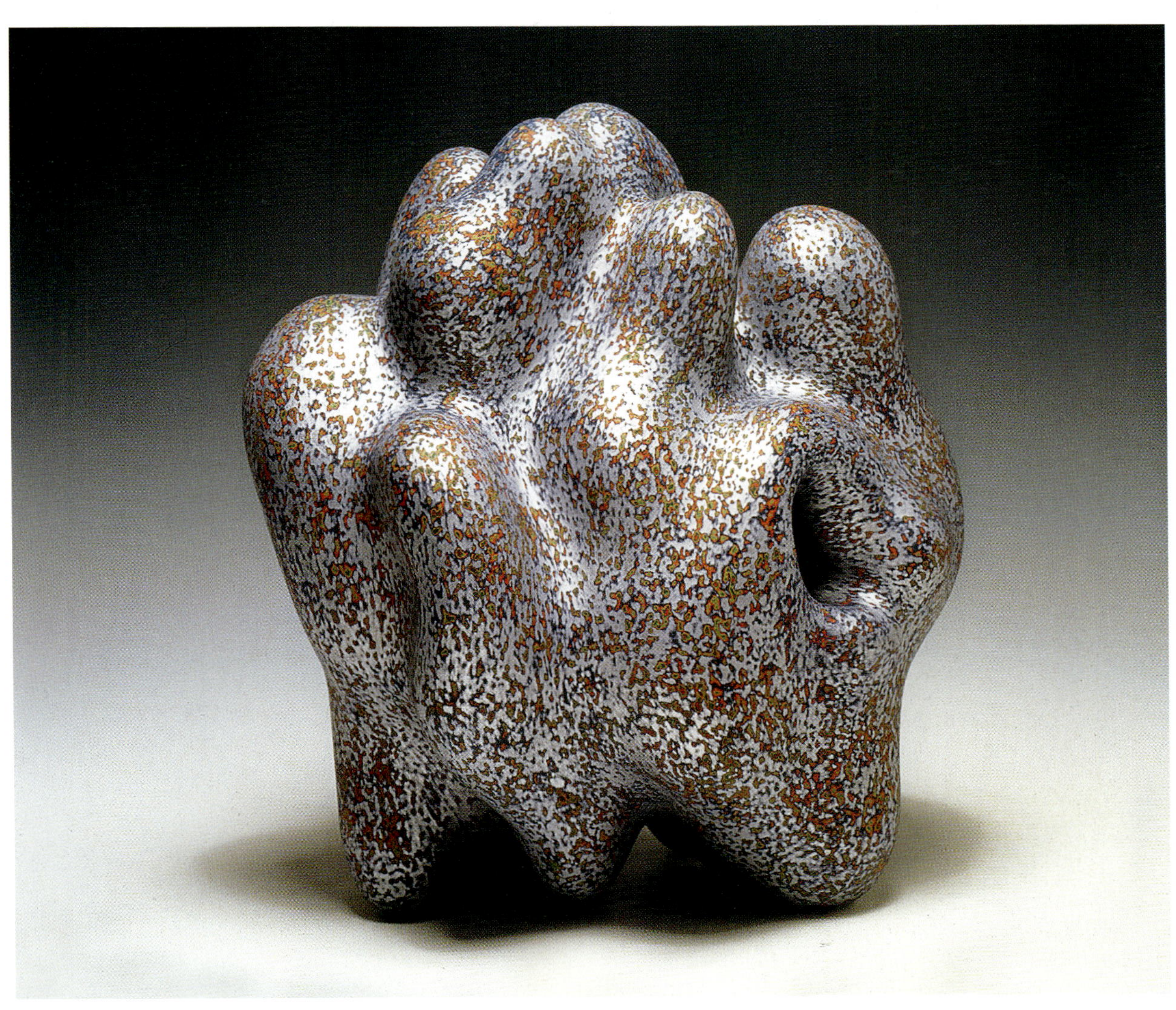

PRINCESS, 2001
FIRED AND PAINTED CLAY
20 X 18 X 13 INCHES

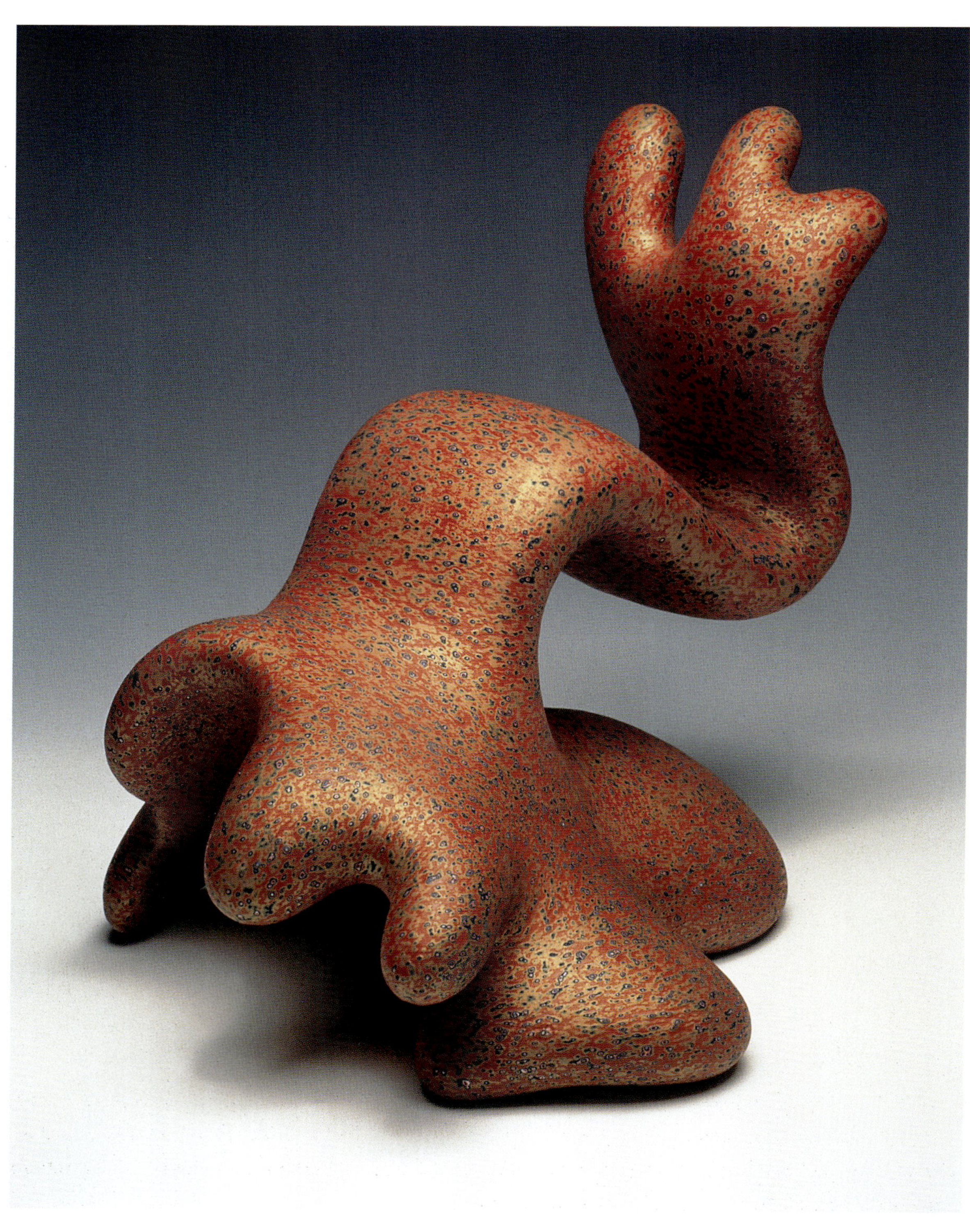

LULU, 2001
FIRED AND PAINTED CLAY
11½ X 13¼ X 10½ INCHES

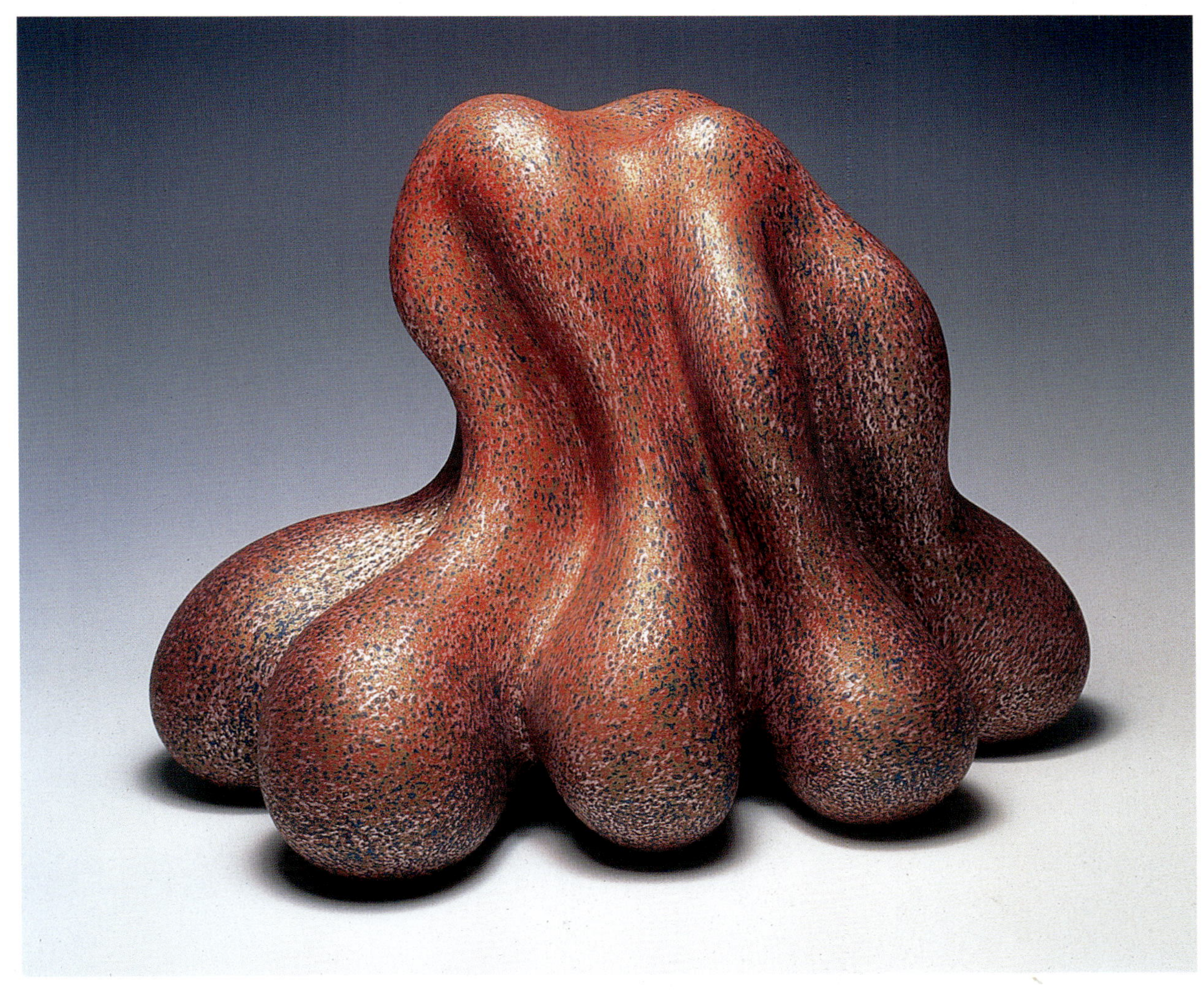

KEN PRICE b. 1935 Los Angeles. Ed: BFA Univ. Southern California, MFA New York State College of Ceramics at Alfred University. Coll: Metropolitan, Whitney, and MOMA NY; Los Angeles County Museum; Dallas Art Museum TX; Kruithuis Museum, s'Hertogenbosch, Netherlands. Representation: L.A. Louver, Venice CA; Fenix Gallery, Taos; Franklin Parrasch Gallery, New York.

KABONGY BALLS
FIRED AND PAINTED CLAY
16 X 21½ X 16½ INCHES

SAM SCOTT

One of life's finest pleasures is a conversation with an articulate, fully conscious artist. Ideas may dart back and forth swiftly, or may be savored together like a great wine. Shared experience colors the moment. Certain words jump into high definition as they pin down a thought precisely. Anecdotes and jokes, laughter and tears, shouts and whispers create a unique texture. Often, what is left unsaid is more important than what is thoroughly described.

The subject may range widely, yet the experience remains whole. Even within various discussions there may be many nonlinear tangents that loop out and then return to the central topic. The direction is forward and backward, inward and outward. Communication on the deepest level both encompasses and defines.

Ultimately the conversation connects two or more people. However, when the language is visual, it may connect as many people as are able to see the image and comprehend it. Painted lines and forms, like spoken thoughts, impact the senses directly. They are interpreted within the mind more exactingly than verbal truisms because they are not bound by custom and convention.

Sam Scott is one of the world's great visual conversationalists. He engages the viewer in an intimate and mutual discourse, eliciting as much involvement as he himself contributes. Scott's forms are approachable because, unlike those of the Abstract Expressionists, they are not self-generated from a purely intellectual basis. Instead, his attention is firmly fixed on the world around him. He celebrates the joy of nature not by limning it but by inhabiting it.

Scott arrived in Santa Fe in 1969 as a well-educated prodigy. He became a catalyst for a group of other young artists whose work has stood the test of time. Now an éminence gris, he continues to teach, stir up, and inspire others while producing at the top of his form. "Everything is there that was there before," he says, "but it's completely new. This is my fortieth year of painting, and this is the great gift that has come to me: I am always at the beginning."

Taking to heart the words of Phil Ochs, who said, "In these terrible times the true protest is beauty," Scott has devoted himself to working for peace. His recent sojourn in Vietnam, where he collaborated with one of the country's top artists, taught him a lot. "It made me understand that this thing we call painting is just little particles of clay on paper," he says. "At the same time, it's an opportunity for humans to offer each other windows to the absolute. We enter this field of pure potentiality through significant acts. I hold the intention of painting as a significant act to be the most important fact of life; to walk in beauty in a heartbroken world is the painter's job."

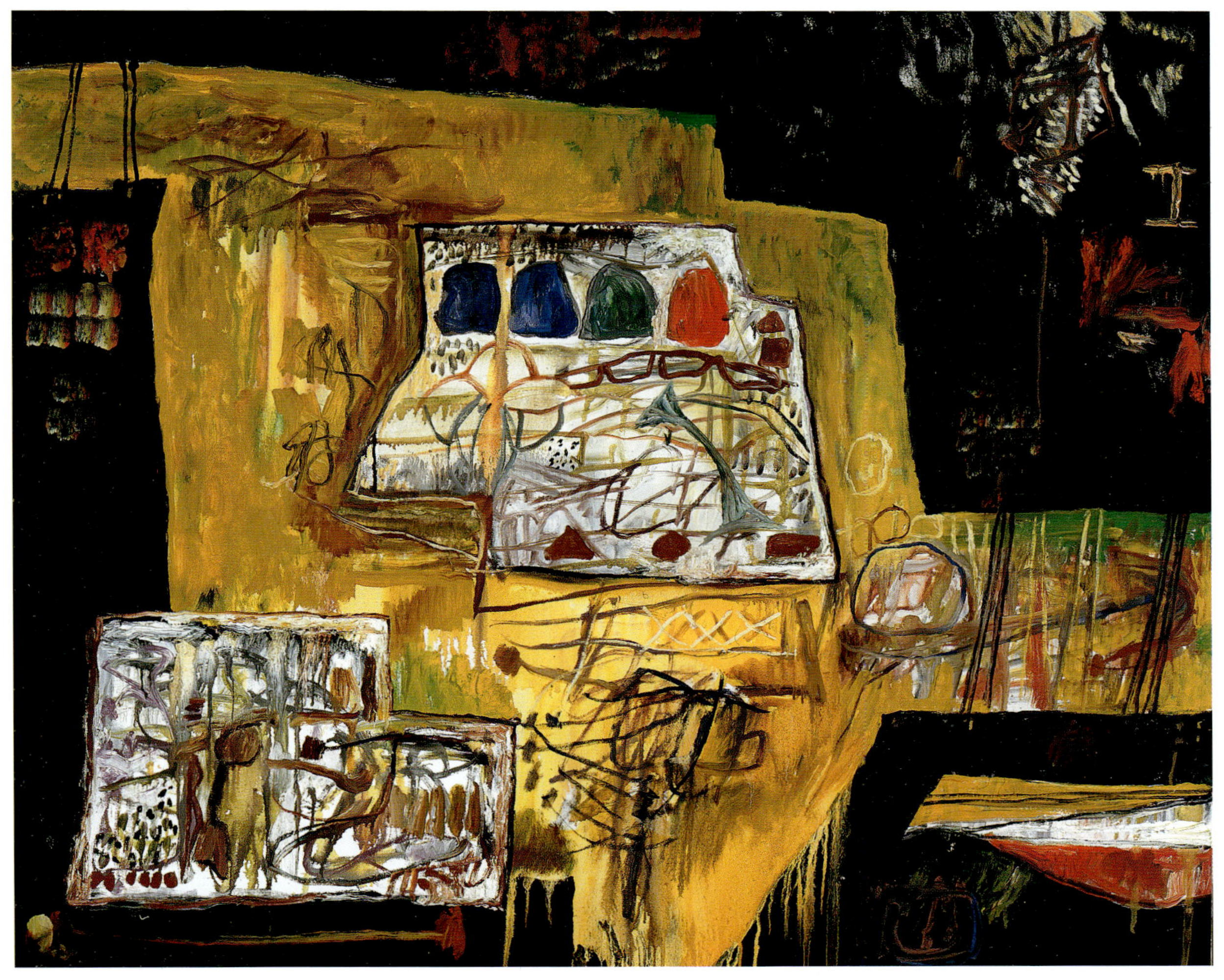

SONG OF THE CANYON WREN, 2002
OIL ON CANVAS
42 X 54 INCHES

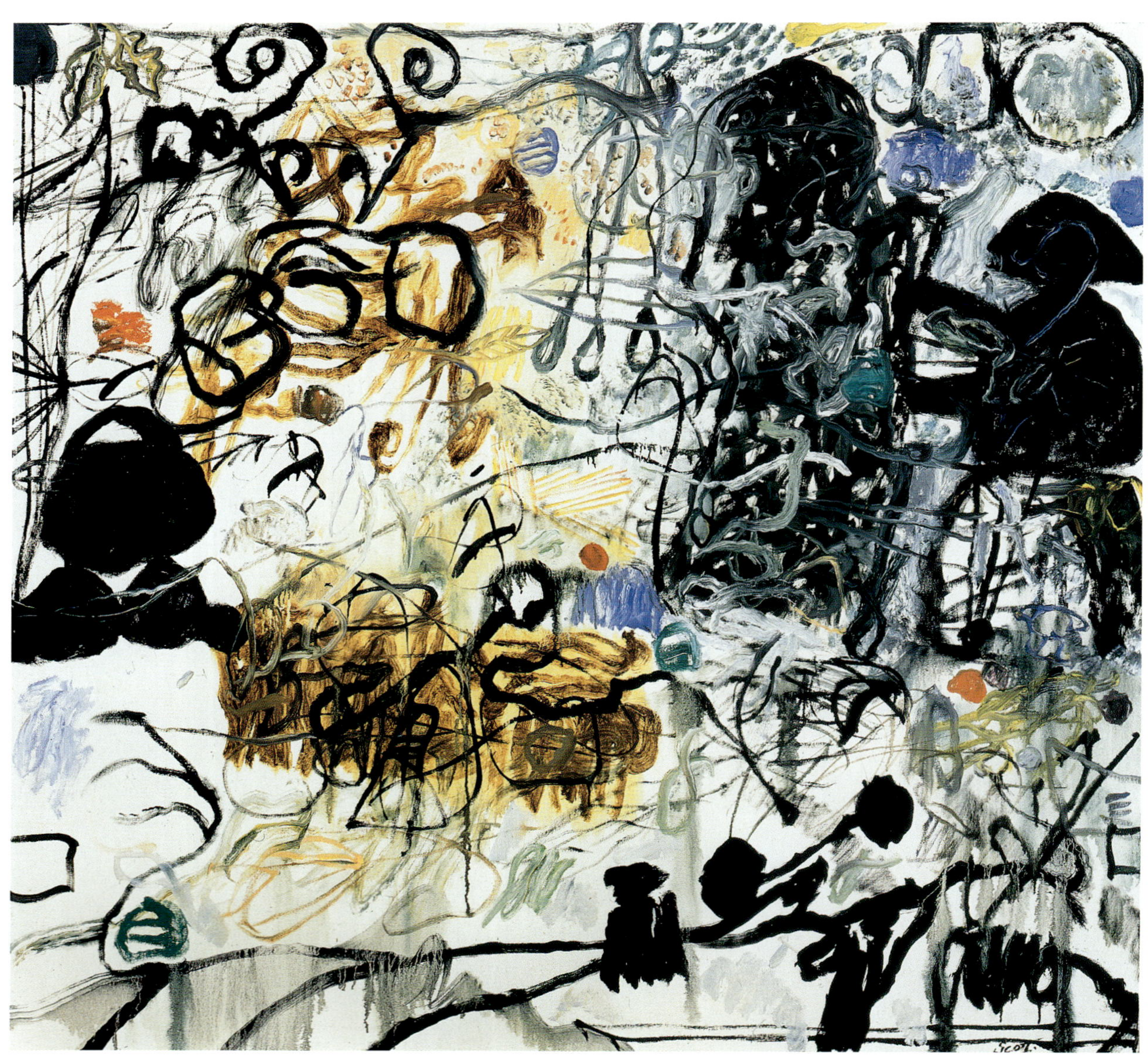

VIOLINS OF THE FLEETING AUTUMN, 1996
OIL ON CANVAS
60 X 66 INCHES

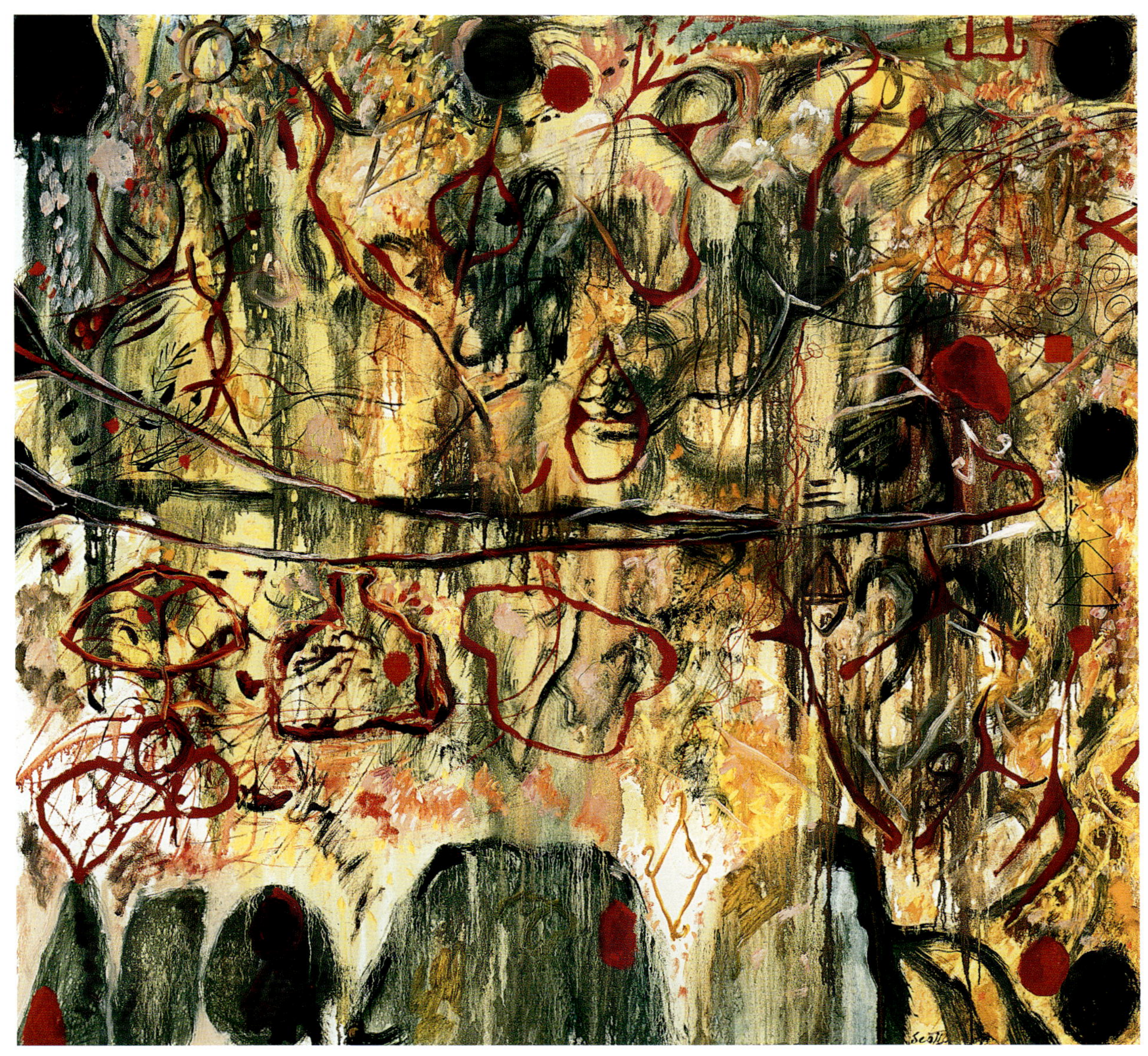

BREAD OR WOOD, 1997
OIL ON CANVAS
66 X 80 INCHES

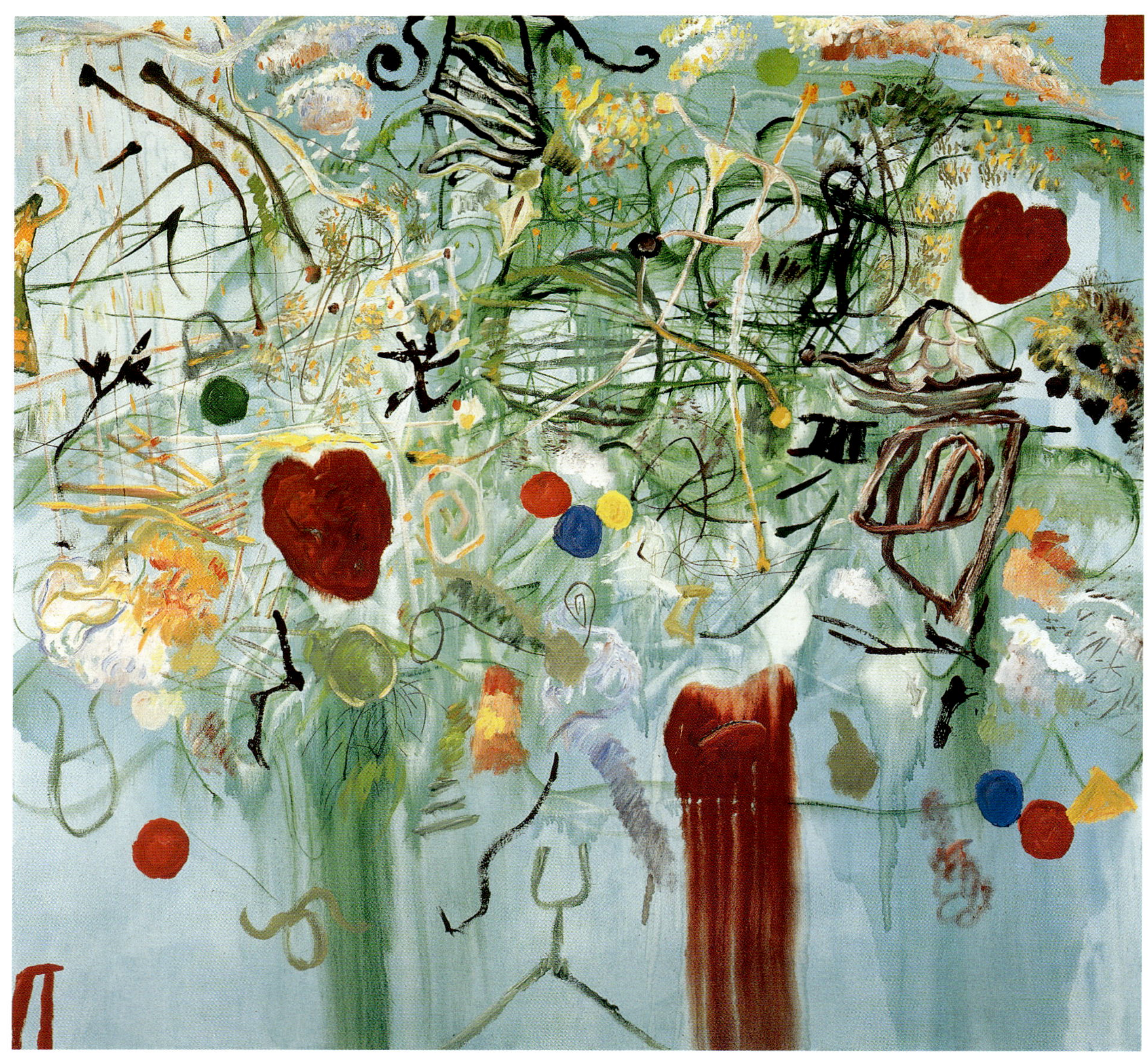

THE MAGIC OF BLOOD, 1996
OIL ON CANVAS
60 X 66 INCHES

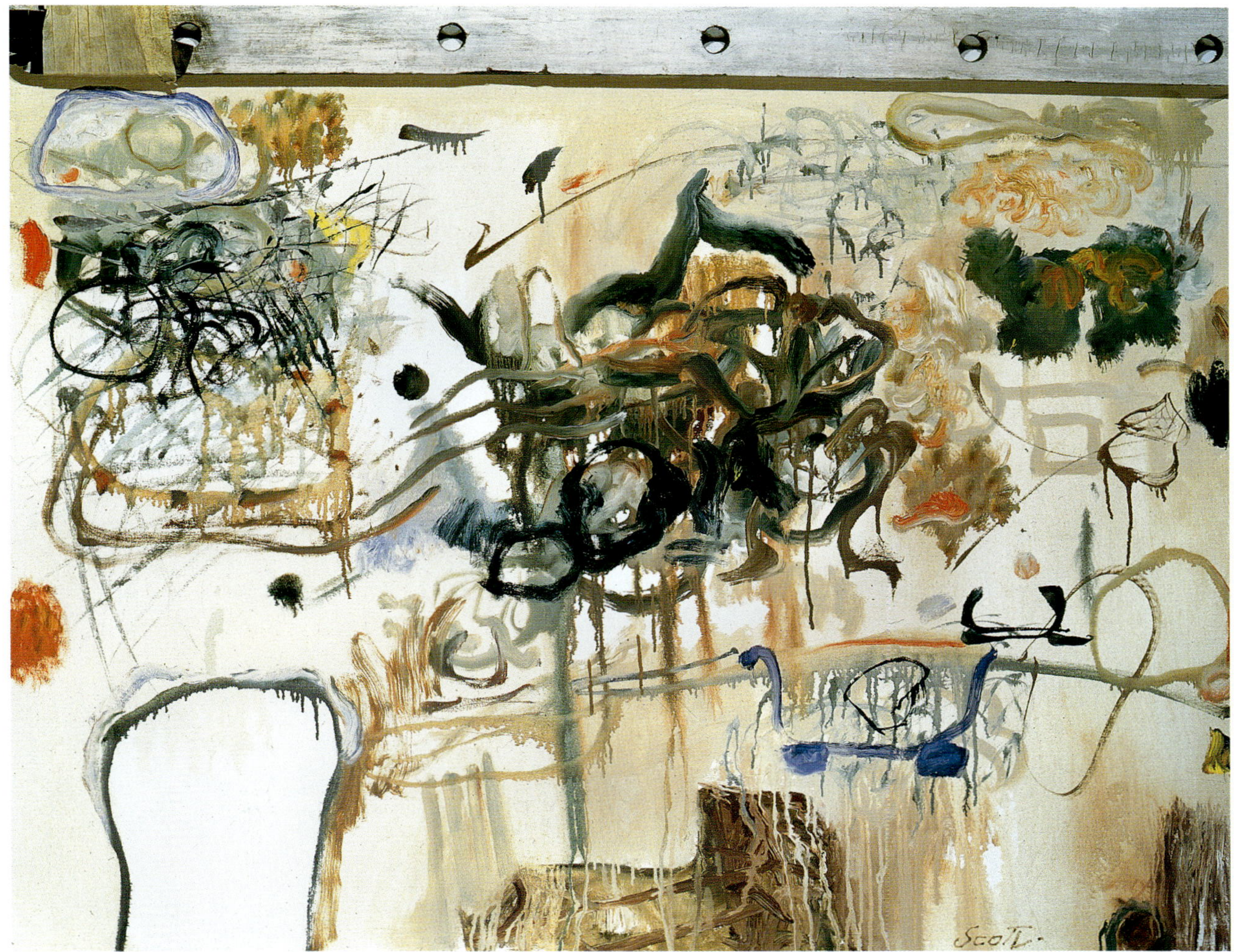

SAM SCOTT b. 1940 Chicago. Ed: MFA Cum Laude Maryland Institute College of Art; BFA Univ. Michigan. Coll: Albuquerque Museum, Capitol Art Collection NM; Denver Museum; Musée de Digne, France; IBM; Hyatt; AT&T; Dore Ashton; etal. Representaion: Wiford & Vogt Fine Art, Santa Fe; Parks Gallery, Taos; Robischon Gallery, Denver.

APPOINTMENT WITH CLOUDS, 1999
MIXED MEDIA AND OIL ON CANVAS
48 X 60 INCHES

LARRY BELL

Artists through the ages have addressed the most severe social issues in order to make it possible for people to form an emotional connection with the unthinkable, and thus reconcile the experience within themselves. Goya's etchings of the disasters of war, Picasso's Guernica, even the Romantic agonies of Delacroix's battle scenes serve as vehicles for the collective unconscious to come to terms with events it can neither act upon nor dismiss.

Repetition is a key element in the assimilation of information that the mind resists knowing. Like a nightmare that recurs throughout a crisis period, the appallingly beautiful icons of horror reverberate endlessly. From the mushroom clouds at the dawn of the Atomic Age to the Challenger explosion to the events of September 11, 2001, they have fallen upon the public eye and ear in a concatenation of still and moving images, appearing in all periodicals simultaneously, repeating and repeating like a deadly mantra on TV newscasts.

Larry Bell was among the millions who watched as the World Trade Center collapsed. The shock had a primal impact on him, slicing through his mind and detonating in his art. He produced a series of death's head images that have the same visceral impact as the media representations of the original event. The red-hot boom and bloom of explosions, the majestic and obscene choreography of the plane hitting the tower, the splintering, twisting, melting disintegration of life as Americans had known it until that moment, are recorded indelibly in these powerful works of art.

Bell brought a lifetime of experimentation and dedicated work to bear on these pieces. Although he is internationally renowned, he has, like many another artist, chosen the seclusion, camaraderie, and esthetic pleasure of living in New Mexico while managing a career centered in the major cities. Bell, one of the most famous of all those who have made that choice, has lived and worked in Taos since 1973.

Long recognized for his constructions and vapor drawings, he has in recent years fragmented and reassembled his images into energetic, hypnotic collages. He has also turned the concept of major work upside down by producing large numbers of modestly scaled pieces that work together like notes in a concerto.

His is a closely considered and wholly abstract art, so this series of images, tied to a specific event, came as a surprise to him. "I never had an experience like that," he recalls. "Every artist works on different levels. For me, these were a catharsis. I worked intuitively, spontaneously. Skills I didn't know I had came out. It was completely different from what I was expecting, but I couldn't deny the honesty."

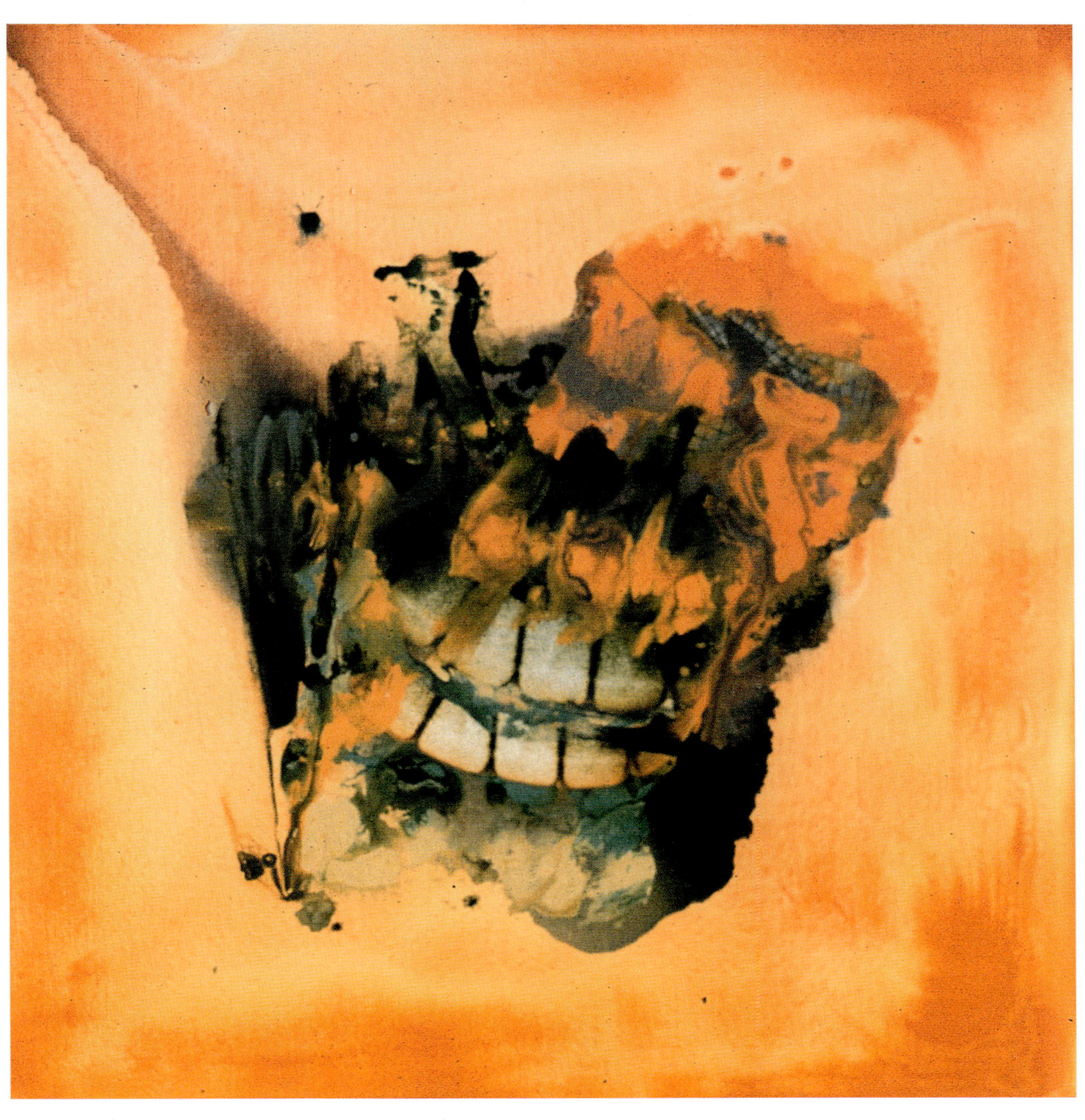

HTTHOJ 6
MIXED MEDIA COL_AGE ON CANVAS
42 X 42 INCHES

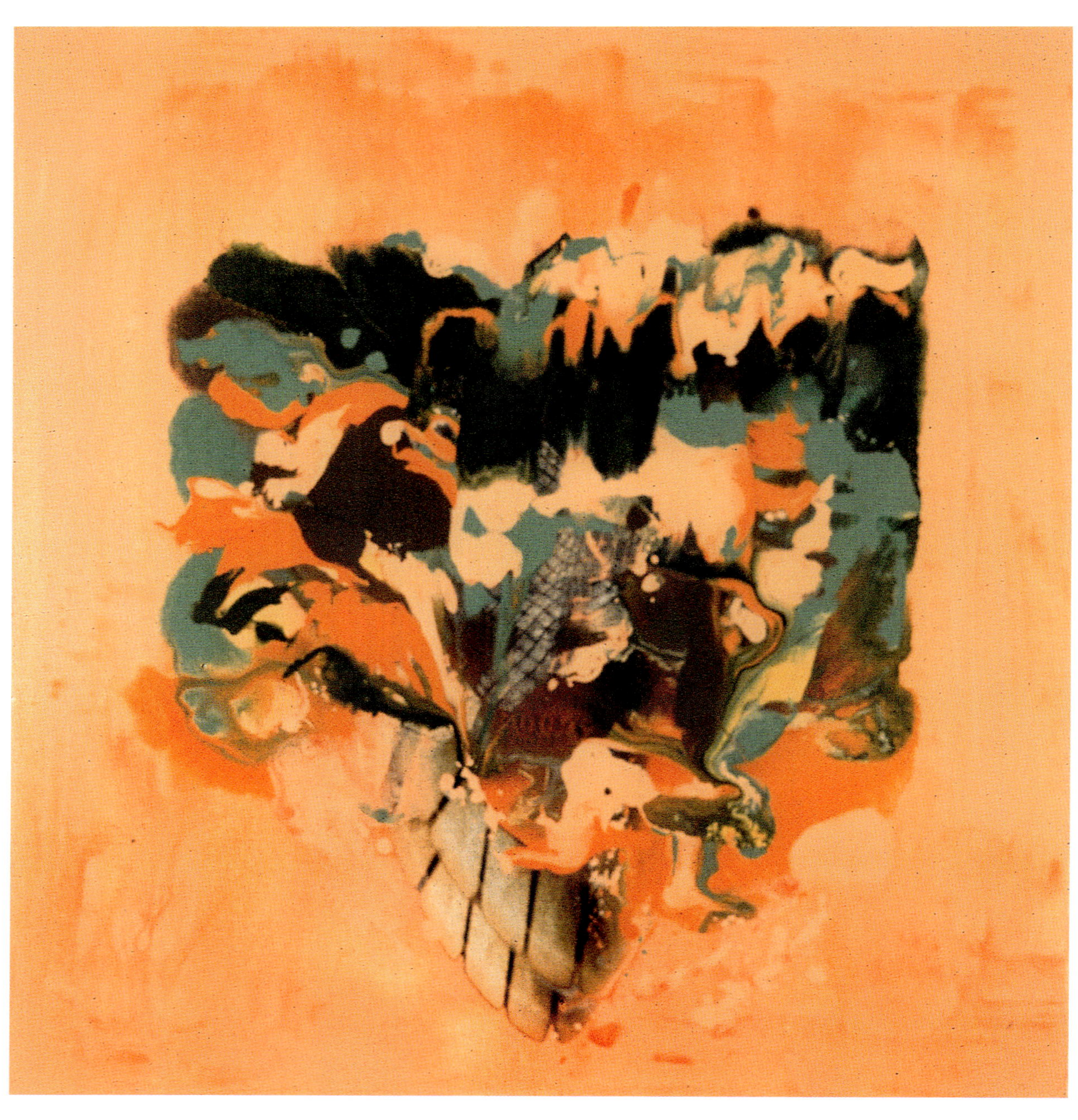

HTTHOJ 7
MIXED MEDIA COLLAGE ON CANVAS
42 X 42 INCHES

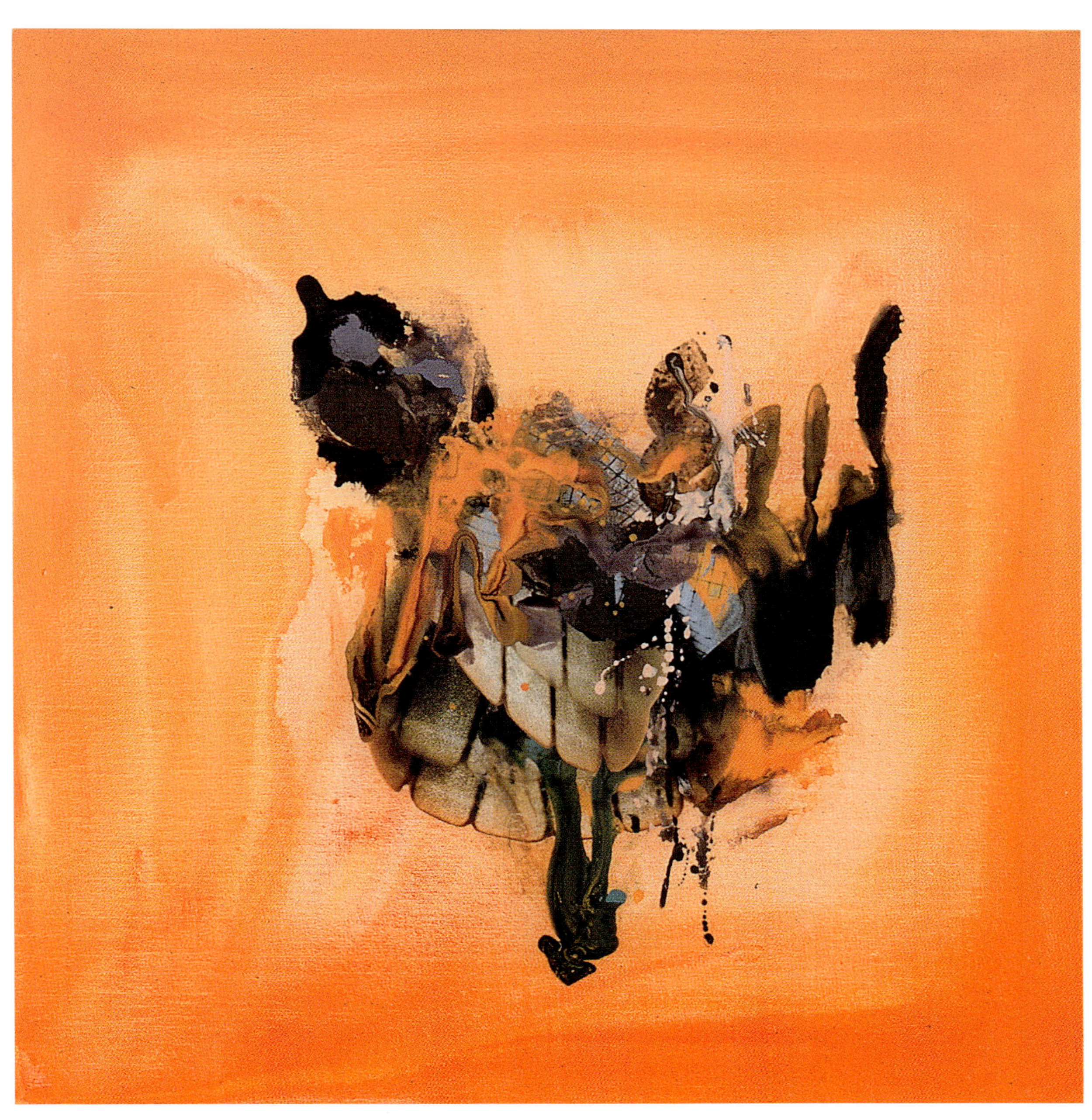

HTTHOJ 10
MIXED MEDIA COLLAGE ON CANVAS
42 X 42 INCHES

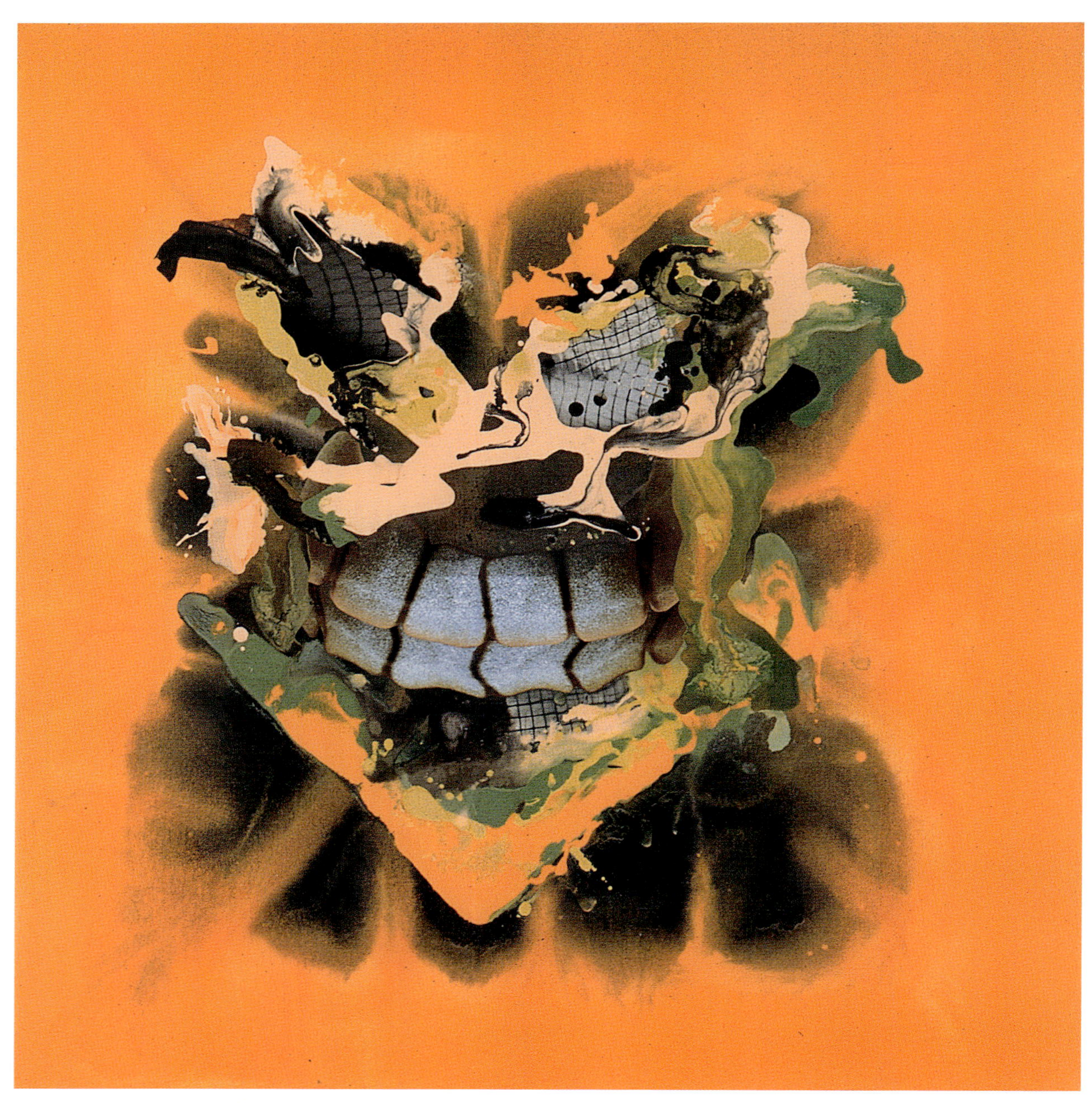

HTTHOJ 32
MIXED MEDIA COLLAGE ON CANVAS
42 X 42 INCHES

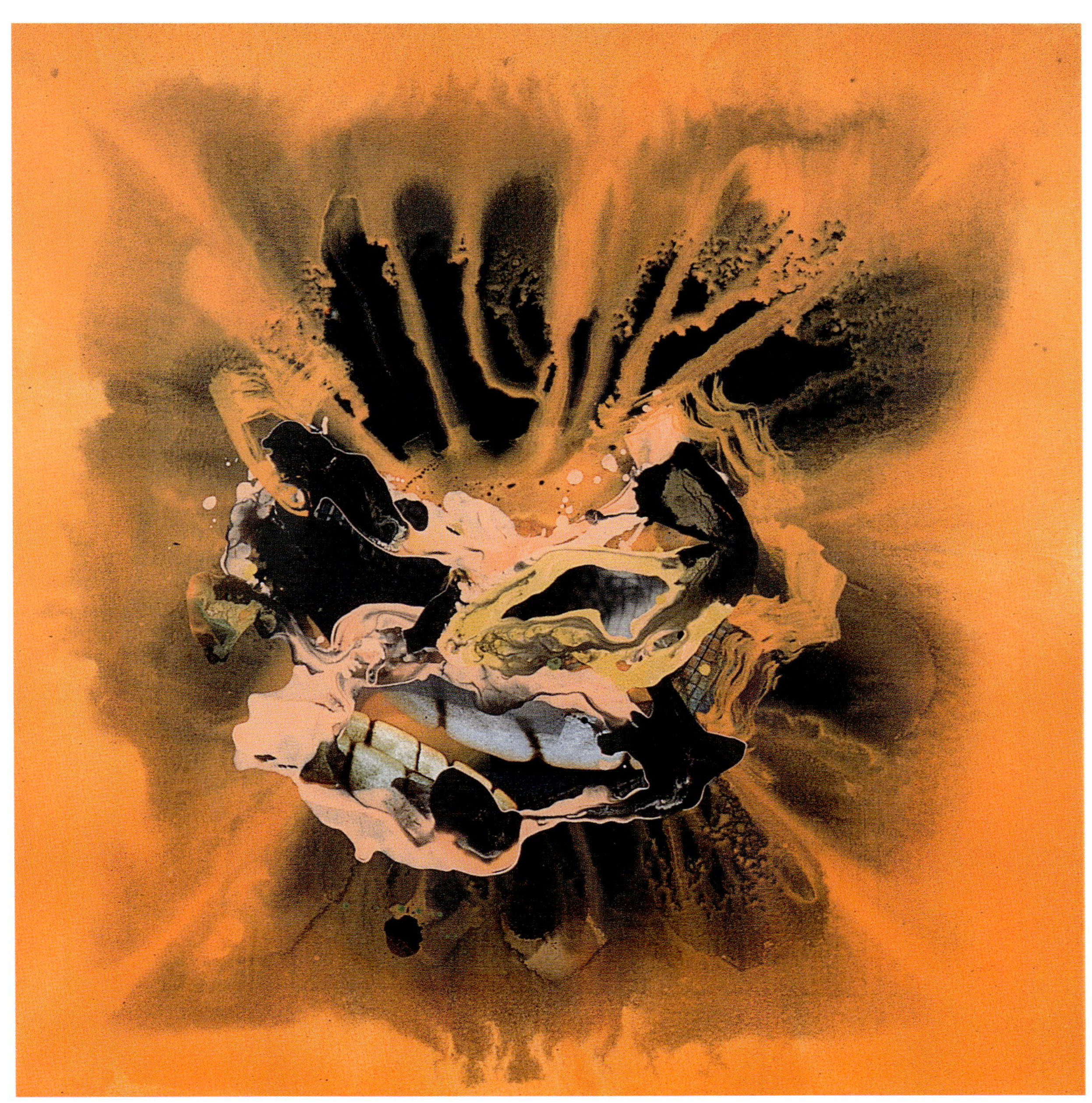

LARRY BELL b. 1939 Chicago. Ed: Chouinard Art Institute (now Cal Arts), Los Angeles. Coll: Albright-Knox, Guggenheim, MOMA NY, Whitney NY; Hirshhorn Museum, National Gallery DC; San Francisco Museum of Modern Art, Los Angeles MOCA CA; Tate Gallery, London; Centre Georges Pompidou, Paris; etal. Representation: Larry Bell Studio Annex, Taos.

HTTHOJ 34
MIXED MEDIA COLLAGE ON CANVAS
42 X 42 INCHES

KEVIN TOLMAN

Those who spend a lot of time outdoors have a different sense of time than those who measure their lives by holidays, semesters, and business deadlines. In the natural world, every year is shaped differently. Seasons come and go at slightly irregular intervals. Time moves at its own pace, whether howling through the desert or sleeping beneath the snow. Time rests beside a campfire, scuds with the clouds, jolts through the rapids, riffles through the treetops, plummets down an avalanche, and stops to watch a butterfly emerging from a chrysalis. Often it does several of these things at once.

The natural flow of time saturates Kevin Tolman's art. One could almost use his work as a clock or a calendar. Definitely, it is a record of all his days. Ever since he was a small child, he has painted and drawn constantly. Even now, whenever he is not painting, he is drawing, sketching, or writing. "If I don't do that," he explains, "I might lose the thread of the ongoing dialog I maintain with my work." Over the decades, those who watch his development can see an organic, ever-changing response to the natural world that is reflected in each painting as well as in his art as a whole. He likens his work to an ever-evolving garden he tends. Reminiscing about one springtime series, he says, "A sort of spring fever led me to think about this flowering and pollination, and how erotic and sensuous a place my orchard and back yard had become."

Tolman enjoys being outdoors as much as possible. During his frequent travels to places like the Iberian Peninsula, he spends as much time in nature as he does in observing the culture or visiting the great museums. At home in the Southwest, he hikes and camps out frequently. "Once," he remembers, "for a season, I slept outside every night just because I think there's something there, something that informs us in some subtle manner."

Kevin Tolman has an easel built outside his studio so he can work in the open – not, obviously, in the manner of the plein air artists who paint what is before them, but in the way of an artist who is tuned to nature with all his senses. He interprets this sensory information even as he concentrates on all the other aspects of painting – his dialog with the work, his interaction with the materials, the moment by moment decisions he makes as the painting progresses in its own time.

"Sometimes I feel that the paintings are much like sitting and looking into a little tiny bit of the ground," he says. "There is a sort of chaotic composition of leaves, grass moving in the wind, sticks, bugs crawling, dewdrops glistening while crickets chirp, birds tweet – a kind of simple, thick, almost unfocused beauty."

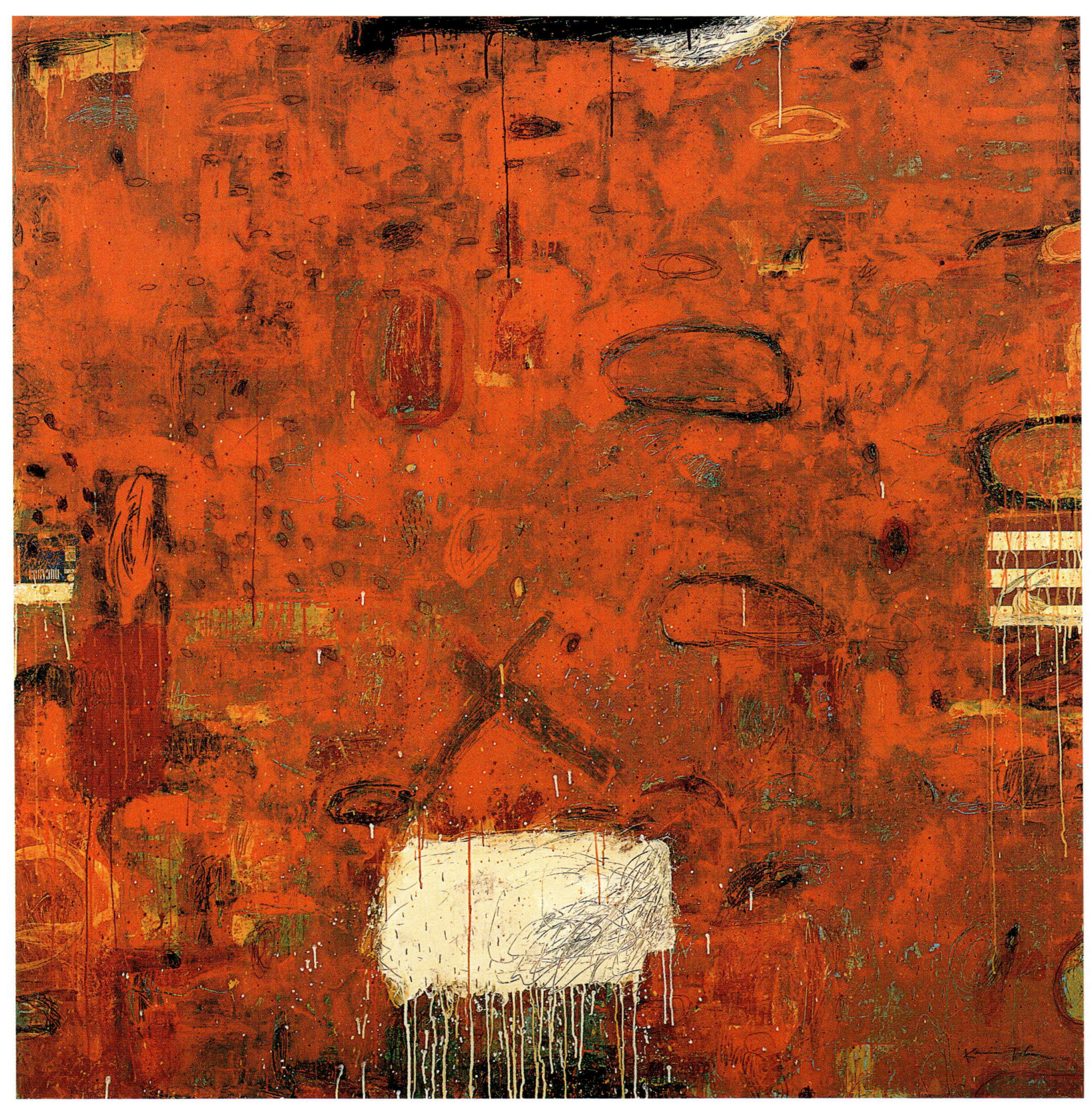

TURNING TABLES/CORDOBA
ACRYLIC AND COLLAGE ON CANVAS
60 X 60 INCHES

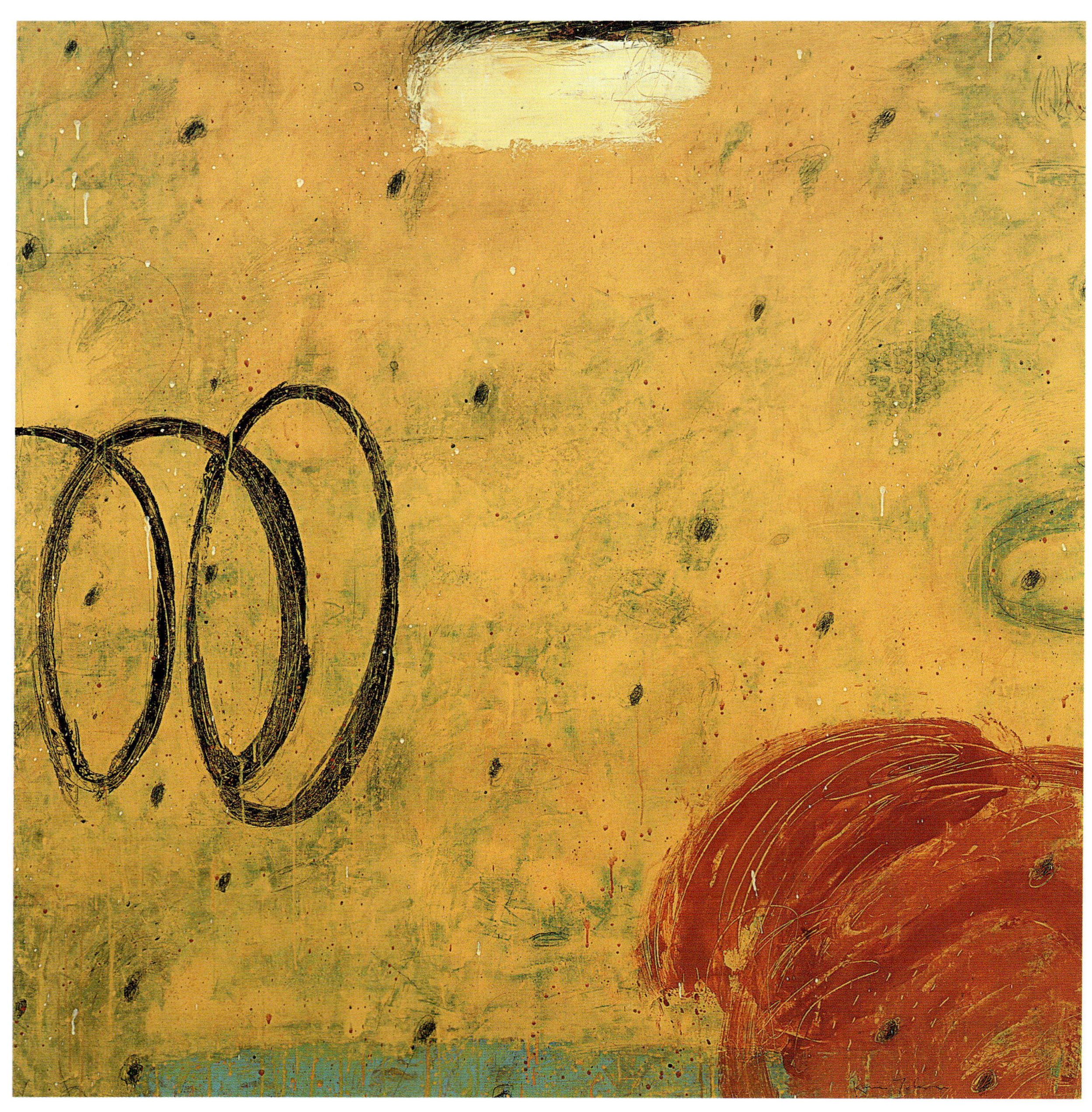

FOUNTAIN/LIFT
ACRYLIC ON CANVAS
48 X 48 INCHES

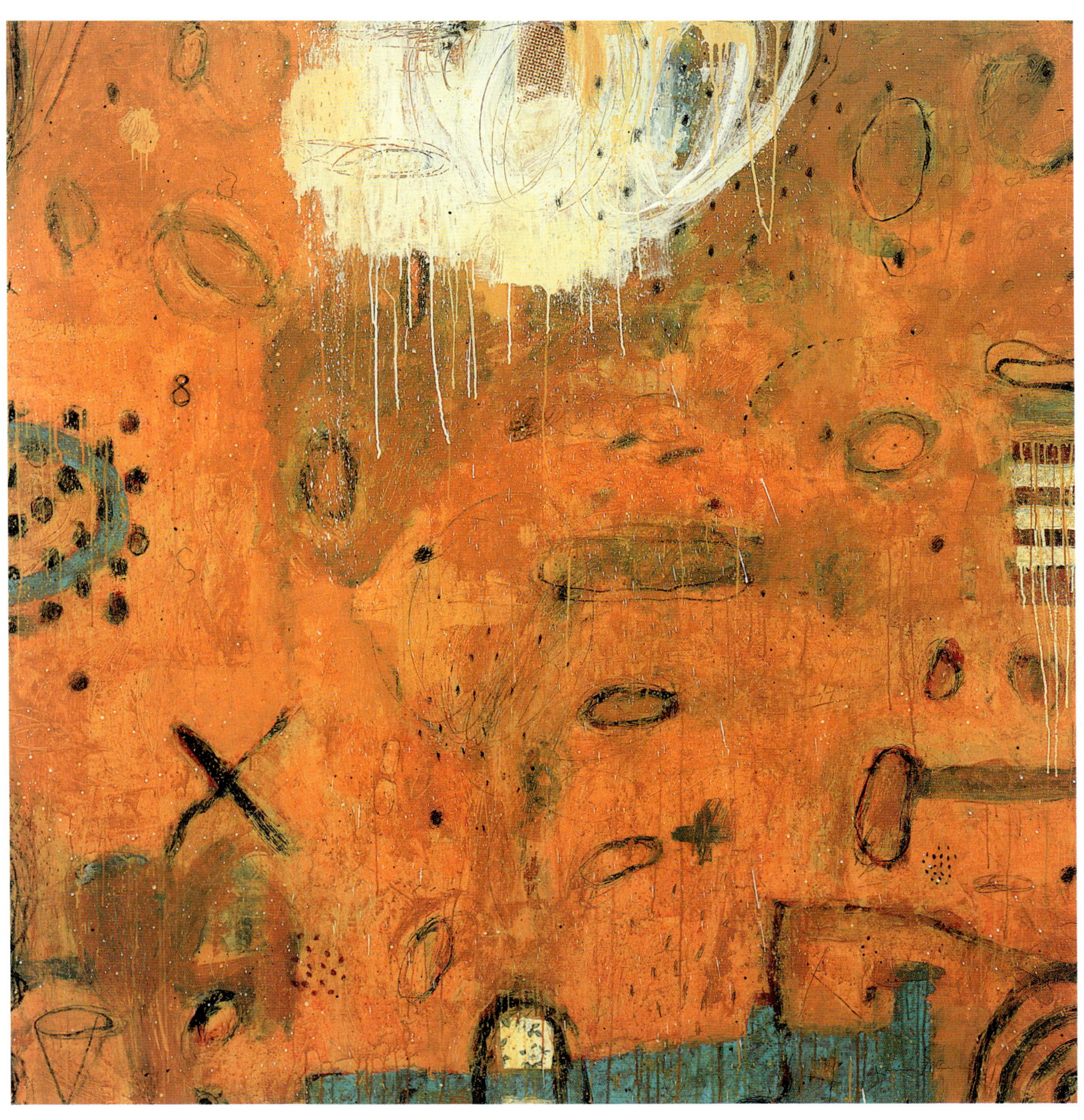

SANTA SEMANA
ACRYLIC AND COLLAGE ON CANVAS
60 X 60 INCHES

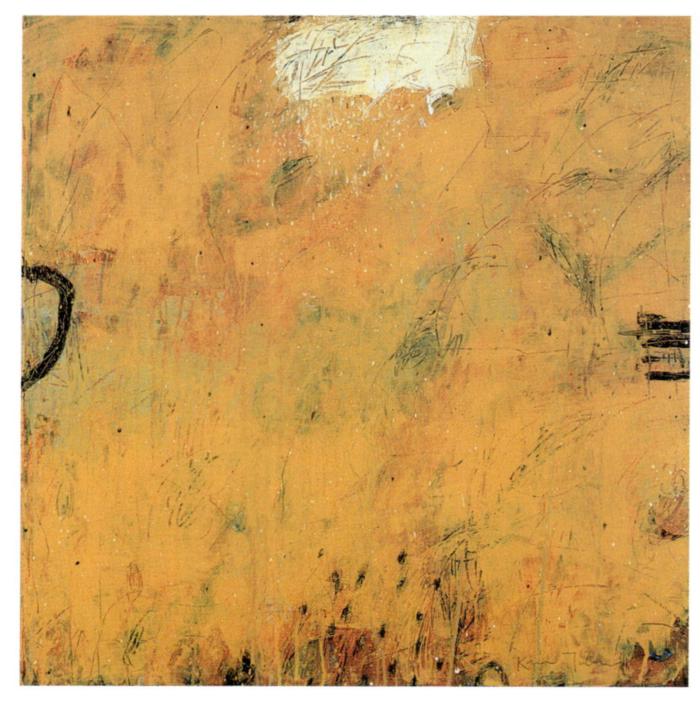

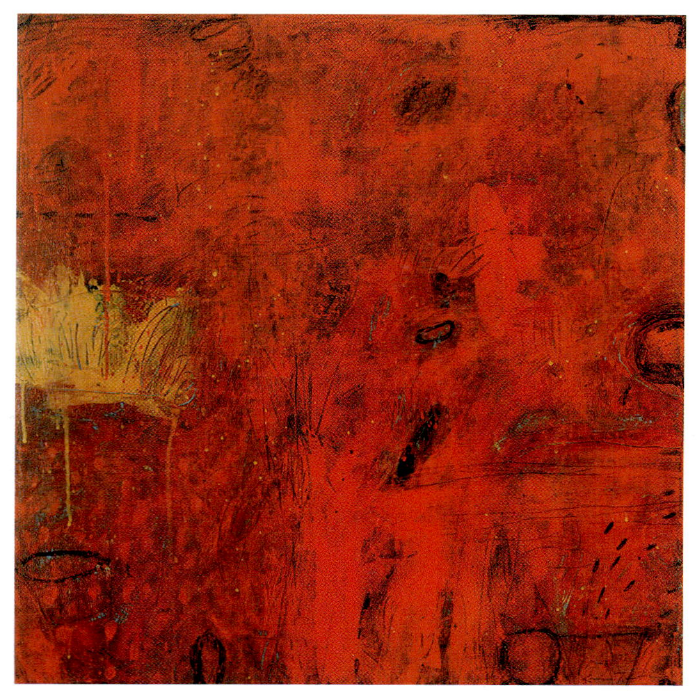

SURFACE TENSION I & II
ACRYLIC ON CANVAS, DIPTYCH
24 X 24 INCHES EACH

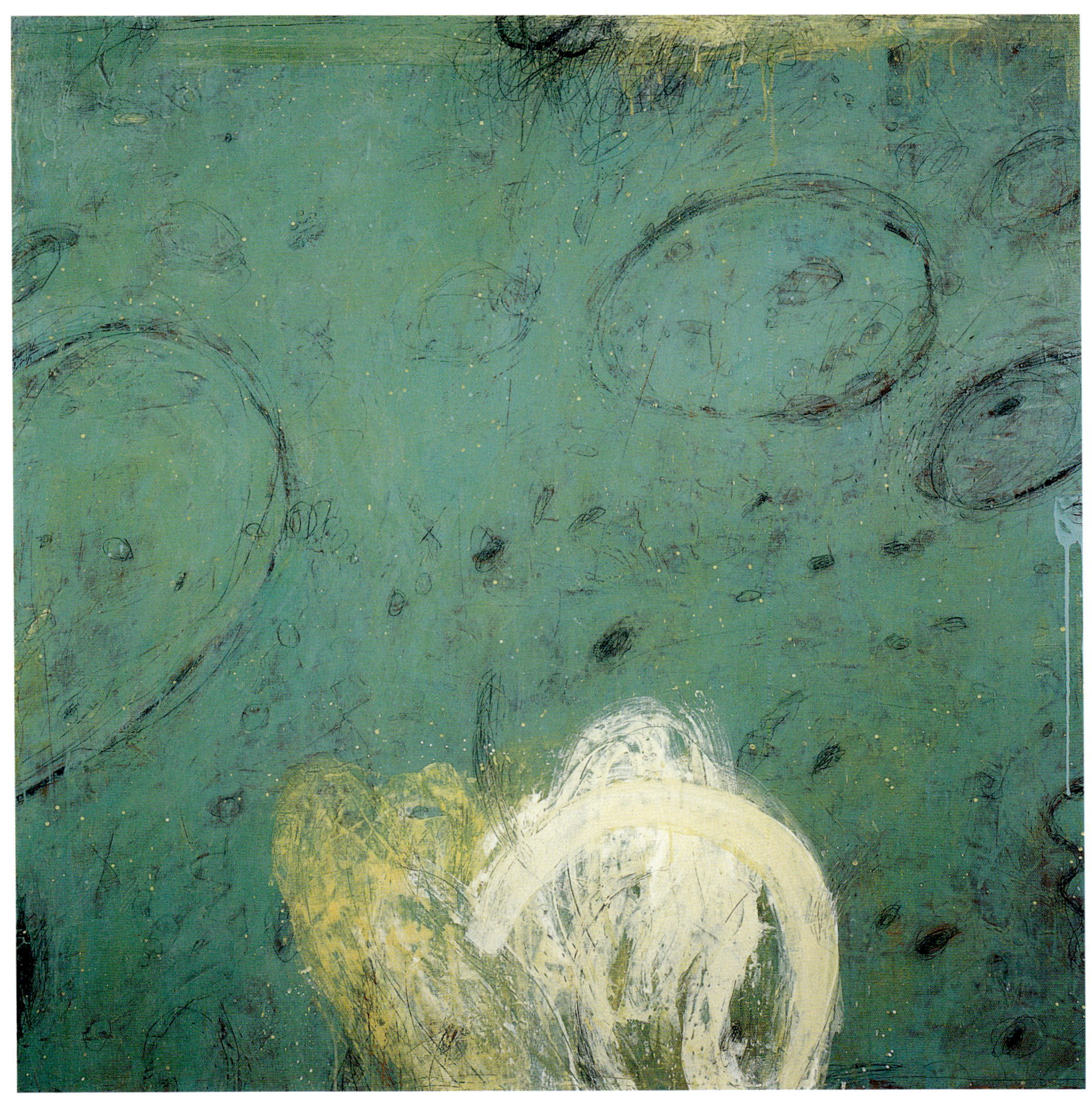

KEVIN TOLMAN b. 1949 Detroit MI. Ed: Art School of The Society of Arts and Crafts/Center for Creative Studies, Detroit; Art School of the Society of Arts & Crafts, Detroit. Coll: Bank One; Neiman-Marcus; Hyatt Hotels; Harcourt Brace; Capitol Art Collection NM; etal. Representation: Karan Ruhlen Gallery, Santa Fe.

SEASIDE/ECHO
ACRYLIC ON CANVAS
48 X 48 INCHES

EMMI WHITEHORSE

The light dawns. Bits and pieces of dreams, like retinal floaters, hover for a moment and then subside into the darkness or go scattering out into the sunshine. Where daybreak meets the water, the mist ripples, dissolves, and rises to meet the sky. The night retreats and bides its time.

The light spreads slowly across the land, crowding out the cool and secret places in the backs of valleys and the folds of shorelines. Dreams, stripped of cover, lie exposed and diminished. In much the same way, the future erodes all cumulative wisdom and subtle history with its sovereign blankness. Saturated color empties itself as slowly as a river into a calm afterglow. The stillness is absolute as civilization waits, parched, for the sunset of time.

Emmi Whitehorse holds nothingness at bay with a rich and durable tapestry of natural symbols. Using the simplest of materials, she has created a body of work that rests lightly but authoritatively in the world of contemporary abstract art. She remains a major figure because her art moves inexorably forward.

Whitehorse was born and raised on the Navajo Reservation. She attended the University of New Mexico, graduated, and began showing her art immediately, before going on to graduate school. "I really didn't plan on career as an artist," she says. "But I have had a good long run."

Her medium and technique have remained the same while her work has evolved. Using chalks and oil bars, she works on large sheets of heavy paper attached to a wall support. The finished piece is affixed to a stretched canvas, then framed.

Within those parameters, a lot has taken place. "My work has been very geometric at times," says Whitehorse. "It has been all black and white. It has swung to figurative, then to very bizarre dreamlike images and odd colors. Then back to figurative again, with mystical, anthropomorphic beings. Then back to vegetative organic images of growing things such as seed pods, cotyledons, or ruffled leaves. I make these forms up. I don't study. I just look at things."

Right now her major interest is in color field work. The light leaks into the borders of the image as if it were prying up the edge of a photosensitive curtain. The edgy, delicate drawing, always a dominant element, recedes into the mysterious depths. "It's almost like looking through a fixed lens," says the artist. "You can see deeply, but you can't see what's beyond that round lens."

Emmi Whitehorse has maintained her crystalline focus through the decades. "It's always been a very personal effort," she says. "As you grow older, you get different ideas and your vision changes. What remains for me is the sense of solitary wonderment."

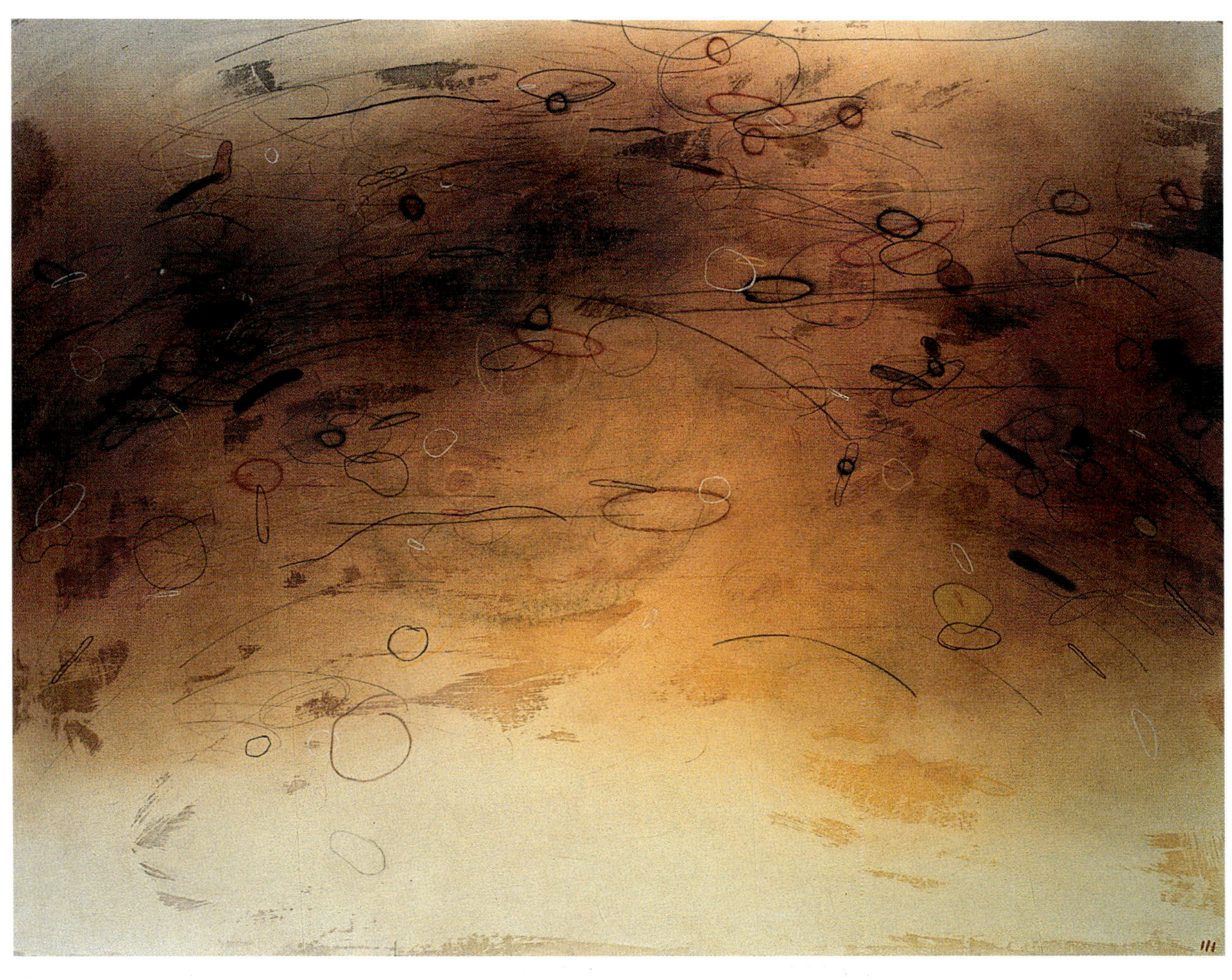

ARC
OIL/CHALK/PAPER/CANVAS
40 X 51 INCHES

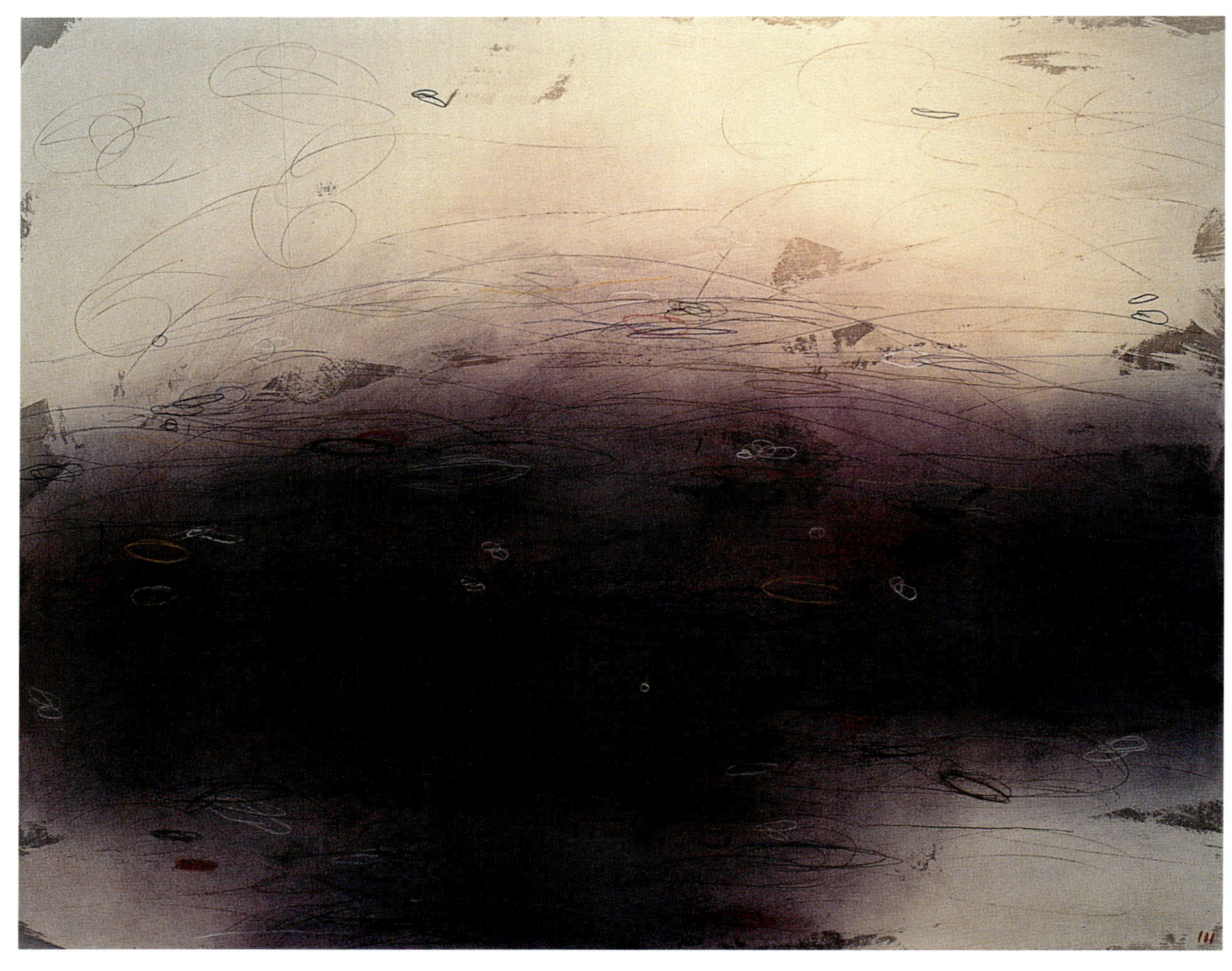

UNTITLED
OIL/CHALK/PAPER/CANVAS
41 X 29 INCHES

EMMI WHITEHORSE

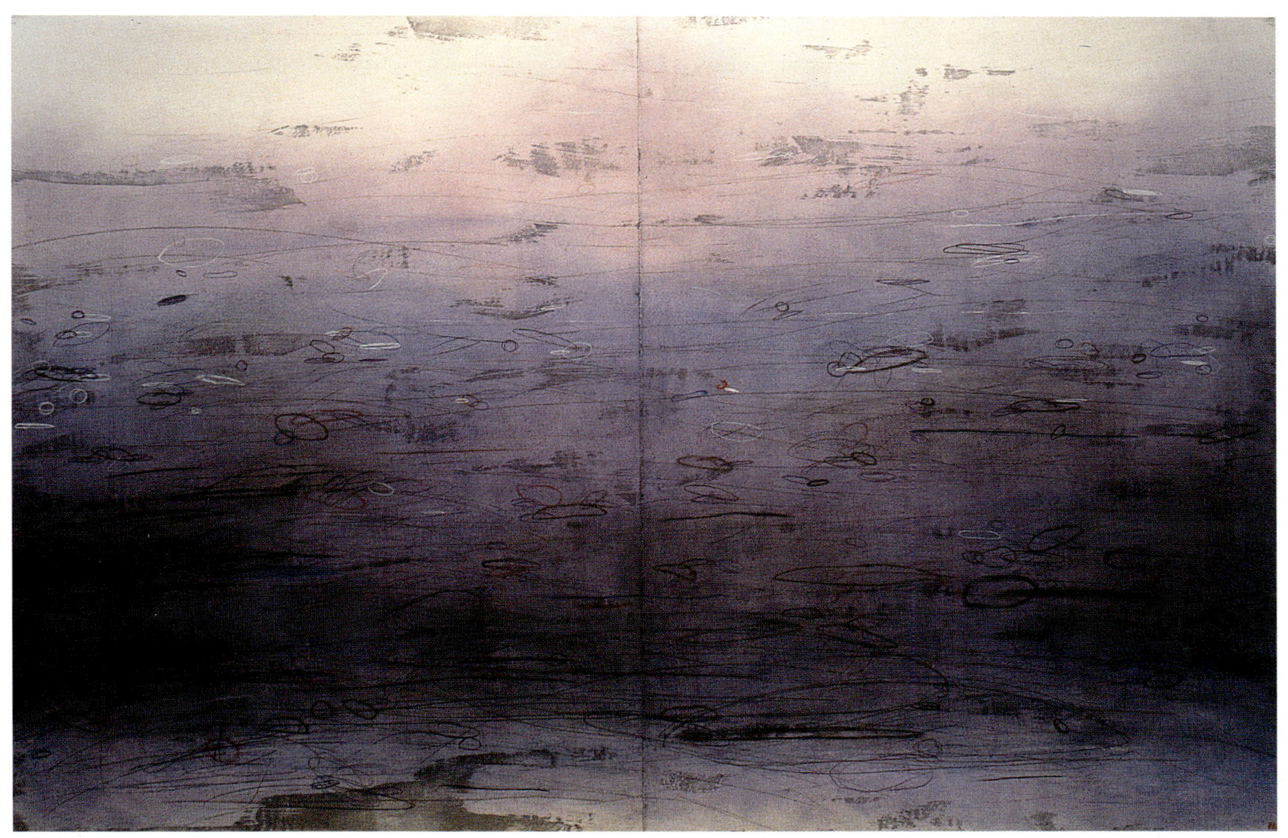

WATERED
OIL/CHALK/PAPER/CANVAS
51 X 79 INCHES

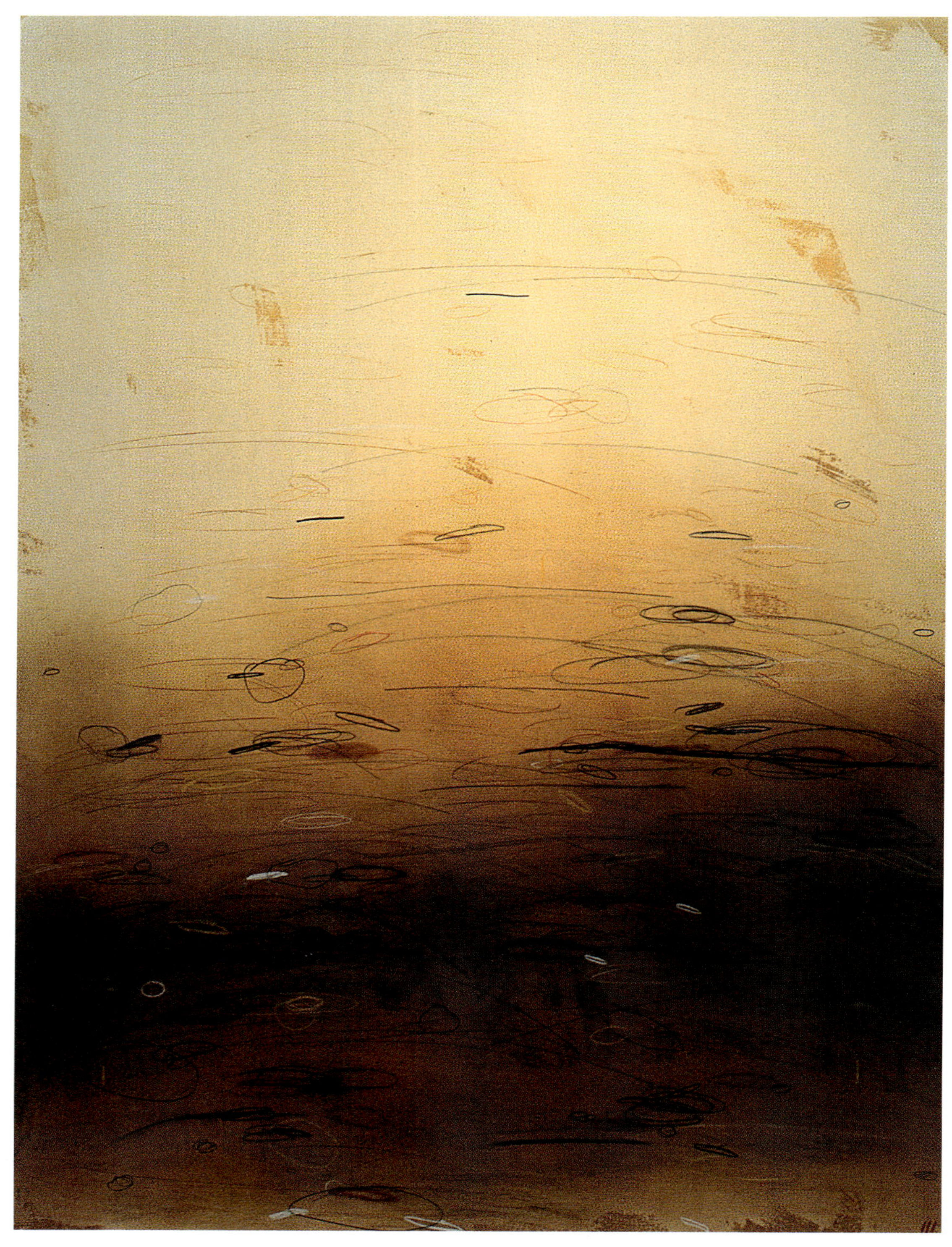

WATER'S EDGE
OIL/CHALK/PAPER/CANVAS
40 X 51 INCHES

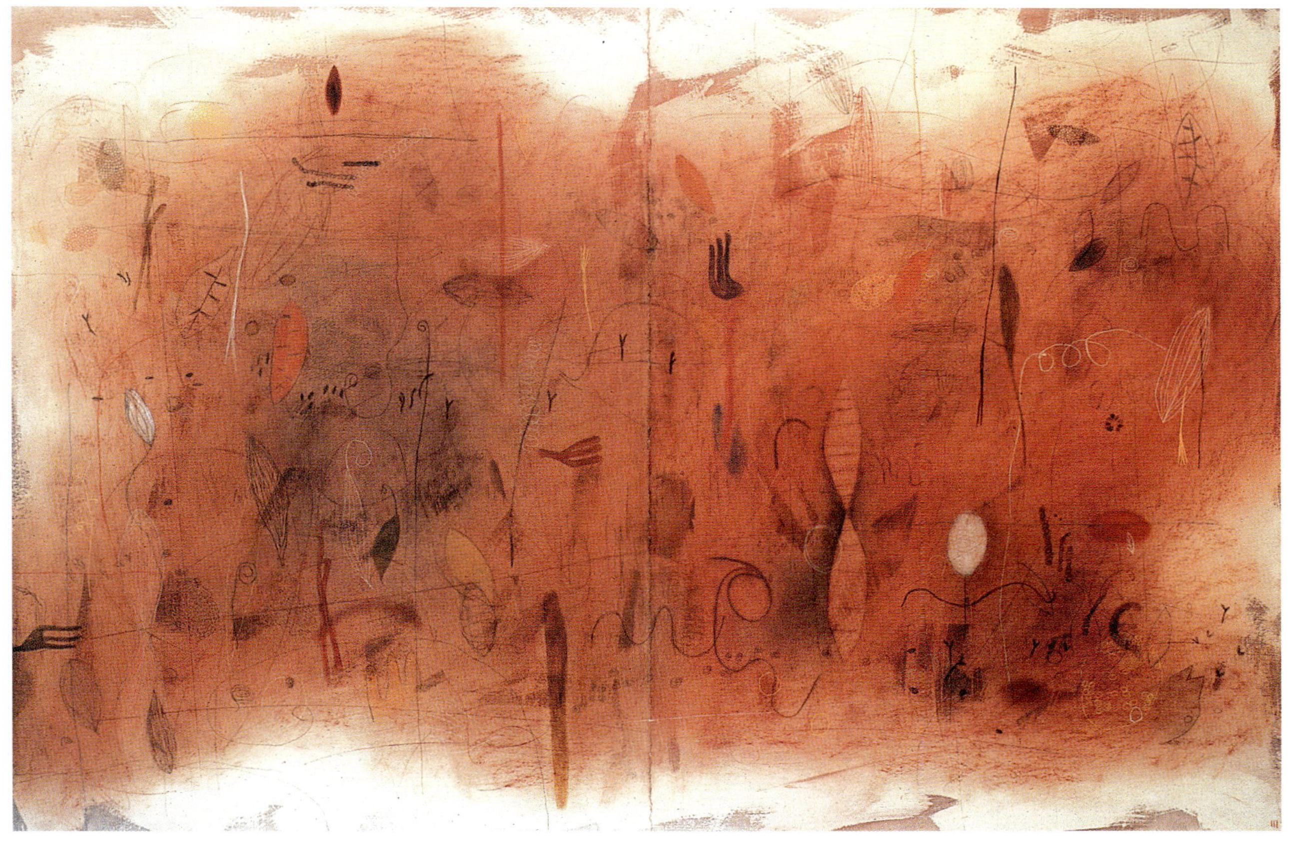

EMMI WHITEHORSE b. 1957 Crownpoint NM. Ed: MA, BA Univ. New Mexico. Solo exhib: Joslyn Art Museum NE; Tucson Museum of Art AZ. Group exhib: American Acad. of Arts and Letters, NY; Albuquerque Museum NM; Denver Art Museum, Westphälisches Museum, Germany. Coll: IBM; Hallmark; etal. Representation: LewAllen Contemporary, Santa Fe; Carson-Matsuoka, Denver; Telluride Fine Arts CO; Mainsite Gallery, Norman OK; Vanier Galleries AZ.

VESTIGE OF A GARDEN
OIL/CHALK/PAPER/CANVAS
51 X 79 INCHES

ZACHARIAH RIEKE

Some explorers, like Marco Polo, are discoverers who travel to the ends of the earth to bring back treasures and new information to those whose lives are limited by their own horizons. Others are like Henry David Thoreau, who stayed in one place and mined it, saying, "I have traveled a good deal in Concord."

So it is with artists. On the one hand are the Thoreauesque ones who establish a certain closely considered and deliberately limited imagery, repeating it over a lifetime in order to embrace every possible nuance contained therein. On the other hand is Zachariah Rieke, a Marco Polo of the interior universe who constantly plunges ahead into uncharted territory.

Although his distinctive surfaces and his enigmatic compositions remain identifiable as his alone, the point of inquiry moves, and moves, and moves. He has addressed one idea after another down through the years, always with a depth of focus that cuts through to the gist of the subject. Organically constructed and irresistibly magnetic, Rieke's art takes command of any space it occupies.

Rieke's paintings are suspended in a profound, meditative silence that is all the more remarkable for the energetic application of earthy materials that produces it. Whether he is building up a thick substratum of ashes, sand, and dirt, or applying a delicate wash of color across the surface of an unprimed canvas, his paintings create a doorway into the unknown. The viewer's mind may step through it as through a looking glass, catching faint threads that become paths, then roads to everywhere.

These individual works of art are resolved in a state of dynamic equilibrium, while Rieke's work as a whole continues to weigh possibilities, to seek ever more elusive destinations, even to gear up and start out again. What would be unthinkable to another artist is a necessary part of Rieke's process – the return to a place once visited, the altering of one's original perspective, and the departure on another journey from a point that was once fixed but has become tenuous and penetrable.

Rieke's process is not unlike that of the early discoverers who used dead reckoning for their explorations. Dead reckoning is defined as "estimating position without astronomical observation, by calculating or guessing the course and distance traveled from a previously determined position." Rieke sees his art as a personal journey from the safe harbor of the known into the maelstrom of the unknown and unknowable. In this spirit he quotes Kierkegaard: "Originality means to stake everything, to risk everything."

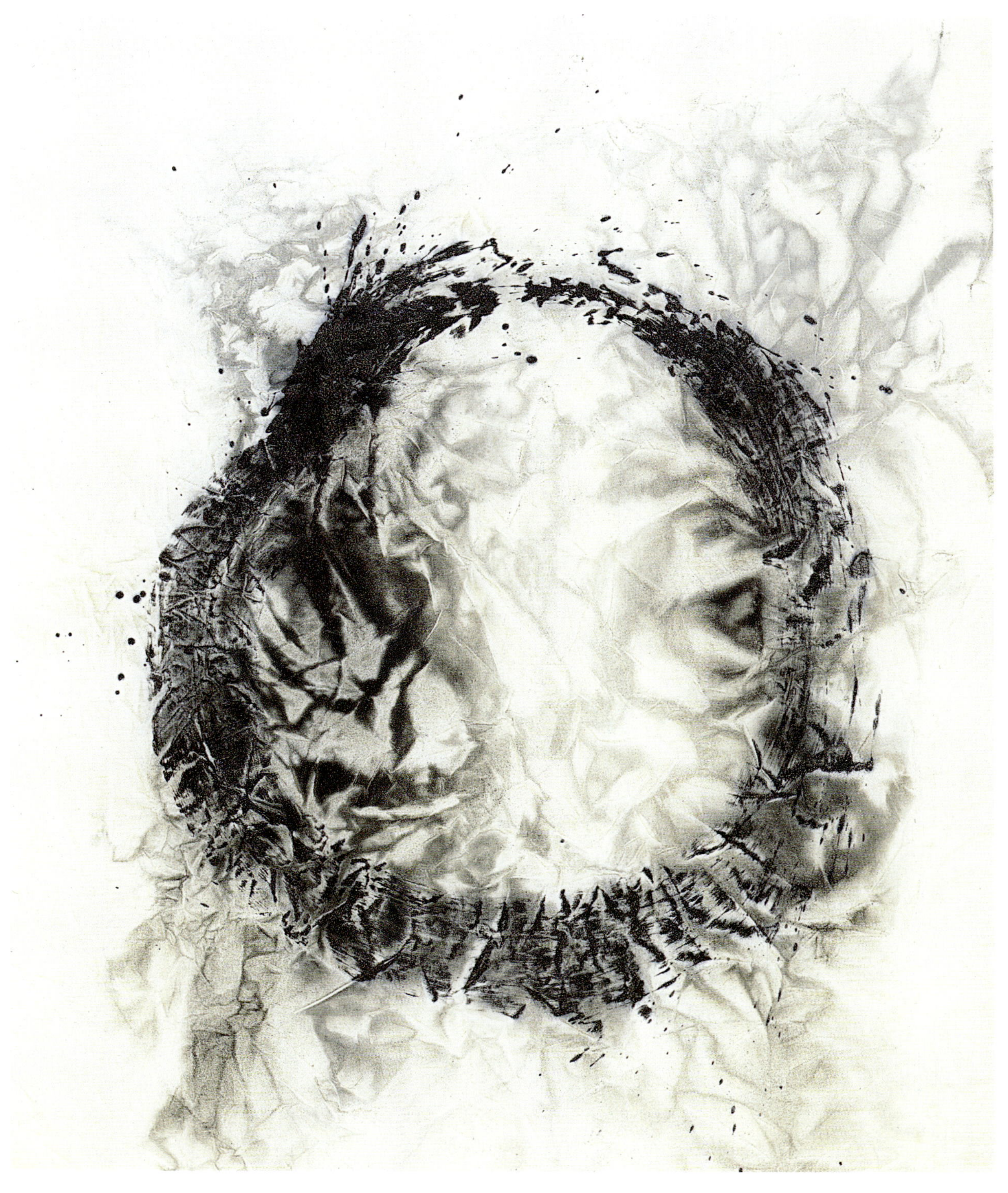

SMOKE RING, 2003
MIXED MEDIA ON CANVAS
72½ X 62 INCHES

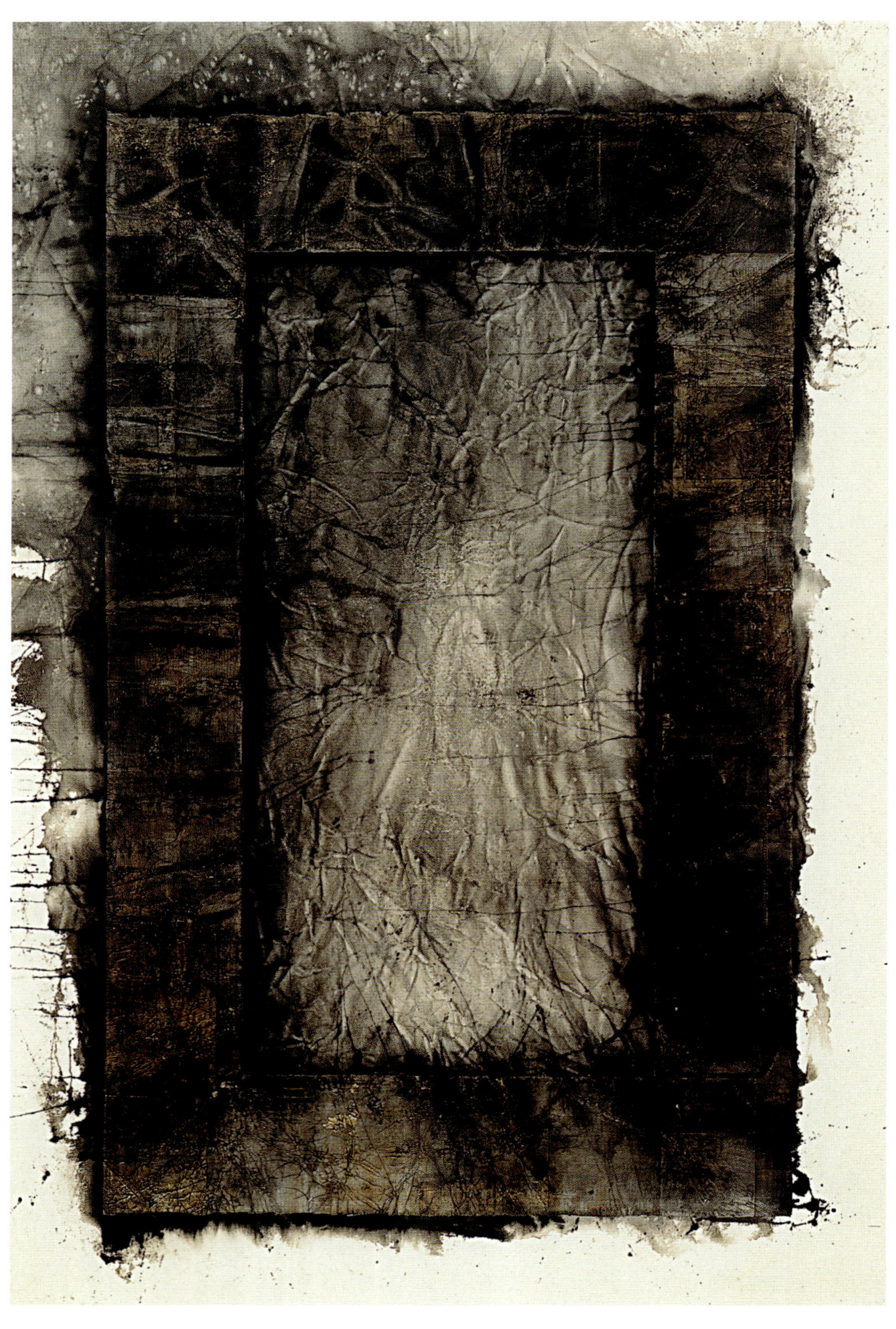

THRESHOLD-2, 2002
MIXED MEDIA ON CANVAS
84 X 58 INCHES

REPOSE, 2002
MIXED MEDIA ON CANVAS
51½ X 44 INCHES

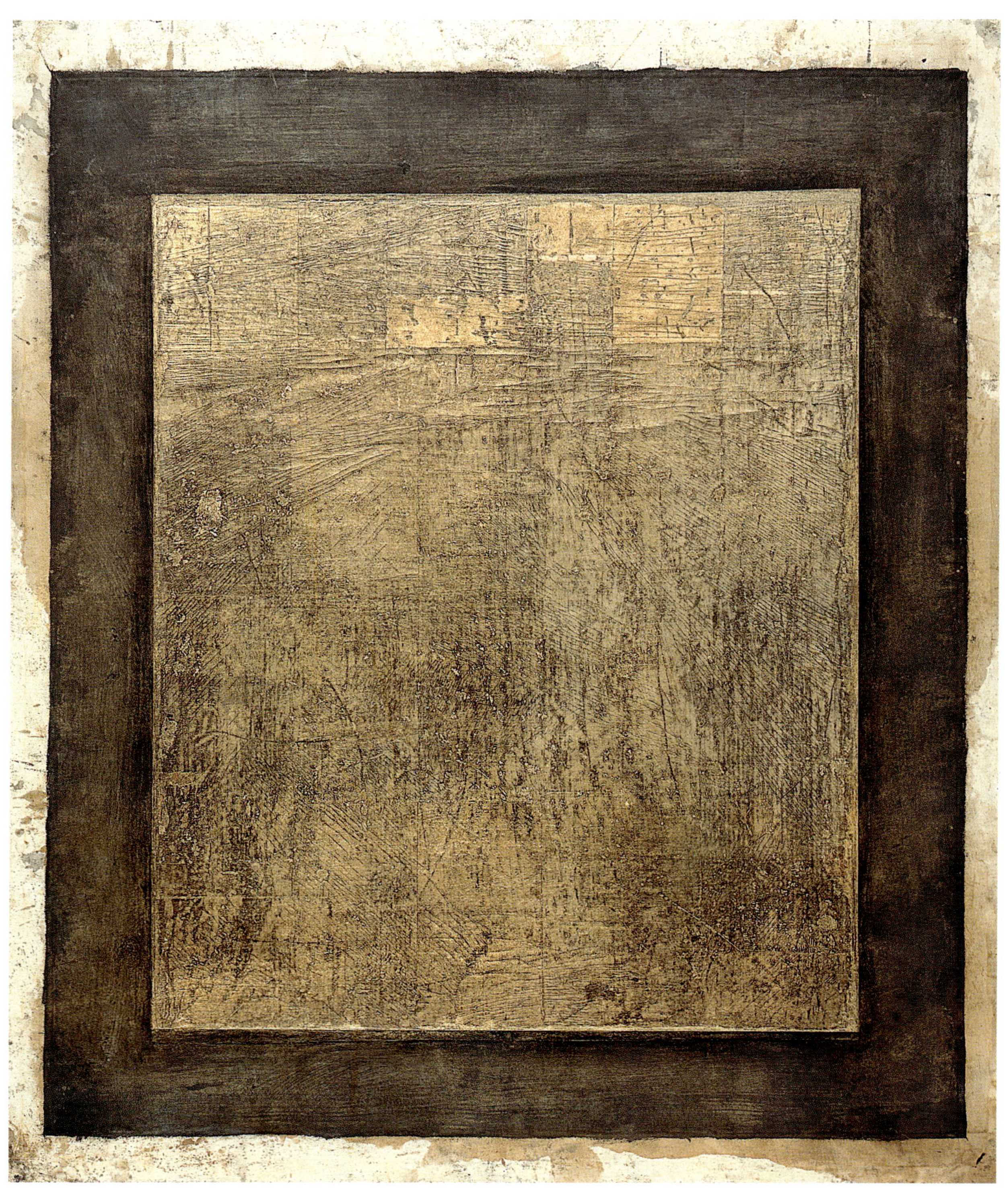

SHROUD, 2001
MIXED MEDIA ON CANVAS
71 X 60 INCHES

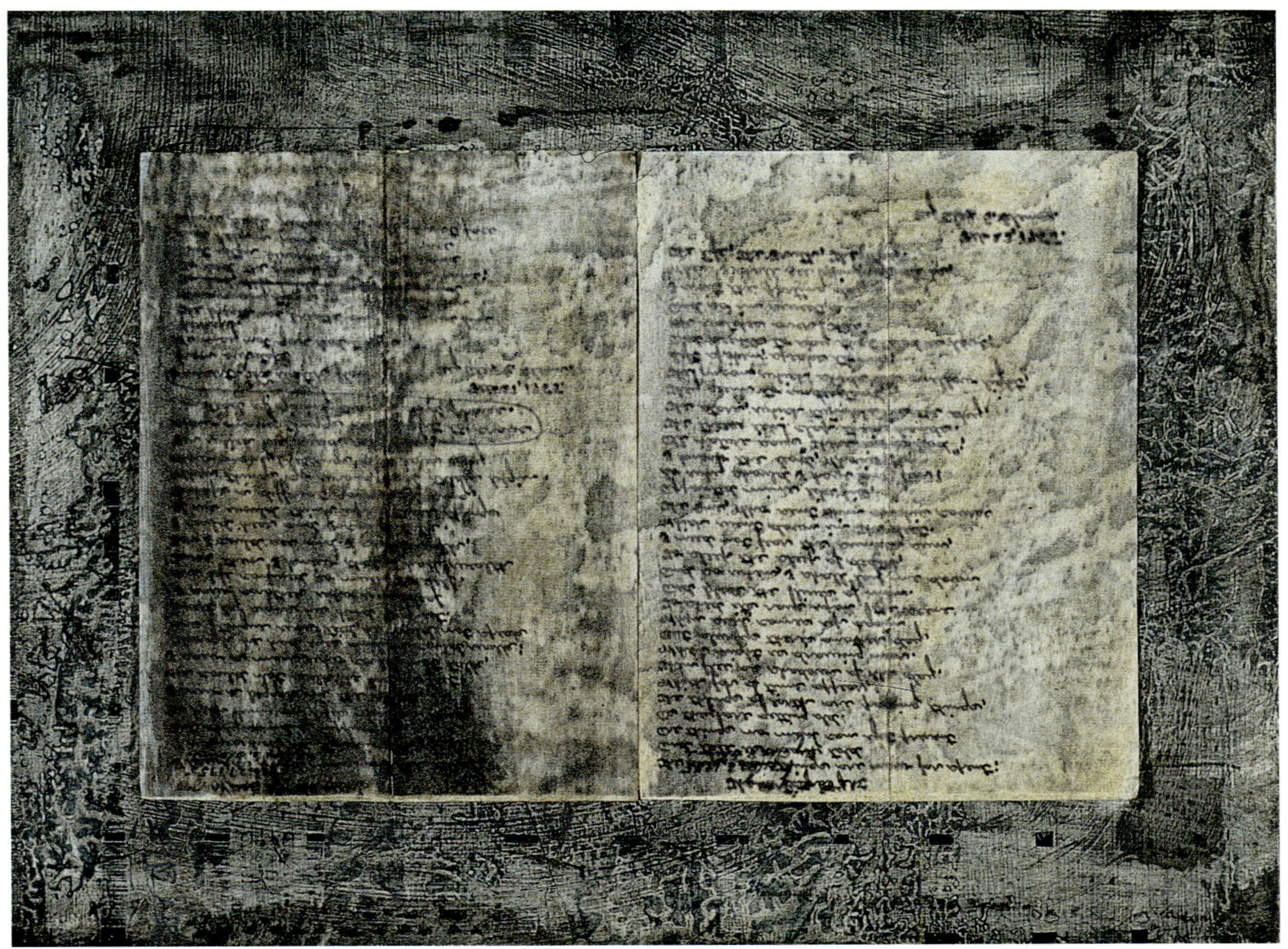

ZACHARIAH RIEKE b. 1943 Belleville KS. Ed: MFA Univ. Florida; BFA with honors, Wichita State University KS. Coll: Museum of Fine Arts, Santa Fe; Albuquerque Museum NM; Univ. Nebraska; Sheraton Hotel, Singapore. Representation: EVO Gallery, Santa Fe.

OPEN BOOK, 1993
ACRYLIC, OIL AND PAPER ON WOOD
16 X 22 INCHES

HELMUT LÖHR

Art can forge a connection between word and image. It can cross language barriers, bridge sound and silence, fuse sign and symbol, and retrieve lost memory.

Music and literature, like visual art, begin as concepts. There is no concrete form of language until it is uttered or written, nor of music until an instrument or a voice projects it, or until it is set down as musical notation. When visual artists work with these ideas, deconstructing and reassembling them, they can transcend the science of linguistics and the mathematics of music.

Helmut Löhr moves freely through these rarefied realms. A multimedia artist and visual poet, he has published several books and created innumerable works of art based on books, music, and language. He has done collaborative work with musicians, composers, and fellow artists. His work has been exhibited all over the world, including European and American museums, libraries, and art and book events.

Löhr works with visual poetry the way John Cage works with sound. Cage believed that "the purpose of music is to sober and quiet the mind, thus making it susceptible to divine influences." Several years ago, Dick Higgins, one of the founders of the Fluxus movement, read spontaneously from Löhr's Visual Poetry book in a gallery in Germany. He felt that Löhr's work should be translated into music and had wanted to introduce him to John Cage, who was already into his final illness. Löhr never had the opportunity to meet Cage, but has since become involved with other experimental musicians and composers. A former student of John Cage is working on the music for The Mushroom Sonate.

In 1986, Löhr started a project called The International Library, with a hundred and fifty artists worldwide creating covers for book objects that he gave to them. This collection is on view at the Frederick R. Weisman Art Museum in Minneapolis.

"There are formulas and blueprints stored in the life forms on earth for all kinds of realities to be developed," says Löhr. "Other libraries, located in various sectors of the universe, store their knowledge in light forms of collections of molecules that we would not even recognize. Our genius frequency can be very helpful to reconnect with these libraries. Genius is not a genetic, physiological, psychological product of academia, a fluke of chaos, and it is not an IQ. It is a frequency of light, in which our mind swims as we search for water."

Over the years, people have tried to label Helmut Löhr's language, only to come up short against the sheer range of information contained in its enigmatic code. "My work started where the Dada artists stopped," says Löhr. "I tap straight into the power of nature, where we get all messages and all knowledge, and I try to hear what nature presents to us. Language is about communication, communication in the creation in which we all participate."

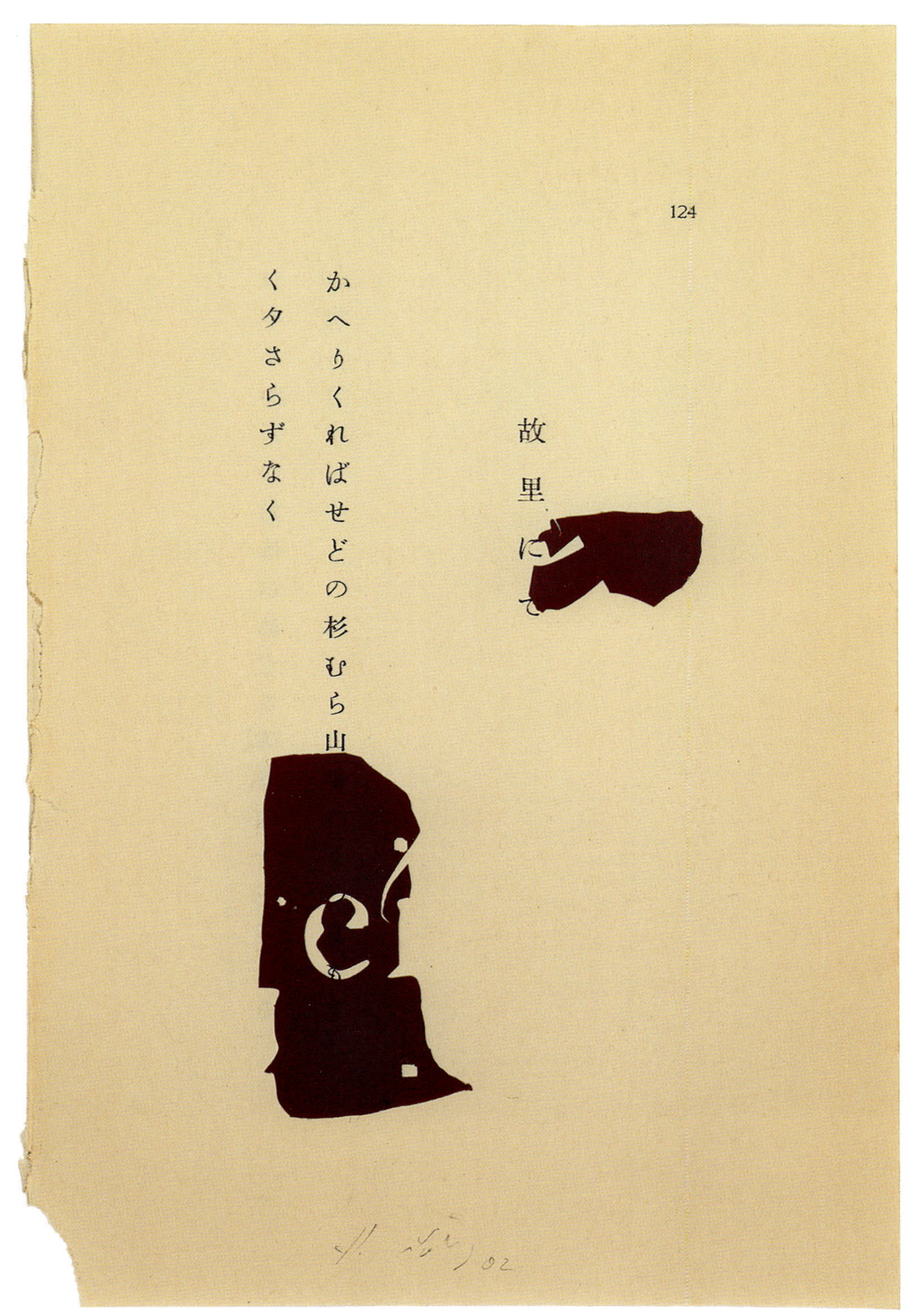

POEM FOR HIROSHIMA, 2002
MIXED MEDIA COLLAGE
7½ X 5 INCHES

LIGHT WITHIN THE HEART OF HEARTS, 2001
MIXED MEDIA
20 X 20 INCHES

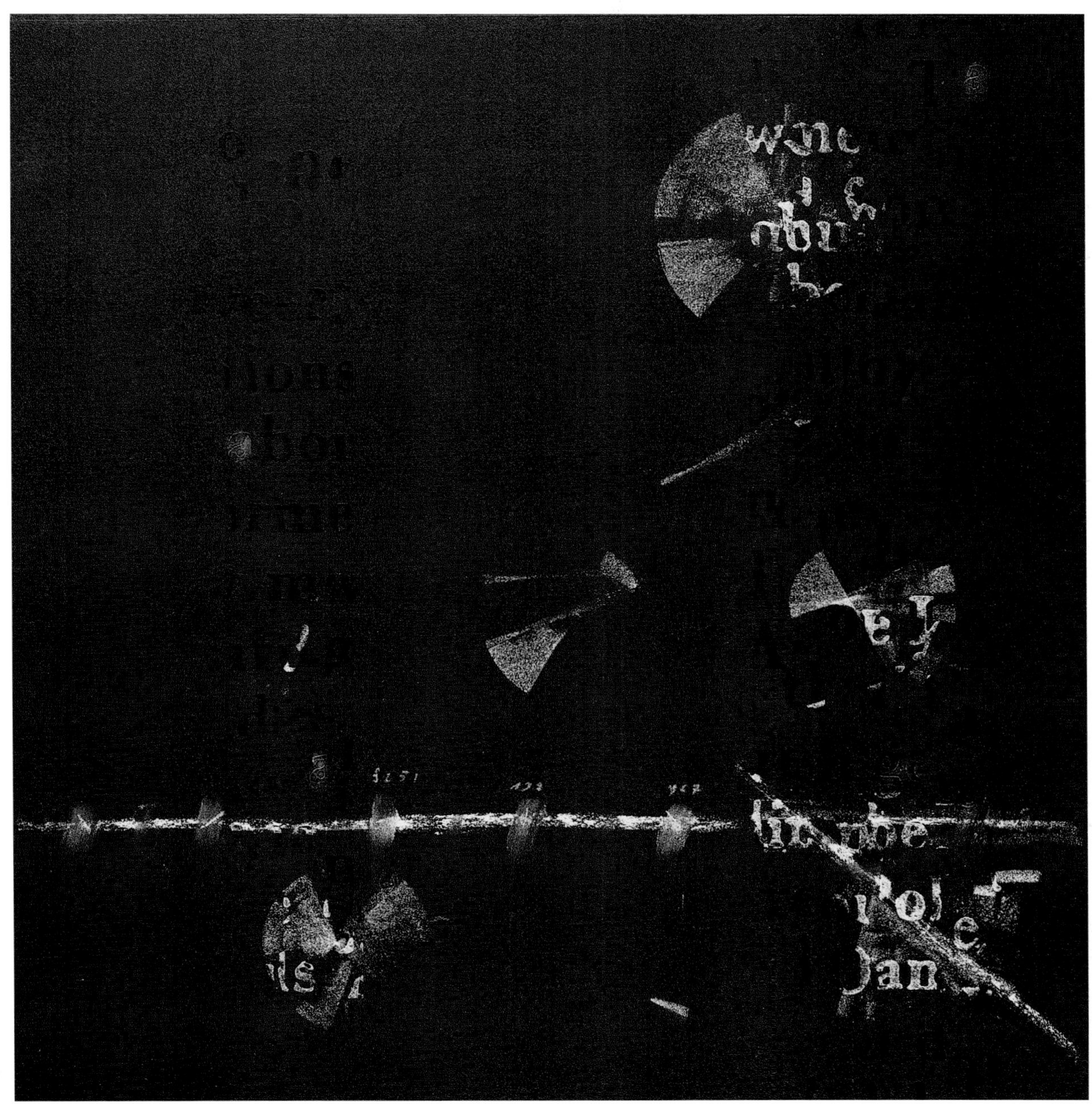

MOVING THROUGH THE FOURTH INTO THE FIFTH DIMENSION, 2001
MIXED MEDIA
20 X 20 INCHES
Accompanying Music: Obertonfantasie:
Hans-Joseph Winkler, Germany
Courtesy Archive of the Artist

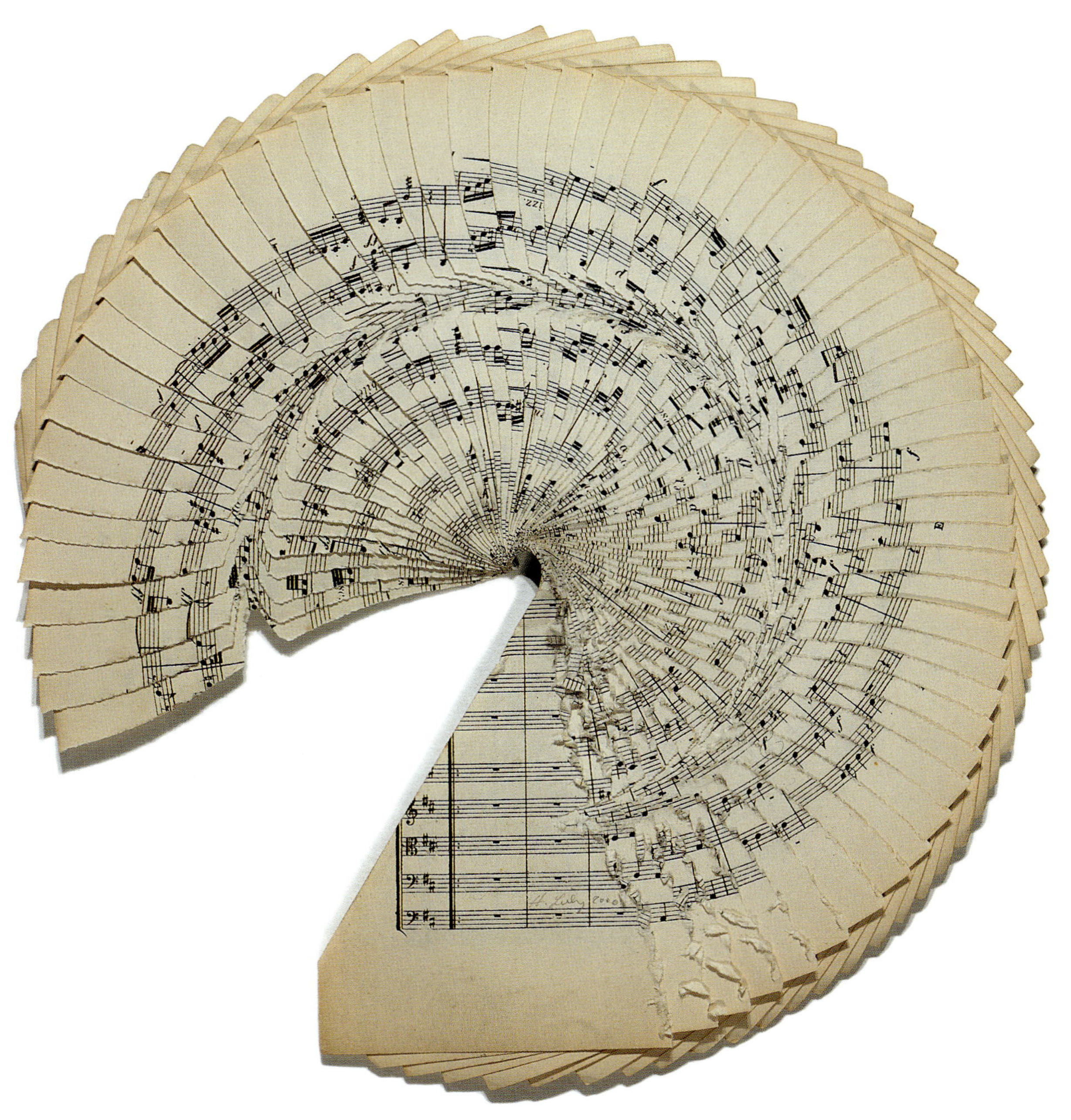

UNTITLED, 2000
MUSIC CIRCLE COLLAGE
10 INCH DIAMETER
Collection Ali MacGraw

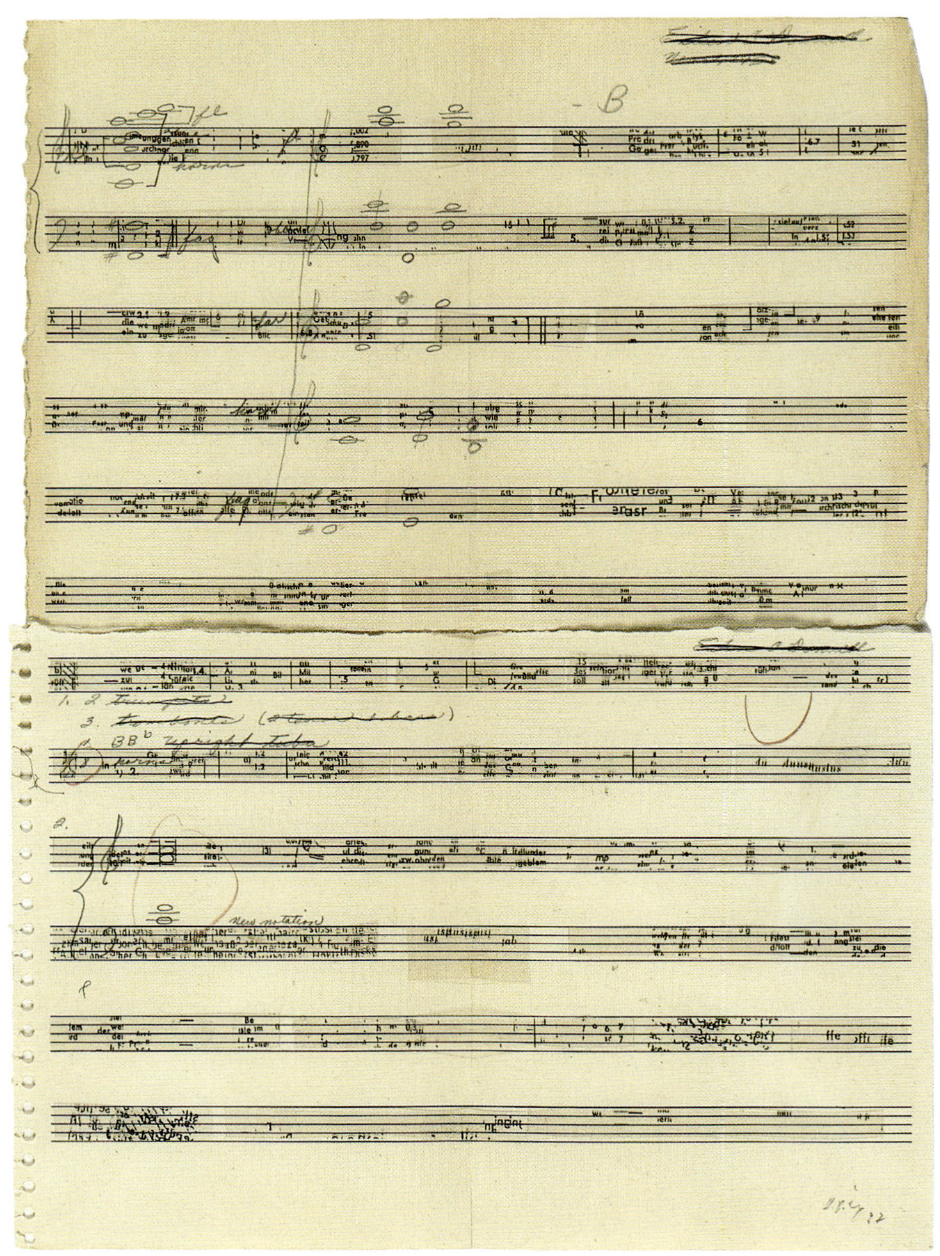

HELMUT LÖHR b. 1955 Germany. Coll: MOMA NY, Brooklyn Museum NYC; Getty Museum, Stanford Univ. CA; Chicago Art Institute; Rijksmuseum, den Haag, Netherlands; Victoria and Albert Museum, London; The Berlin Museum, Germany; etal. Representation: EVO Gallery, Santa Fe.

MUSHROOM SONATE FOR JOHN CAGE, 1997
PARTITUR COLLAGE
9 X 12 INCHES Music: Pat Irwin, NY
Courtesy Archive of the Artist

MICHAEL WRIGHT

Desire rises up where it is least expected. It pushes out against the darkness; it insinuates itself between the numbered hours of the calendar; it projects itself on the mind's inner walls like graffiti.

Desire generates possibilities from nothing, then creates the energy to pursue them. It drives children and corporations, scientists and sailboats, novelists and nations. Sometimes desire is erotic; more often it is not.

Michael Wright's abstract art bursts from the canvas as if propelled by its own energy. The forms nudge and jostle; the imagery is a feast; the mood is coolly ecstatic. These large-scale canvases paint tomorrow's emotional landscape with old-fashioned warmth and energy.

To reach this radiant and uncharted territory, Wright has traveled the high road since birth. As a boy, he explored both the woods of New England and the ideas of his literary parents and their circle. As a young painter, he became friends with several giants of Abstract Expressionism. Psychoanalysis, method acting, and science fiction were the topics of the day. Charlie Parker played upstairs. The beatniks had not yet become hippies.

Wright absorbed the ambiance and stockpiled its energies for future use. He went to Korea when the military conflict arose, then came home and spent some time processing that experience. He moved to East Hampton and worked for Willem deKooning as a studio assistant for several years, doing his own work in a studio that DeKooning found for him. Wright, who had always worked in a realistic mode, reached a point where he had to expand his vision.

Thus began a lifetime of internal and external exploration that never let up, as the artist went in search of a wider terrain. He first visited New Mexico in 1974. Immediately, he recognized the clarity of light and the variety of forms as somehow familiar and true. It took him more than ten years, but he finally sold his studio in New Hampshire and made the move.

For the first few years, he gave in to his excitement about the landscape. He made many plein air sketches, took them back to his studio, and created forceful paintings that had already begun to move toward abstraction. Finally, he let go of representation altogether and plunged into nonobjective art.

His work today concerns itself with the sweep of life experience, with the wild and windy motion of time, with the wheel and turn of ideas that embrace all outdoors. "It's complicated to keep everything going," says Michael Wright, "but I'm happy most of the time. I remember how it all started to work for me when I came out to New Mexico, and I think – my God, this is all made for me."

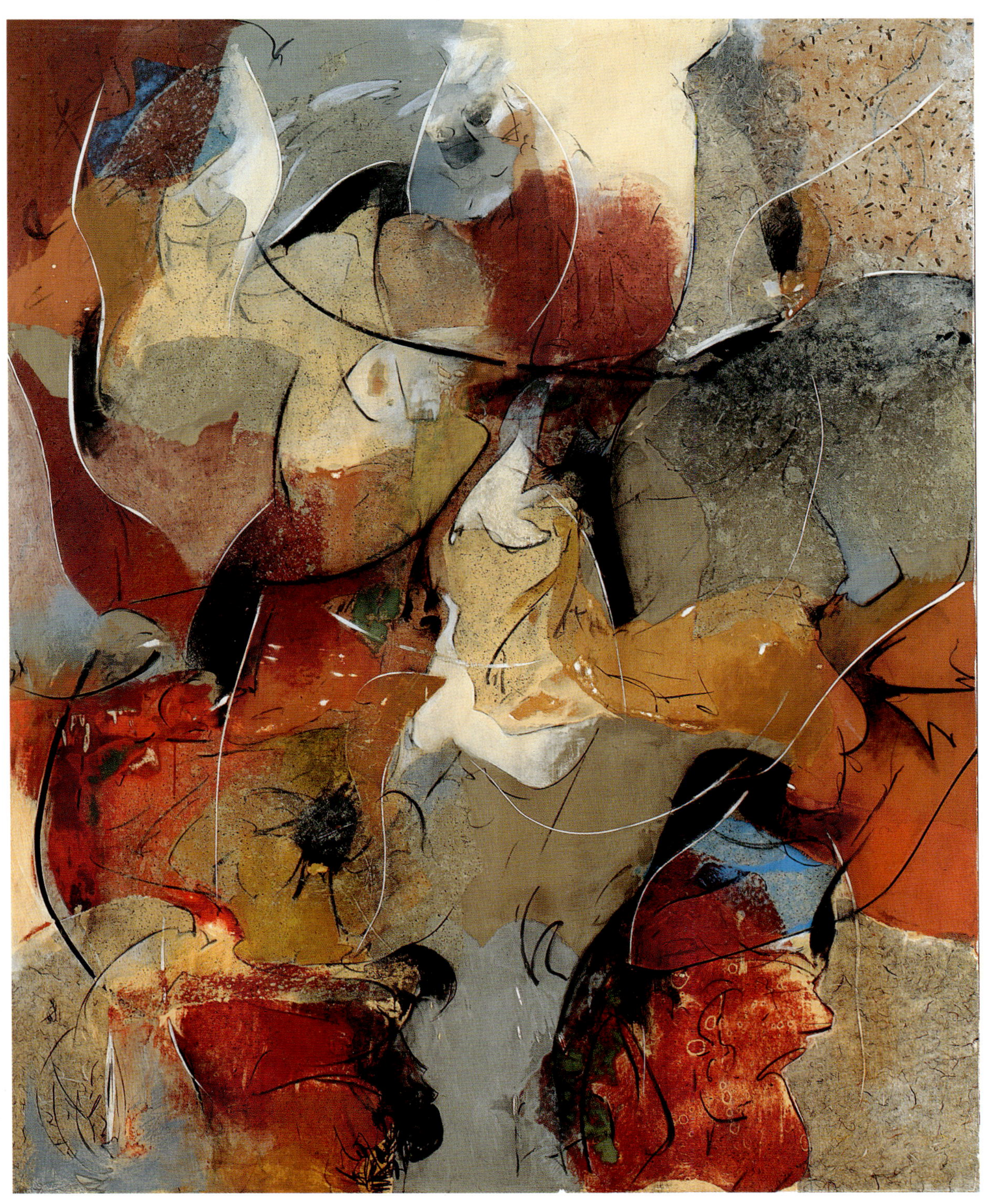

WHERE THE TAWE FLOWS, 1997
MIXED MEDIA ON CANVAS
80 X 68 INCHES

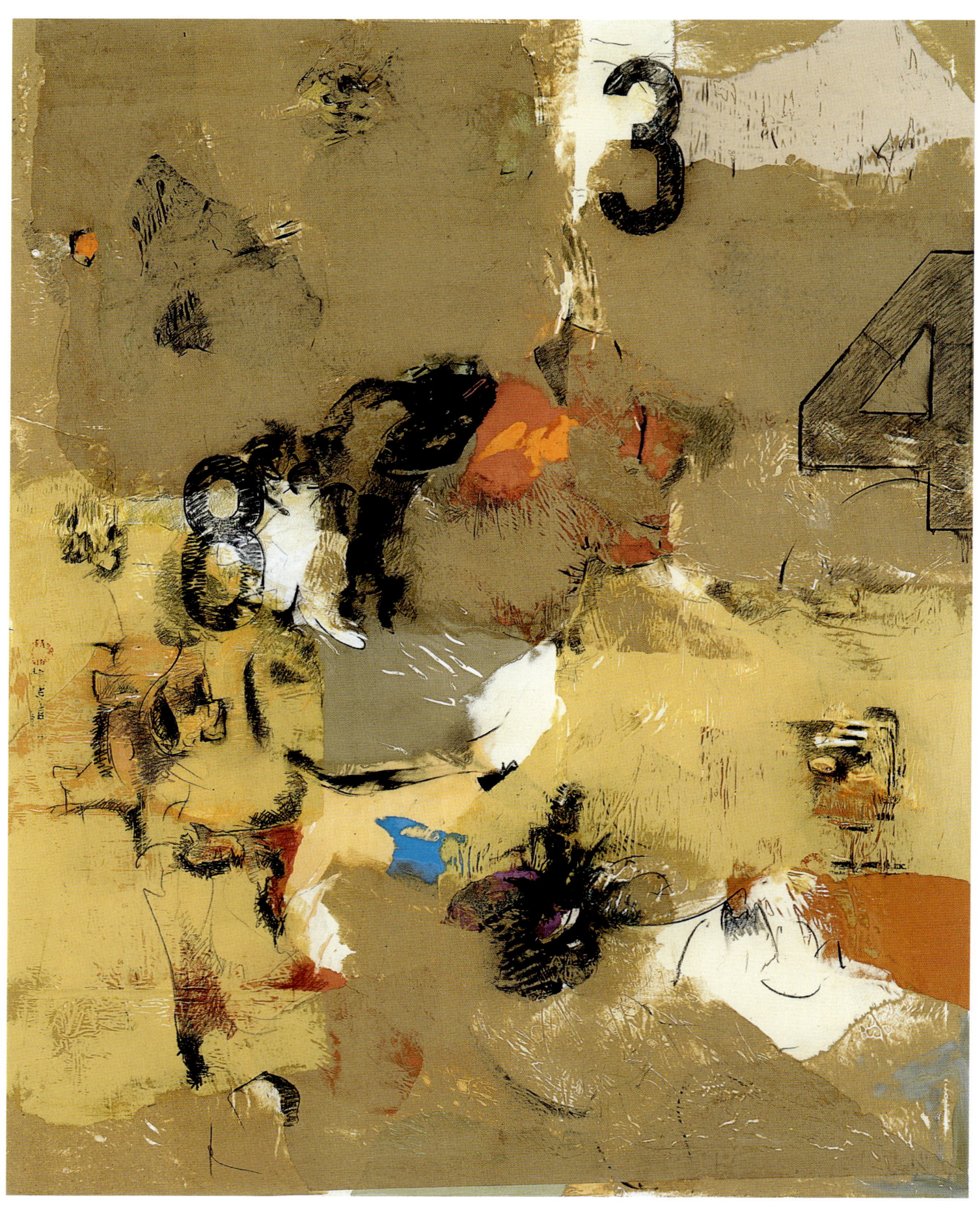

RIVA'S NUMBERS 3-4-8, 1998
MIXED MEDIA ON CANVAS
80 X 66 INCHES

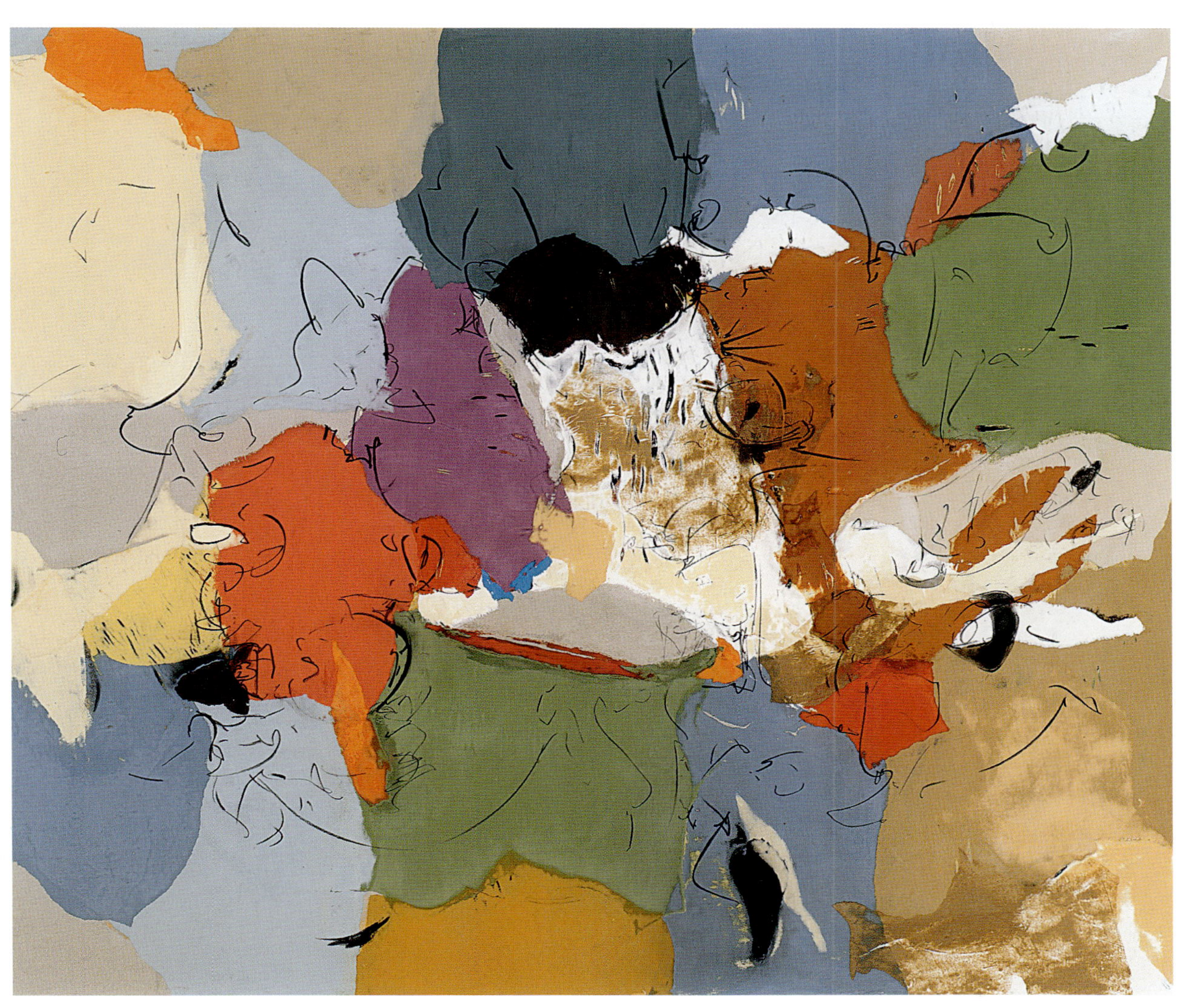

CARNIVAL #2, 1996
MIXED MEDIA ON CANVAS
66 X 80 INCHES

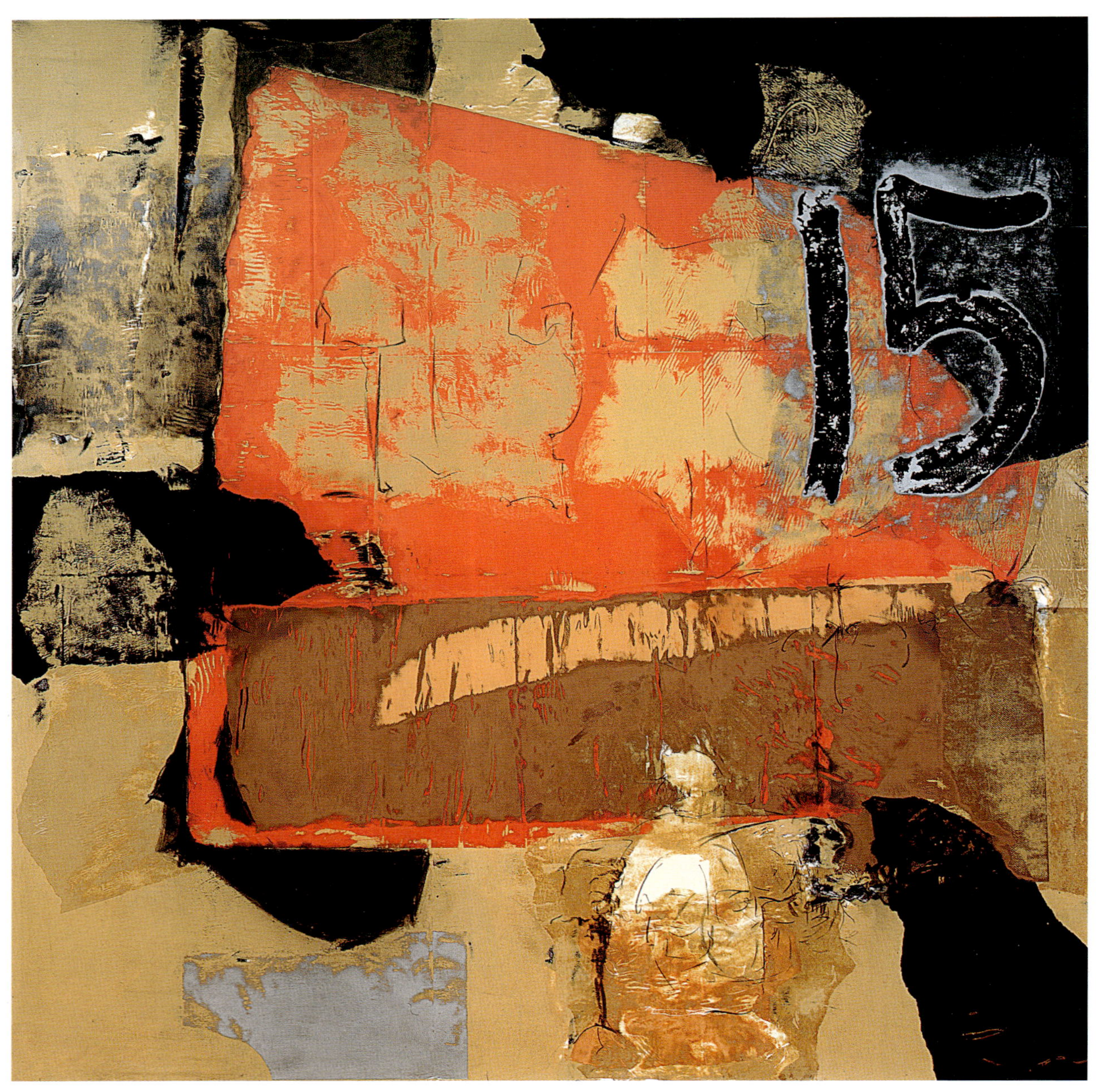

RIVA'S NUMBERS #15, 1997
MIXED MEDIA ON CANVAS
96 X 94 INCHES

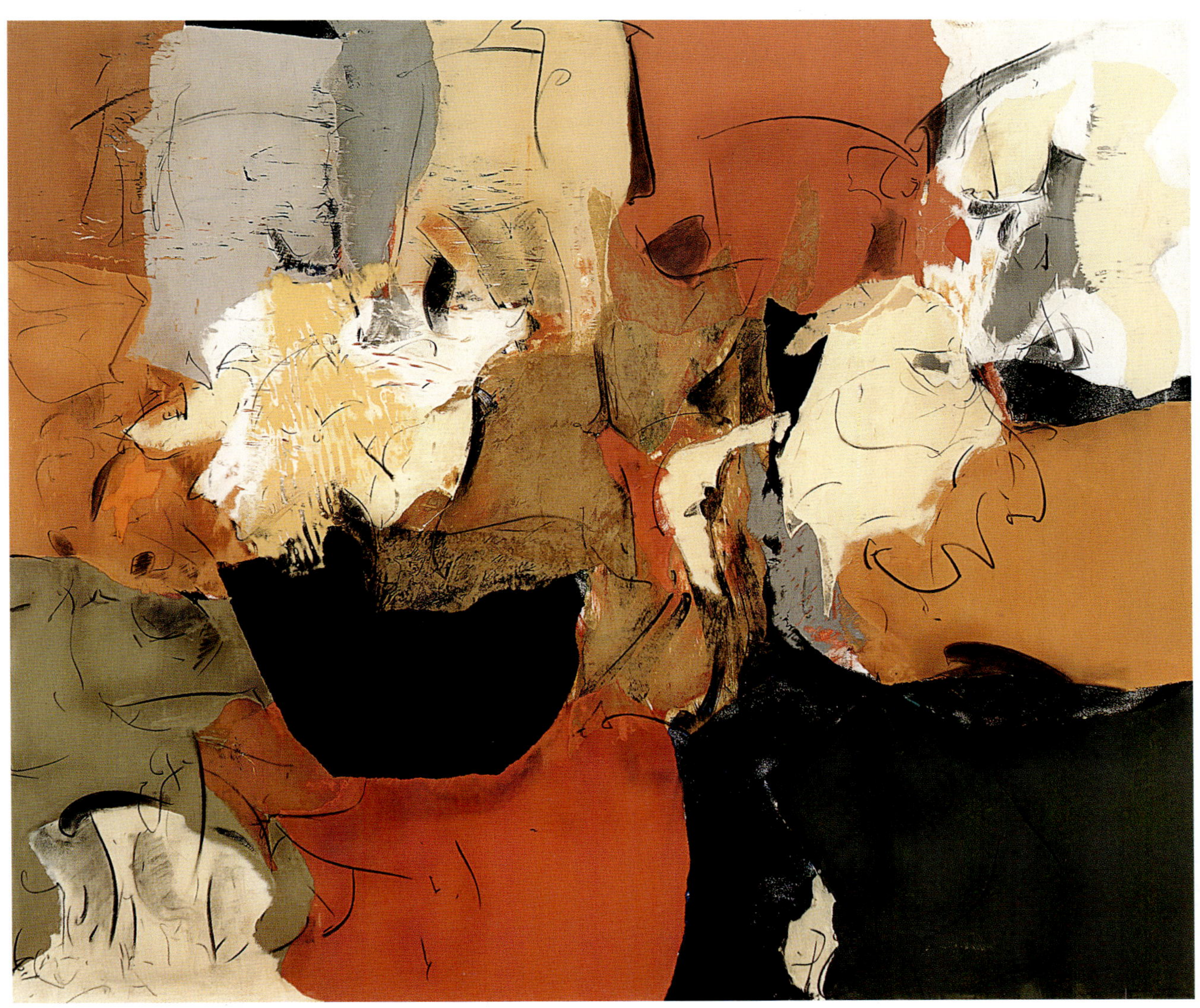

MICHAEL WRIGHT b. 1931 New Rochelle NY. Ed: Yale Music and Art School CT; Albright Art School NY; Brooklyn Museum School NY. Faculty, College of Santa Fe. Exhib: Denver Art Museum CO; Museum of Fine Arts NM (touring). Coll: Museum of Fine Arts NM; Guild Hall Collection, East Hampton NY. Representation: Anderson Contemporary Art, Santa Fe.

MIGRATION SERIES #1, 1996
MIXED MEDIA ON CANVAS
66 X 80 INCHES

SALLY ANDERSON

Some art contains such a dominant subject that the viewer is reduced to the role of a spectator, a vessel into whom the artist pours insights and messages and interpretations. Other art, particularly abstract imagery, steps out and involves the viewer directly. This art derives its entire presence and meaning from those who relate to it, just as a stranger becomes a friend or a house becomes a home. The intensity of the connection depends both on the inclination of the observer and the strength of the work of art.

Sally Anderson creates solid, commanding art that provides a rich range of form and texture for contemplation and eventual intimacy. Neither a passive projection screen nor a confrontational statement, each piece exists in a state of accessible containment. One is reminded of that rare acquaintance whose personal integrity is his or her sole identity, who is not defined by social position or career or the opinions of others, who just is.

Anderson's own energy is the mechanism by which her art relates to the viewer and elicits a vital response. She creates shapes that are authoritative yet approachable. Her supremely complex surfaces invite communion; her beautifully organized compositions promote clarity. She chooses rich colors and metallics that speak of human aspiration; she burnishes them with the patina of time.

Anderson is an established presence in New Mexico abstract art. She arrived in the 1960s, fresh from a climate of lakes and trees, and has mined the color and scale of the high desert for her art. Anderson has received numerous awards, two National Endowments and from the 1970's to the present has had over forty one-person shows. Her designs for furniture, rugs, textiles, and wall coverings have been licensed as home furnishings collections by top companies in the United States and Europe.

Anderson's art reflects her command of a complex medium. She works in acrylic and oil paint on double-coated Mylar™ which is then bonded to aluminum, bronze or board. Successive layers of paint and wax are built up to achieve rich textures, then hand-rubbed with a final layer of oils and wax giving each piece a rich luster.

"I see things in a dimensional way," says Sally Anderson. "My ideas come from many different places. I start with a feeling or an attitude rather than a subject, and begin putting a piece together. I communicate with the work and then the work itself leads me to the place where it's going. It's a continuum: each piece is informed by those that went before it; one piece leads to the next, and the next."

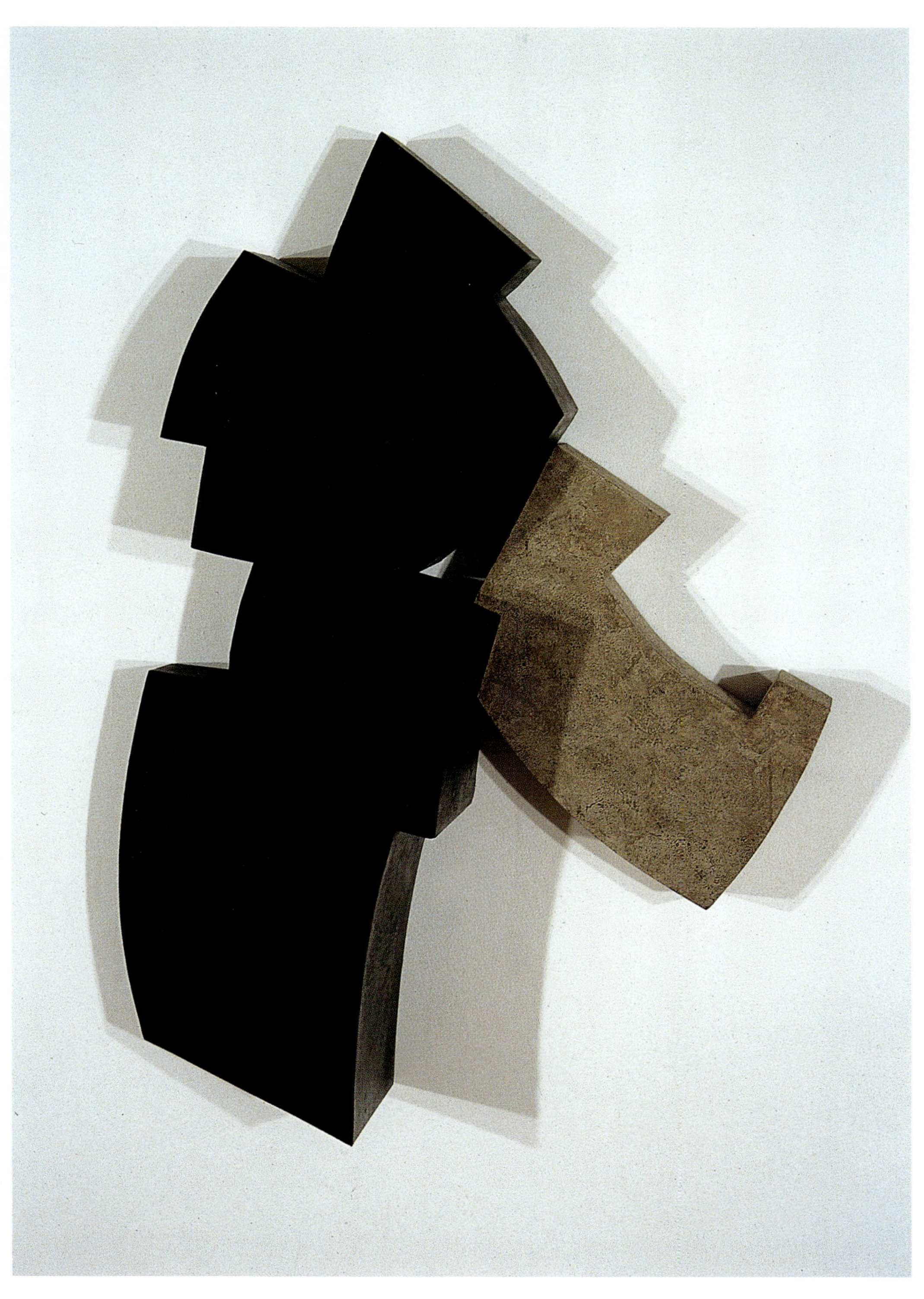

PUZZLE
MIXED MEDIA ON MYLAR ON WOOD
40 X 40 INCHES

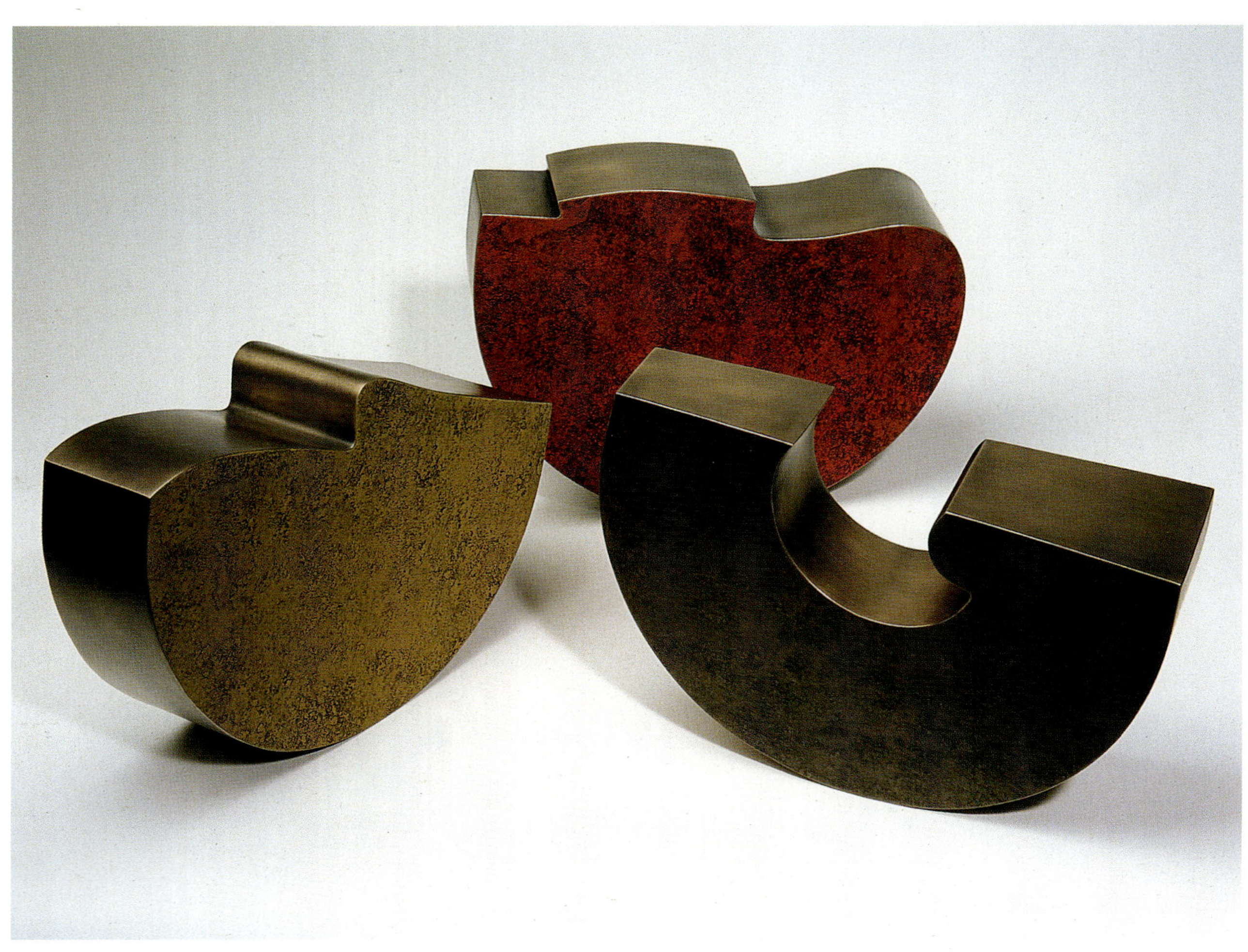

THREE DUCKS
MIXED MEDIA ON MYLAR ON BRONZE
10½ X 13¼ X 4¼ INCHES EACH

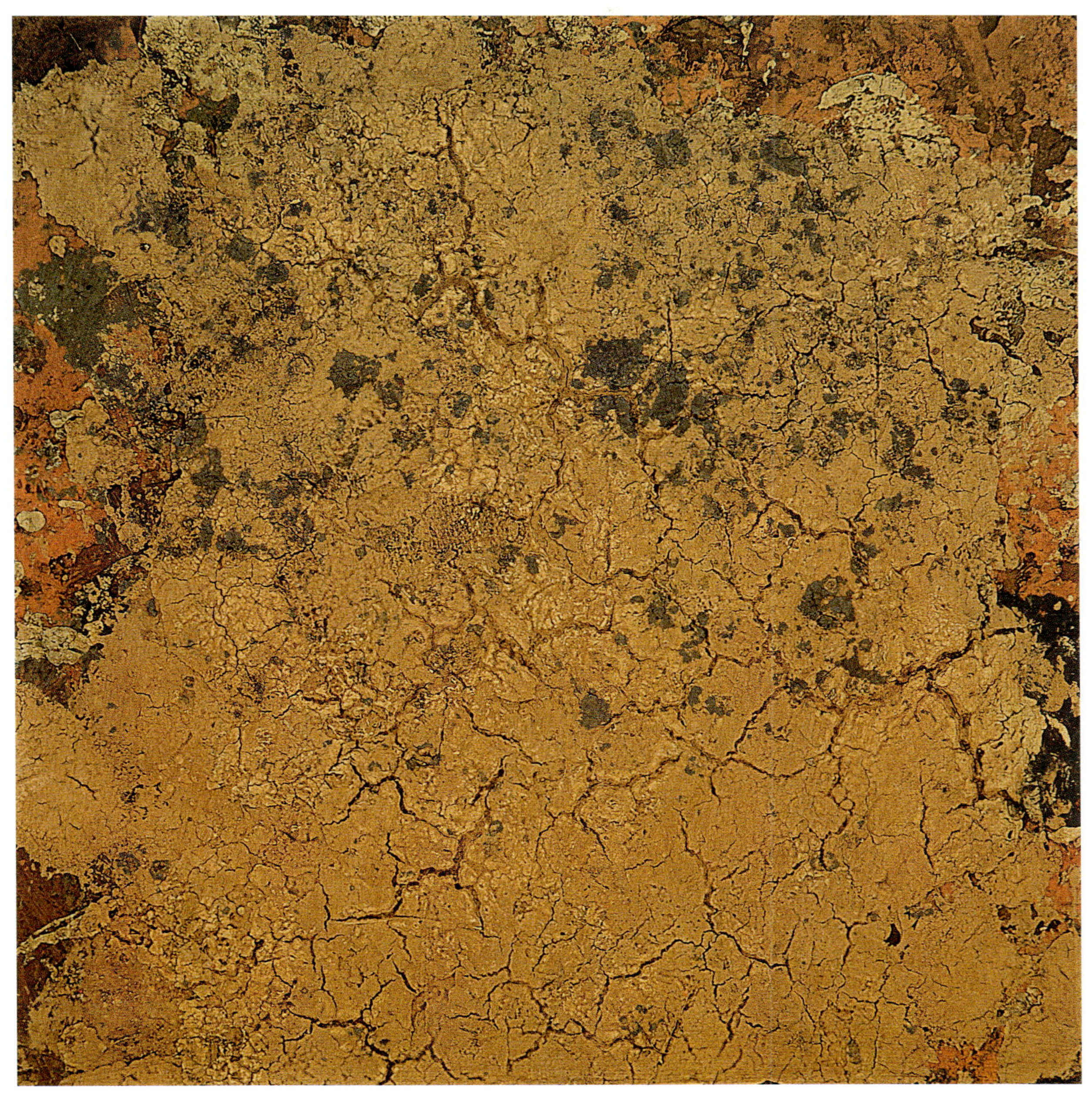

UNTITLED GOLD
MIXED MEDIA ON MYLAR ON ALUMINUM
12 X 12 INCHES

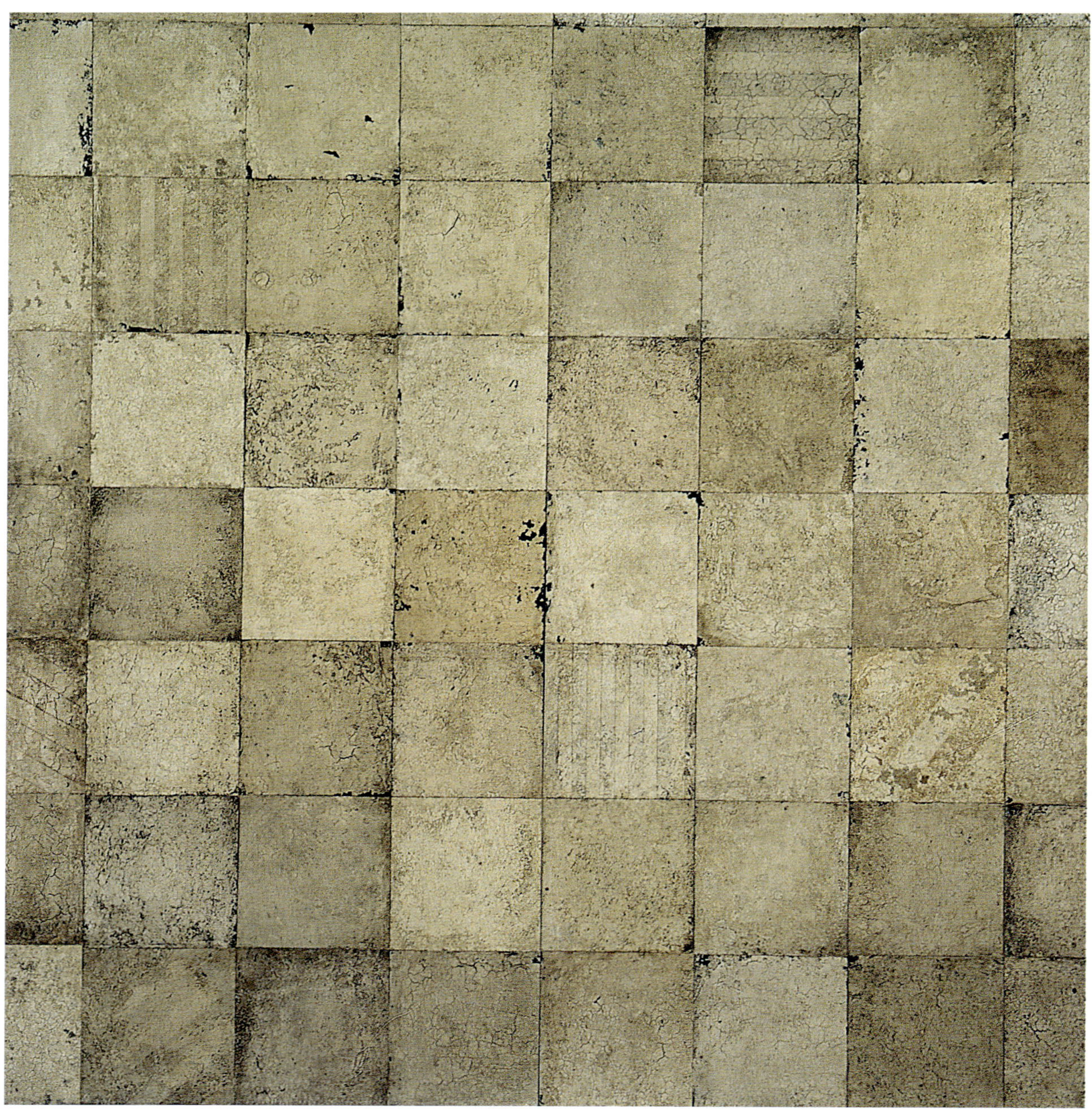

CROCKERY
MIXED MEDIA ON MYLAR ON WOOD
72 X 72 INCHES

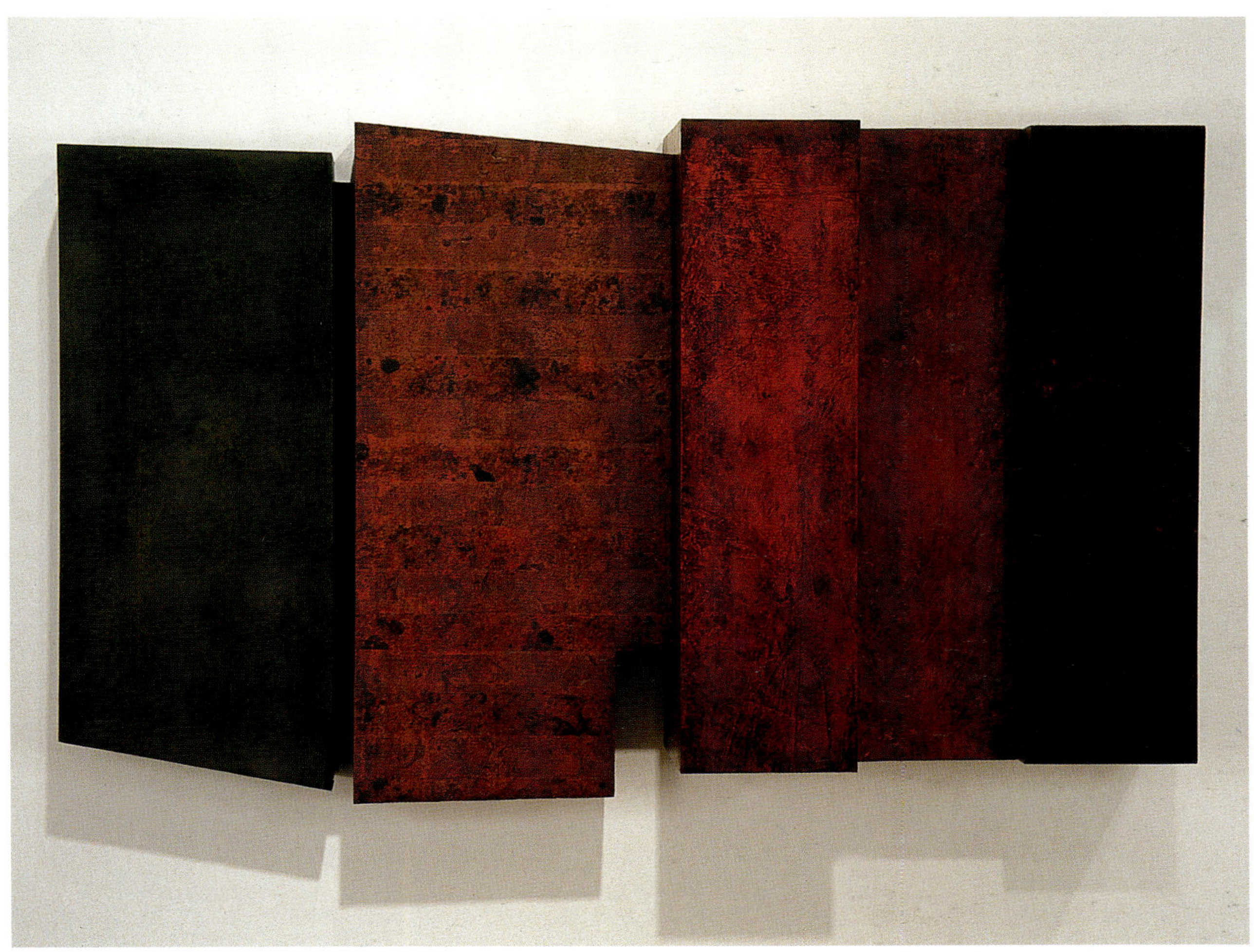

SALLY ANDERSON b. Rockford IL. Ed: Beloit College WI; Instituto de Allende, San Miguel de Allende, Mexico; Univ. Wisconsin. Invitational exhibits: Beloit College Art Museum WI; Phoenix Art Museum AZ; El Paso Museum TX; Carnegie Institute Museum PA; Albuquerque Museum, Museum of Fine Arts, Santa Fe and International Folk Art Museum, Santa Fe; one-person exhibition, Roswell Art Museum NM. Representation: Anderson Contemporary Art, Santa Fe.

RED, RED AND MORE RED RETHOUGHT
MIXED MEDIA ON MYLAR ON WOOD
23 X 39 X 6½ INCHES

BILL BARRETT

Filling up space is much more exacting than carving into mass. A sculptor may begin by working with mass, but the finished work organizes and sculpts the space around itself. Whether a sculpture forms brackets that hold an intense emptiness, or sends out delicate probes that explore the outer reaches of thin air, or resolutely pushes against its surroundings in order to occupy its own space solidly, it establishes and holds onto its rightful presence.

The sculpture of Bill Barrett does all these things and more. His largest pieces, towering thirty-two feet or more and weighing thousands of pounds, rest as lightly on the ground as acrobats. His more intimately scaled pieces move indoors and assume command of their surroundings while remaining approachable and empathetic. Every sculpture invites the mind in for a tour of ideas and a high-level discussion of truth and beauty.

One of the most significant aspects of Barrett's bronze sculpture is his use of fabrication along with casting. He casts his models for his larger pieces, but he fabricates his monumental pieces in bronze. "I've been making bronze models since the beginning of my sculpture career," says Barrett. "Fabrication is the most important part of what I do now. The welding permits me to be an additive sculptor."

Remarkably, Barrett is able to create the most calligraphic, balletic forms in this demanding medium. These fluid shapes dance together and reach forth toward the viewer. They speak of life, of freedom, and of the contortions a body has to go through just to maintain physical and interpersonal balance. "I'm really about interrelationships with people," says the artist. "If that is what the work communicates satisfactorily to other people then I'm accomplishing the goal I've set for myself."

Barrett has kept up a staggering schedule of one-person and invitational group shows for forty years, beginning with the San Francisco Museum of Art in California and the Whitney annual in New York, and crisscrossing the nation and the world in the decades since.

After twenty years as a prominent New York artist, he established a second residence in New Mexico in 1988. He now divides his time between the two, maintaining his prodigious output from studios in both locations. His reputation has expanded also, and today his work hangs in the permanent collections of fine arts museums all over the country. Bill Barrett occupies his own space solidly, pushing out the parameters of his life, sculpting his environment, and asserting his presence as an international artist.

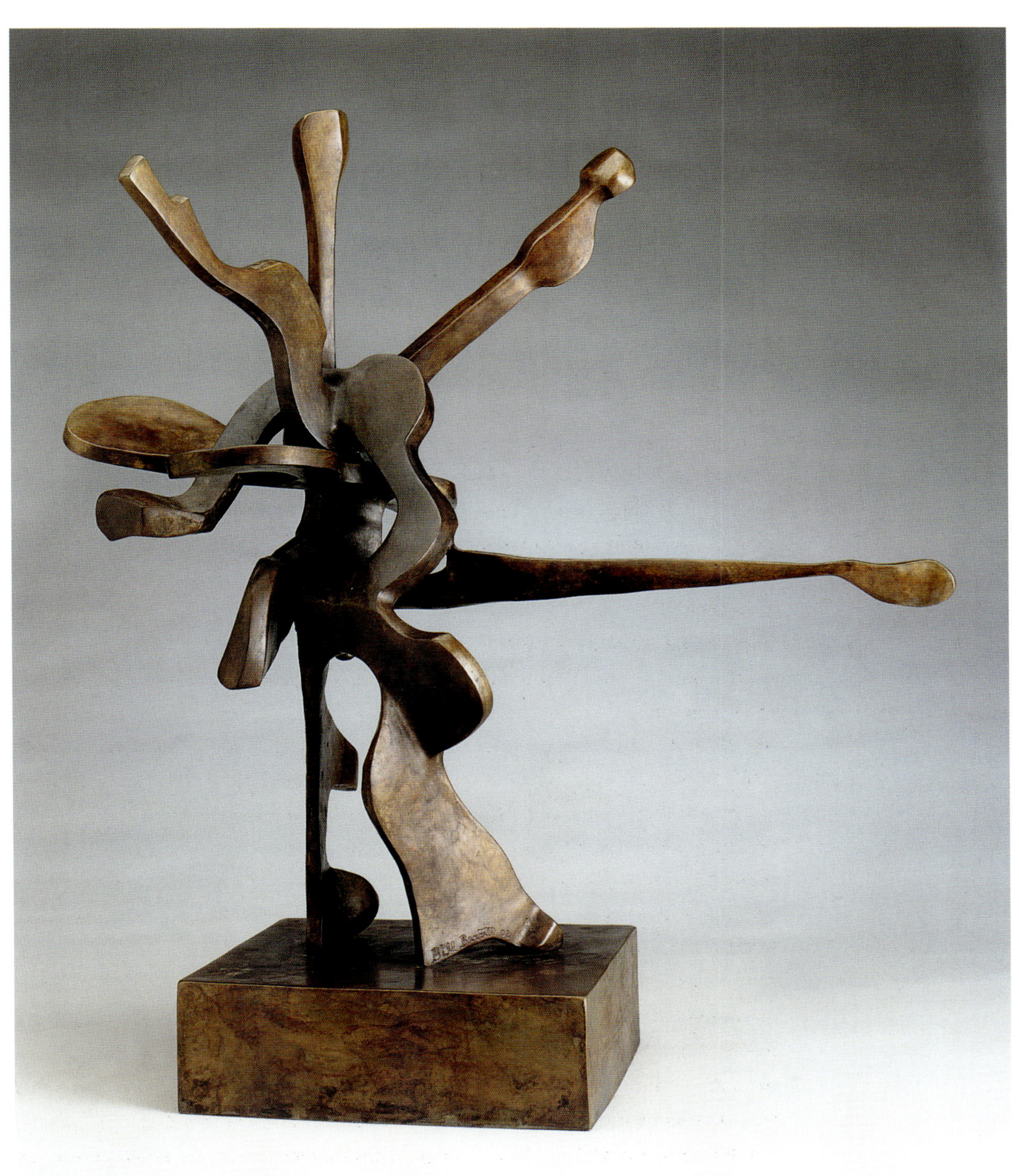

ON GUARD, 2003
CAST BRONZE
23½ X 22 X 10 INCHES

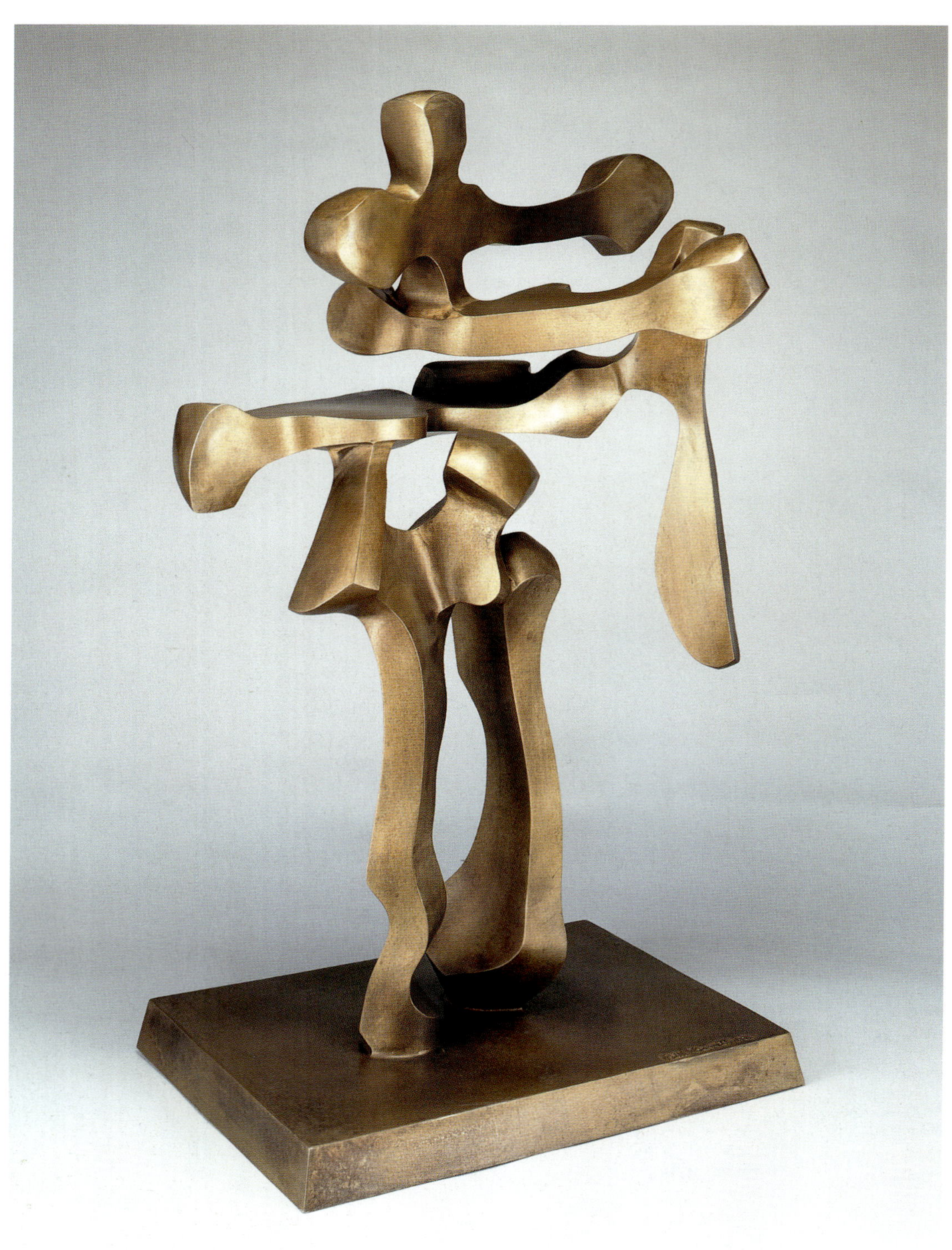

NY113, 2002
FABRICATED BRONZE
66 X 48 X 32 INCHES

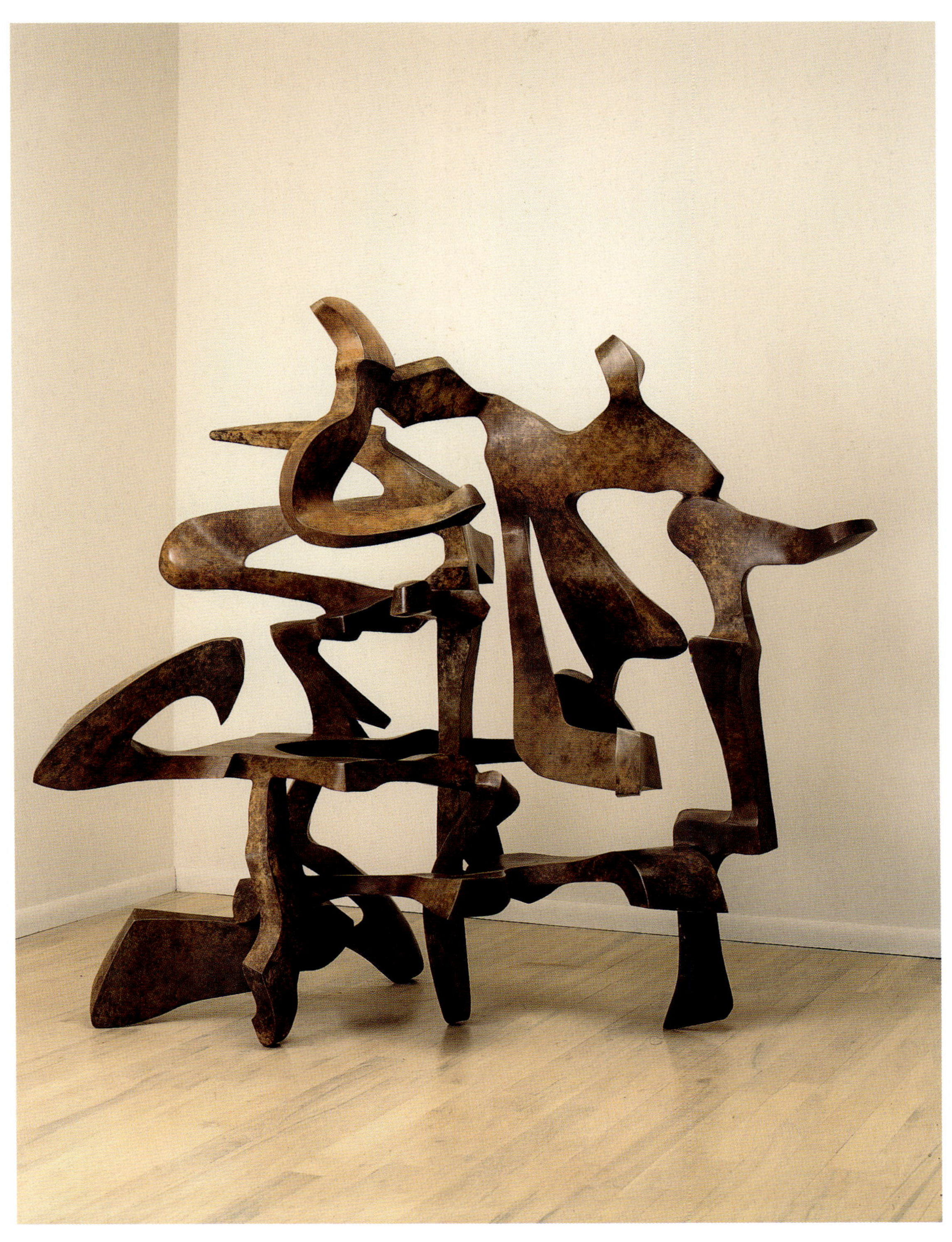

INQUIRE WITHIN, 1998
FABRICATED BRONZE
54 X 60 X 48 INCHES

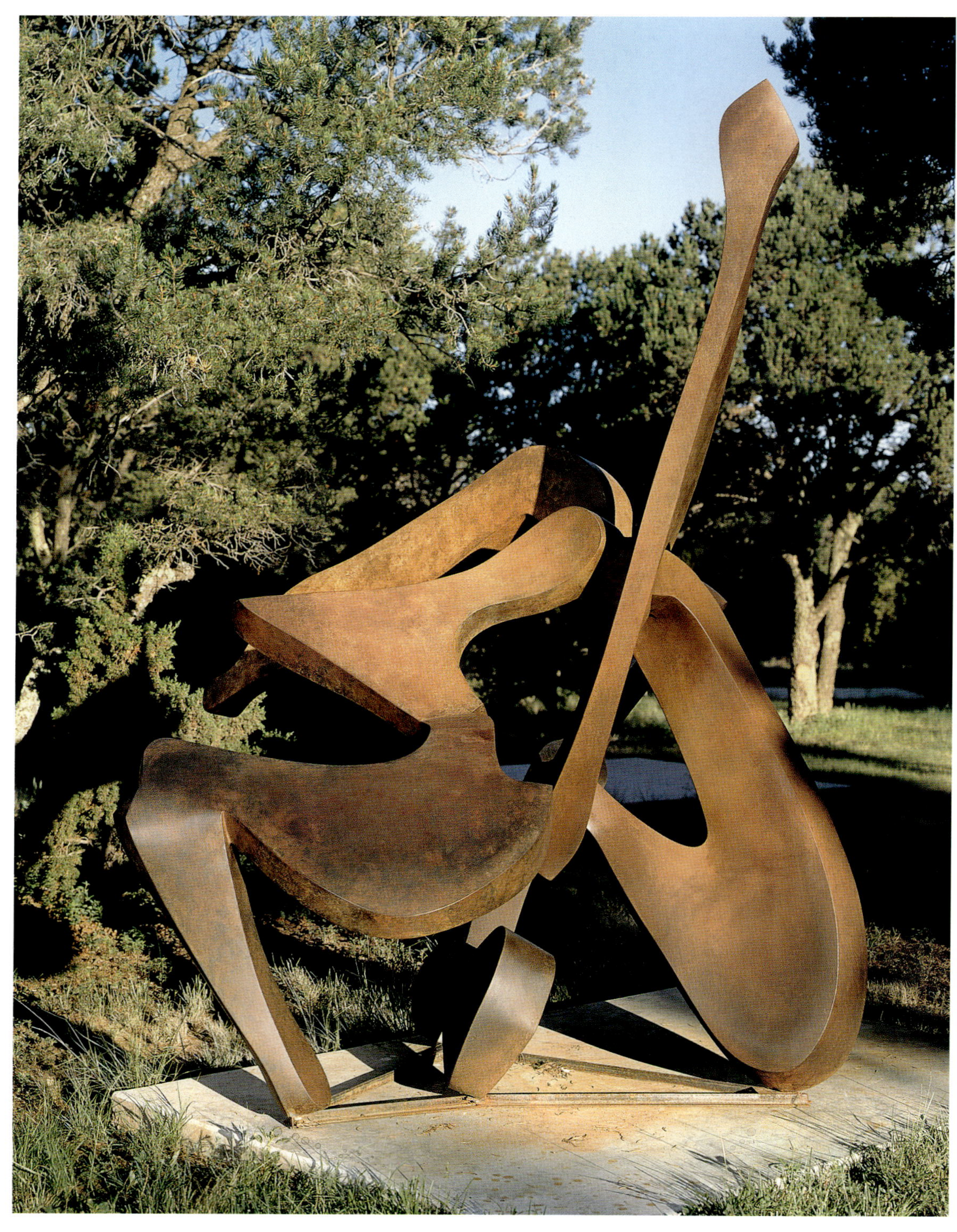

STARGATE 6, 2000
FABRICATED BRONZE
120 X 108 X 96 INCHES

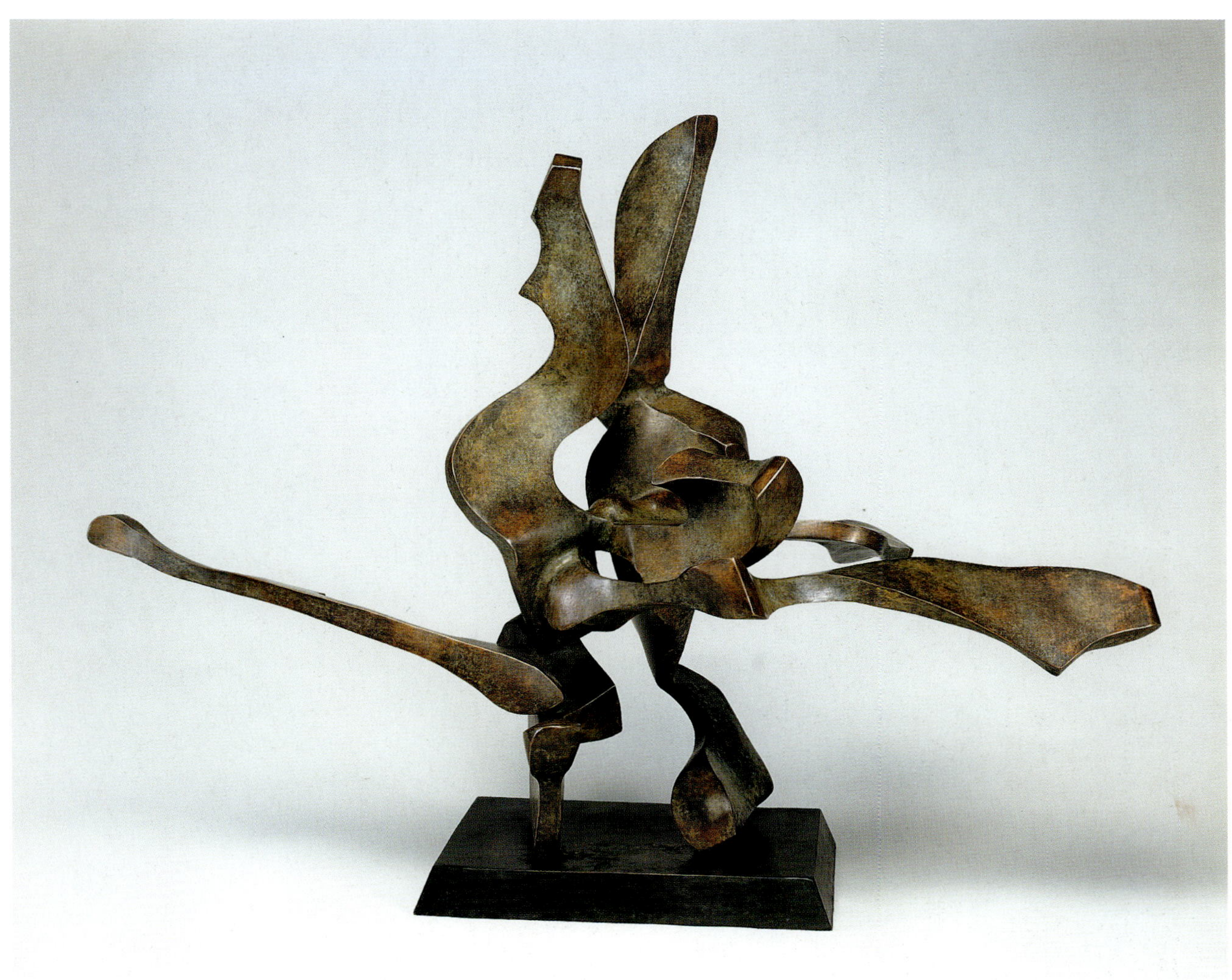

BILL BARRETT b.1934 Los Angeles. Ed: BS, MS, MFA Univ. Michigan; Coll: Utsukushi-ga-Hara Museum, Tokyo; Cleveland Museum of Art OH; Virginia Museum; Santa Fe Museum of Fine Art; Jniv. Michigan; Neiman-Marcus; Trammel-Crow; Hitachi; etal. Representation: Kouros Gallery, New York; Thomcs McCormick Gallery, Chicago; Santa Fe; Shidoni Sculpture Gallery, Santa Fe.

ELAN, 2003
FABRICATED BRONZE
33 X 45 X 17 INCHES

RICHARD HOGAN

Ideas make tracks in the mind. They rise like growing things; they descend like bolts from the blue. They move and glow and bend, leaving afterimages like vapor trails. They stop and then start up somewhere else. They recede into the background of thought, then come up to the forefront and preoccupy all consciousness. They build up in layers. They crowd the memory and the vision like pale electric forests, creating energy; they scatter out and lighten up, affording rest and contemplation.

Richard Hogan has made his own tracks as a seminal and highly influential artist whose work is a benchmark in New Mexico, and who is becoming known as such in the larger arena. Quietly, persistently, he has worked to help establish and maintain a viable contemporary art scene in Santa Fe and Albuquerque since the 1970s.

Hogan's signature style consists of marks and smudges that speak in a language all their own. The smudges are the result of erasures, which function in several ways. They are records of the process; they add dimension; they set off the final marks, making them glow like radioactive isotopes. "My intent," he says, "is that the paintings be perceived not as being about something, but as being something, being what they are. They are abstract, not abstracted from something else."

Scale is important; the pieces are large. "I paint actual size," says Hogan. "It's the size they're supposed to be in relation to the human body." The artist prefers that they be hung low on the wall so that they occupy the same space as the viewer, inviting closeness and involvement.

Hogan's interests range over the world and time. Southwestern paleolithic art, Eskimo and Inuit art, Celtic stone circles, Giacometti, all contribute to the sense of his work without projecting the slightest trace of representation. "I intend my work to be nonreferential," he says. "I don't want it to look like anything. I hope part of the reason I'm trying to keep it nonreferential is that I have so many references."

Richard Hogan's paintings project high energy. "It must be something I want in there," he says. "Other people don't spend as much time with my paintings as I do. I always feel that they're not successful unless I can look at them a long time without getting bored. As long as I find them continually interesting, then I'm happy. I always want my work to sit there and vibrate."

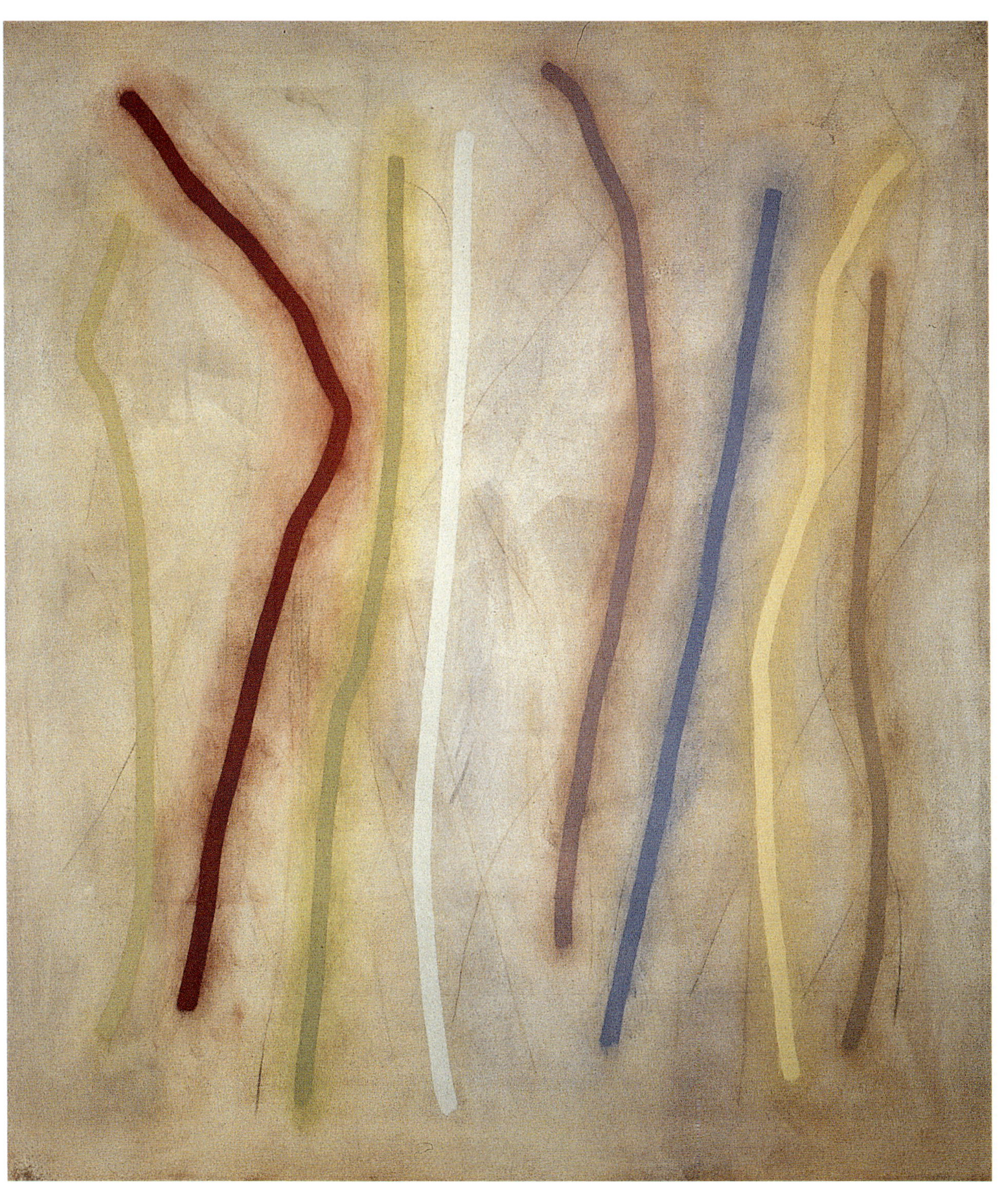

WHITE LADY, 2001
OIL ON CANVAS
84 X 72 INCHES

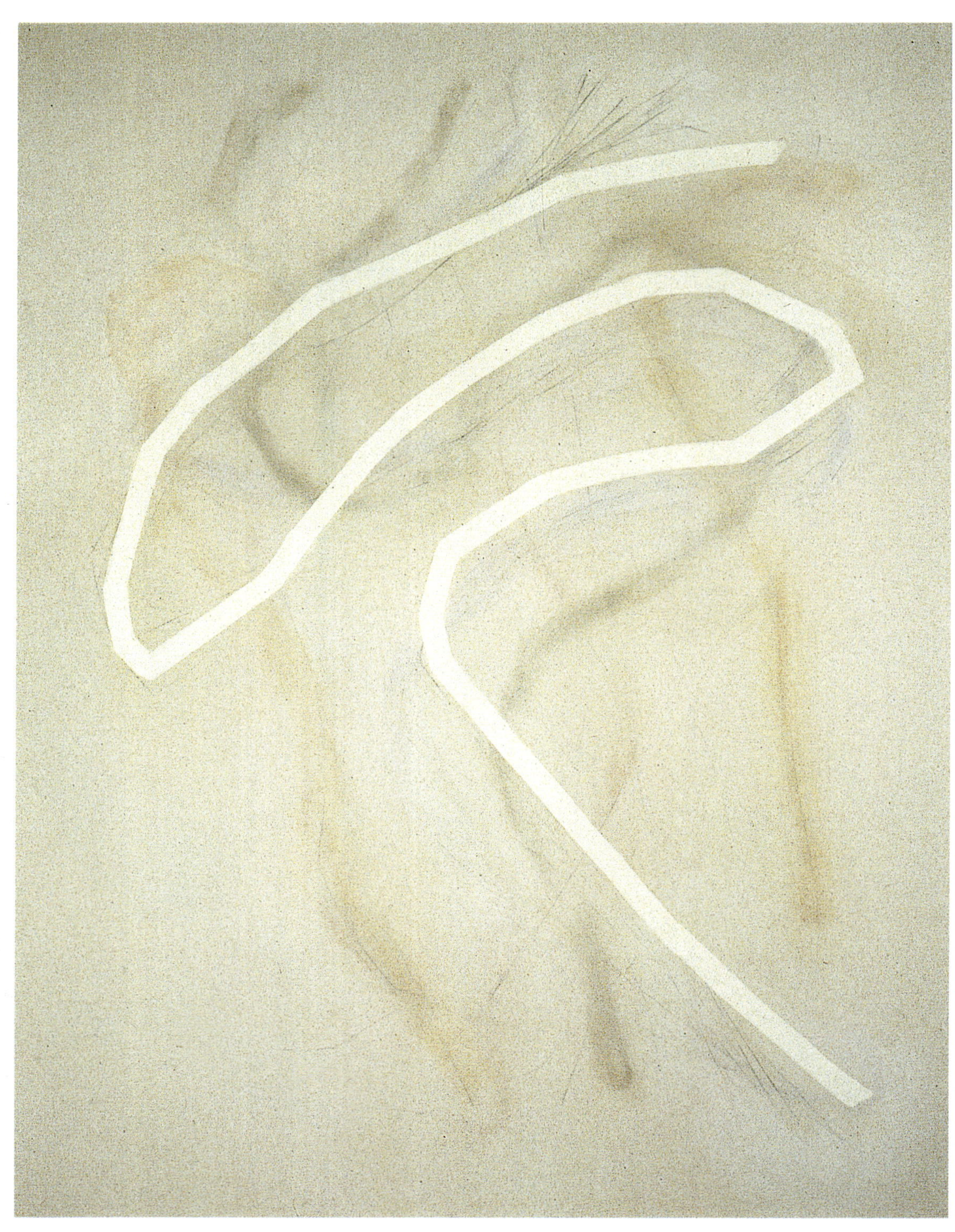

JURA, 2002
OIL ON CANVAS
84 X 66 INCHES

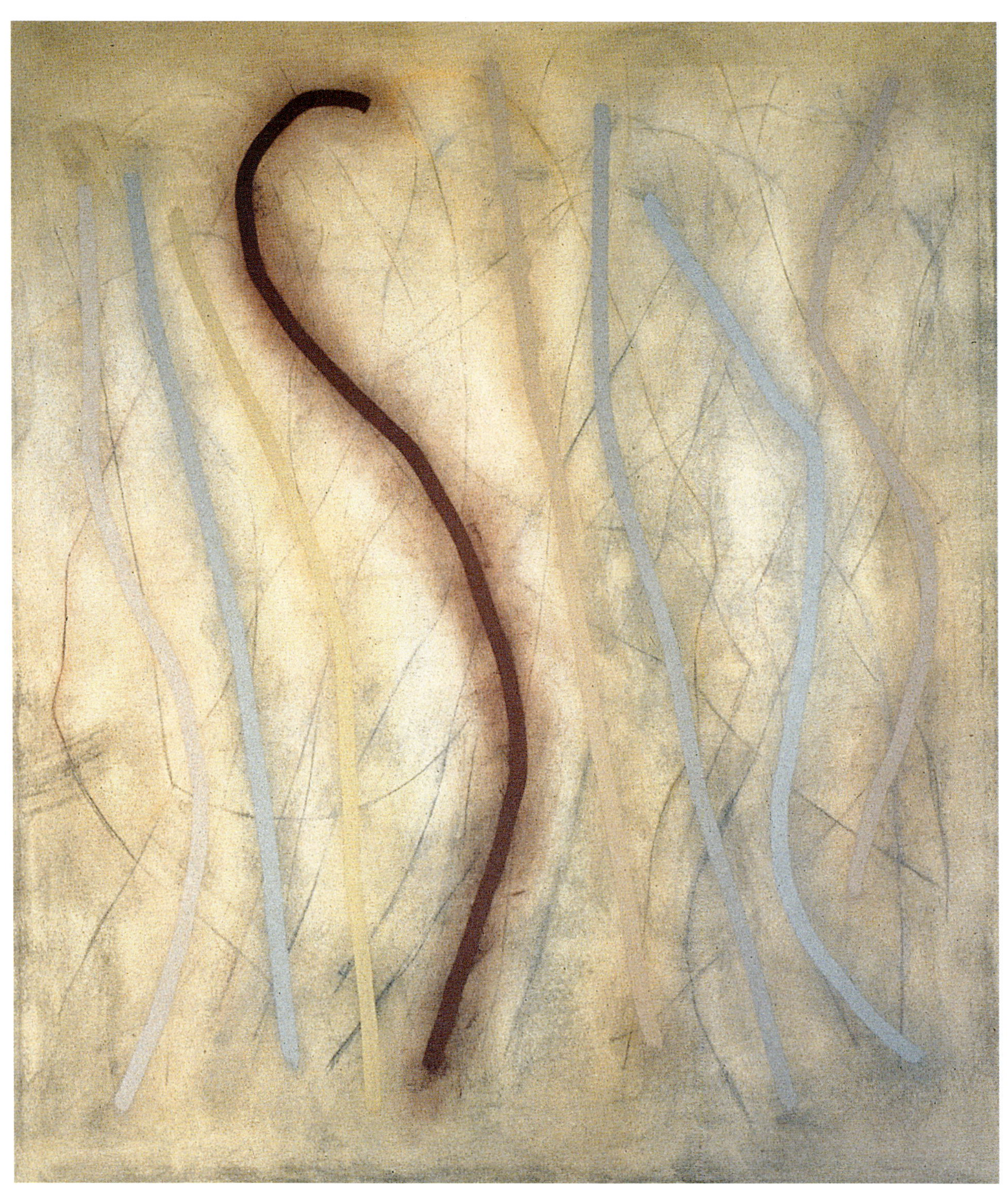

LONG MEG, 2001
OIL ON CANVAS
84 X 72 INCHES

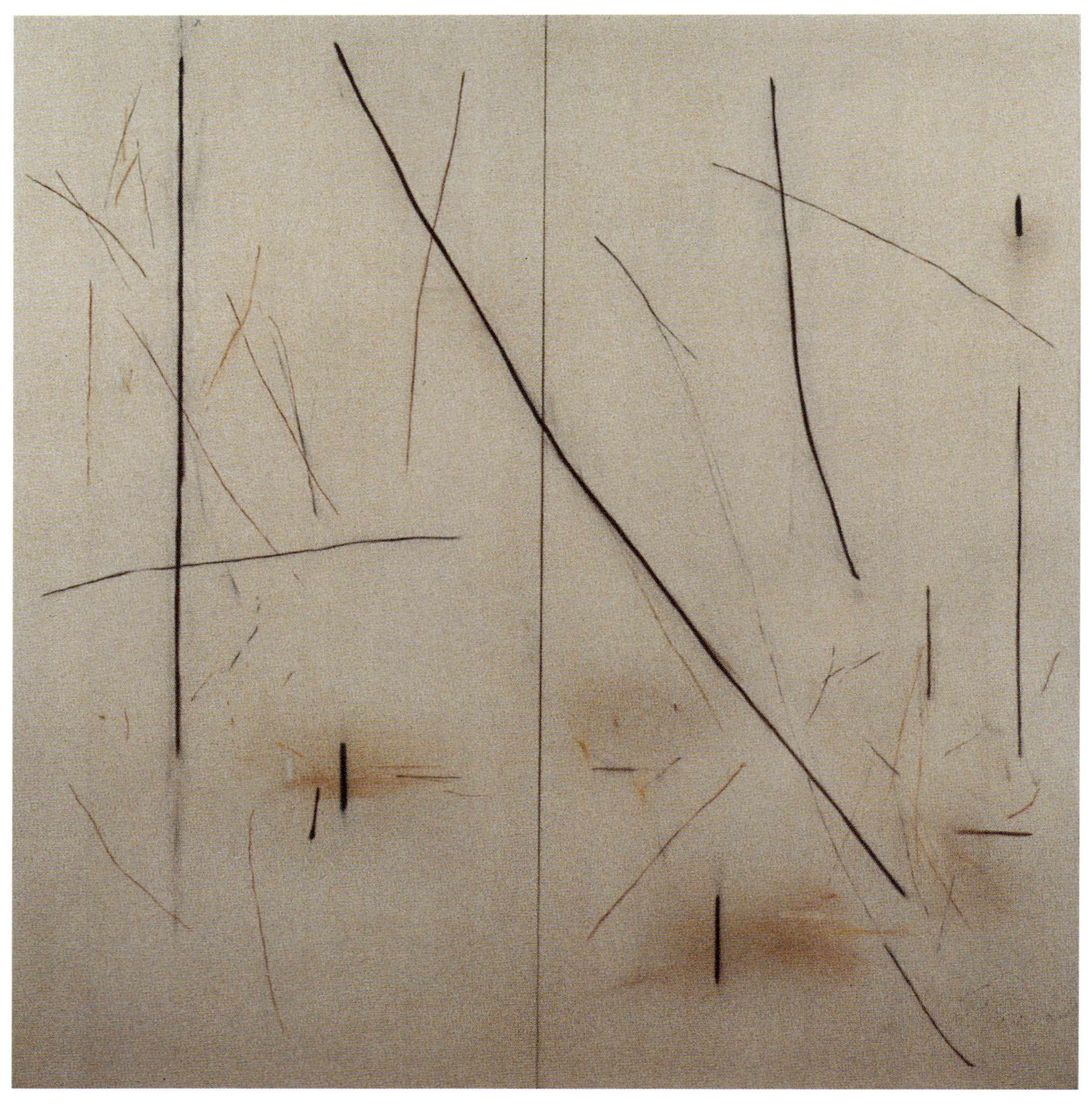

CAPITAN, 1981
OIL ON CANVAS
84 X 84 INCHES

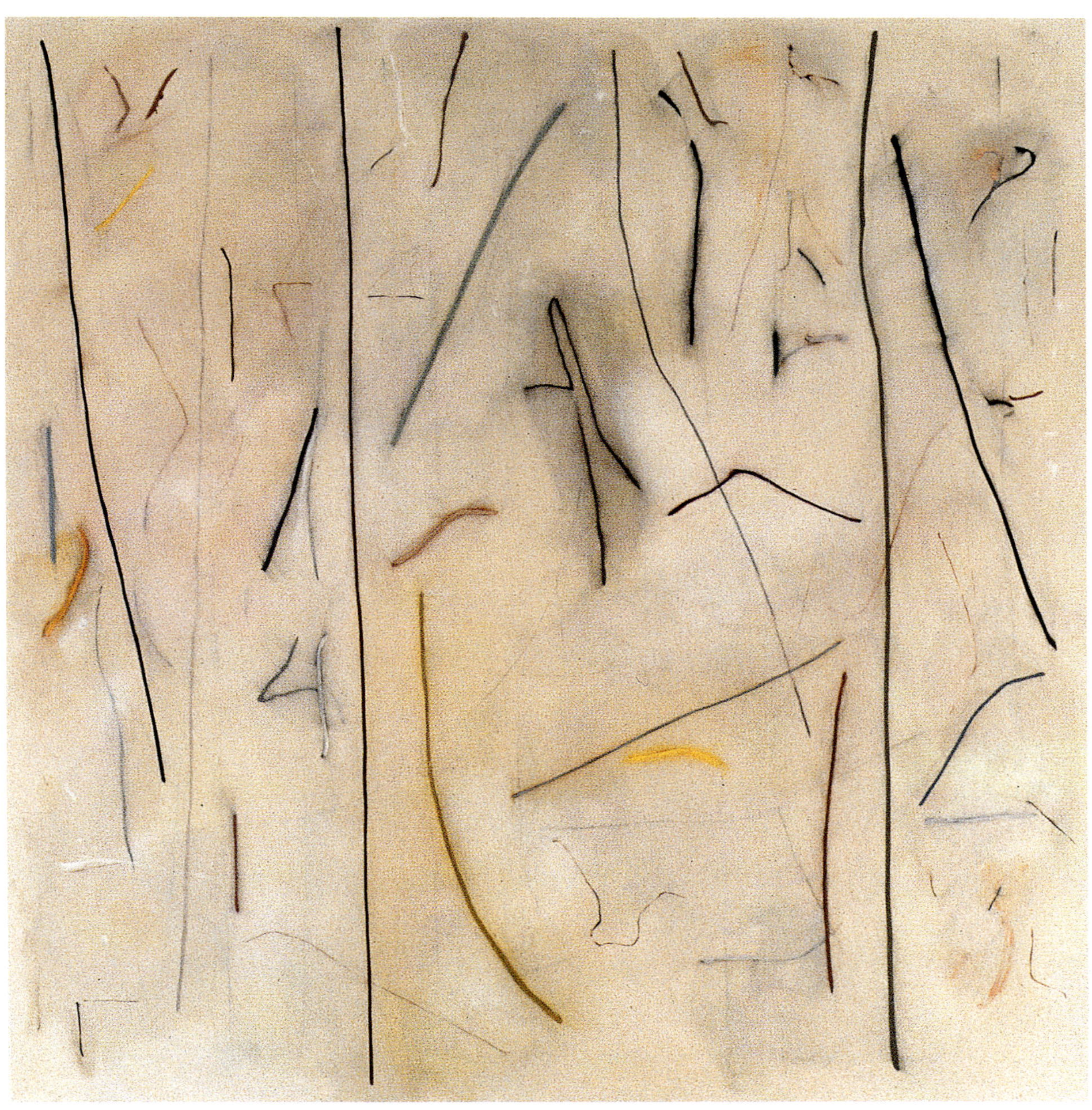

RICHARD HOGAN b. 1941 Youngstown OH. Ed: MA, Univ. New Mexico. Coll: Albuquerque Museum, Museum of Fine Arts, Santa Fe; Roswell Museum NM; Pepsi; IT&T; etal. Representation: Linda Durham Contemporary Art, Galisteo NM and New York.

QUATRO, 1981
OIL ON CANVAS
78 X 78 INCHES

JOHNNIE WINONA ROSS

Read between the lines. What is not there might be more important than what is there. The virtue of omission is that it clears the page and makes room for interaction. When all the words disappear, what is left is the meaning.

Dig downward through eons of geological strata and locate the time line that links them together. Dig upward through the encrustations and buried hopes of daily life. Find the clarity that brings order to chaos.

Johnnie Winona Ross finds clarity by excavating a world of information from deceptively simple substrata of form. His tools are as simple as an archaeologist's picks and brushes; his ideas are as complex as ancient cultures; like pictographs, his paintings transcend their own rich physicality.

Ross spends many hours investigating prehistoric rock art found in the canyons and the caves of the Southwestern desert. He is particularly interested in sites within a seventy-five mile radius of Barrier Canyon, Utah, which contain a mixture of cultures and time periods dating from approximately 5000 B. C. to 1200 A. D. There, he finds "multitudes of images layered on top of each other and specifically related to the surface they are painted upon."

Ross takes the ideas behind these sites and abstracts them absolutely. Not a trace of pictorial narrative remains. He sets down more than a hundred layers on each painting. Between each layer he takes a razor blade and scrapes down the paint until it is smooth, revealing the history of the painting. Then he burnishes it until he achieves a soft, warm gloss, a process that is traditional to Native American potters.

Ross is an investigative abstract artist whose direction was shaped during the height of Minimalism. His ideas are greatly respected, as evidenced by the fact that he has received a number of awards, fellowships, and residencies. Each term yielded a body of work that garnered critical acclaim.

After three decades of painting and exhibiting, Ross resigned his position as professor and department chair at the Maine College of Art and moved to New Mexico. For the past five years he has supported himself and his wife as a full time artist. He has benefited greatly from his proximity to the archaeological sites that inspire him. "I don't know what role the pictographs have played," he says, "but my work has changed significantly. Some aspect or spirit seems to be transferred from the rock into my paintings."

That aspect may involve a very subtle but important change in one's perception of the world after viewing Johnnie Winona Ross's work. The artist distills nature and culture into pure consciousness, creating in the process a beautiful object that ultimately transcends even beauty.

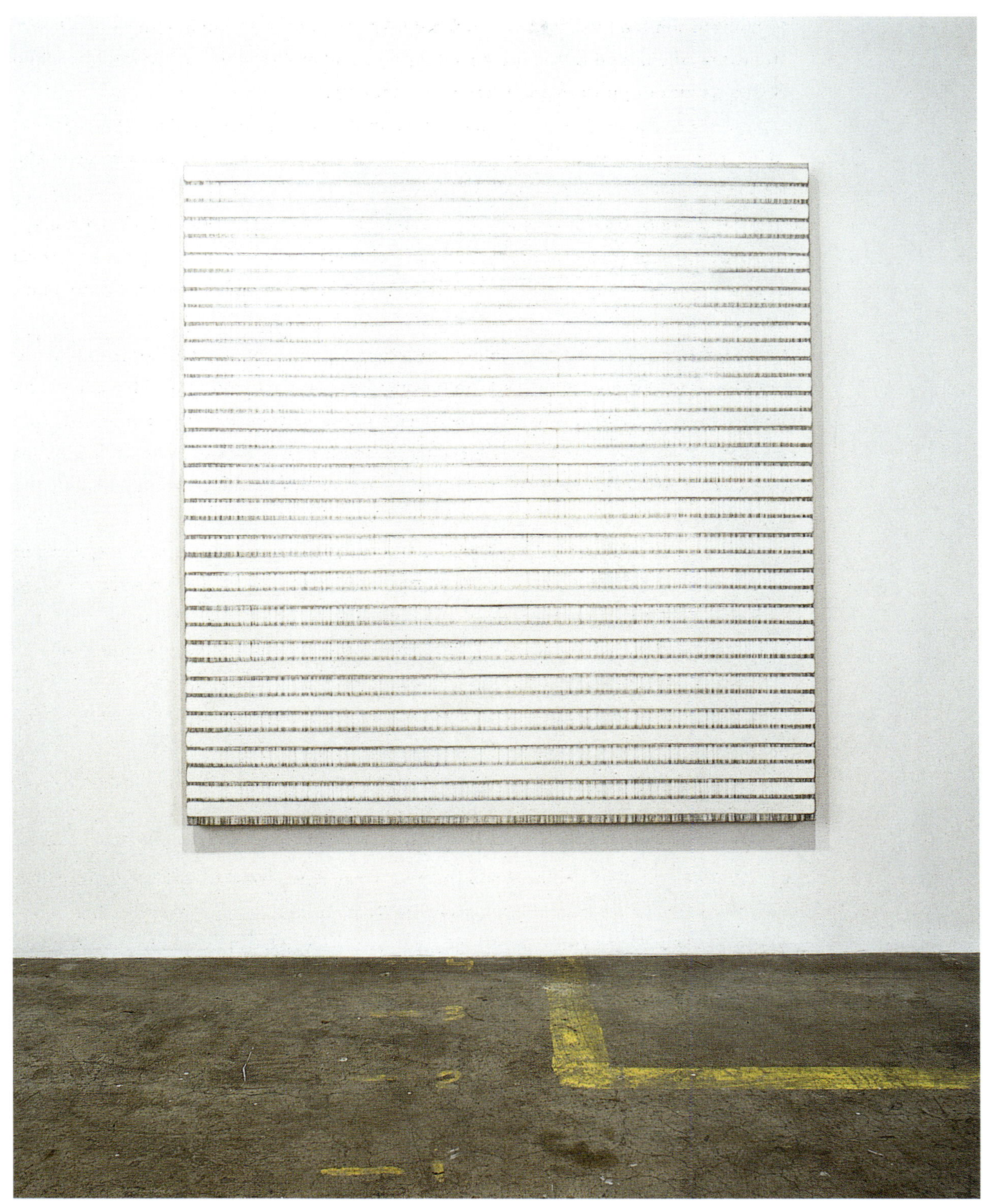

SALTCREEK SEEPS, 2003
OIL ON LINEN
60 X 57 INCHES

SEEPS I S 02, 2002
OIL ON LINEN
48 X 46½ INCHES

WIRE CANYON CUTOFF I WCC 06, 2002
OIL ON LINEN
60 X 57 INCHES

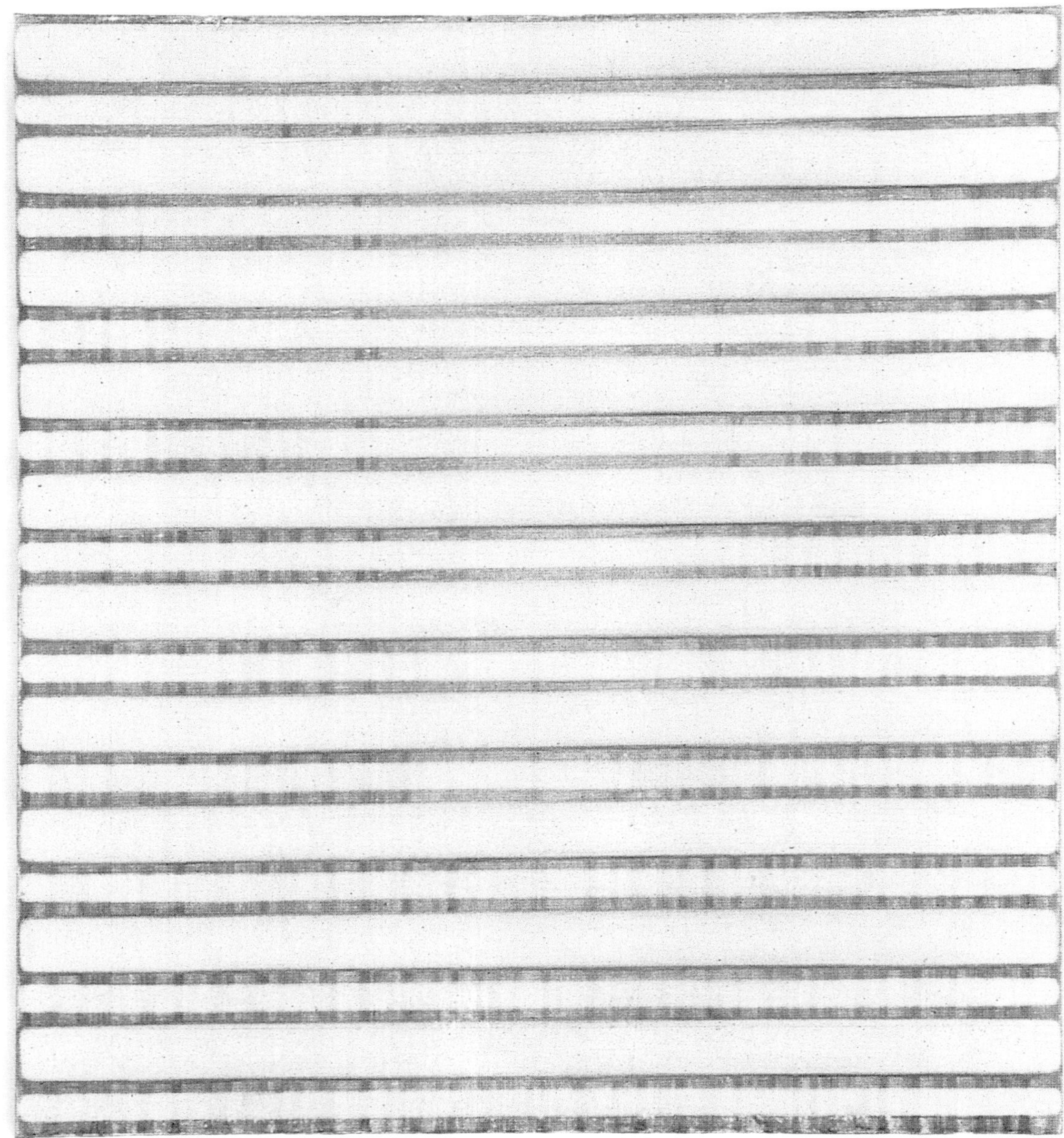

WIRE CANYON CUTOFF I WCC 10, 2002
OIL ON LINEN
24 X 22½ INCHES

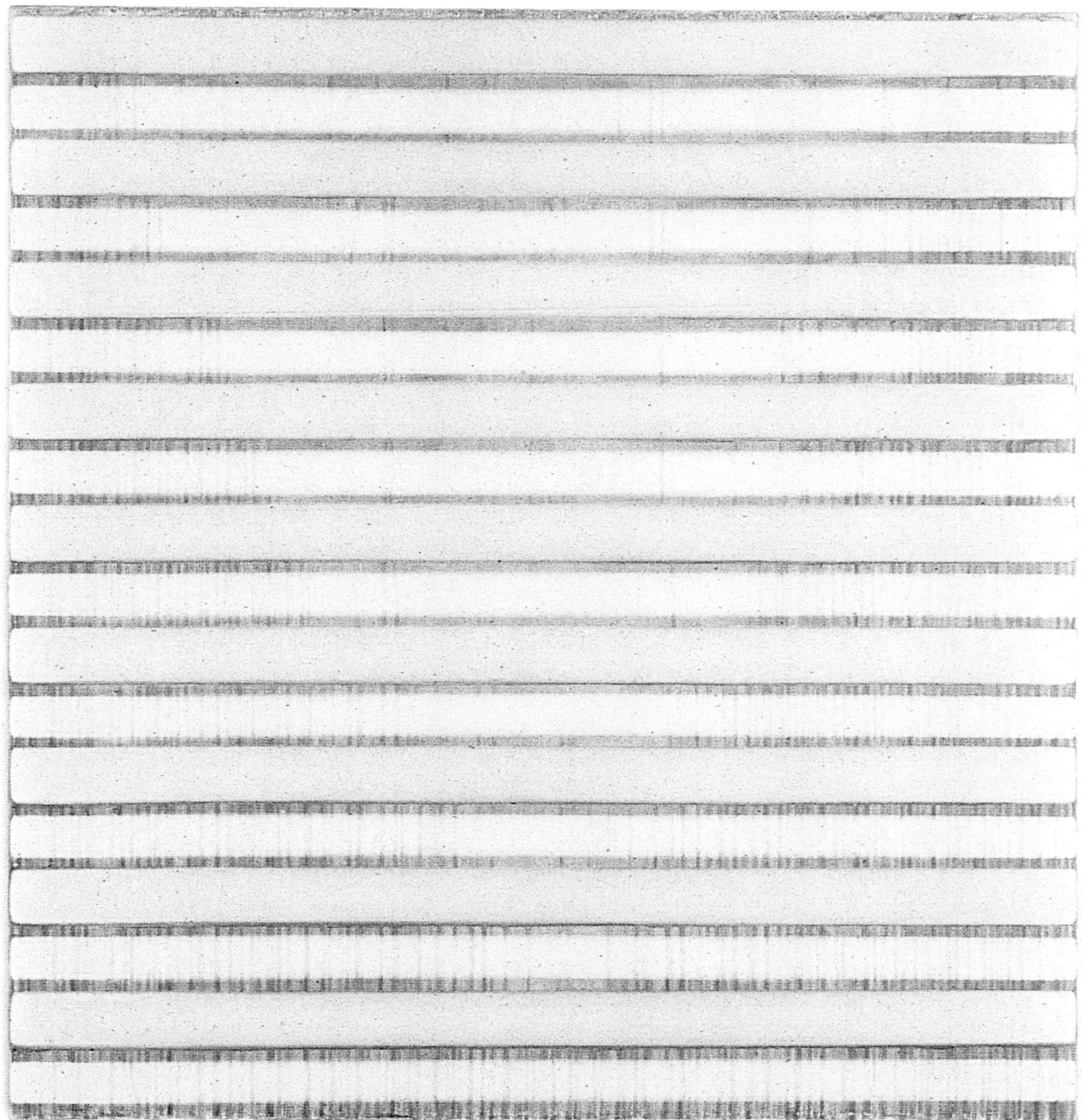

JOHNNIE WINONA ROSS b. 1949 Missouri. BFA Washington Univ. MO; MFA Univ. Illinois. Coll: Portland Museum ME; Harwood Museum, Roswell Museum, Anderson Museum of Contemporary Art NM. Representation: James Kelly Contemporary, Santa Fe; Richard Levy Gallery, Albuquerque; Parks Gallery, Taos.

WIRE CANYON CUTOFF | WCC 12, 2002
OIL ON LINEN
48 X 46½ INCHES

FLORENCE PIERCE

Light is an element in every work of art. Light creates shadow in sculpture; it is interpreted, manipulated, replicated, and cited as inspiration in painting. Artificial lighting is carefully controlled in museum and gallery installations of artworks so as to reveal their essence.

Florence Pierce takes it a step further. She literally gathers great armfuls of the intensely clear New Mexico light into her images by pouring layers of resin on mirrored Plexiglas™. The mirrored surface refracts light back through the translucent resin in infinite colors and densities. The hypnotic, sensuous images beckon from across the room, then change when the viewer walks from one side to the other. Sometimes they seem to glow in the dark.

The artist arrived in Taos in the 1930s as a teenager named Florence Miller. She had previously attended the studio school at the Phillips Collection in her native Washington, DC. She was interested in studying with Emil Bisttram, who had embraced abstraction and had co-founded, with Raymond Jonson, the Transcendental Painting Group. These artists were interested in the most fundamental aspects of creation, such as the language of geometry and the truth that lies beneath appearance. They also studied a variety of spiritual disciplines, including Zen Buddhism, in their pursuit of transcendence. Miller became the youngest member of the group, and one of only two women. She married Horace Towner Pierce, who was also in the group. They settled in Albuquerque, raised a family, and maintained parallel art careers until his death in 1958.

Pierce continued her experiments in form, concept, and medium, creating abstract paintings and sculptures, always remaining true to Transcendentalist principles. One day in 1969, while mixing some resin to reinforce the structure of a sculpture, she spilled a few drops on a piece of tinfoil. Turning it this way and that, observing the light as it reflected from the tinfoil and moved through the resin, she realized that she had discovered a new way to produce art. She promptly lost interest in the piece she had been doing, and began working with the difficult, toxic, but supremely rewarding medium of resin.

At that point, her already flourishing career took off. Through the decades, she has remained a leader in the rarefied field of monochromatic Minimalism. Pierce sailed into her eighties with a full exhibition schedule, a formidable history, and smashing personal style. Tall, white-haired, and regal, she continues to challenge herself by producing works of art that project luminous elegance and clarion force. These images of living, breathing light function as talismans, presences, statements, beacons. Ultimately, however, they are artifacts of a process that Florence Pierce refers to simply as "stilling and freeing the mind."

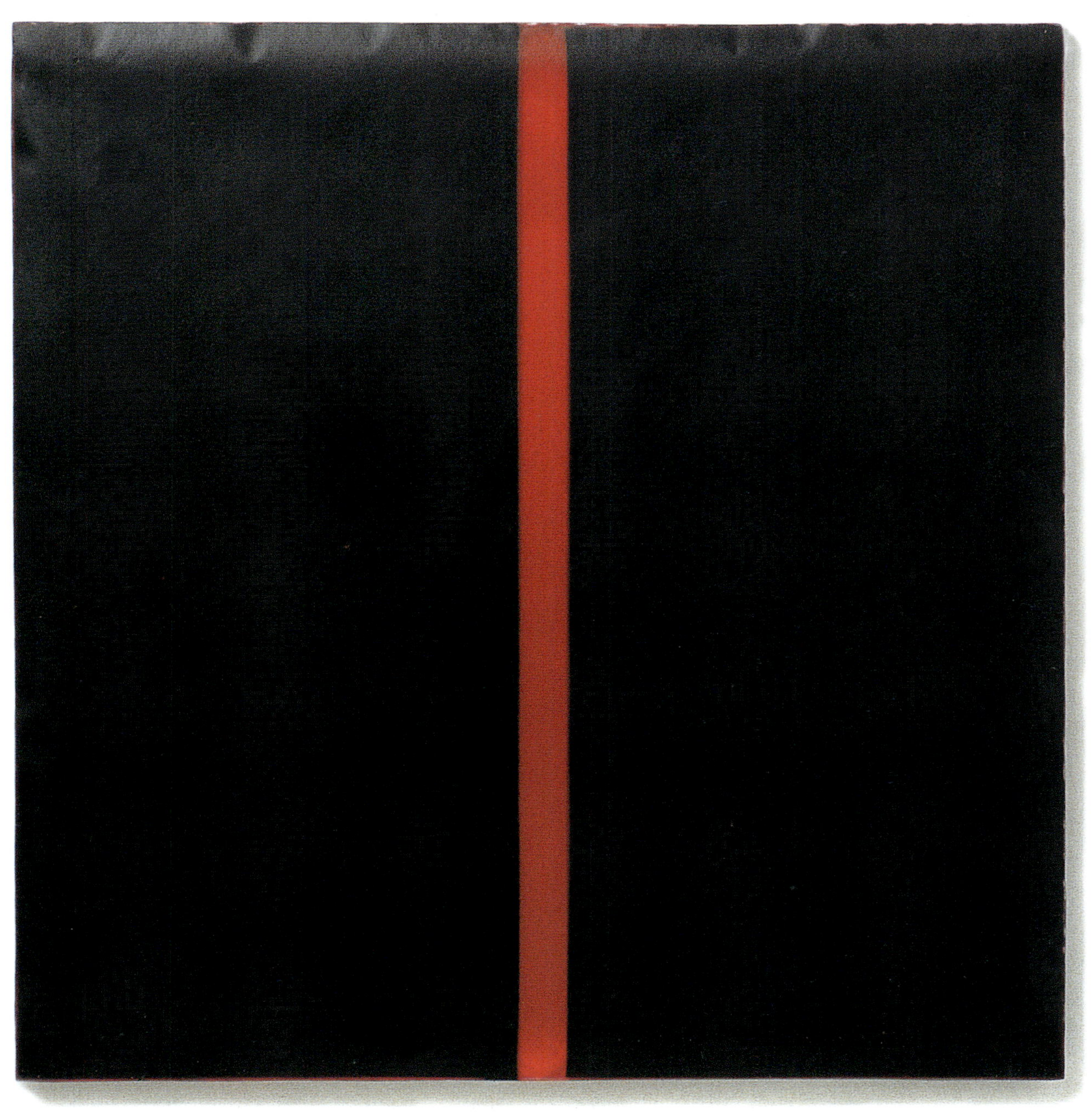

UNTITLED #117
RESIN/PLEXIGLAS™
24 X 24 INCHES

UNTITLED #119
RESIN/PLEXIGLAS™
24 X 24 INCHES

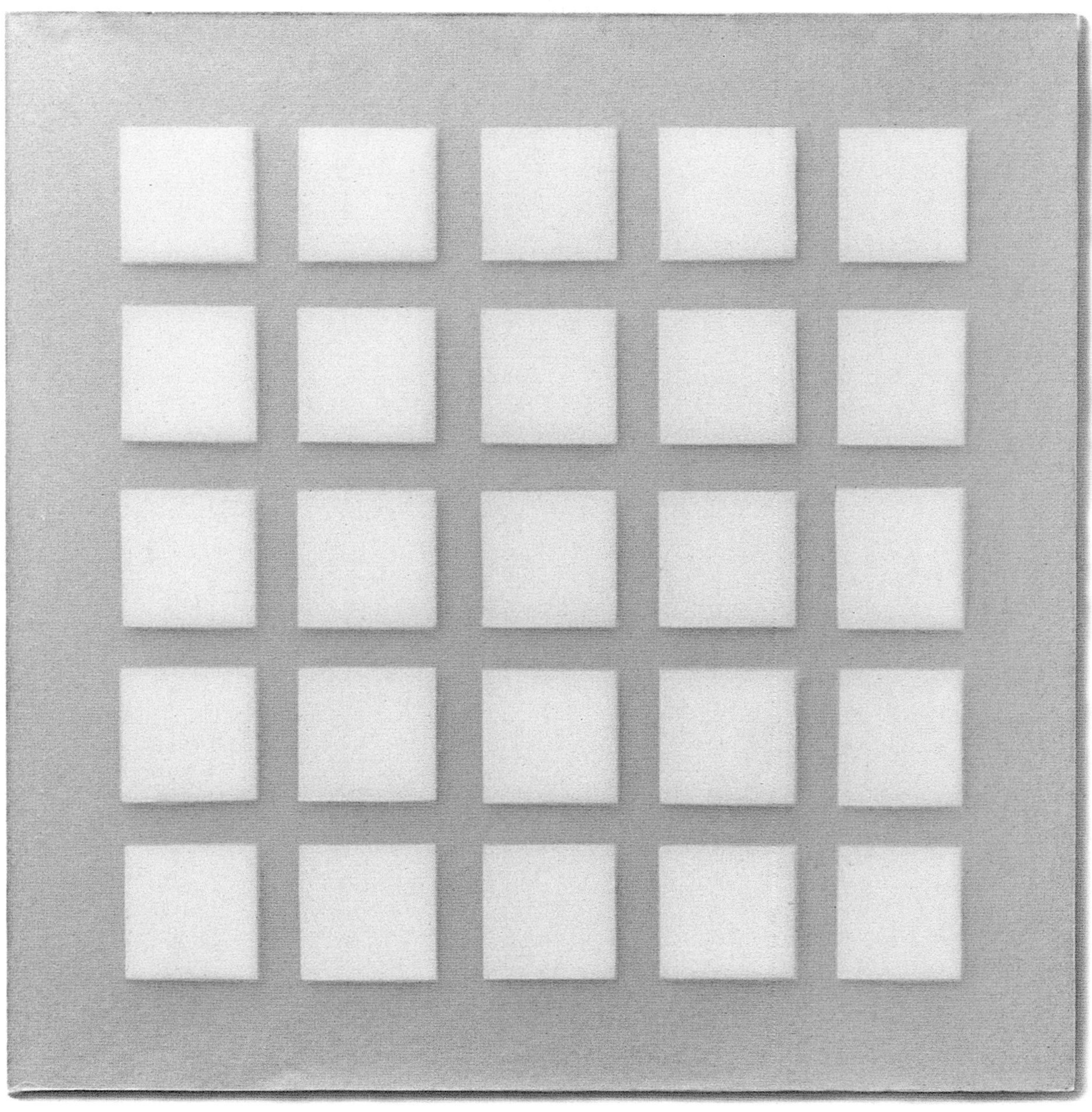

UNTITLED #11A
RESIN/PLEXIGLAS™
24 X 24 INCHES

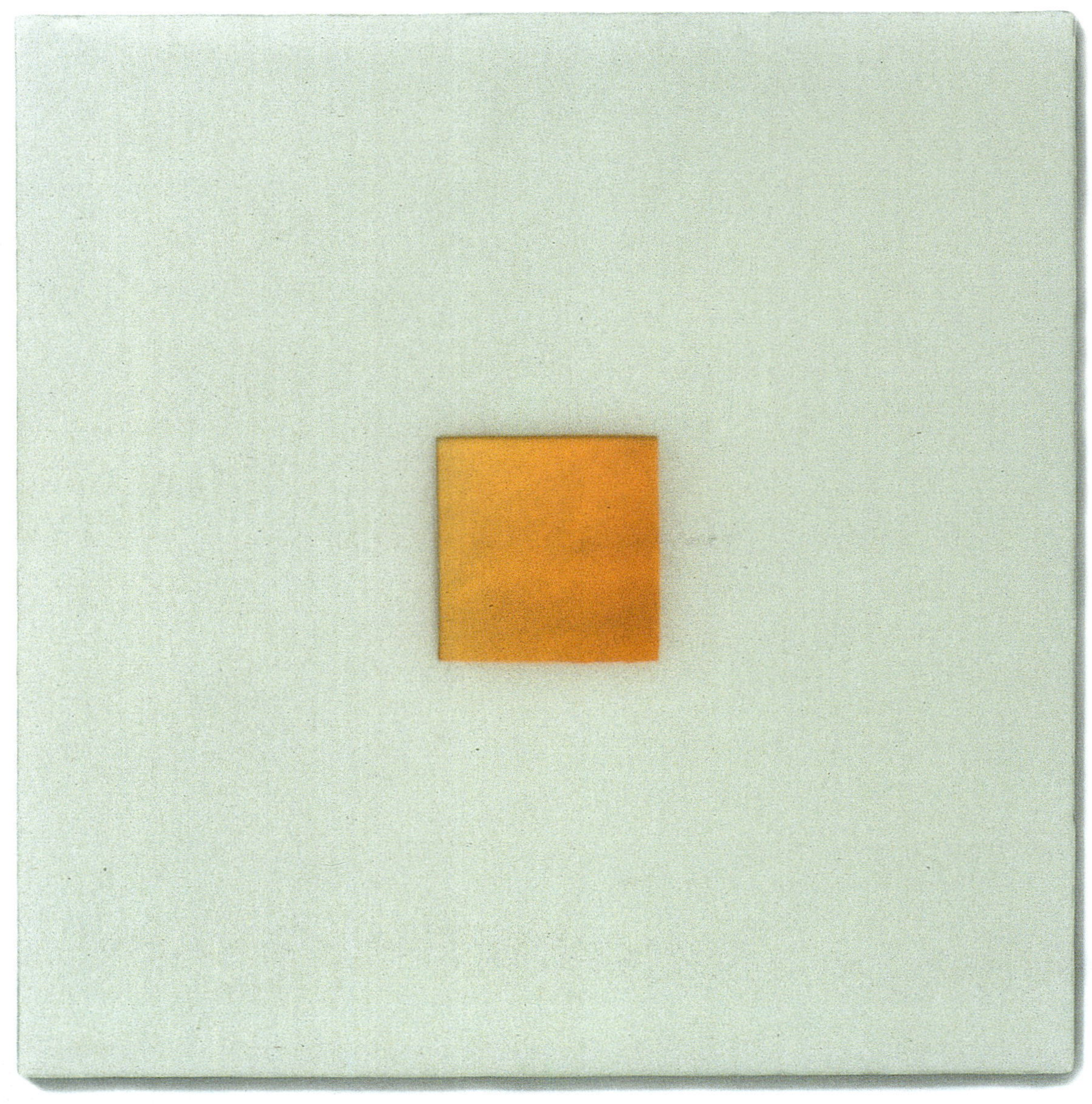

UNTITLED #12
RESIN/PLEXIGLAS™
24 X 24 INCHES

FLORENCE PIERCE b. 1918 Washington DC. Ed: Duncan Phillips Collection, Studio School DC; Emil Bisttram School of Art NM. Solo exhib: Museum of Fine Arts, Santa Fe NM; Amarillo Art Museum TX; Jonson Gallery, Univ. of NM. Honors: Governors Award for Excellence In the Arts NM. Coll: McNay Museum, San Antonio TX; Albuquerque Museum NM; Rockefeller Univ. NYC. Representation: Charlotte Jackson Fine Art, Santa Fe.

UNTITLED #149
RESIN/PLEXIGLAS™
16 X 16 INCHES

KAREN YANK

It is no wonder that the ancients believed their world was flat, with its horizon drawn around it in perfect symmetry and the sky bowed above it. Even in more recent times, Emerson spoke of life as "a self evolving circle." Mother Earth and all eternity still exist in the human mind as a rounded wholeness, steady under the feet when all else crumbles. The full moon and the sundial mark the passing of our days and years.

Karen Yank has created a long series of disc-shaped steel sculptures, choosing to focus on one form - the circle - and one material - steel - in order to mine it for associations, metaphors, and variations. Her imagination rolls past all limitations that might be imposed by this discipline, and she creates a kaleidoscope of ideas. She pares each piece down, then abstracts it further with additions and subtractions, carving and scratching, polishing and weathering until the art comes alive. "My sculptures reflect the emotional impact of my chosen environment and close personal relationships," says Yank.

Working with arc- and gas-welding equipment on Cor-Ten™, stainless, and mild steel as well as bronze, she creates wall pieces and freestanding sculptures as large as eight feet in diameter. Many difficult steps are involved, giving the sculpture a robust physicality. Yank welds together two discs with a hollow between them. The resulting thickness allows her to create depth on various levels. Her patinas are similarly subtle, ranging from deep black to burgundies and greens, enticing the senses to touch them. She juxtaposes highly polished stainless steel with these tactile surfaces to set up endless interplays and inferences, and incises them with the most evocative lines.

Her father, noted sculptor Paul Yank, set her on a lifelong course in the arts. He helped shape her esthetics from childhood on, and continues to be a great source of inspiration. Her other creative colleague has been her artist husband Rodney Hamon, with whom she is raising a daughter.

In 1987, she earned a scholarship to the Skowhegan School of Painting and Sculpture in Maine. It was there that she met and studied under Agnes Martin, her most significant mentor. Their frequent conversations continue to enrich their friendship to this day. "Much about the way I work is influenced by her," says Karen Yank. "Agnes Martin has given me a lifetime of extraordinary insight." When one looks at the work, a direct influence is immediately apparent, even though the forms are different. Both express abstract emotion. The line quality is strikingly similar. And there is about both a beauty and wholeness that transcend time. When all else in life turns flat, this art remains inviolate.

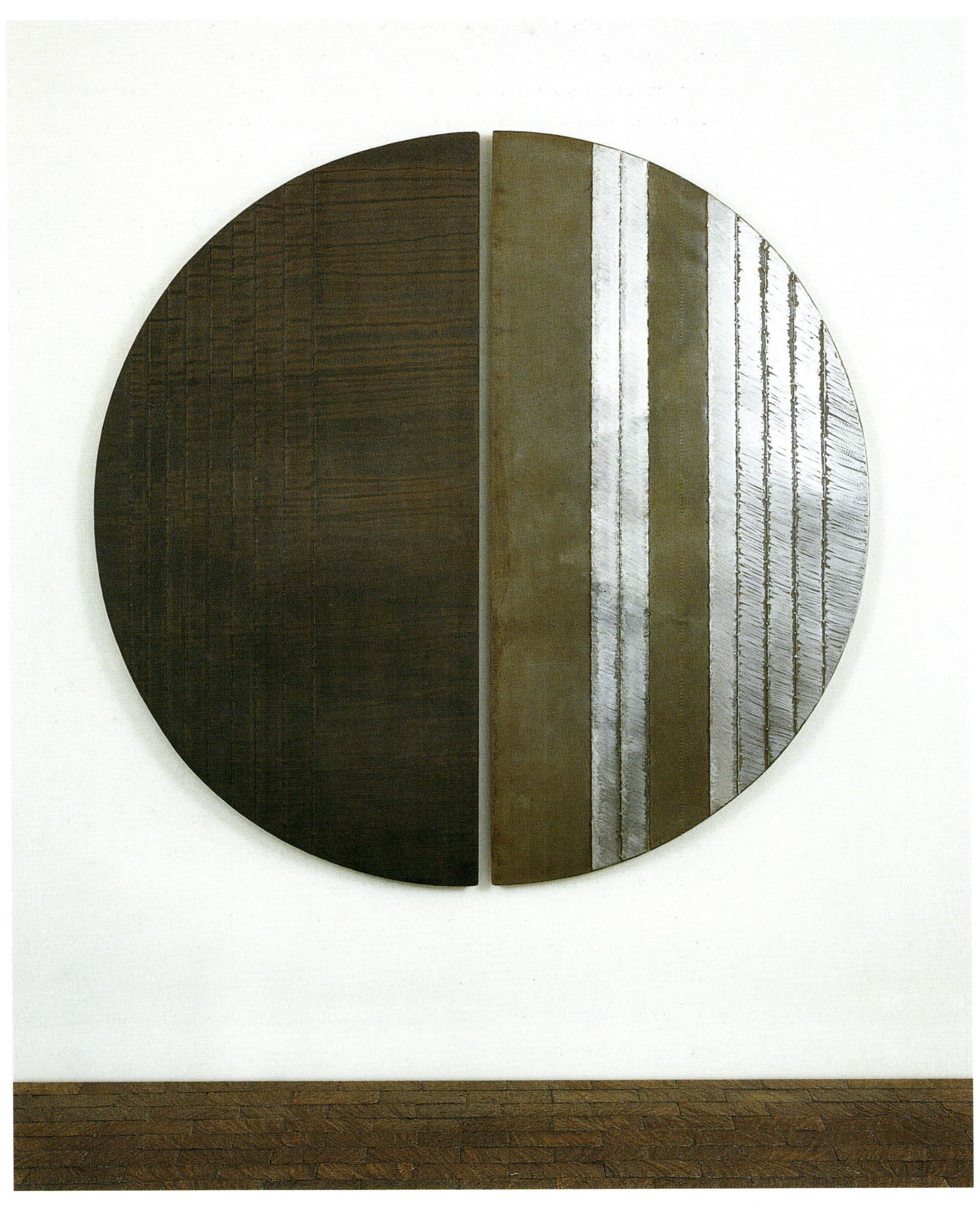

IN THE GROOVE II
COR-TEN™ STEEL
72 X 72 X 1½ INCHES

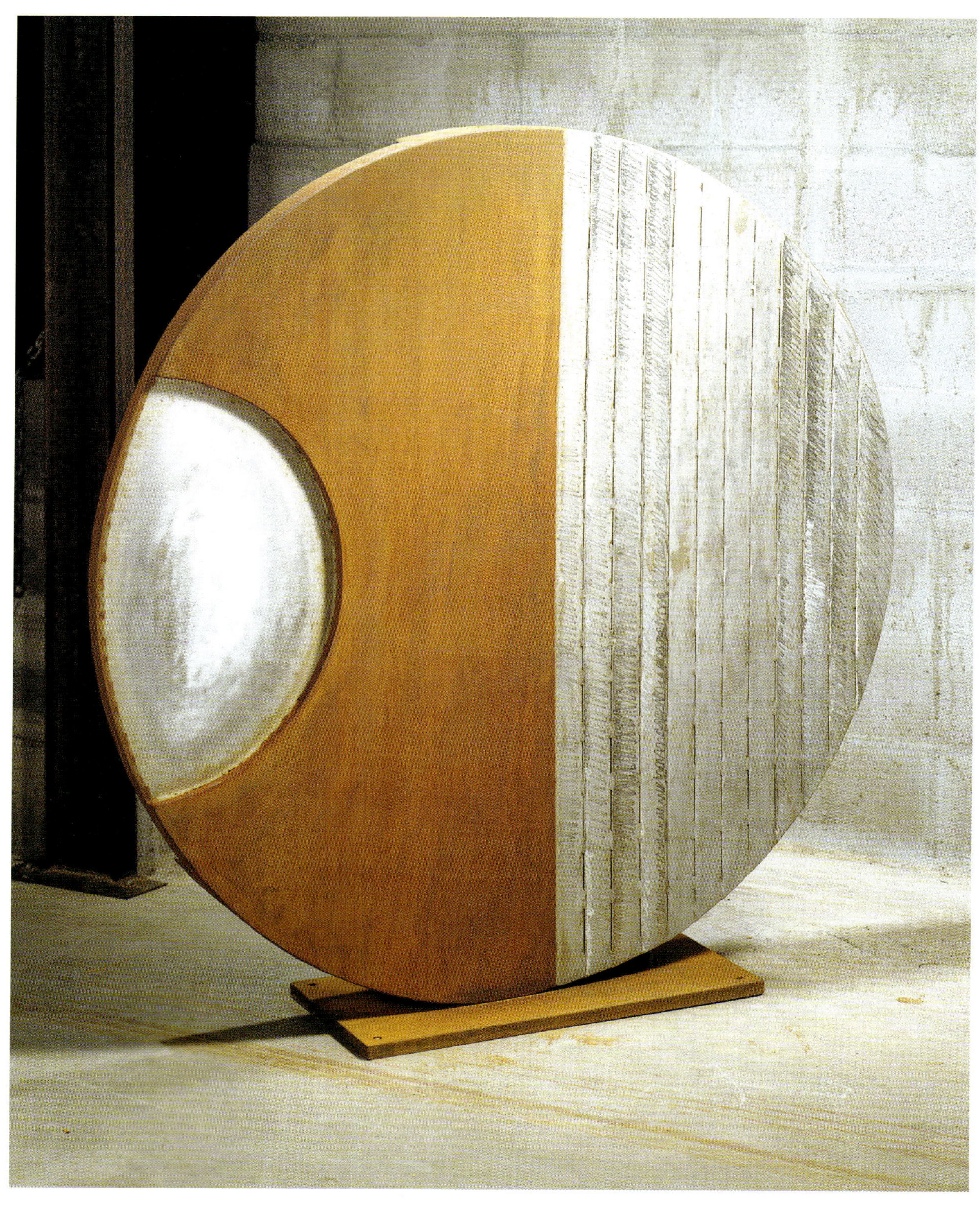

REFLECTIONS
COR-TEN™, STAINLESS, STEEL
48 X 48 X 12 INCHES

KAREN YANK

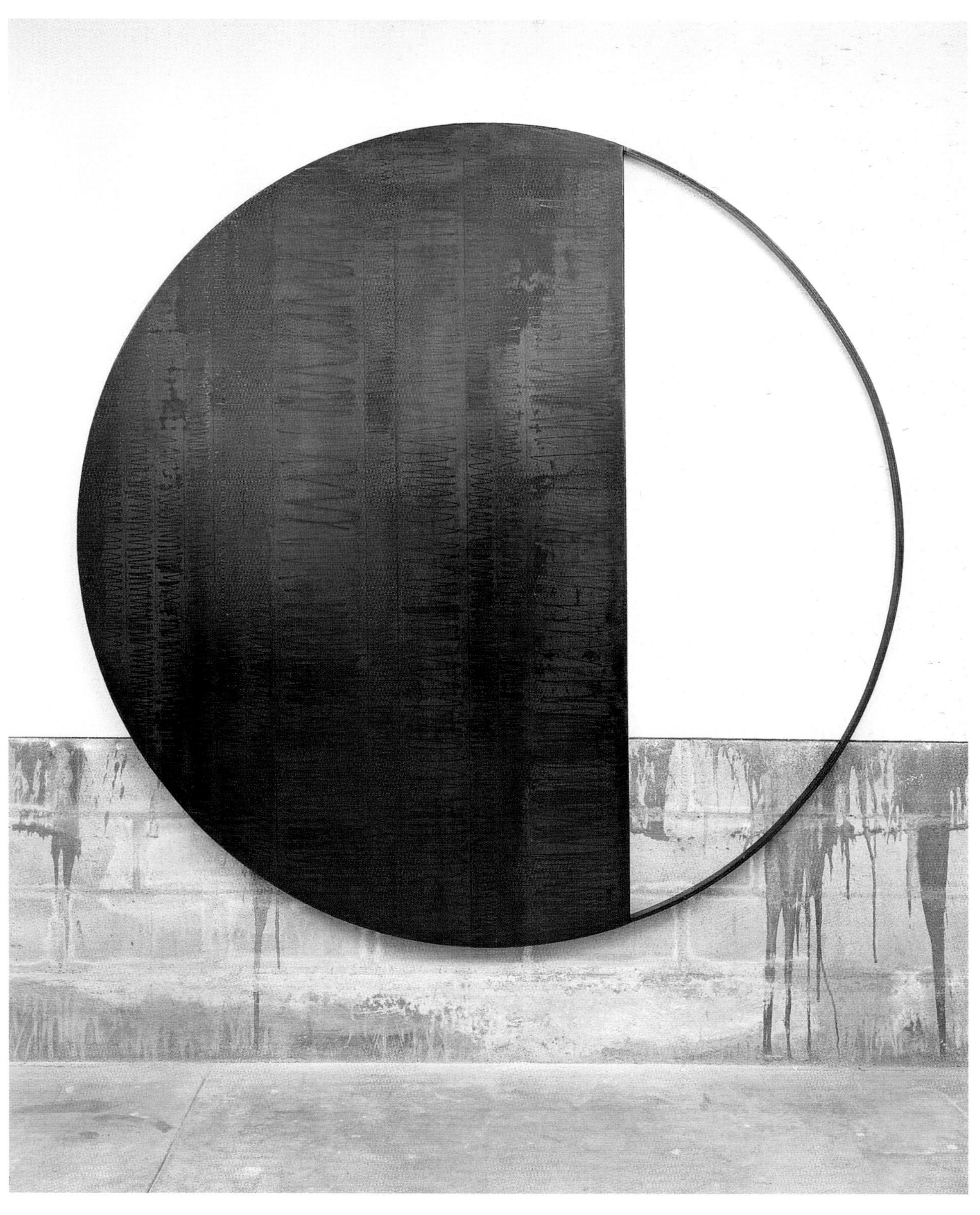

UNEQUAL HALVES
STEEL
84 X 84 X 1½ INCHES

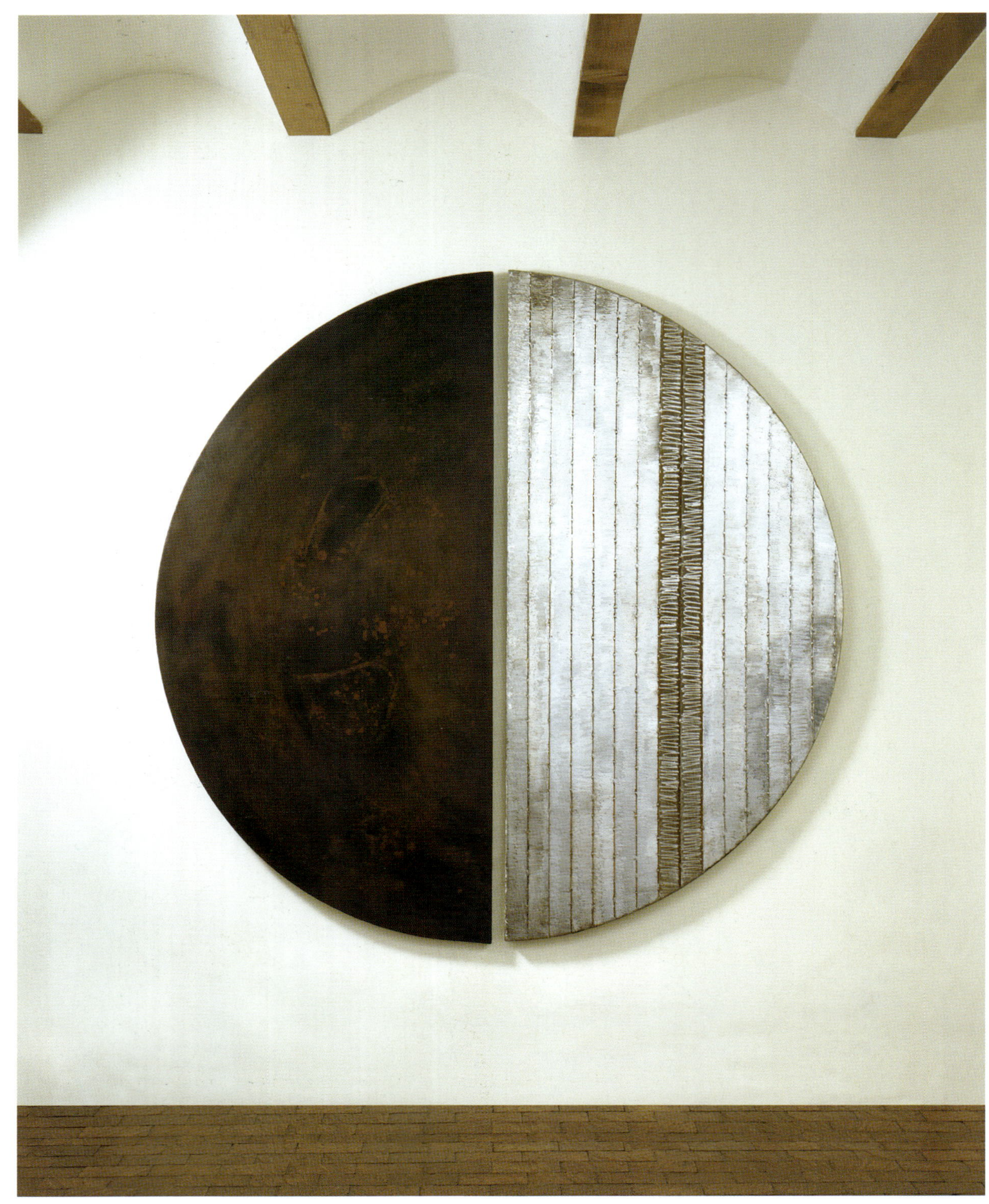

AT A POINT CLOSEST TO YOU
COR-TEN™, STEEL
84 X 84 X 2 INCHES

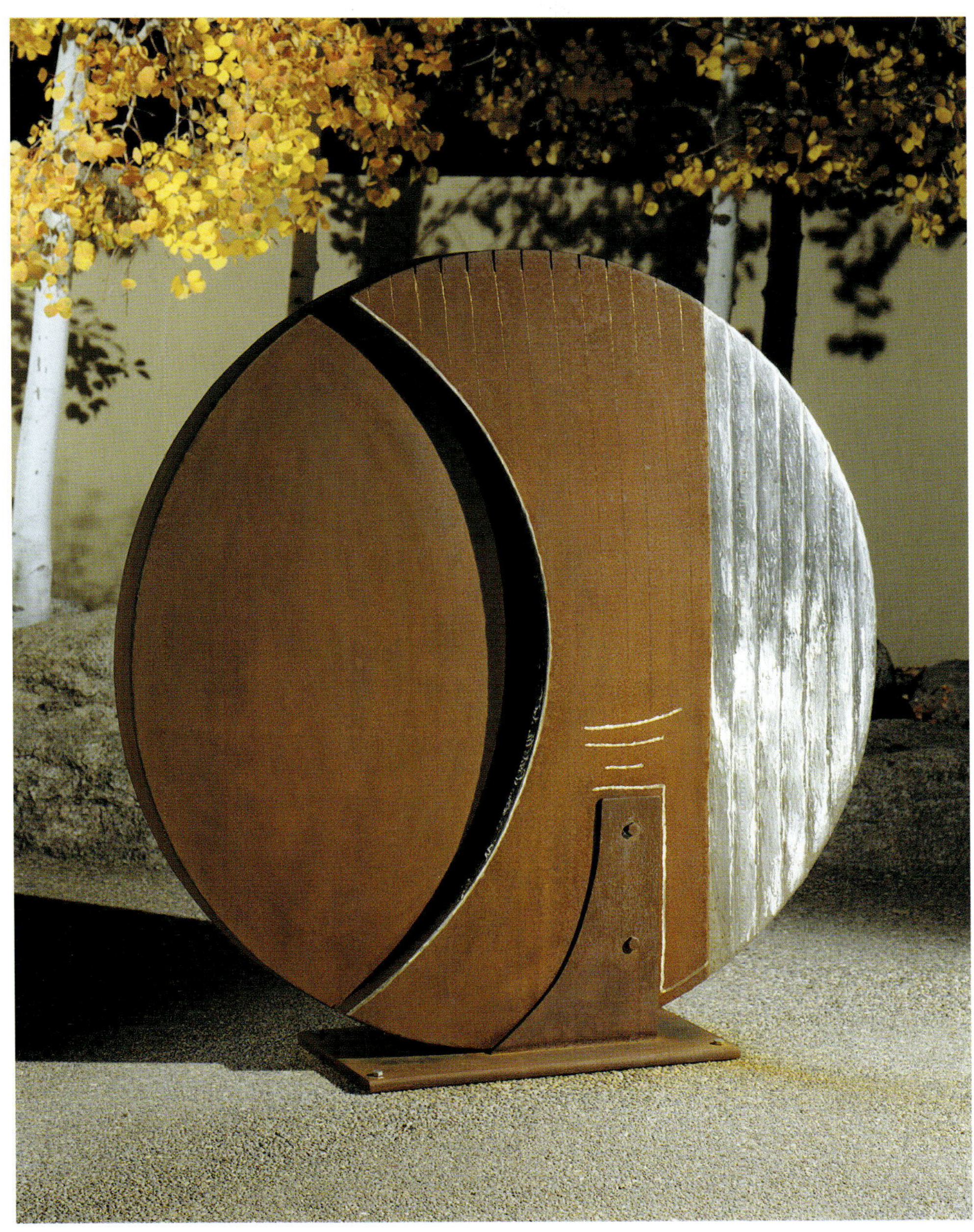

KAREN YANK b. 1961 Milwaukee WI. Ed: MFA Rutgers Univ. NJ; Univ. New Mexico; BA Univ. Wisconsin/Madison. Coll: Capitol Art Collection NM, State Library, Santa Fe NM; Albuquerque Museum, University Hospital, Sandia National Laboratories, Albuquerque NM. Representation: Munson Gallery, Santa Fe; New York; Aspen; Scottsdale.

ELUSIVE RIPPLE
COR-TEN™, STAINLESS, STEEL
48 X 48 X 12 INCHES

ALAN PAINE RADEBAUGH

Our field of vision takes in fragments only. When we reassemble them in our minds, we see the whole picture, or so we believe. But what we have really absorbed is a series of sensory impressions like the scattering of clouds, the reaction of oil with water, the erosion of earth and relationships, the active surface of life as it peels away and flakes off to reveal its majestic and arbitrary incompleteness.

Fragments and inferences make up our consciousness. Art transforms our perceptions into wholeness. Alan Paine Radebaugh is an artist who understands these verities, and who maintains a clear and down-to-earth viewpoint about them. "I like going out into the world and looking at things," he says. "I wander around the desert, the mountains, the seacoast, the prairies for weeks at a time until something filters in and talks to me. One little shape comes alive. When it does, it's undeniable - it screams to be drawn. It's personal; it's just me and it. So I make drawings of it and then come back to the studio and make paintings."

Radebaugh spends long hours in the studio. When he has completed a body of work, he goes out and looks at the world again. "I can spend three days out there and have a year's worth of material," he says. "I see abstract shapes, forms, and lines. The forms are what speak to me. They're alive; they glow."

Radebaugh is able to transform this vital spark into a work of art because he is adept at many mediums. He studied photography and drawing at the College of Wooster in Ohio, then earned his BFA in printmaking at the University of New Mexico. He designed sculptural furniture for ten years. Since the late 1980s, his predominant medium has been painting. Even within this discipline, however, he ranges widely. For one series, he painted on etched aluminum panels set in eight-foot-tall wood beams with large steel bases. He also paints in conventional oil on canvas.

Alan Radebaugh explains that the act of going out, tuning in to his surroundings, and making drawings is the most soul-satisfying aspect of his work. Last year, while he was walking around the Canadian Rockies, he found something that spoke to him. He started drawing and became oblivious to his surroundings, a dangerous thing to do in bear country. He heard a rustling behind him and came out of his state of total absorption to find two deer displaying an interest in what he was doing. He had come to see nature working; nature was looking back at him.

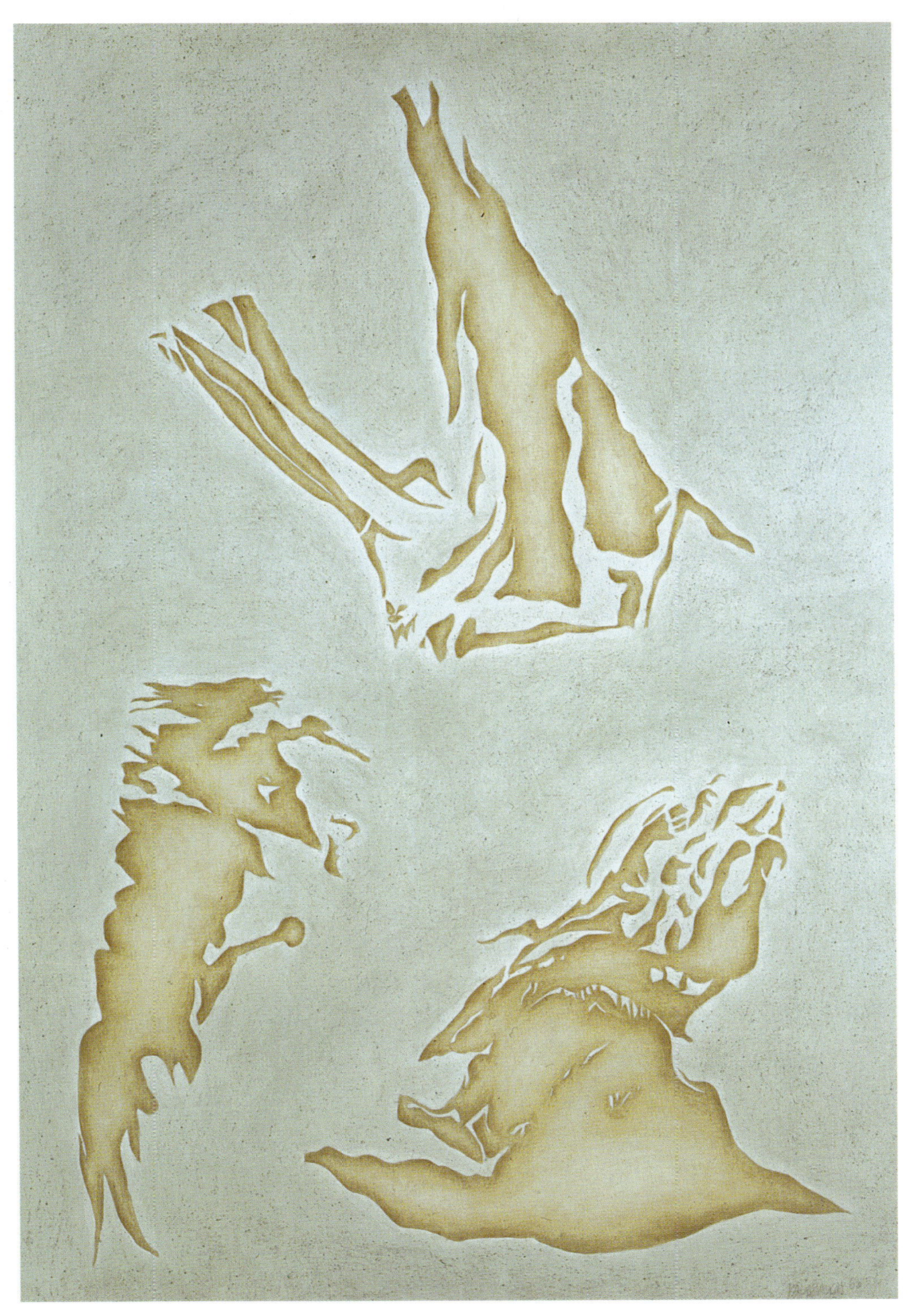

FRAGMENT DIALOGUES II
OIL, WAX, ACRYLIC, PIGMENT, CANVAS
64 X 44 INCHES

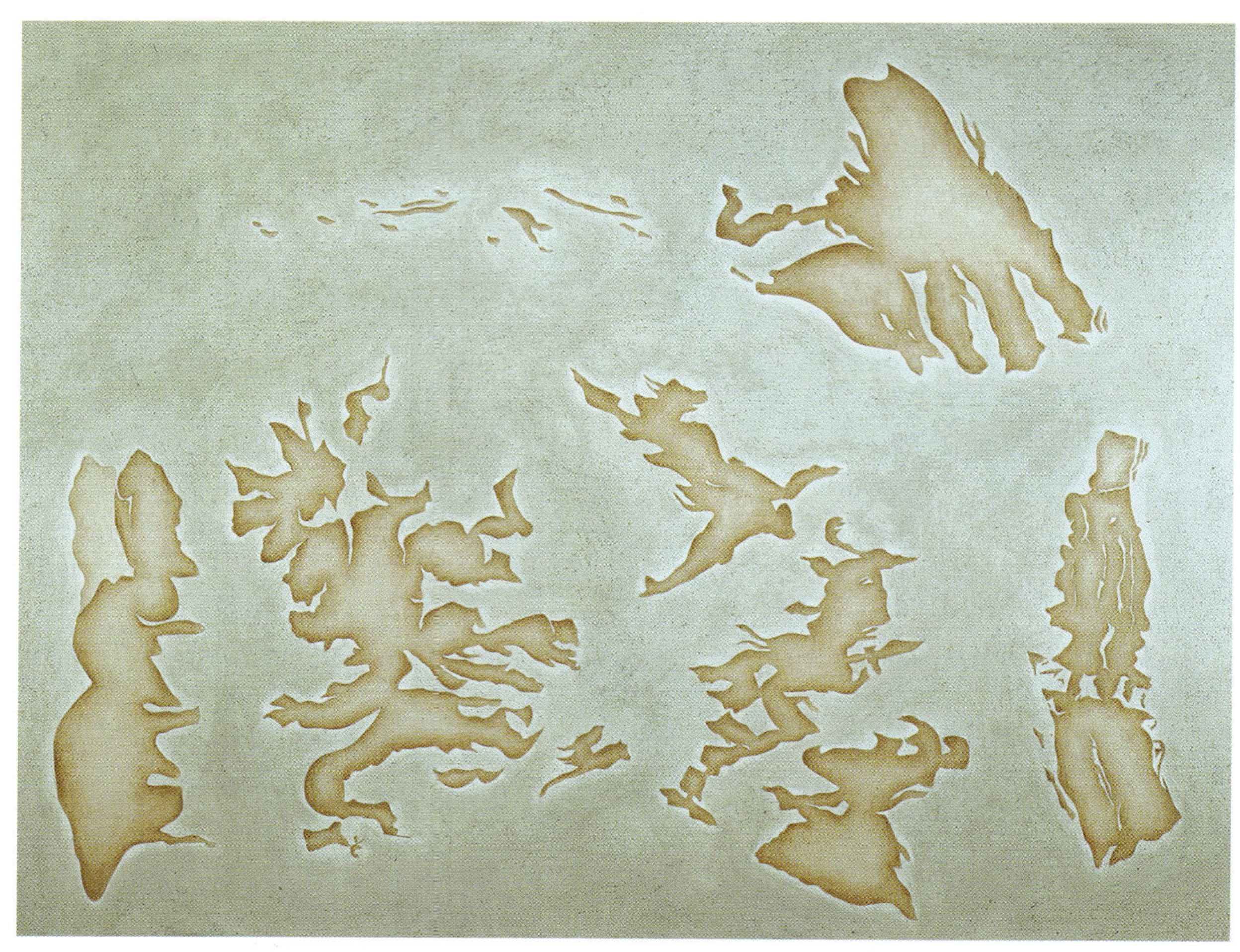

FRAGMENT DIALOGUES I
OIL, WAX, ACRYLIC, PIGMENT, CANVAS
64 X 84 INCHES

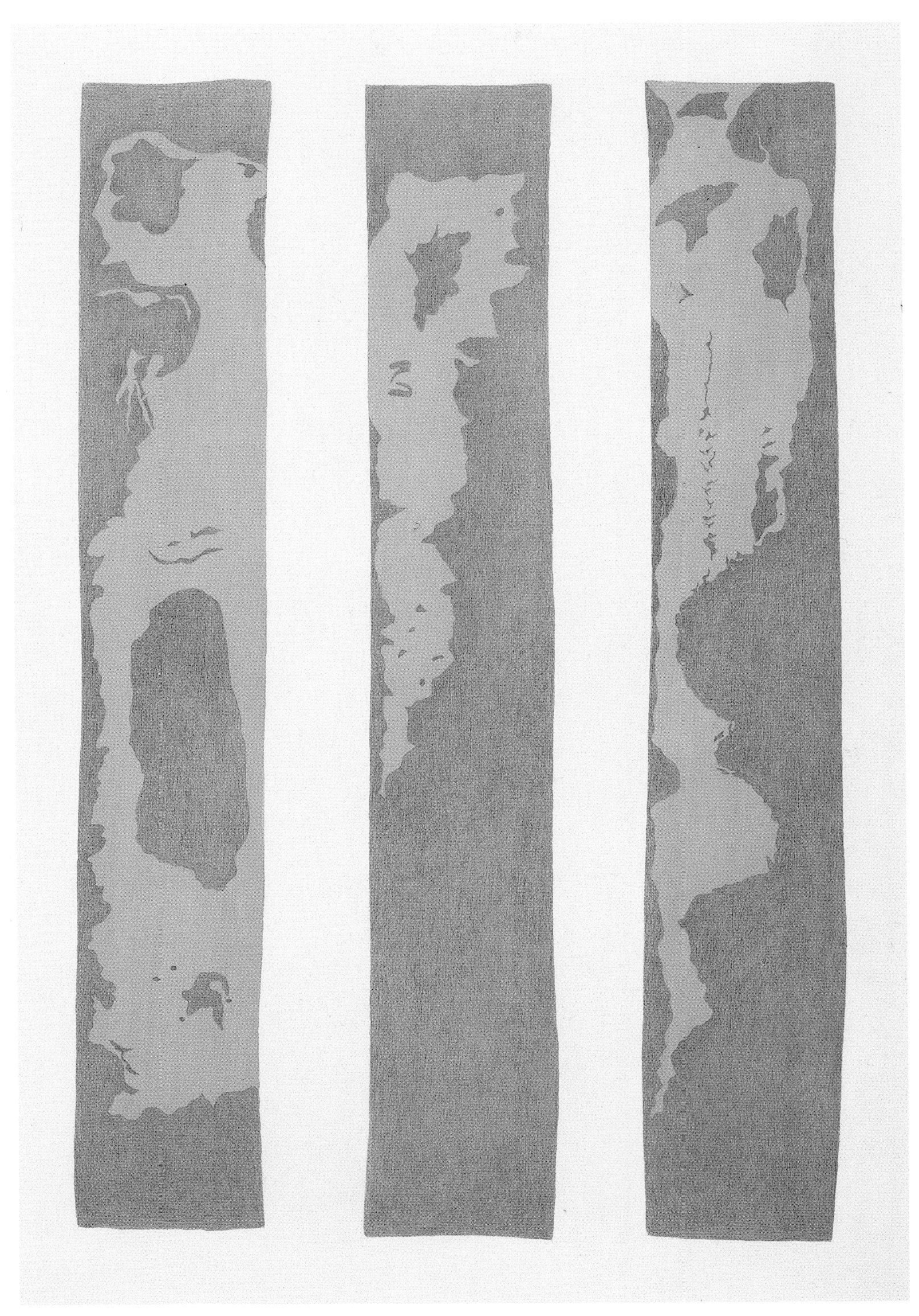

TRI-FRAGMENT I
GRAPHITE, ACRYLIC, CANVAS
46 X 32 INCHES

TRI-FRAGMENT III
GRAPHITE, ACRYLIC, CANVAS
46 X 32 INCHES

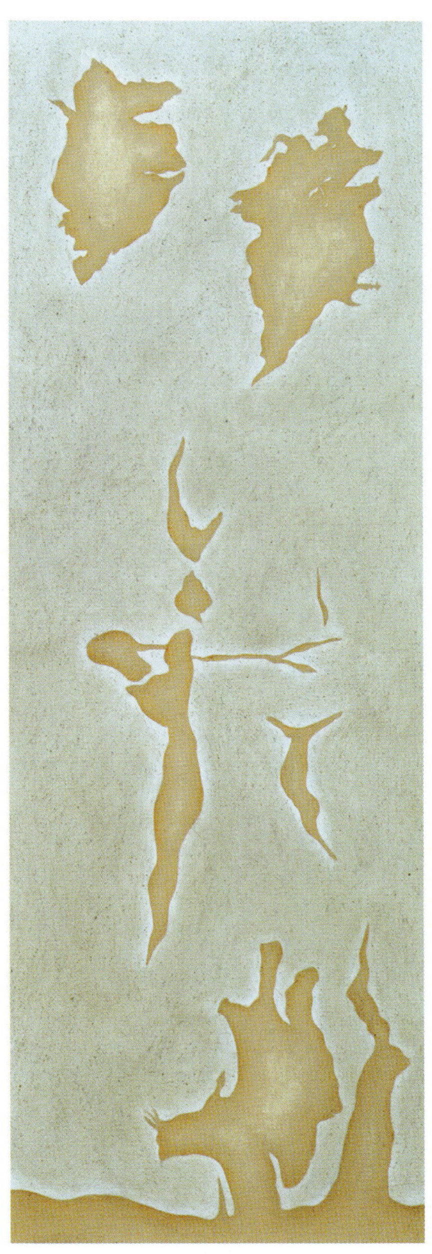

ALAN PAINE RADEBAUGH b. 1952 Boston MA. Ed: The College of Wooster; BFA Univ. New Mexico. Coll: Albuquerque Museum, Museum of Fine Arts Santa Fe, Capitol Art Collection NM; Ohio State; Washington & Jefferson College, etal. Representation: Coleman Gallery Contemporary Art, Albuquerque.

FRAGMENT DIALOGUES III
OIL, WAX, ACRYLIC, PIGMENT, CANVAS
64 X 22 INCHES

VALDEZ ABEYTA Y VALDEZ

Sight and sound converging in the mind create an event larger than the sum of its parts. The sound of a drum vibrates on eyelids; the rhythm of the abstract, its shouts and whispers, adds dimension to the experience. The line between sensibilities fades and opens itself to full consciousness.

Nowhere is this phenomenon more evident than in the art of Valdez Abeyta y Valdez where sound is the keystone. The viewer finds it impossible to register these powerful images on the retina alone. The skin tingles; the eardrum bends reflexively. The mind takes in the experience of the artist and absorbs it into sense memory.

As a child roaming free on foot and on horseback in the glorious Rio Grande Valley of northern New Mexico, Abeyta y Valdez listened to the sounds of the natural world and they became an integral part of her being: the rushing water in acequias, the rhythm of hands plastering ancient adobe walls, the cadence of horses' feet touching the earth. These seeds of memory now fall from her hands to take shape on paper.

Abeyta y Valdez reflects her life in her art. She transposes those life sensations into immaculcte drawings that project resonating tones, subtle syncopation, and powerful bursts of sound. She does not often work in full color, preferring a limited palette of sepias, umbers, and blacks built up from the different textures of selected papers. She says, "The muted colors in my drawings represent my reality of my homeland, the place where I was born." Each finely rendered drawing is comprised of so many layers that the pencil image rises above the surface of the paper.

Her work has caught on with a wide audience - not only for the strength of the work itself, but for the insights that she is able to share with the world at large. "My work is about the breath of things, the primal hum of life," says Valdez Abeyta y Valdez. "It's about how things breathe, and the silence between breaths. I hear my drawings before I see them."

Founder of the nationally recognized Larragoite Drummers, Abeyta y Valdez, a classically trained musician, teaches music to the very young. Five days a week, she "teaches young minds and small hands on drums and translates the abstract language of music into the magical sounds of spirit."

At the close of each day, she returns to her studio in her garden. There, she retreats from the whirling edges of her life to draw the pure, still, quiet center where stones and branches, eggs and seeds breathe and sing of spirit.

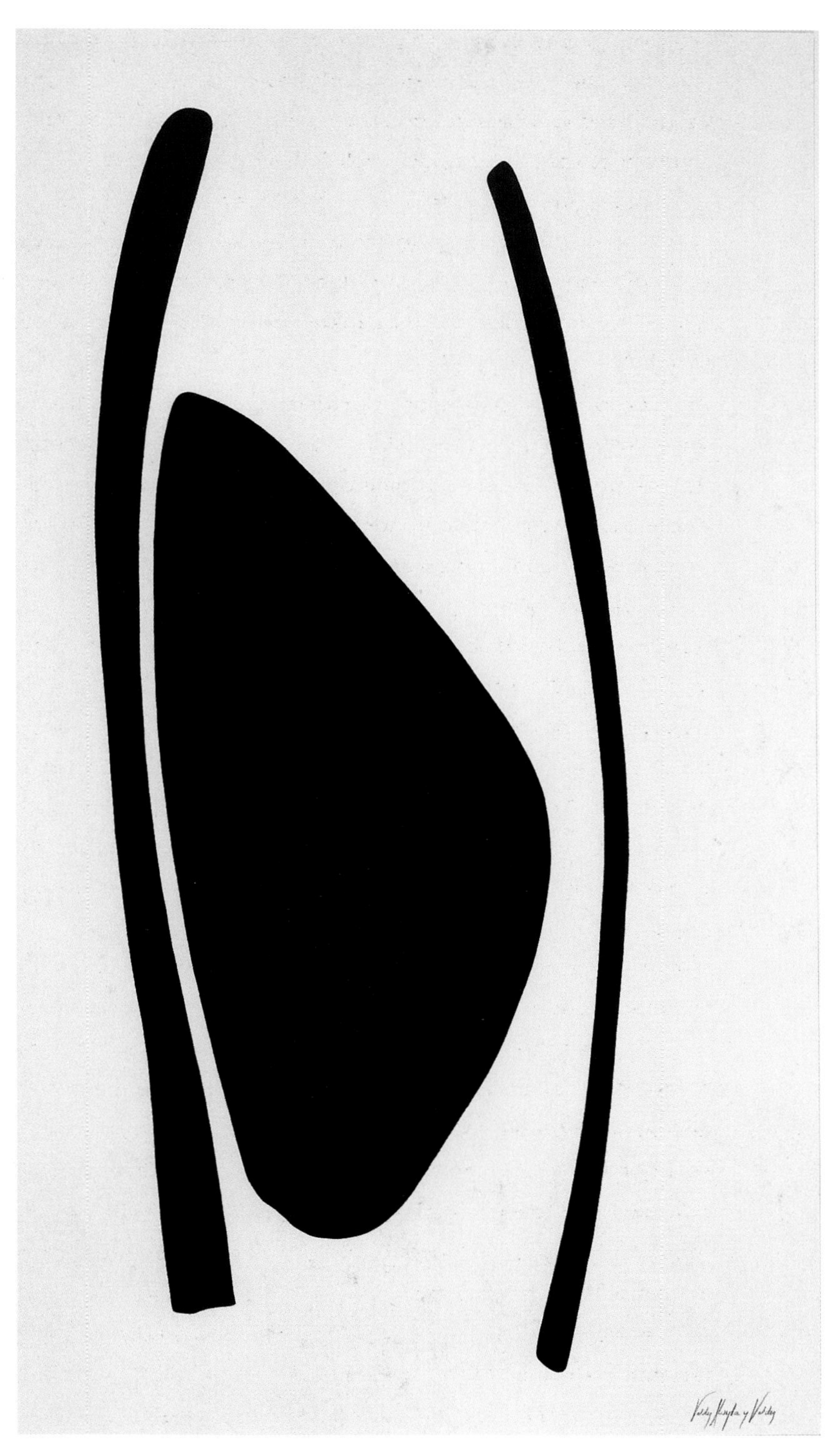

VENUS OF WILENDORF
BLACK LEAD PENCIL
55 X 38 INCHES

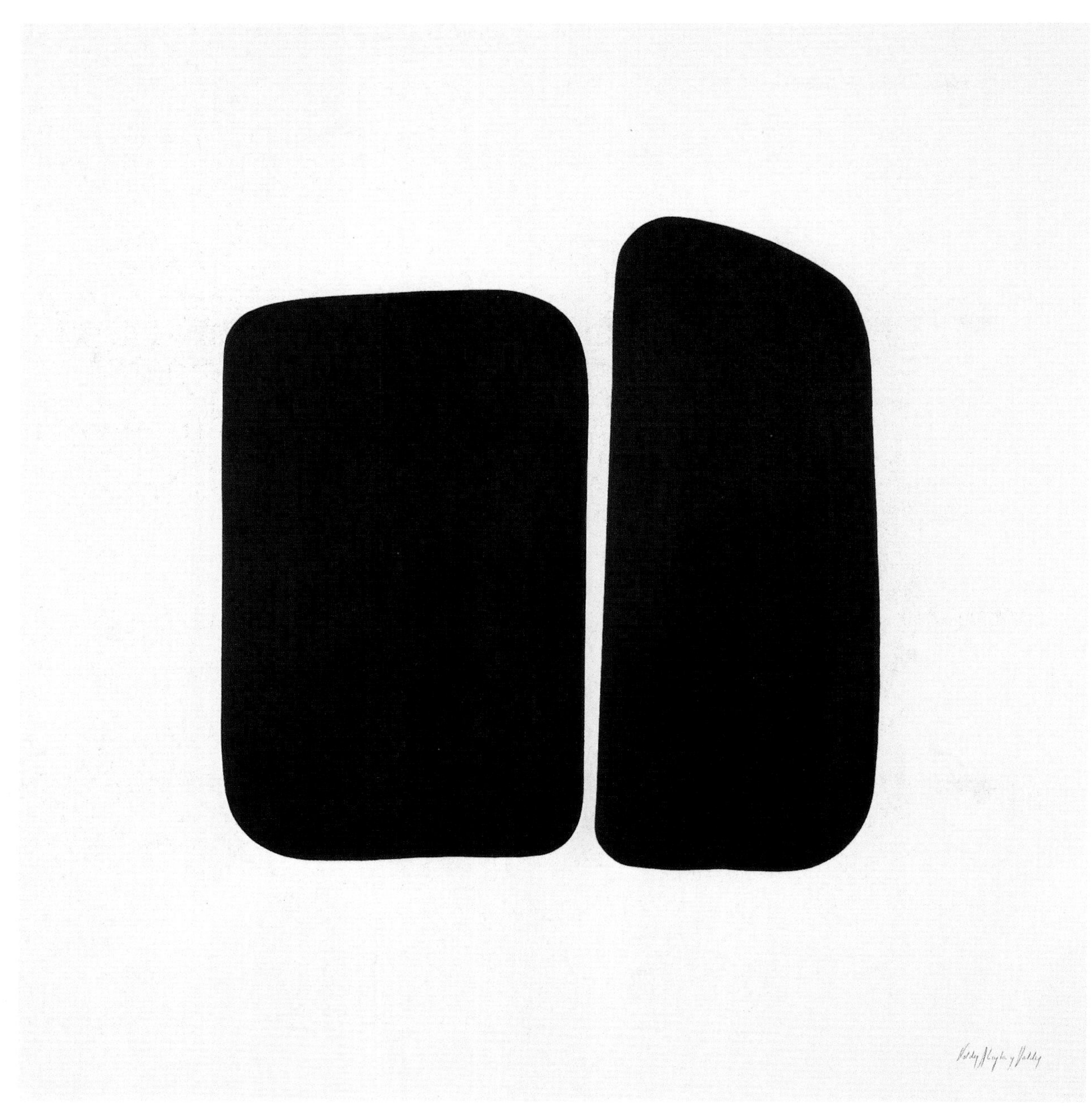

LOVERS ETERNAL
BLACK LEAD PENCIL
42 X 42 INCHES

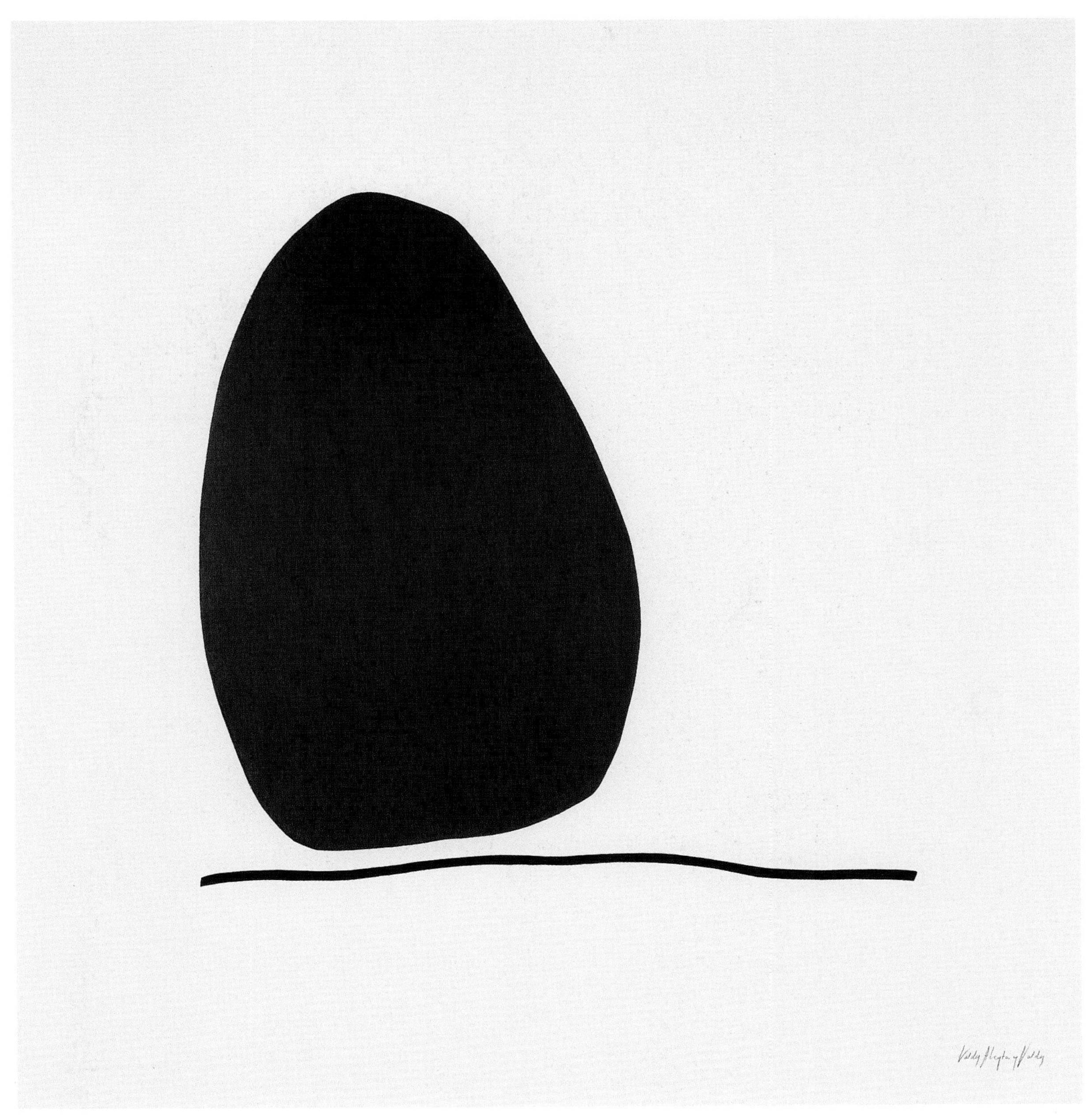

WINTER SEED
BLACK LEAD PENCIL
42 X 42 INCHES

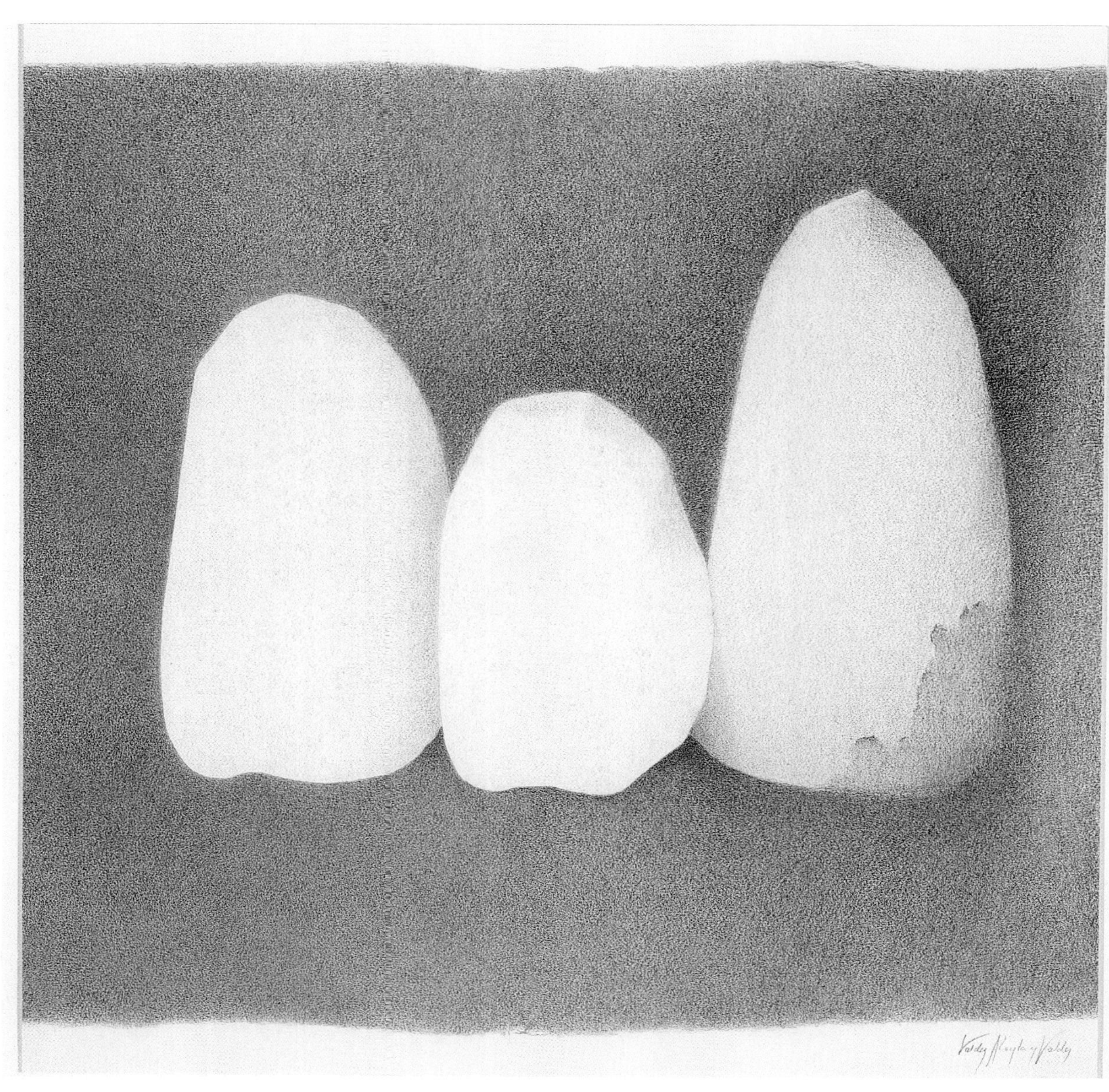

FOR SIMONÉ, STONES OF KNOWING
BLACK LEAD PENCIL
38 X 39 INCHES

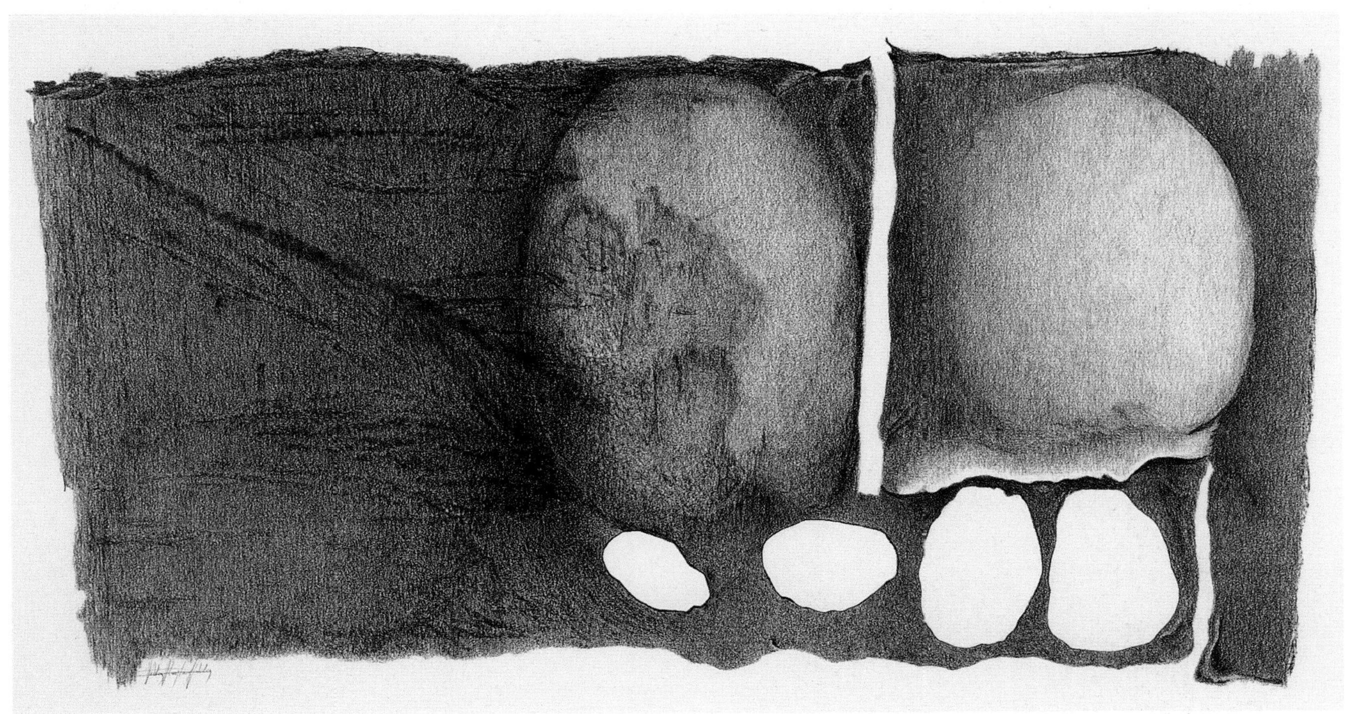

VALDEZ ABEYTA Y VALDEZ b. 1951 Espanola NM. Ed: BA. Humanities, BA, Studio Art, College of Santa Fe. First Director, El Museo Cultural de Santa Fe. Founder, Larragoite Drummers. Awards: Top Teacher of the Year NM; Teachers Who Inspire NM. Contemporary Hispanic Market 1993-1999. Represer tation: Anderson Contemporary Art, Santa Fe.

GENESIS
BLACK LEAD PENC L
32 X 51 INCHES

CONNIE MISSISSIPPI

Find the point where control stops and the natural world takes over. Find what is left after the extraneous is stripped away, leaving only the spark of life. Give it mass and weight and durability. Give it a thousand shapes that signify and symbolize the life of the mind and the body. Go to the essence of it and uncover what Roethke calls "the imperishable quiet at the heart of form."

Connie Mississippi uses living wood, sophisticated tools, and profound ideas to produce abstract sculptures which are more complicated and complex than they may at first appear. The artist finds a three dimensional voice to give tenable shape to the seasons, the laws of physics, the art of dynamic imbalance.

One of her most ambitious pieces was a suite of one hundred white lacquer sculptures, one for each year of the twentieth century. A handwritten page accompanied each, amplifying its content in reflected historical text. Another piece was inspired by physicist Stephen Hawking, who observed that we will never be able to see a black hole because of how it pulls energy, including light, into itself. Mississippi was drawn to the issue of declared impossibility and created an abstraction of the black hole, countering the scientist's assertion.

Mississippi was a painter until 1980. Her work acquired a third dimension when she began experimenting with collage and shaped canvases. "One day I realized I was making sculpture," she says. "I knew I wanted to make organic forms, so I found someone who could teach me to use a lathe, which for me is a sophisticated carving tool. However, its standard size limited me, so I had a special lathe built. Now I can carve a piece that is almost four feet in diameter and eight feet in length, a different scale entirely from what is usually done on the lathe. In addition to the lathe, I may use power carving tools, chisels, and sanders. The possibility of the increase in size led to the use of laminated plywood. When I couldn't find natural wood large enough for the work I had in mind, I began laminating plywood blanks to the sizes I needed."

Mississippi finds wood to be an ideal medium to express her abstract concepts. No other material binds the natural world with human creation in quite the same way. She appreciates how wood responds to the artist's hand, yet maintains its own integrity. Sometimes she deliberately references the tree itself in a piece by incorporating remnants of the bark. Other times, as she s carving, she may change the design of the piece to honor what she finds within the tree

"Using wood, which is a living element and which yields to change so gracefully, allows me to experience in the doing of the work the revitalization of one of nature's most magnificent creations," says Connie Mississippi. "It is my belief that by using the wood of a tree, I give the tree another life, a different force of existence."

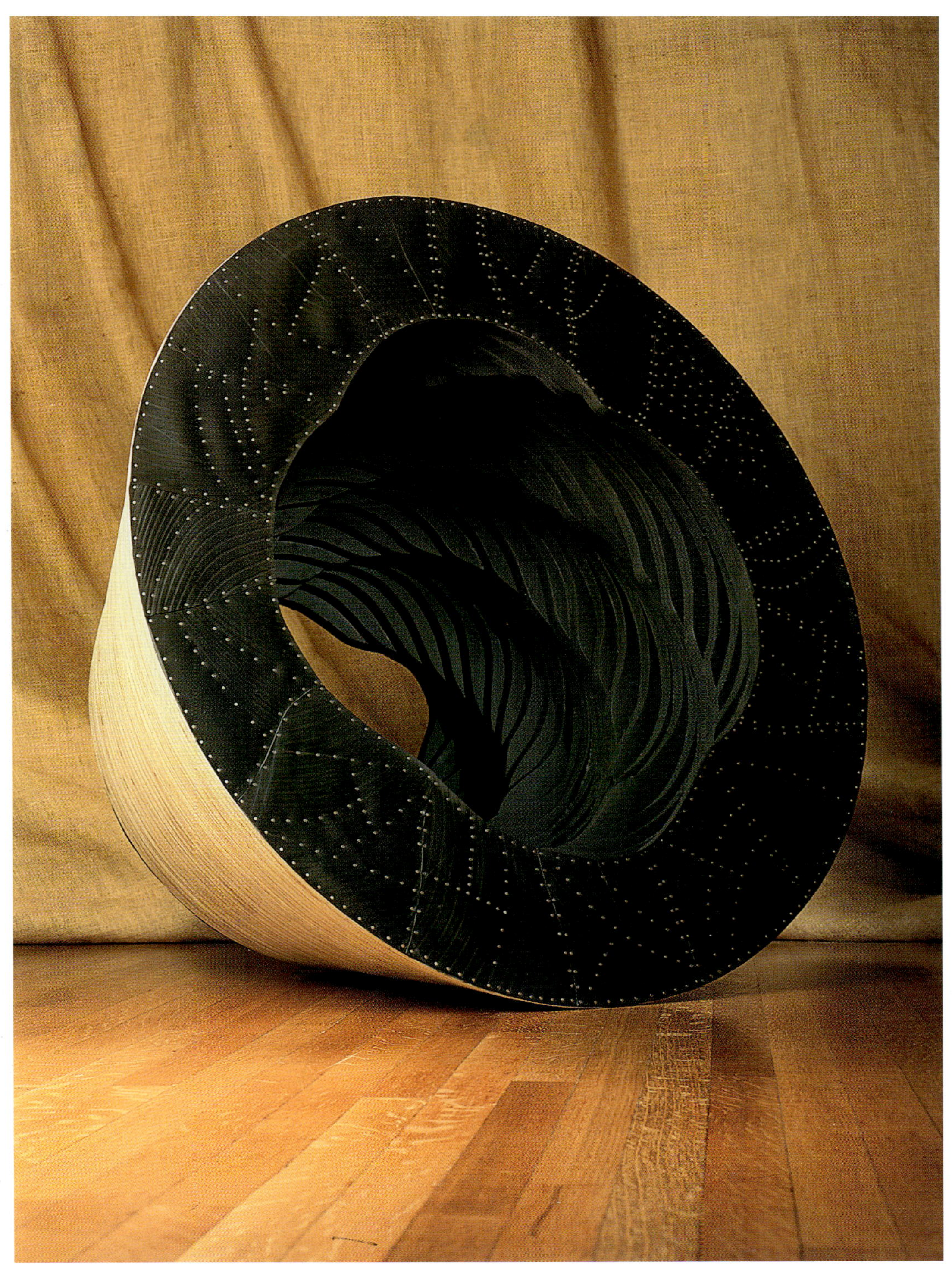

THE BLACK HOLE
LAMINATED, TURNED AND CARVED PLYWOOD
LAMINATED WITH PAINT & RUBBER
34(HT) X 20(DEPTH) INCHES
Collection Arkanscs Museum of Art

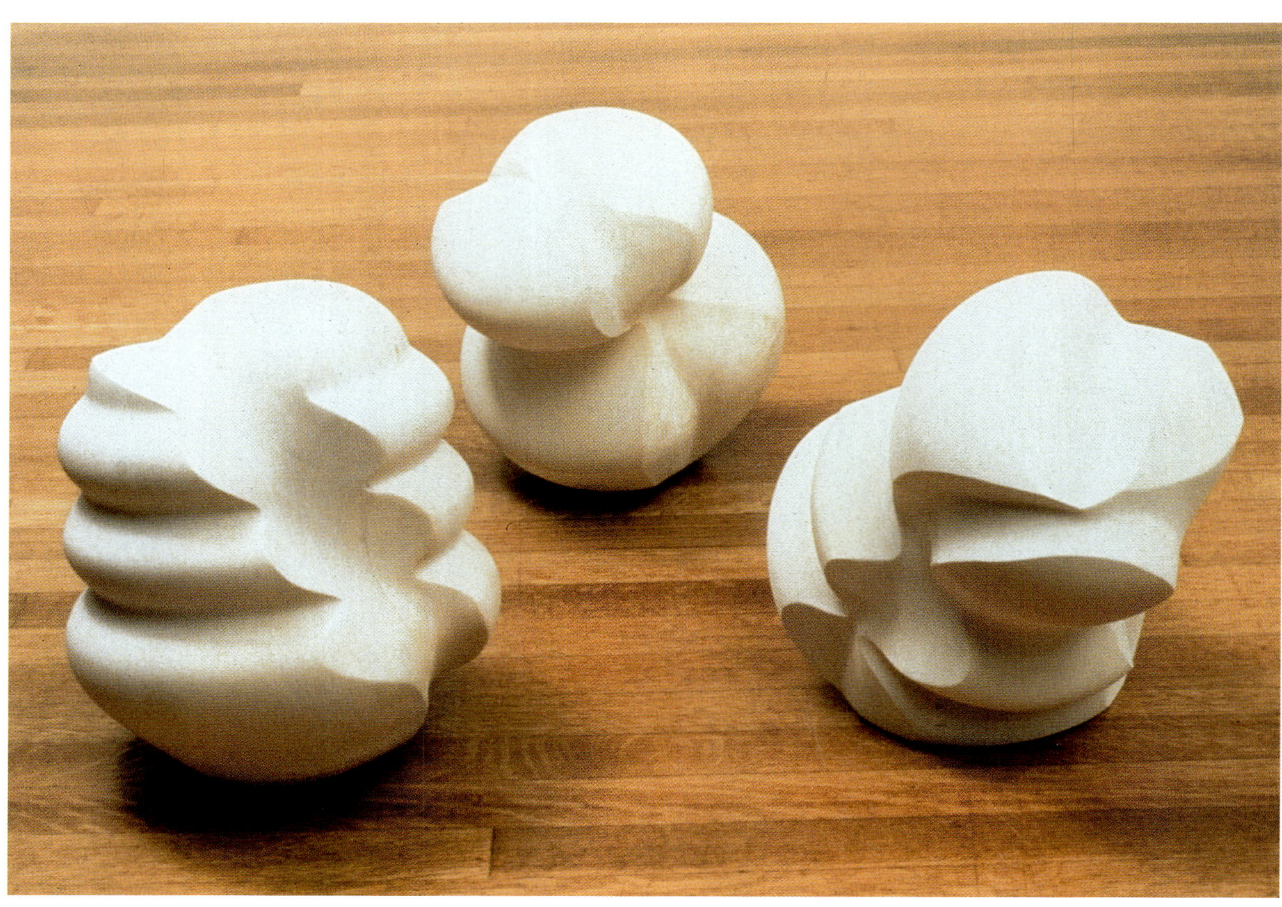

PAST #119, PRESENT #120, FUTURE #121, 1999
LAMINATED, TURNED, CARVED AND LAQUERED BASSWOOD
EACH: 12(HT) X 10(DIAM) INCHES
Past: Collection Robyn and John Horn
Present: Collection Mint Museum of Craft and Design
Charlotte, NC

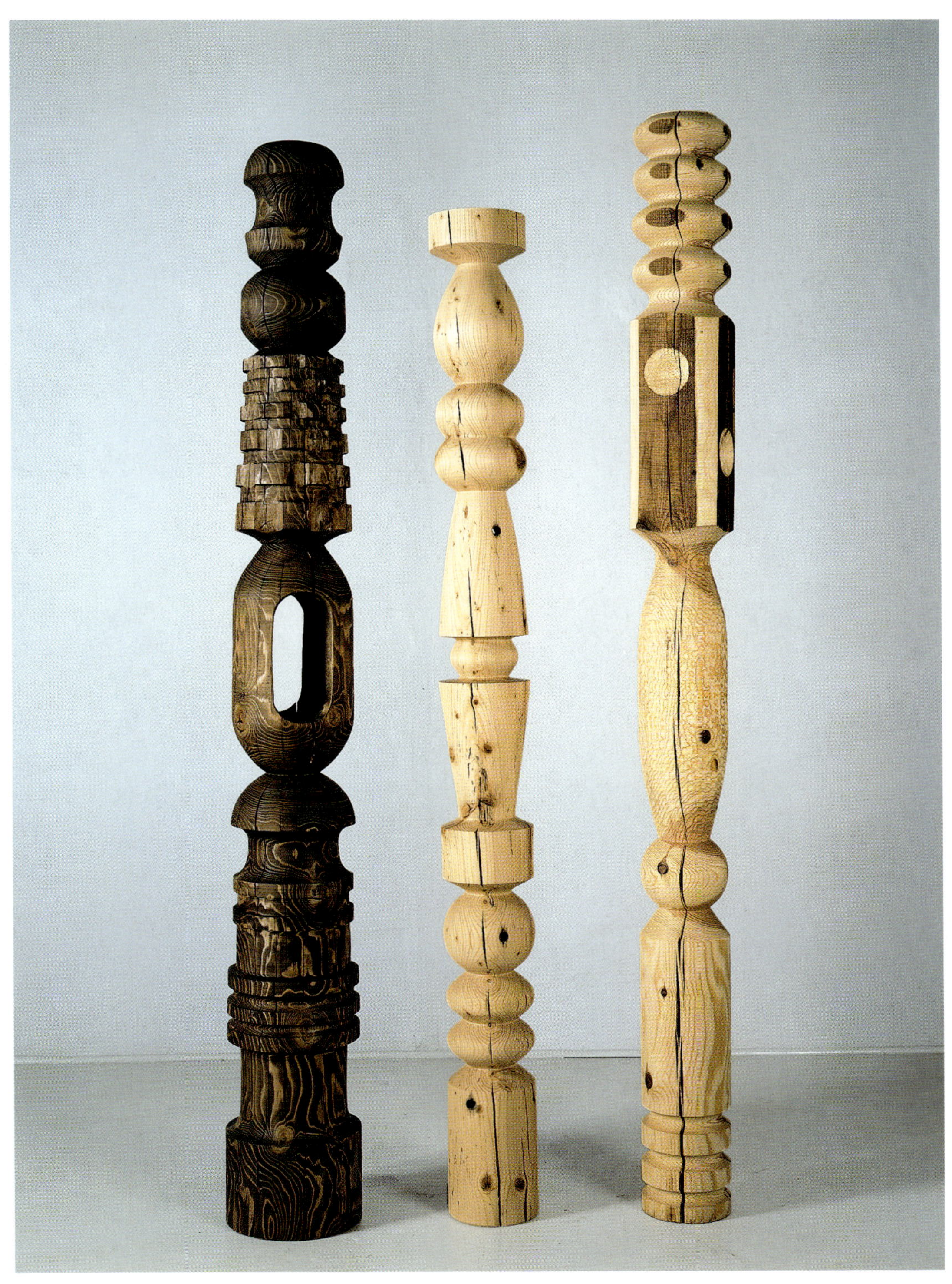

NIGHT TOTEM, STAR TOTEM, MOON TOTEM
FIR STAINED AND OILED
LEFT TO RIGHT:
90(HT) X 10(DIAM) INCHES
85(HT) X 8(DIAM) INCHES
93(HT) X 9(DIAM) INCHES

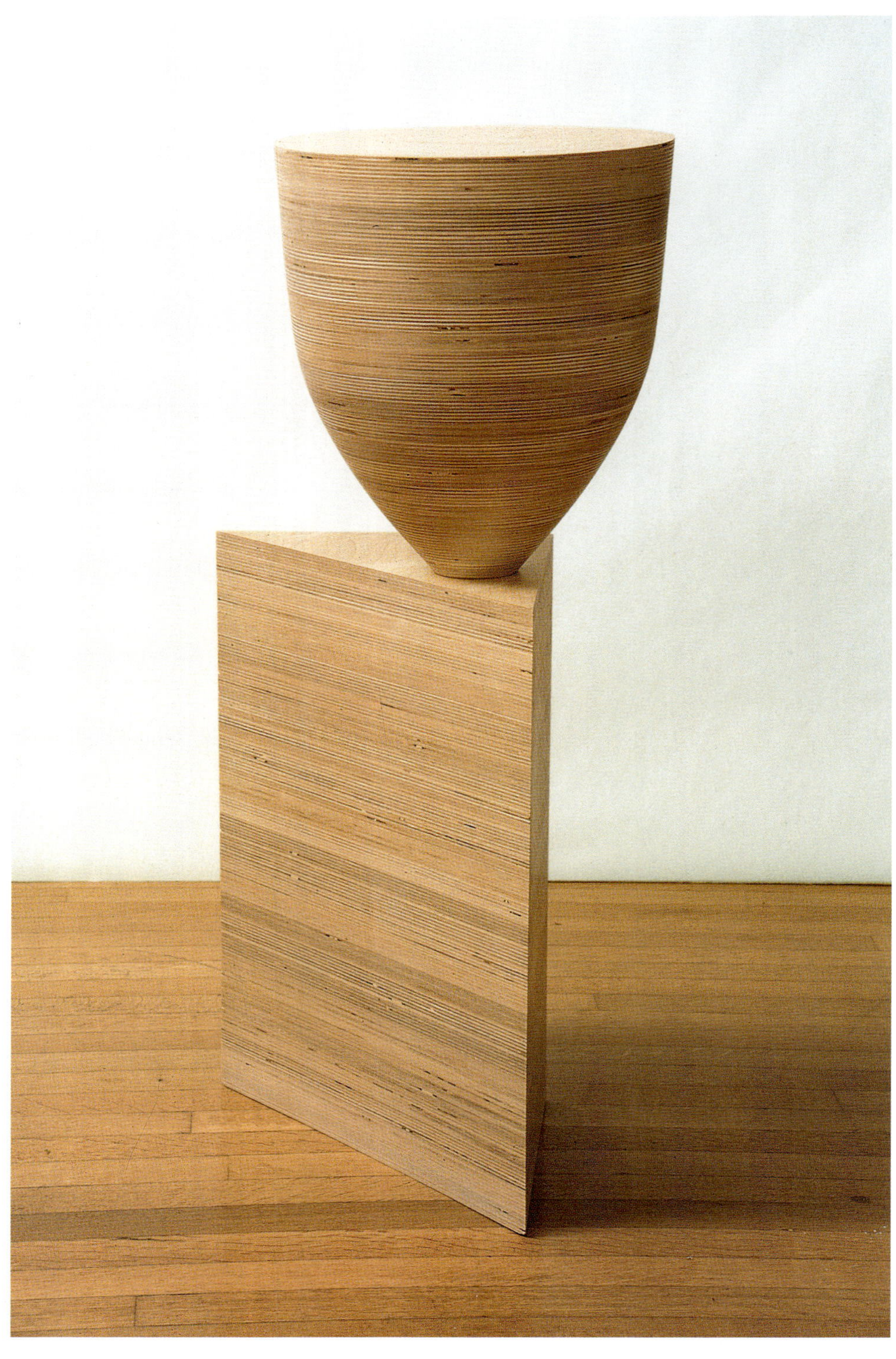

WEDGE, 1998
LAMINATED PLYWOOD, TURNED AND PLANED
34 X 16½ X 13 INCHES

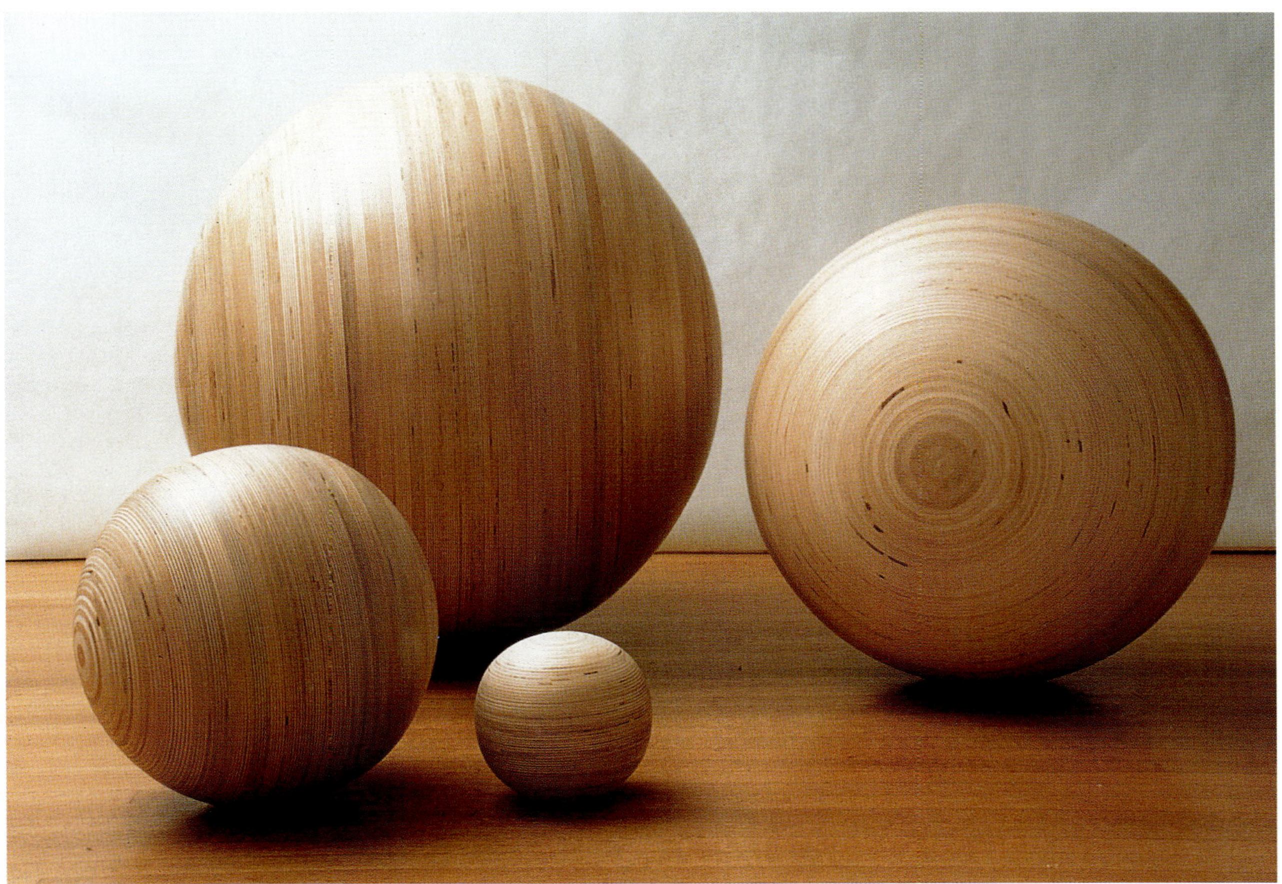

CONNIE MISSISSIPPI b. Greenwood MS. Ed: MFA Pratt Institute NY; BFA Memphis College of the Arts TN. Coll: Los Angeles County Museum of Art CA; Rockefeller University NY; The White House DC; Arkansas Museum of Art AK; Detroit Institute of Art MI; Minneapolis Institute of Art MN; Mint Museum of Craft and Design NC. Representation: Anderson Contemporary Art, Santa Fe.

SPHERES, 2000
LAMINATED AND TURNED BALTIC BIRCH PLYWOOD
30, 25, 16 AND 7 INCH DIAMETER SPHERES

NANCY KOZIKOWSKI

The special province of art and artists is to introduce new elements and ideas into customary ways of thinking about anything and everything. To look at a work of art or to speak with an artist is to expand one's mind. Behind the grid of conventional viewing and personal interaction, endless play and innovation come pouring in. The subject dances. Boundaries are pierced. One can sometimes glimpse the most basic building blocks of thought. Nothing is absolute to an artist, especially not the customary definitions of subject, medium, and style.

Nancy Kozikowski is such a generative abstract painter. In addition to working with pastel on paper, she has become highly skilled in traditional weaving techniques, using them as a non-traditional painting medium in order to create abstract images. "I consider myself a painter who weaves her own canvas," says the artist. "I make my own colors from scratch. Call it very slow expressionism!"

Kozikowski enjoyed one of the most direct and unfiltered educations an artist could ask. She decided on her vocation while she was still in her early teens, and her parents supported her choice. They engaged a relentless art tutor who taught her how to draw anything she could imagine. They took her to see major works by the Abstract Expressionists at a time when they were still the avant-garde. She built an exact copy of a Navajo loom and taught herself to spin, dye, and weave. By the time she finished high school, she was too far ahead of the learning curve to attend art school, so she jumped straight into her career.

"My work has grown out of my environment," she says. "It's not just the Spanish and Navajo traditions, but the landscape as well. Albuquerque's West Mesa is one long hand-drawn line. The way it changes color is stunningly moving. You don't even need an ocean to get that Minimalism, that hugeness. It has challenged me to do really big pieces, and I don't have to make excuses for being abstract."

Nancy Kozikowski is one artist who could easily concentrate on realism because of her fine draftsmanship. Instead, she constantly reconciles the figurative with the abstract, much as Picasso and Matisse bridged the unsophisticated and the modern in their work. "I never try to impose anything on my paintings and weavings," she says. "The most I do is keep eliminating anything that doesn't work. I feel that if a piece communicates with me, it could engage the imagination of someone else. I think that I choose one design over another because any work of art, by any artist, is always a kind of self portrait. Possibly it's an expression of our molecular structure."

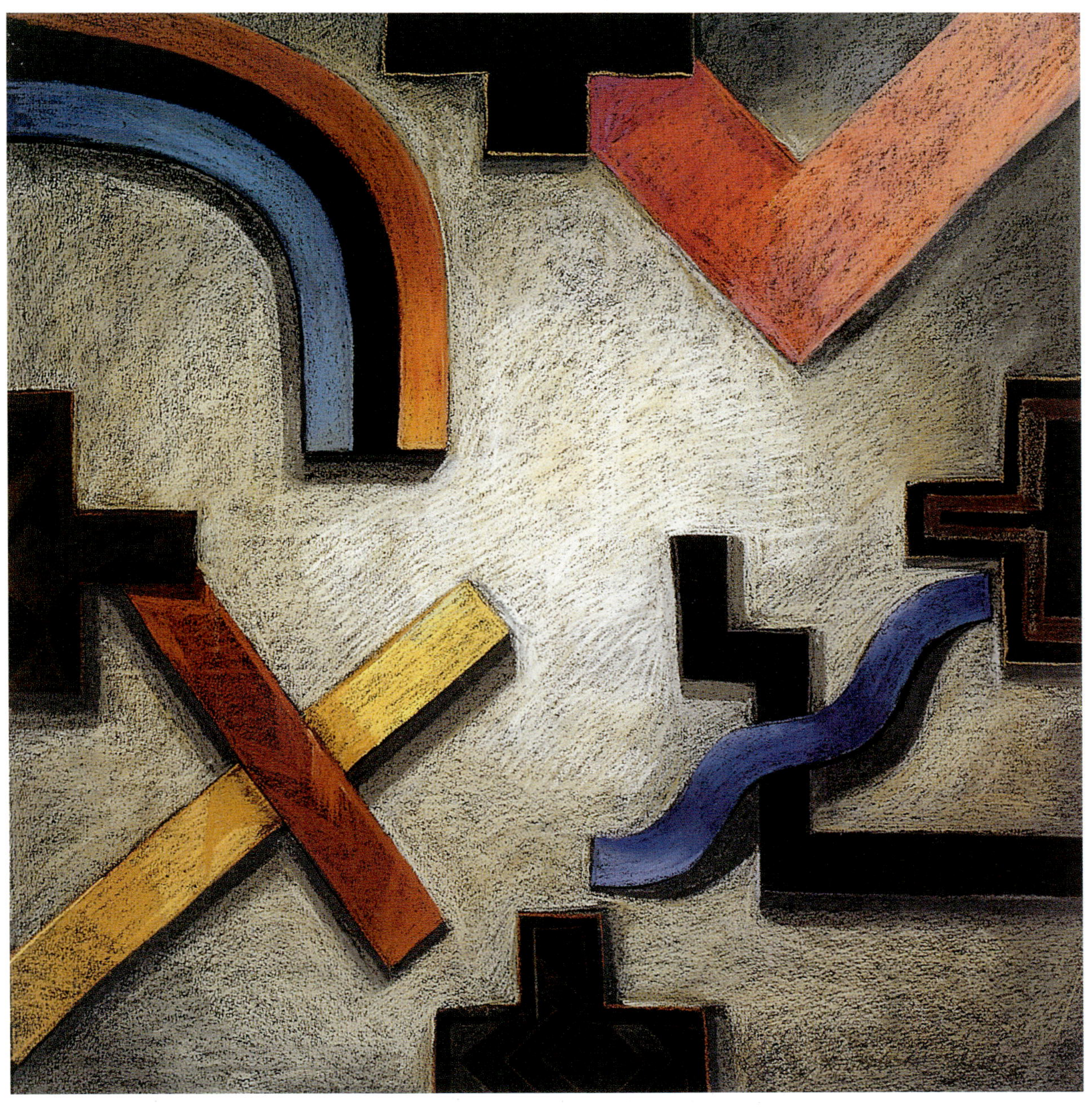

TETRES/PAPER
PASTEL
30 X 30 INCHES

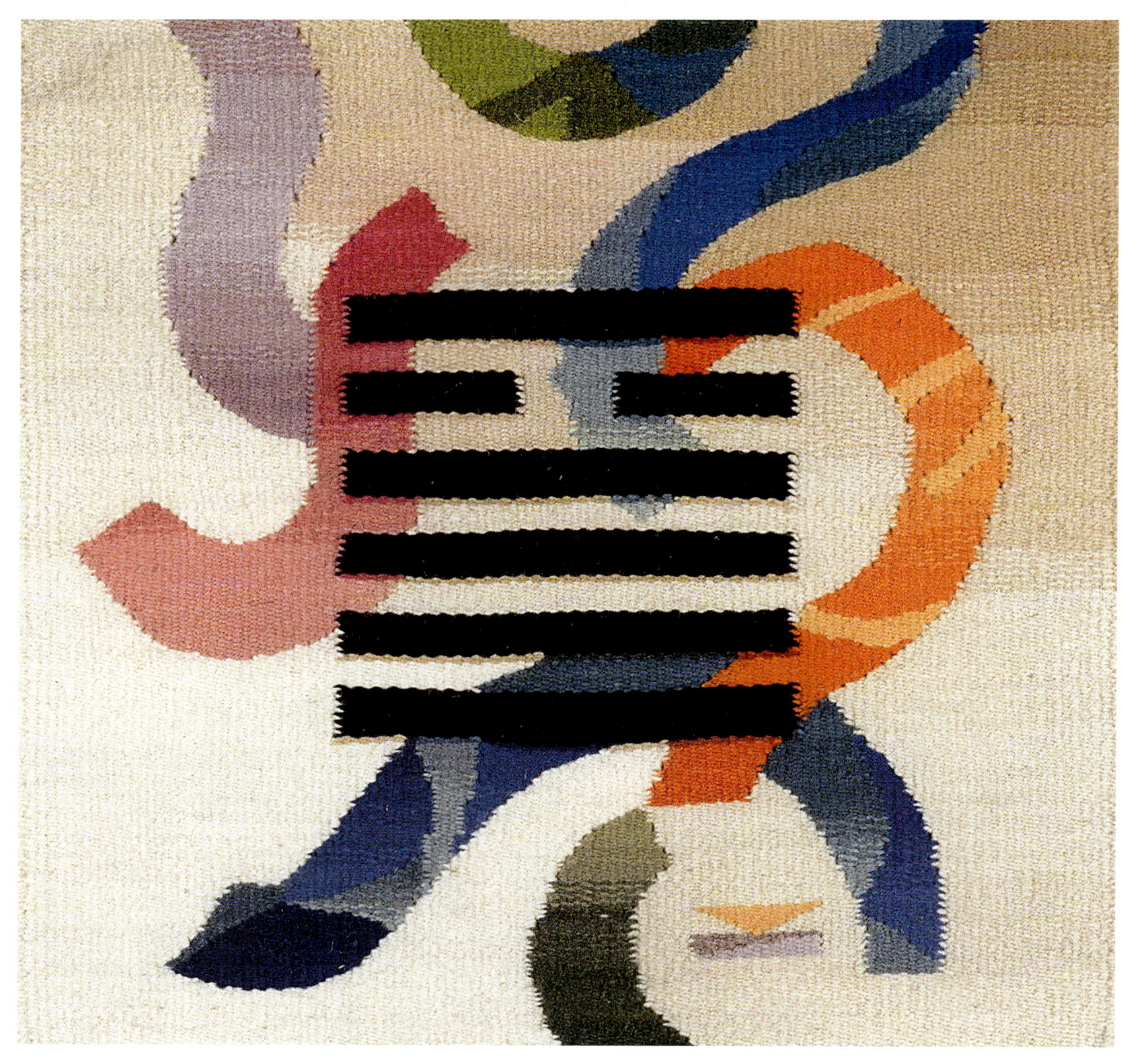

PROSPERITY 2
HAND DYED, HAND WOVEN
20 X 21 INCHES

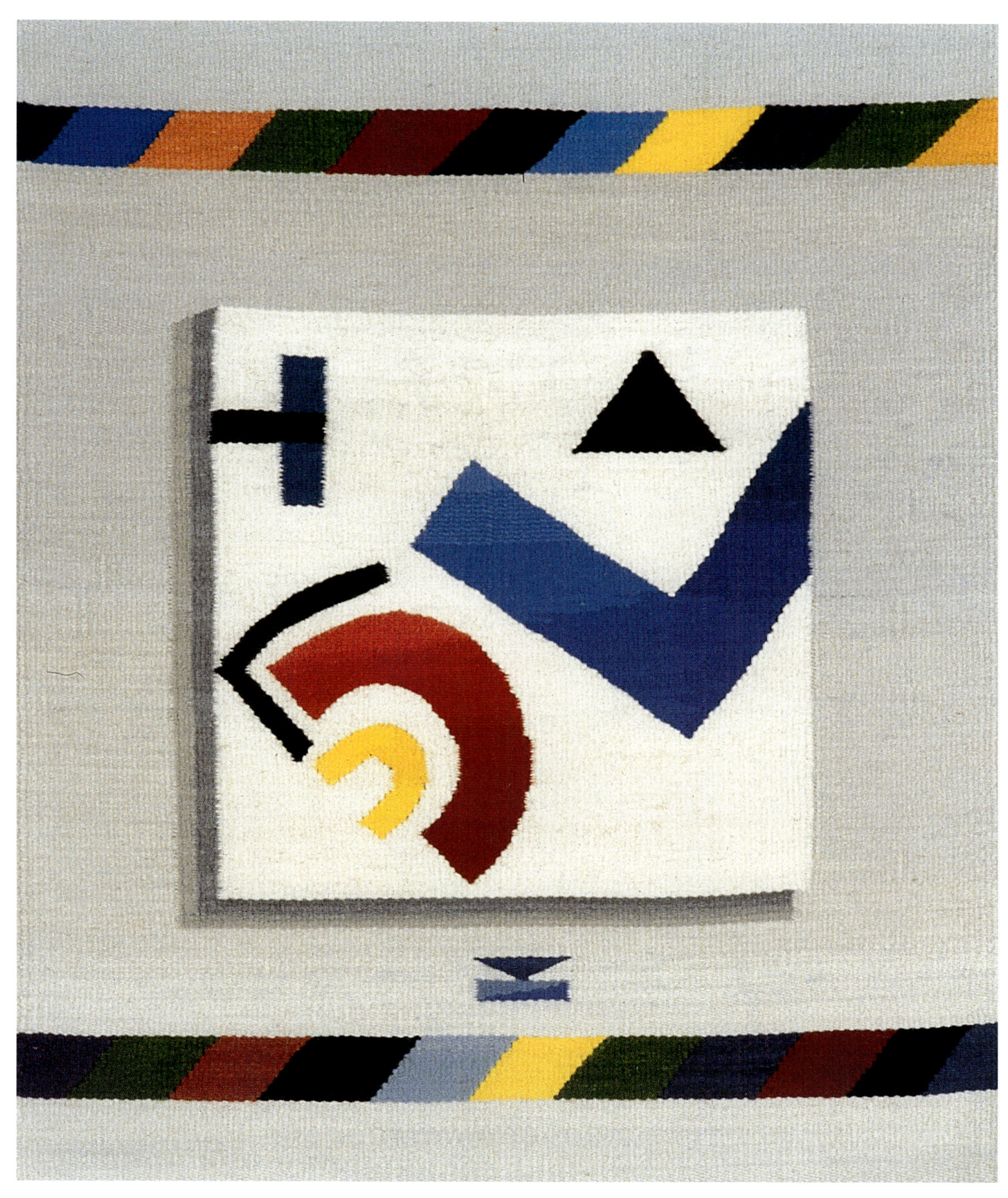

CHARACTERS II
HAND DYED, HAND WOVEN
29 X 30 INCHES

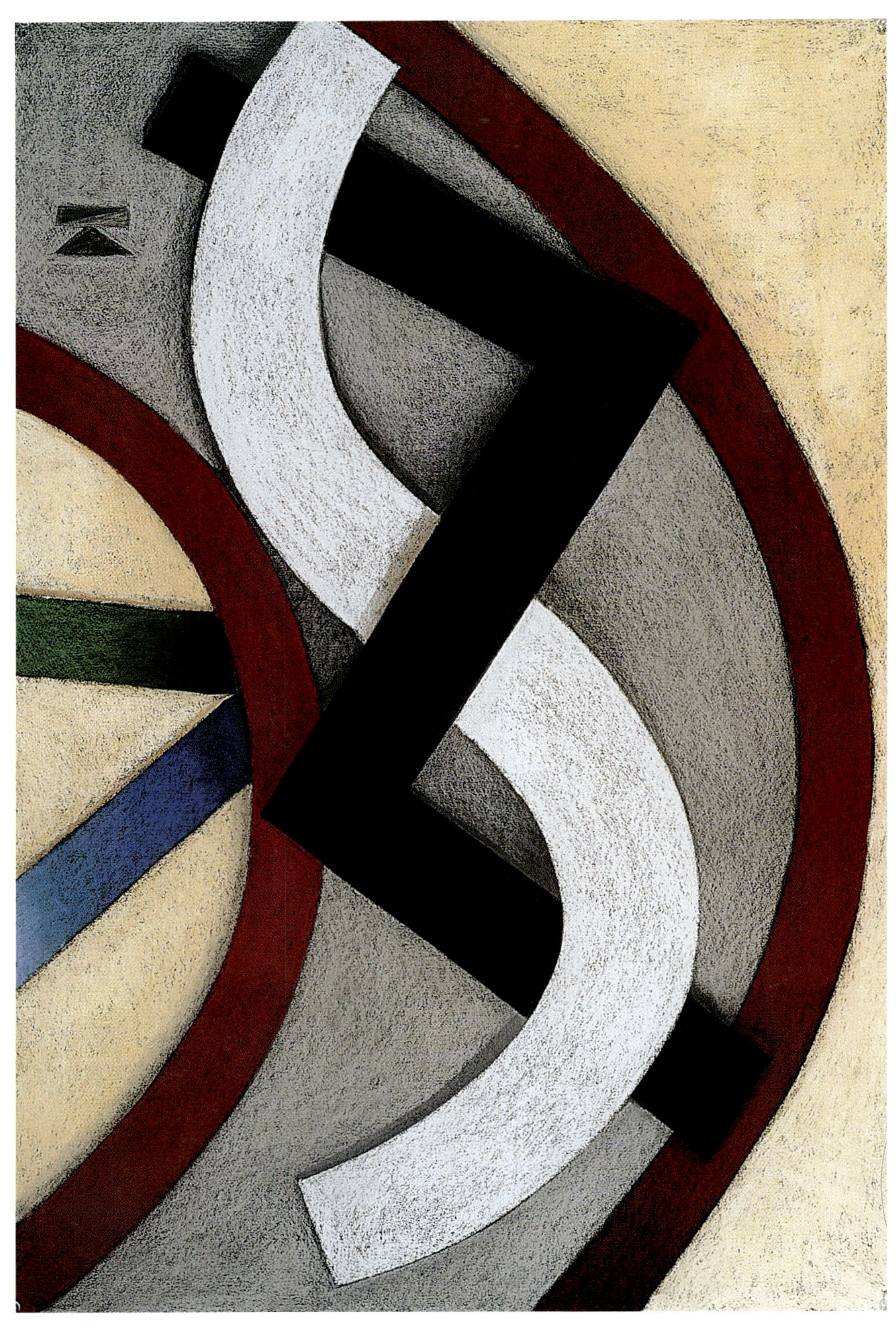

US BELT
PASTEL/PAPER
44 X 30 INCHES

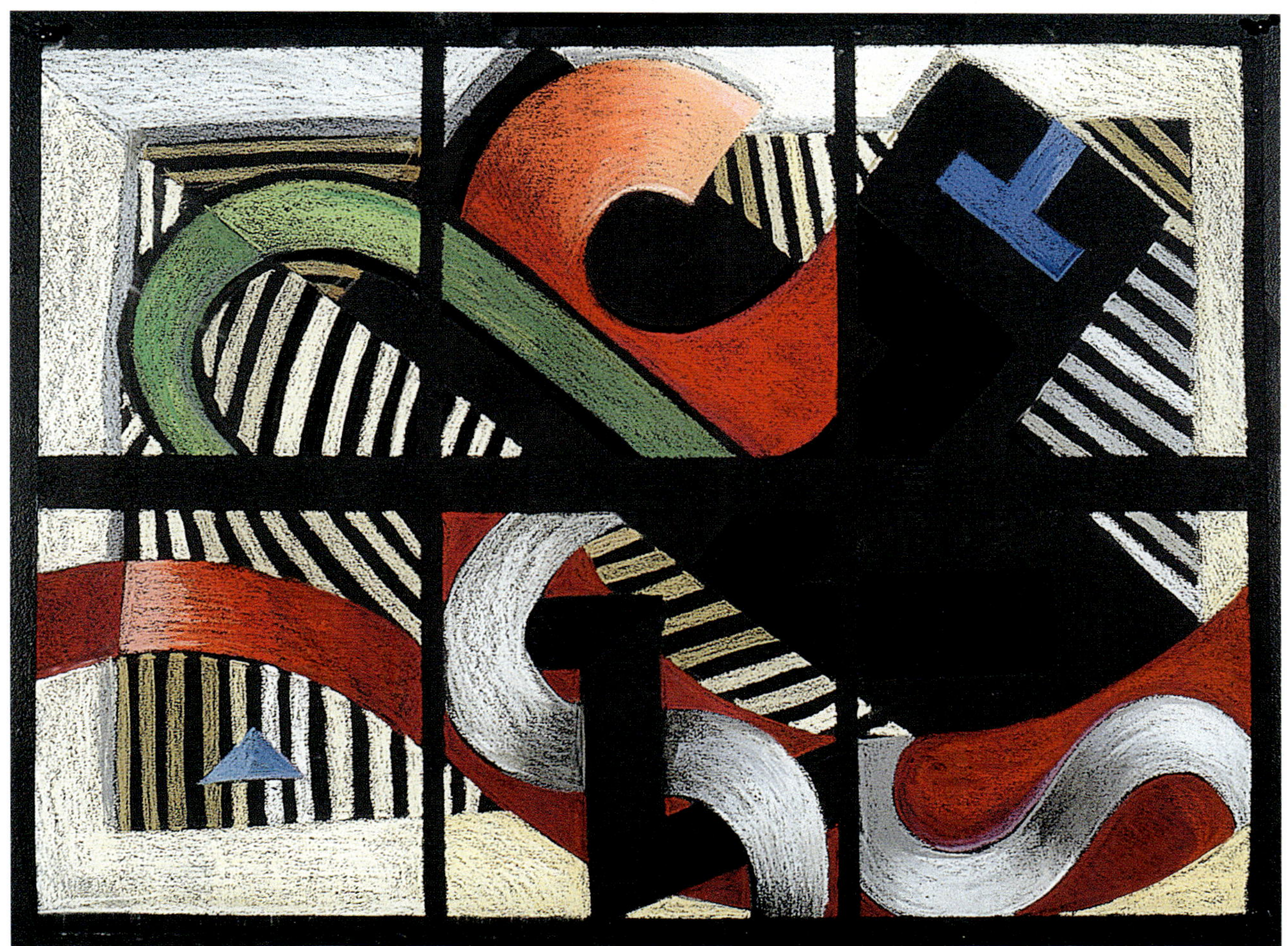

NANCY KOZIKOWSKI b. 1943 Albuquerque NM. Coll: Smithsonian Institution, Washington DC; Albuquerque Museum; Massachusetts General Hospital, Boston; Neutrogena Corporation; The Vatican.

SECOND GRID
PASTEL/PAPER
44 X 30 INCHES

MERCEDES LITTLE CROW VELARDE

The geometry of the natural and built environment, from early civilizations to the present, is fertile ground for abstract art. The crisp, angular forms of quartz crystals and dolomite, the cellular structure of leaves, and the organic asymmetry of constellations and microorganisms lend an organizing structure to our view of nature. The marks of humankind upon the land, from ancient pictographs to aerial views of remote villages to the geometric grace of interstate highways, add a diagrammatic language that can be decoded, interpreted, and reconciled by artists who work in a nonfigurative mode.

Mercedes Little Crow Velarde begins with this structure and language, then takes it a step further, deconstructing the known to reconstruct a new possibility, creating abstract images that whisper to the innermost thoughts while teasing at the outer edges of the mind. In her art, there is no duality between inner and outer, microcosm and macrocosm. There is only the organic whole.

"What you see on the canvas," she explains, "is more like the cellular structure of a much larger idea. In terms of language, it's beyond the dictionary, bigger than an alphabet, more than a concept. You have to get the message through the body, not the mind."

Little Crow Velarde builds her canvases in a very physical way, addressing her ideas directly without drawing anything first. She goes right in and applies many layers of pigment with a palette knife, creating the most intricate textures imaginable. The drawing comes in between the layers as a non-recognizable language surfacing to the top. The result, paradoxically, is a surface that almost looks worn down, as if it carried the memory of messages written through time. Blooming from this rich and fertile encrustation are "windows, oxidations in the form of threads, vortices, open ended pyramids and the hues of organic mulch." The eye synthesizes them into an almost comprehensible pattern.

Recently, Little Crow Velarde has become interested in another optic phenomenon called phosphenes, which are the brilliantly luminous images that spontaneously illuminate the field of vision in quick flashes during altered states of consciousness. They are taking her into new and exciting realms. "I don't know where I'm going next," she says, "but I'm headed toward a bigger area of non-structure."

In the hands of Mercedes Little Crow Velarde, every painting is a step in her personal journey, a curve in the road that leads to viewpoints in time. The signposts have no words or even symbols, yet they mark the way to the past and the future. Like hieroglyphics peeking through the intricate layers of memory and circumstance, these paintings hold out the possibility of communication with other planes of existence. They furnish a code of entry, a map of subliminal experience, a language of all the senses.

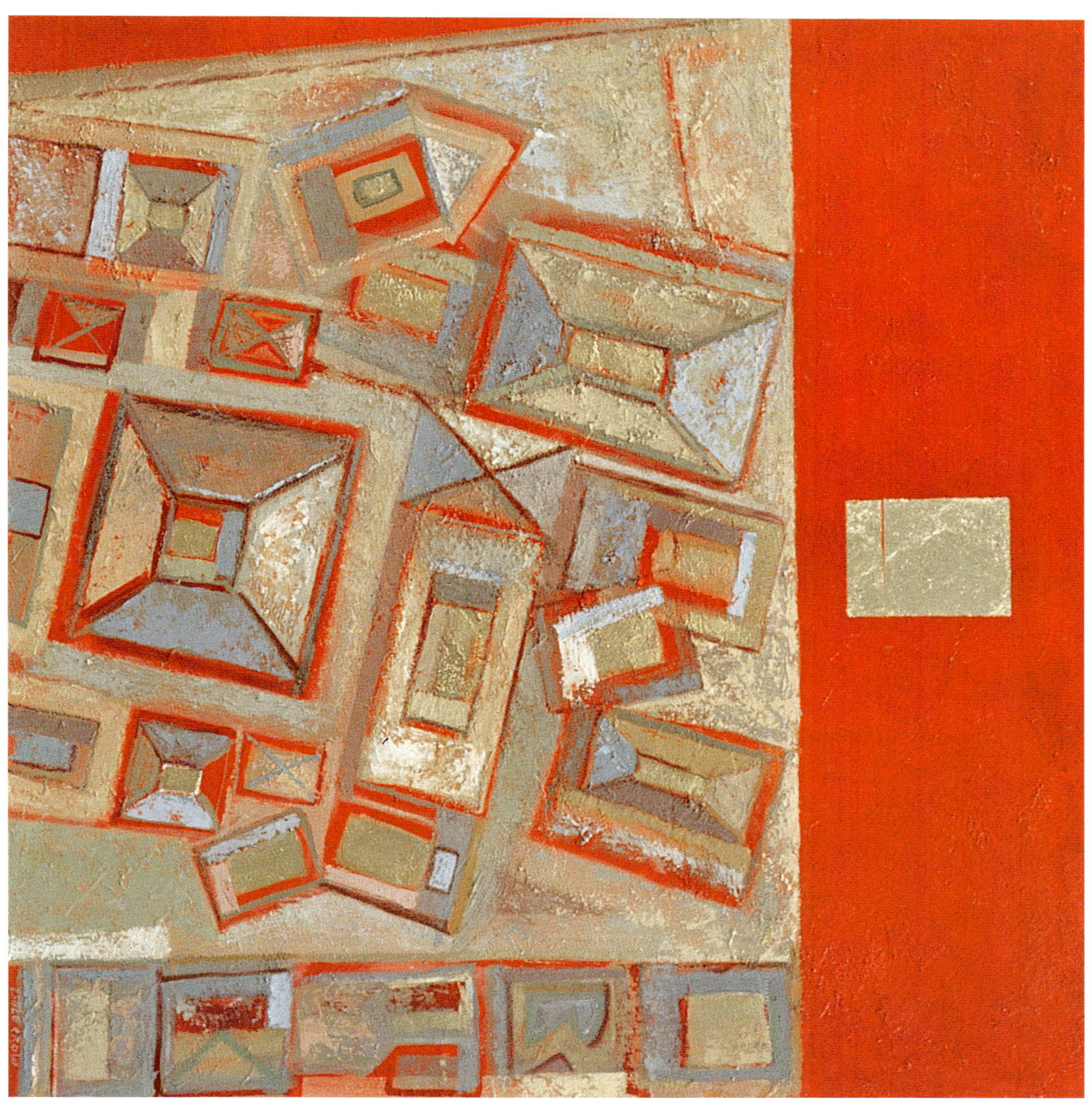

AERIAL SITE
OIL
48 X 48 INCHES

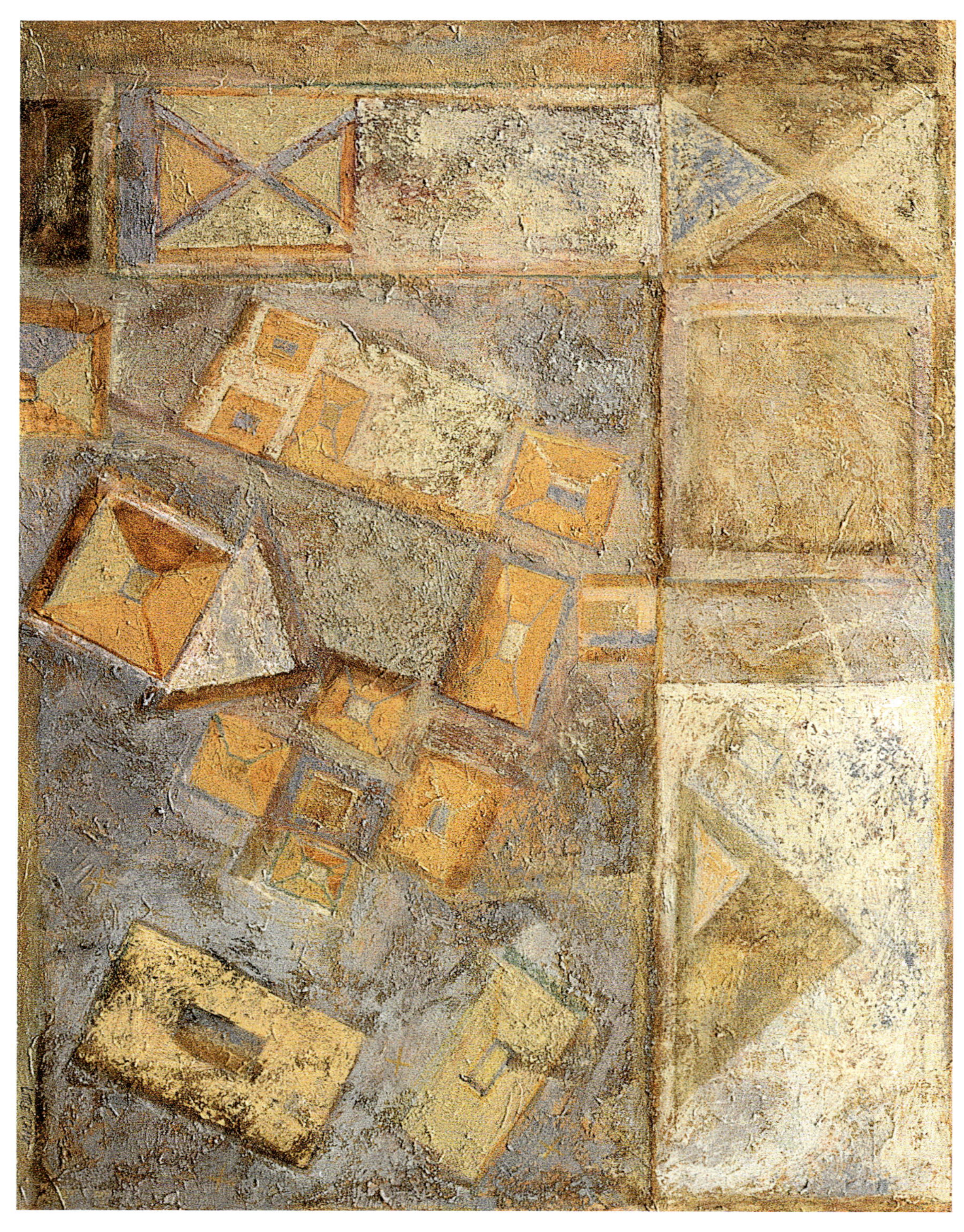

AERIAL SITE II
OIL
48 X 60 INCHES

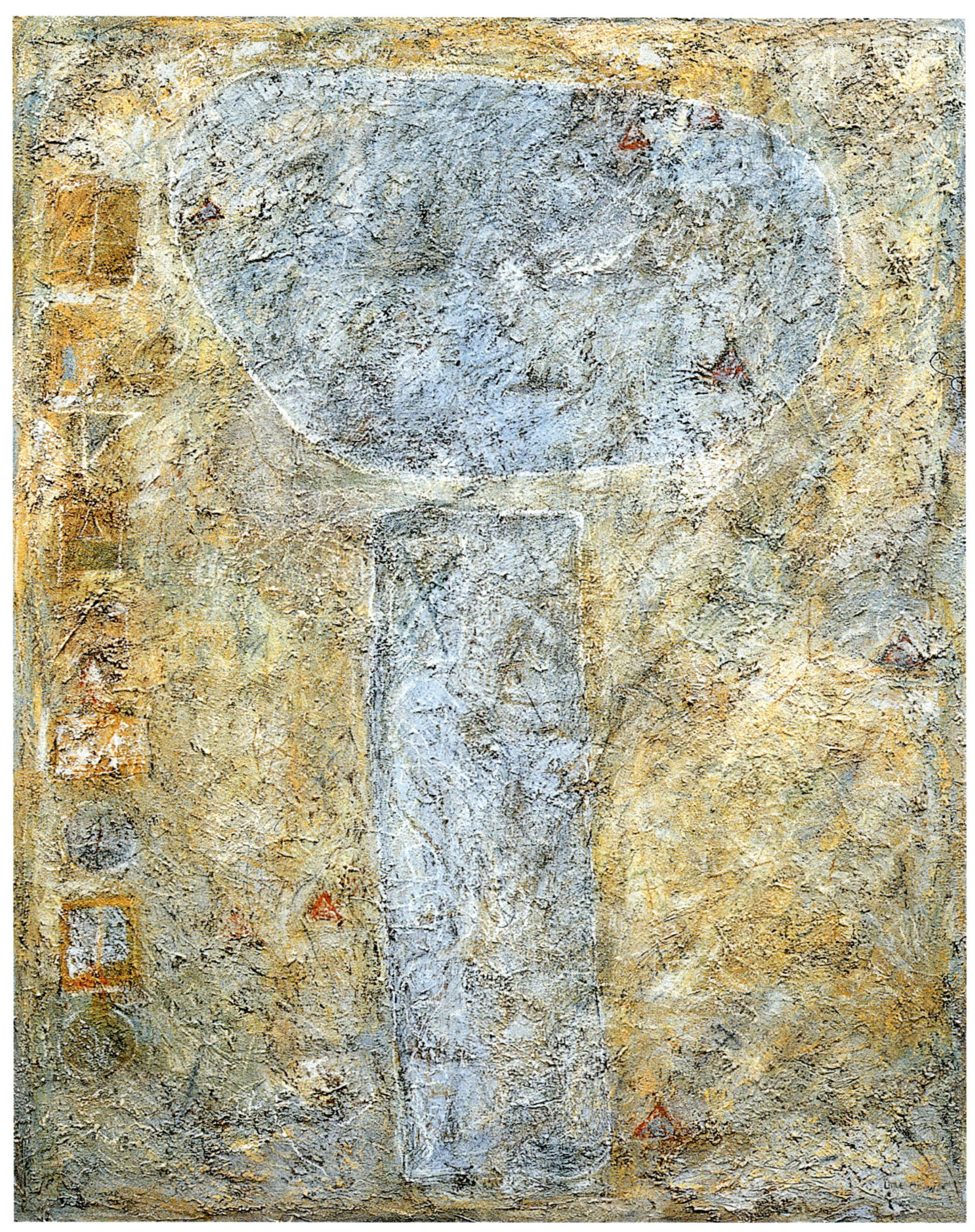

ARTEFACTO SERIES
OIL
48 X 60 INCHES

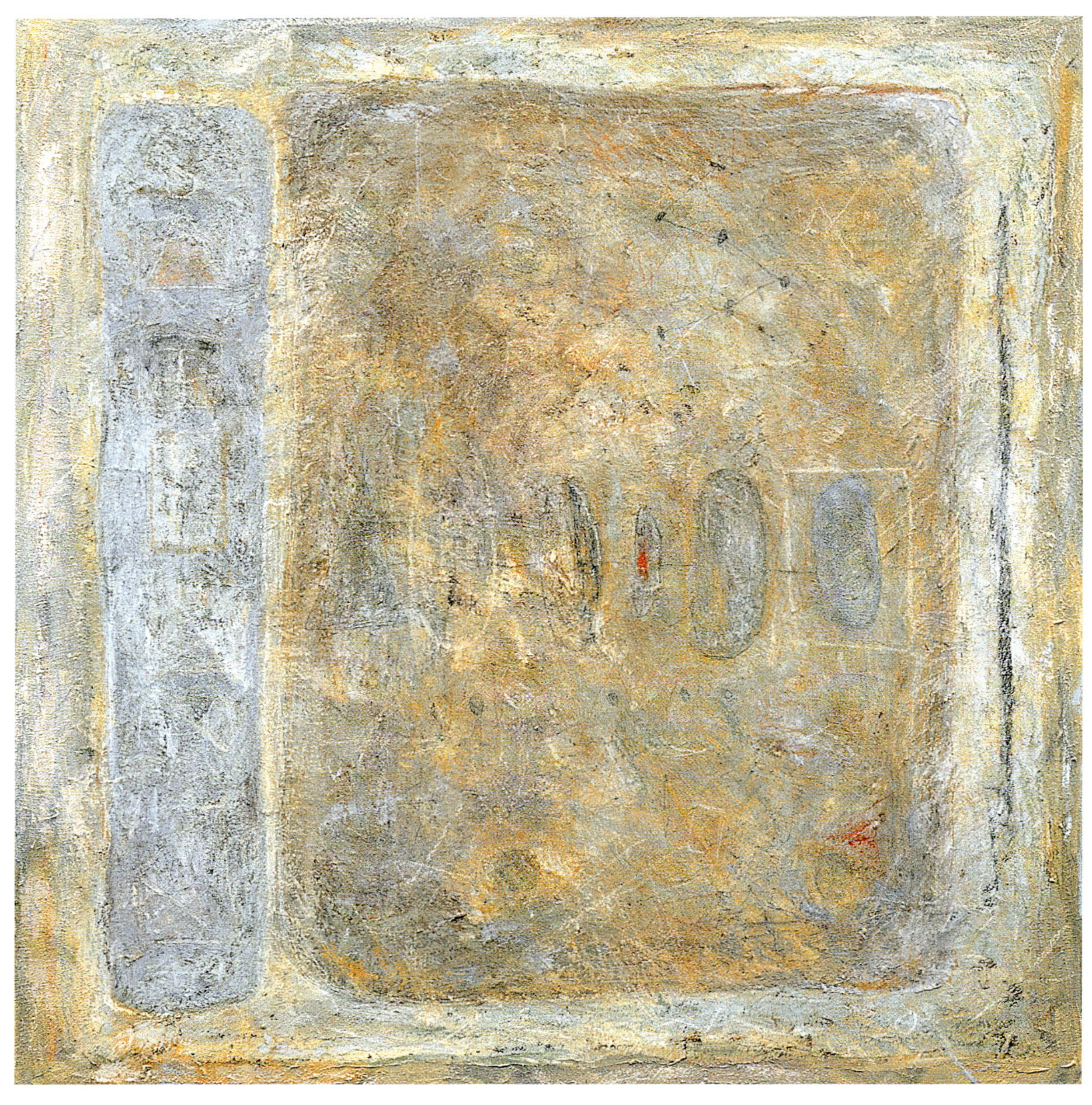

ARTEFACTO SERIES II
OIL
48 X 48 INCHES

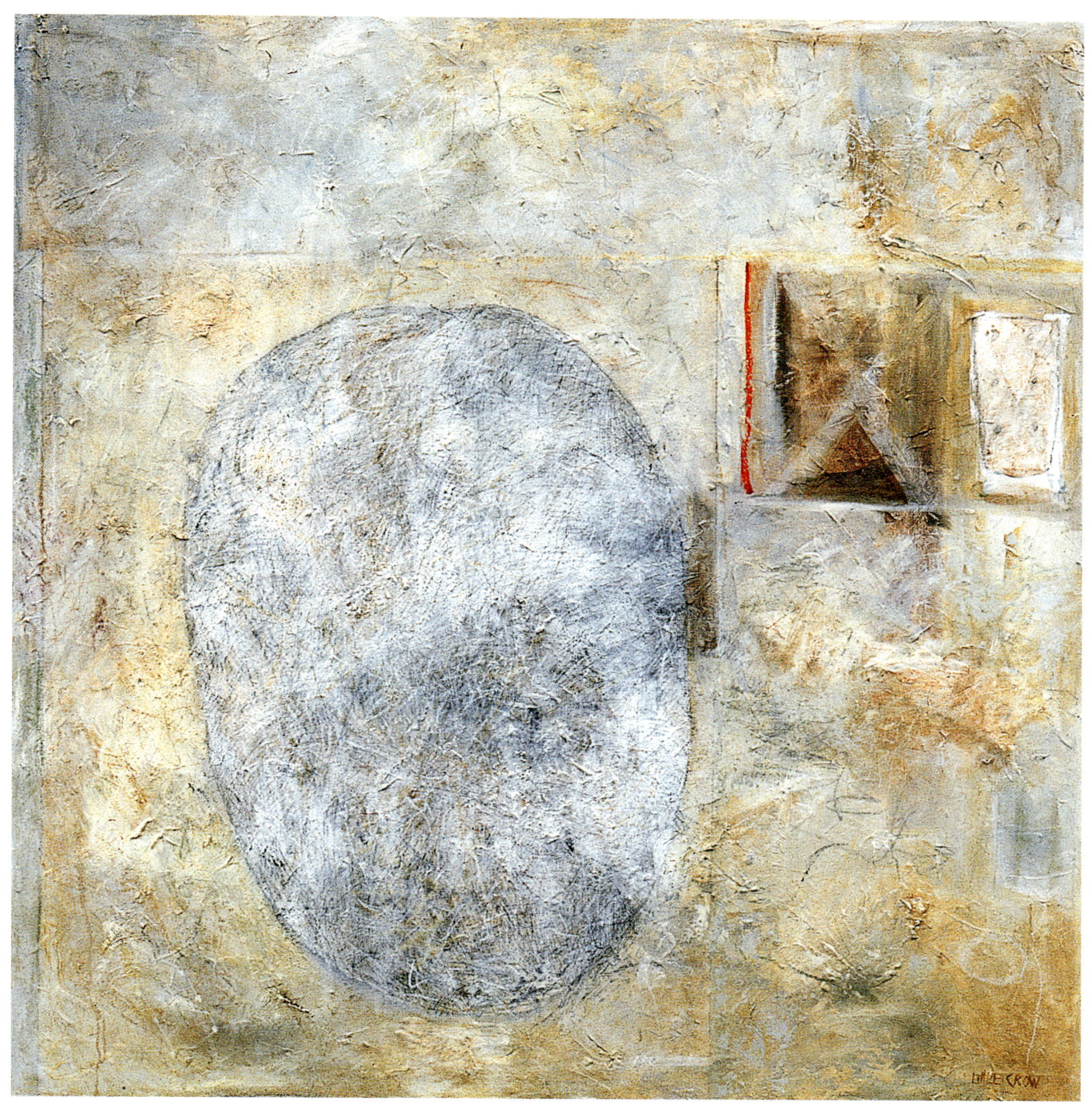

MERCEDES LITTLE CROW VELARDE b. 1943 Mexico. Ed. Universidad National Autonomo de Mexico; Otis Art Institute, Chouinard (now Cal Arts) Los Angeles; MA Univ. Saskatchewan. Exhib: El Museo Museum, Mexico; Hispanic Market NM. Coll: Heard Museum AZ. Representation: Little Crow Gallery, Santa Fe.

ARTIFACTO SERIES III
OIL
48 X 48 INCHES

PASCAL

In the universal tongue that is abstract sculpture, three dimensional objects assume many forms and functions. They serve as symbols and sentinels, totems and signposts, ceremonial objects and freestanding works of art. Some pieces are fortresslike, others almost anthropomorphic. Wood and stone and metal work alone or together, sometimes in surprising ways, as when a wood form appears to break open and reveal a metal interior. Above all, abstract sculpture, particularly when it is made of wood, exerts a tactile appeal that asks the viewer to stand near and share the physical space.

The sculpture of Pascal is a fine example of the compelling quality of wood. Pascal is a Frenchman who settled in Santa Fe in 1997. Prior to that time, he had gained a European reputation as a promising young sculptor. He fielded a series of solo exhibitions in France and Switzerland, and worked on collaborative projects with Pierre Cardin and others.

Pascal's career has blossomed in America. He has been awarded several commissions for large-scale installations. Galleries and collectors alike have responded to the simplicity of his approach, which balances geometric abstraction with organic form. There is an undertone of symbolism as well, a hieroglyphic shorthand that hints at other visual languages.

Pascal was influenced from a very young age by his grandfather, a wood sculptor. It was from him that Pascal developed his love for wood and his passion for working with it. He creates an extraordinary range of abstract meditations that seem to arise directly from the material itself, rather than from a conscious plan. He has an extraordinary rapport with his materials, concocting his own varnishes and resins as well as creating bronze-like patinas on non-metallic surfaces. He works with a variety of precious woods and creates sculptures that express the texture, aroma, and strength of each.

He considers wood to be a feminine material - warm, colorful, full of surprises, and not always easy to control. Therefore, many of his sculptures have a feminine cast, with elegantly swelling contours and subtle curves. Conversely, he sometimes works with more angular, masculine themes, such as his Fleche (Arrow) series, and the wood responds with a robust presence.

Pascal's technique is interactive. Each work of art is characterized by a graceful balance, a meticulous attention to detail. Even as he carves and burnishes, he allows the piece to guide him. "Wood has its own intelligence," he says. "It knows many things, and it teaches them to me. In this way, I understand what I want to do with it, so that the final image reflects its innate qualities as well as my own thoughts and feelings."

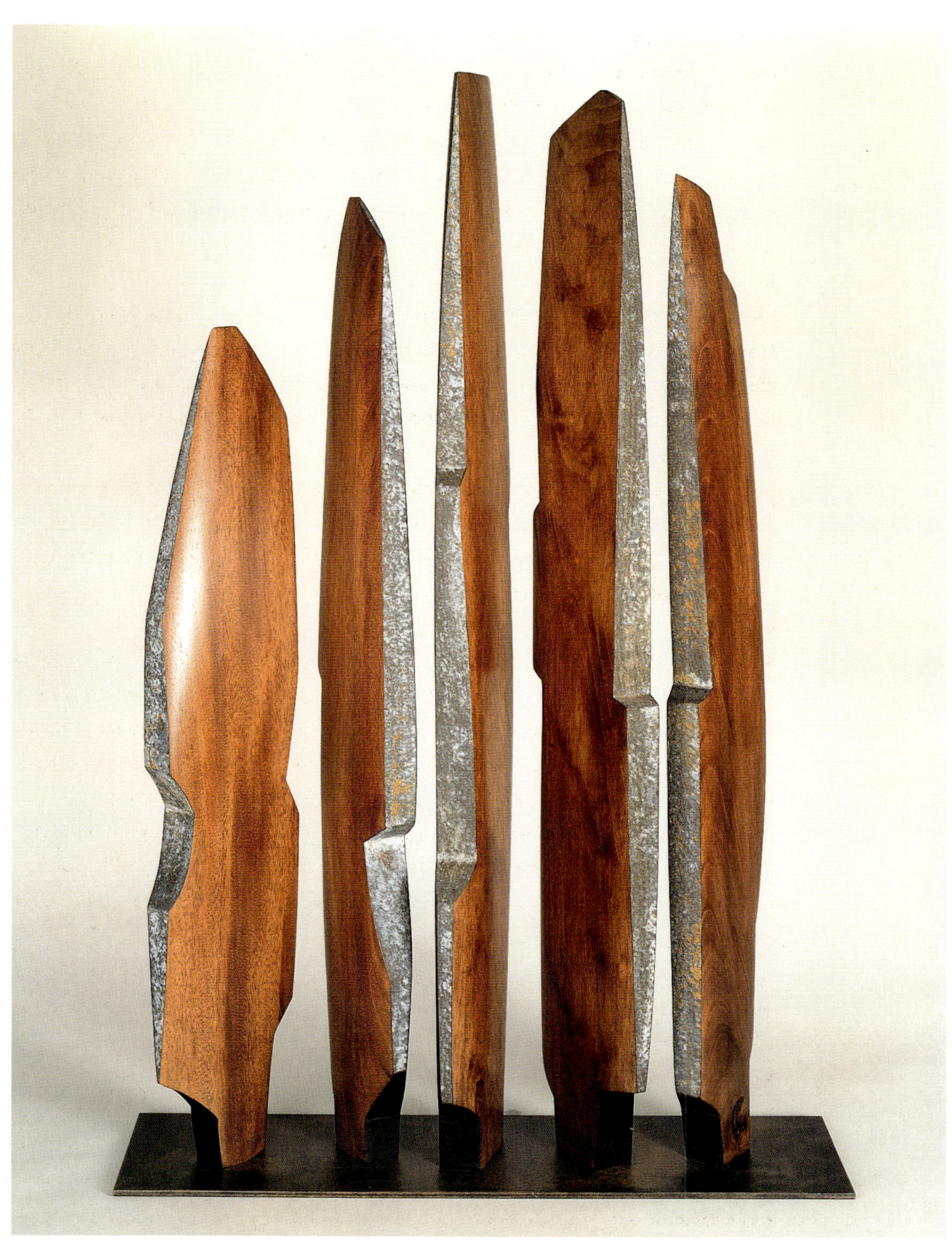

MÉMOIRE EN 3 DIMENSIONS
MAHOGANY
44 X 28 X 8 INCHES

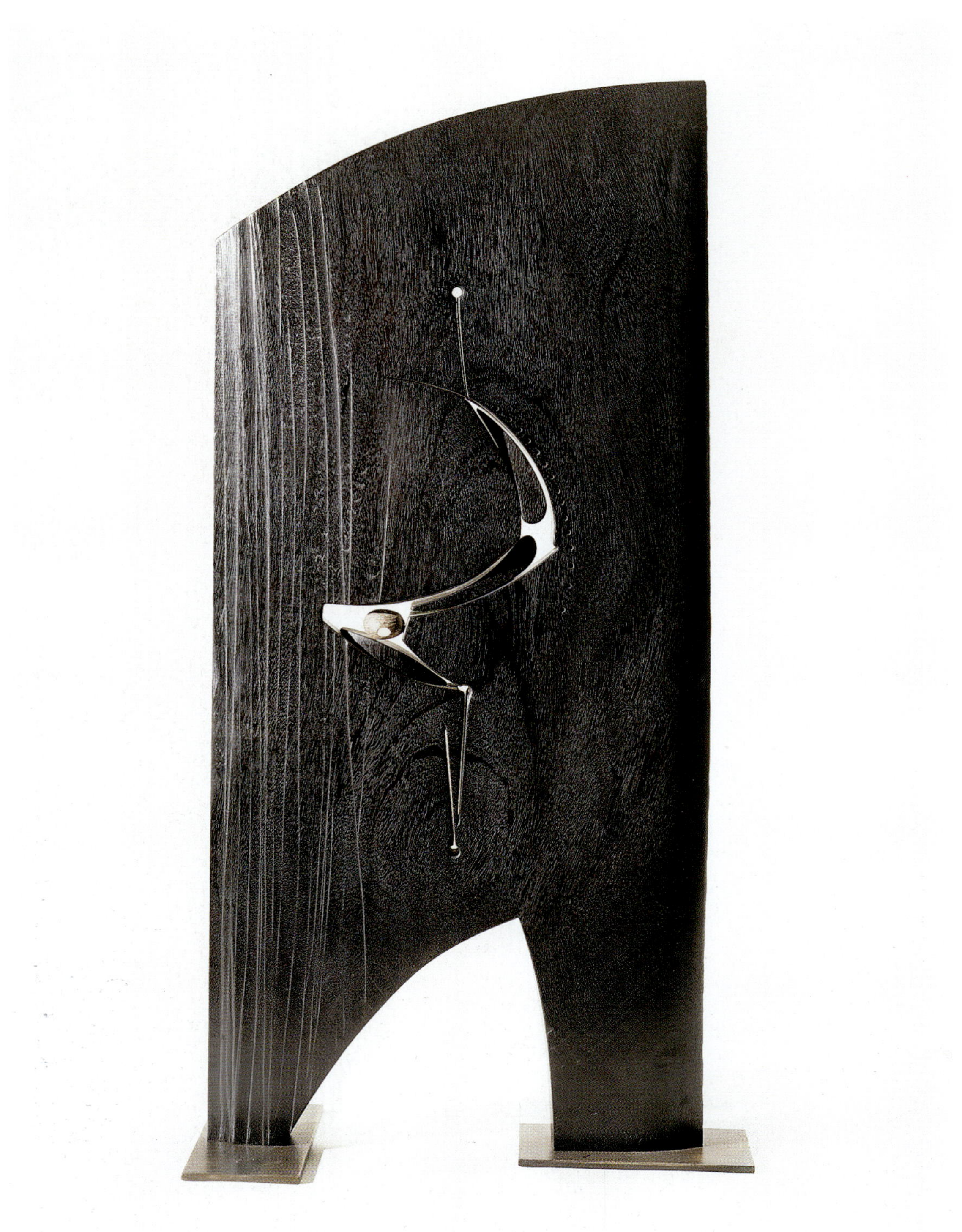

FRACTION I
MAHOGANY
38 X 18 X 7 INCHES

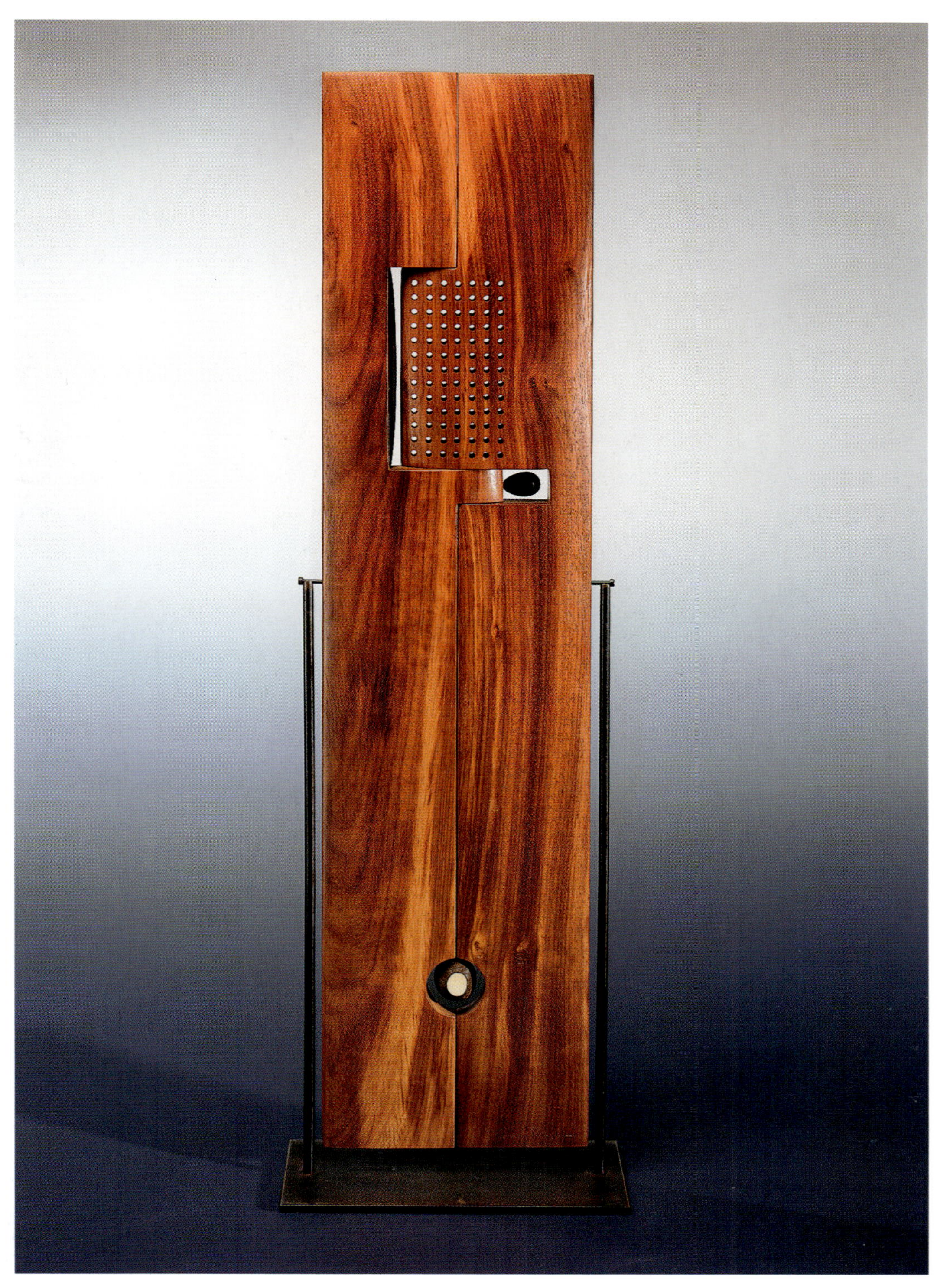

FLÈCHE SYNERGIE
AFRICAN PADAUK
40 X 10 X 6 INCHES

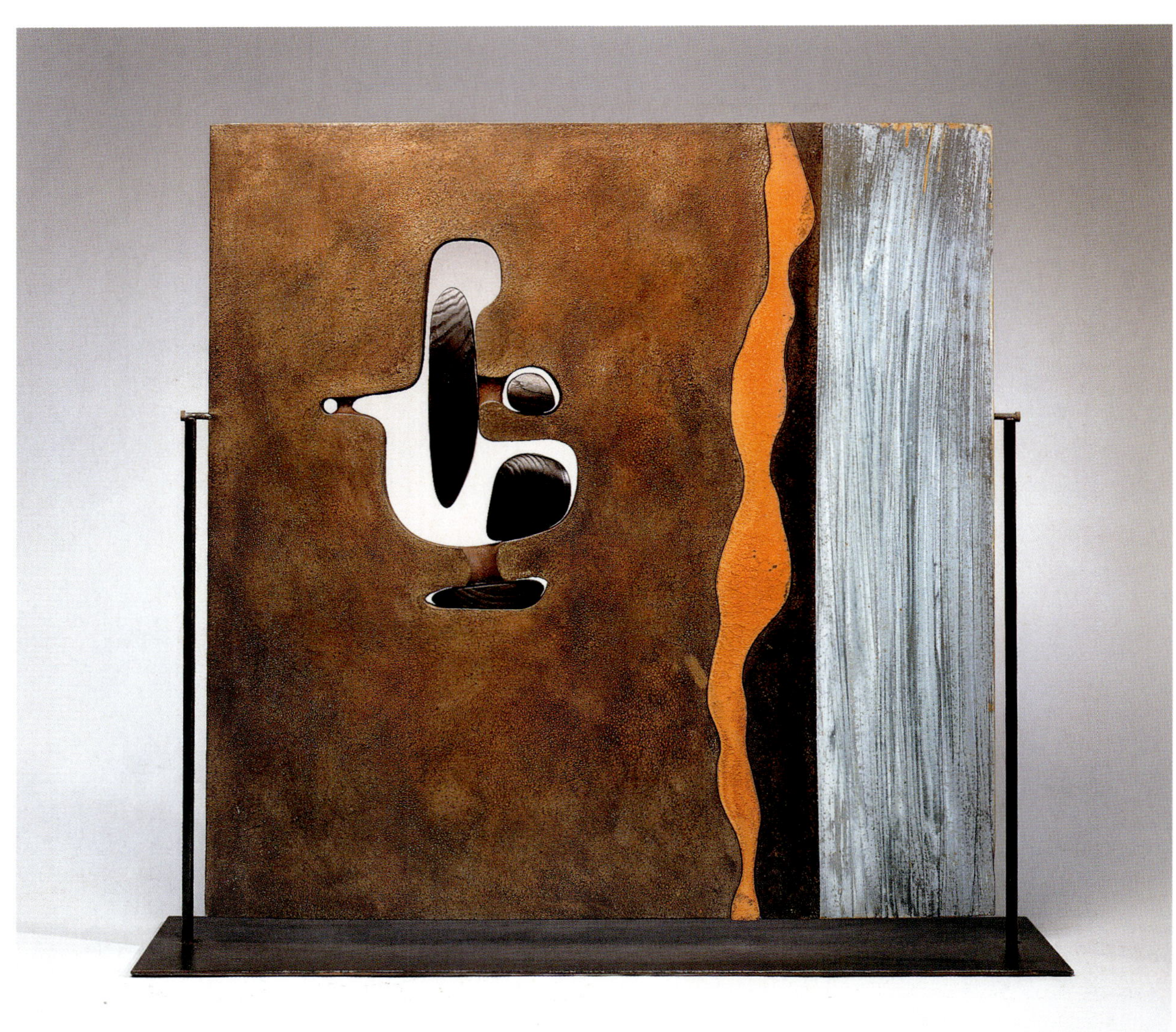

OPOSÉ 8
MIXED MEDIA
42 X 42 X 5 INCHES

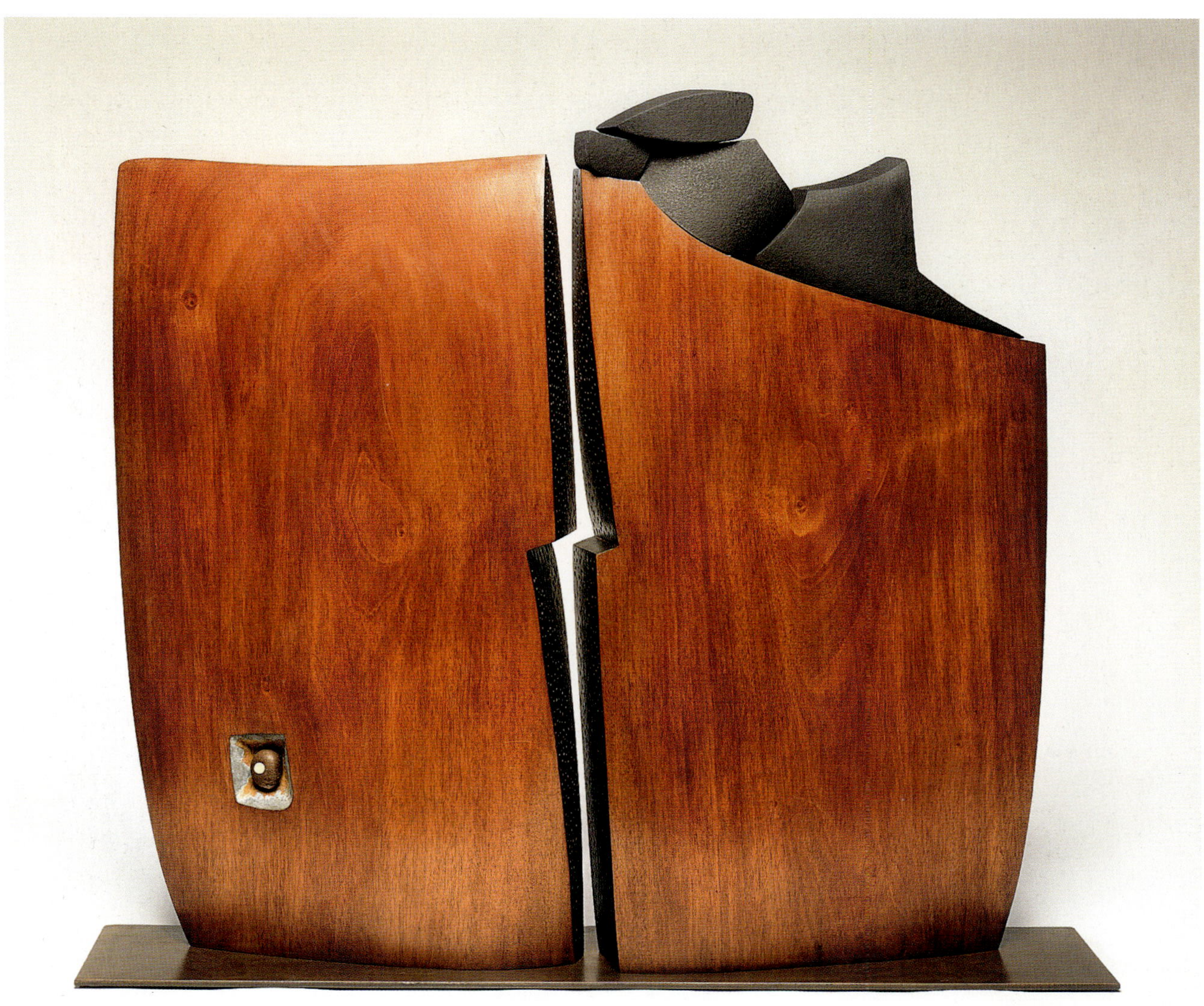

PASCAL b. 1962 St. Raphael, France. Ed. San Rafael, France; San Diego CA; Belfiort, Pietra Santa, Italy. Collaboration for urban project, architect Anti Lovag; assistant muralist, "Pala s-Bulle," a house sculpture, for Pierre Cardin. National Artist Registry, Art in Architecture USA; Art In Embassies Program, USA. Representation: Seven-O-Seven Contemporary Art, Santa Fe.

RENCONTRE
MAHOGANY
37 X 42 X 10 INCHES

ERNEST WILMETH

Silence is golden. It informs ceremony; it reveals the telling detail; it speaks of eternity. It affords the luxury of restraint and the refinement of formality. Silence permits a slow awakening to life.

In the hush of sunrise, immediately before the birds begin their morning chorus, the last moments of an opulent dream rise like incense off the lake. For a moment, there is peace.

Ernest Wilmeth's tranquil art filters out the roar and chatter of the universe, yet it imparts beauty and excitement to the experience of those who see it. Like the untold worlds behind a single face, each painting and collage offers up an inscrutable mask, burnished and vibrant, whole and polished, private and ultimately unknowable. The lovely appearance of each piece only seems to reveal its content.

Wilmeth creates collages of handmade and commercial papers that are torn and applied to an underpainting of acrylic on paper or canvas. Frequently, he chooses translucent Japanese rice papers that are richly textured with fiber and bits of raw natural material, then introduces delicate color to define their placement. Subtle markings, suggesting Kanji characters or the rhythmic design of kimono fabric, bring focus and detail to the composition.

In a related body of work, he arranges precious metals with mathematical precision against inky black acrylic paint. Geometric forms of gold, silver, and copper leaf, set off with an occasional highlight of color, balance themselves serenely between metaphor and abstraction.

Wilmeth's work concerns itself with the structure of the spirit, with the balance and embellishment that set one personality apart from another. "We take our experience and conceal it in our art," he says. "We're all talking in one sense or another about ourselves. Some more than others, of course." The difference, it would seem, lies in the degree of introversion or extroversion of the artist, expressed either as the compulsion to spell it all out or the discretion to allow the work exist in a state of purposeful containment.

"Rather than let the viewers in on everything," says Wilmeth, "I think it's important to leave a little mystery. That way, they can invest the piece with their own thoughts, which are ten times more interesting. My art is quite meditative, of course, but that's not something I set out to do. I just do it. The work is very quiet."

Ernest Wilmeth has left the palace door slightly ajar, and splendor spills into the night. The scent of tea drifts from hidden chambers where black silk sheets rustle, then become still. A distant gong whispers a single long note.

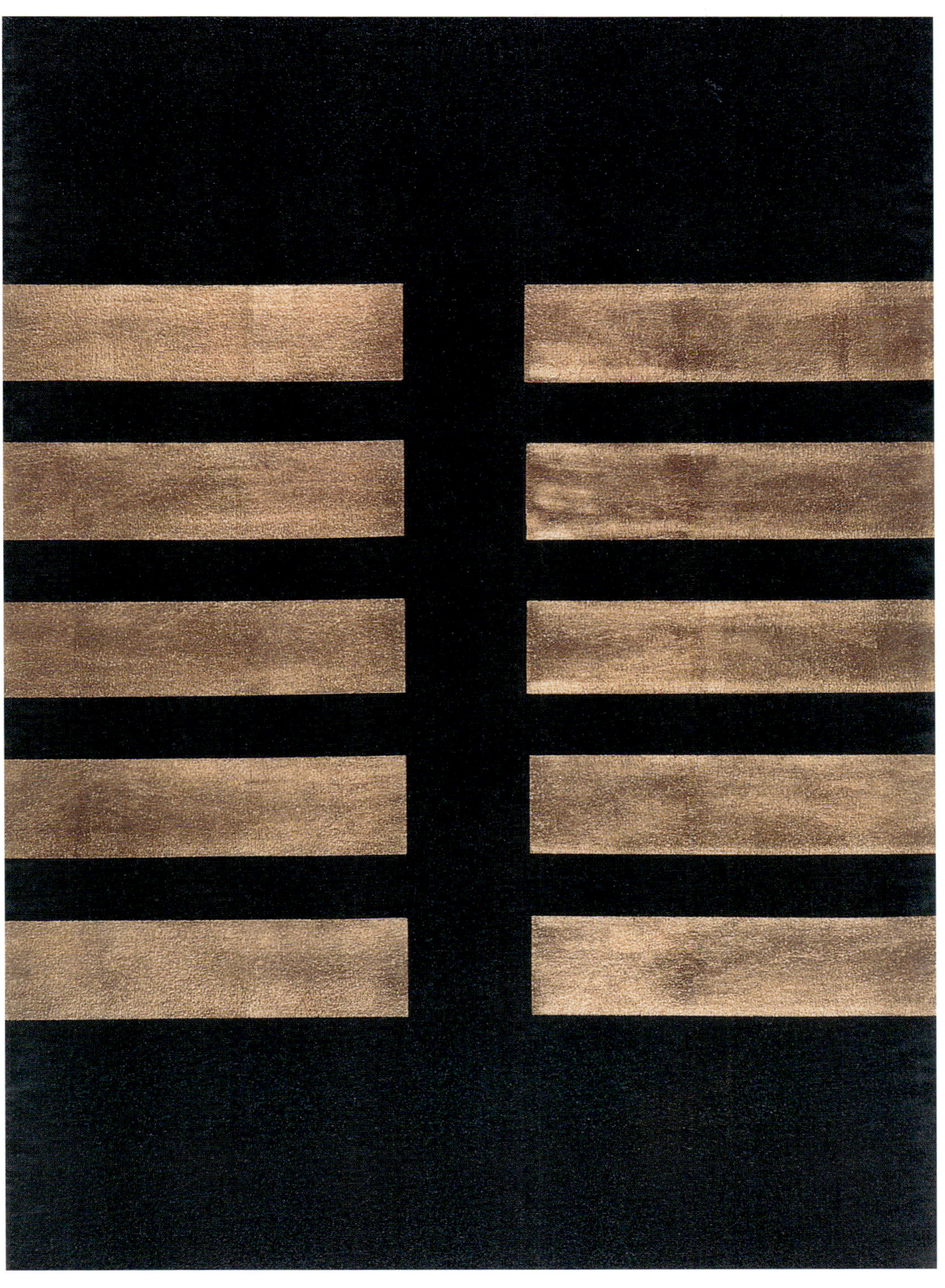

GARDEN ENTRANCE II
ACRYLIC & COPPER LEAF ON CANVAS
40 X 30 INCHES
Collection of the Artist

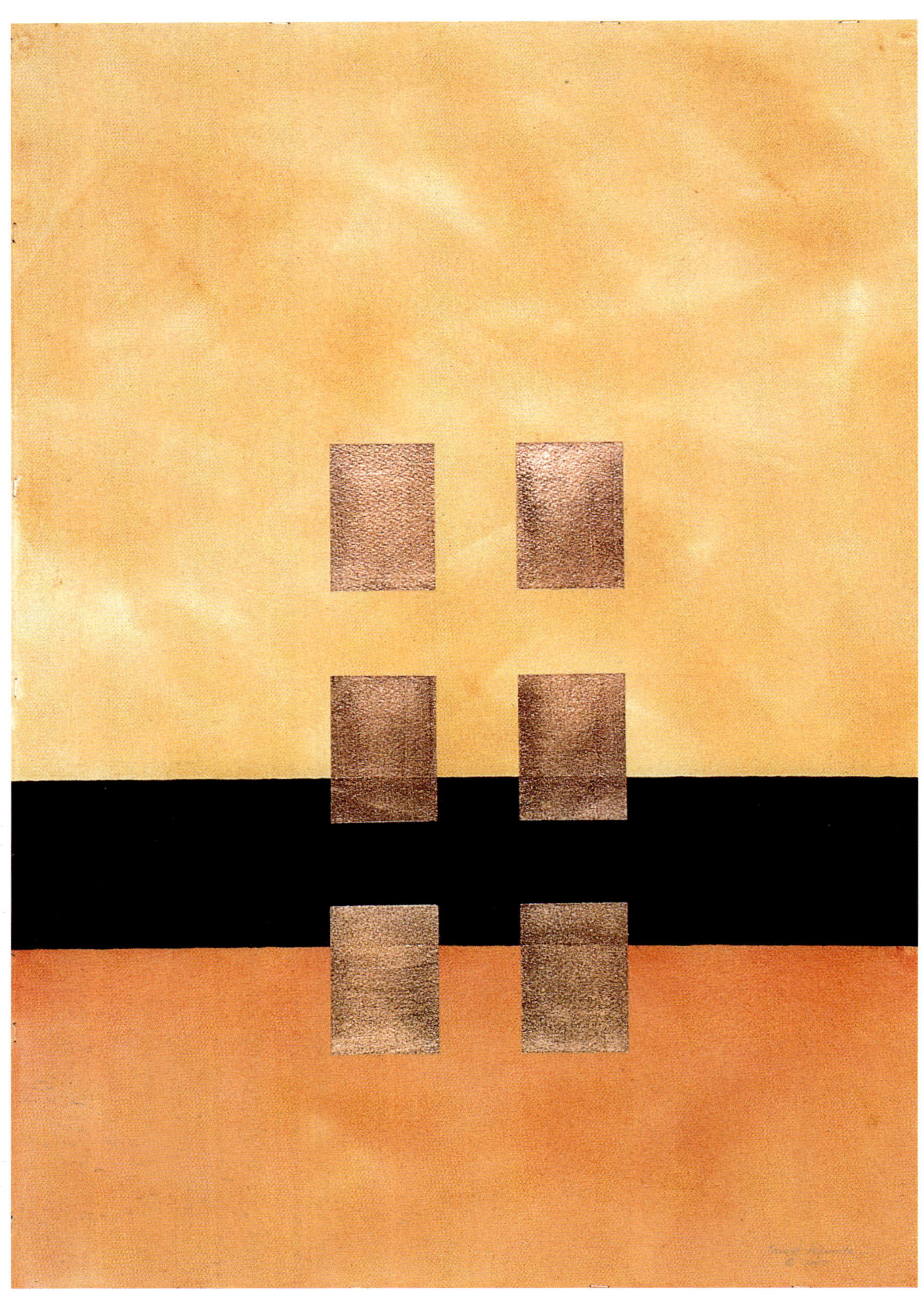

DUSK
ACRYLIC & COPPER LEAF ON PAPER
30 X 22 INCHES
Collection of the Artist

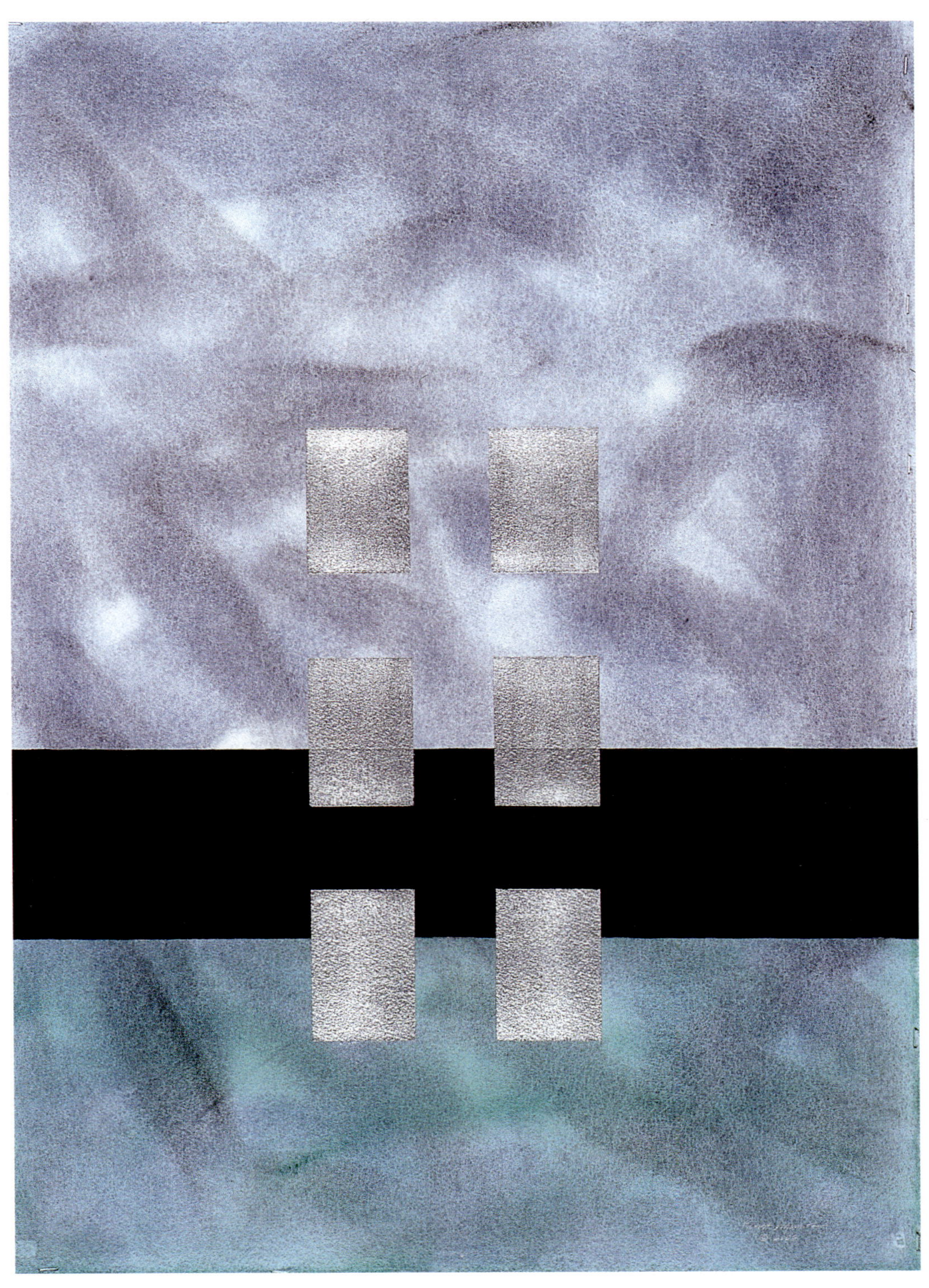

DAWN
ACRYLIC & SILVER LEAF ON PAPER
30 X 22 INCHES
Collection of the Artist

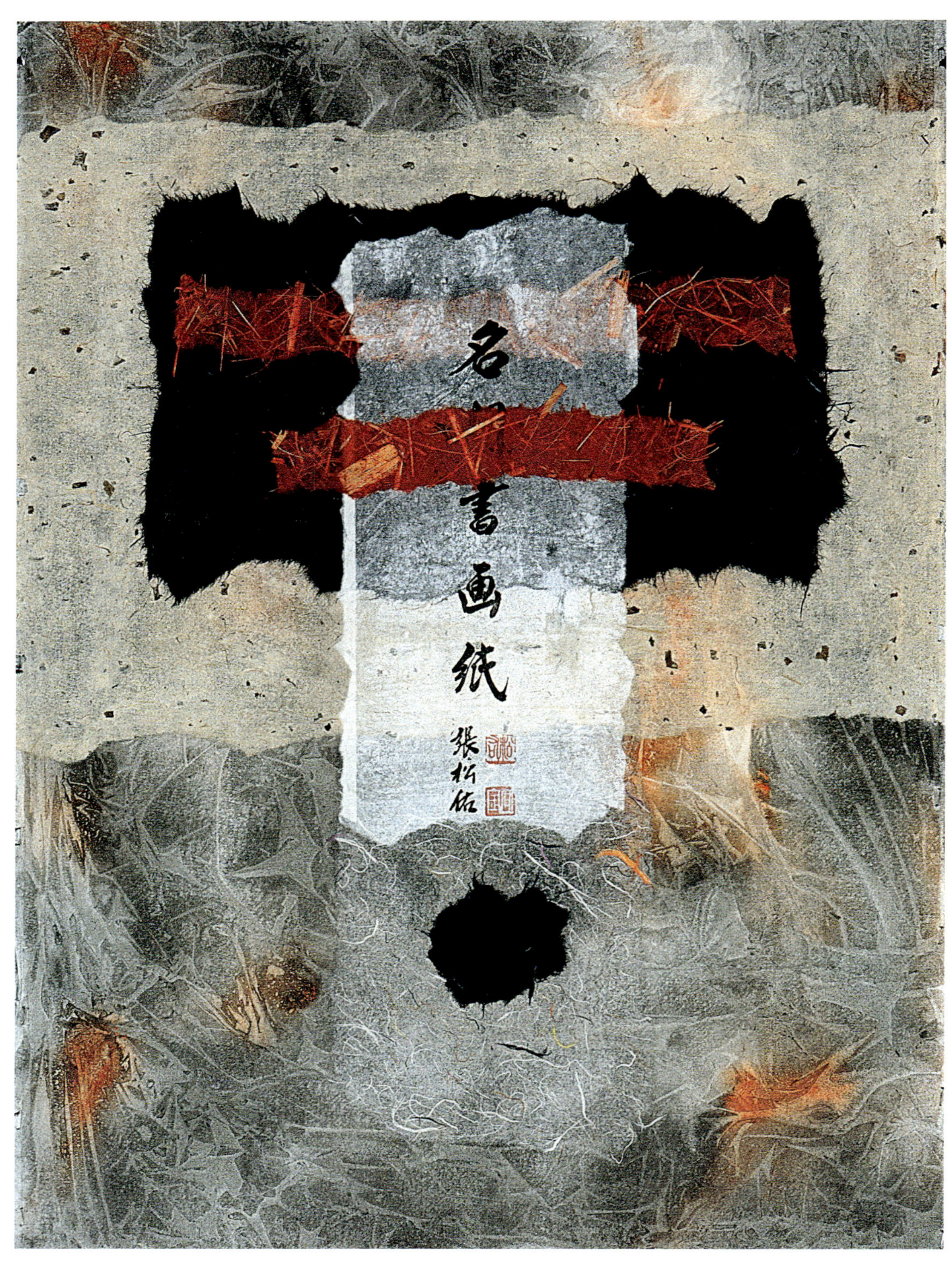

SAN FRANCISCO GIFT
COLLAGE/PAPER
30 X 22 INCHES
Private Collection

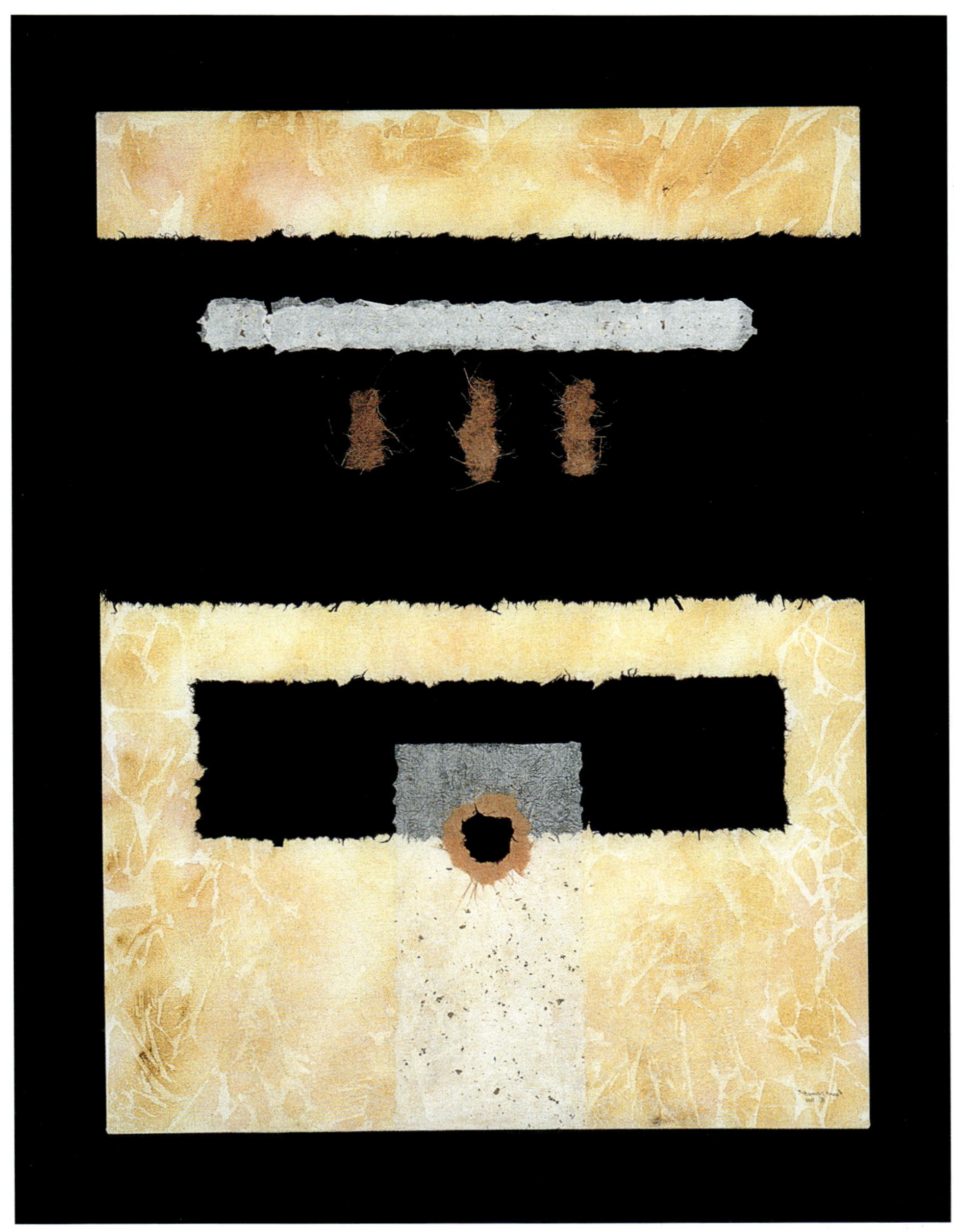

ERNEST WILMETH II b. 1952 Perryton TX. Ed: BFA Northern Arizona Univ. Exhib: Southwest Arts Festival; Santa Fe Festival of the Arts; etal. Affil: Who's Who in American Art; life member, Royal Society of Arts, London. Representation: Shidoni Gallery, Santa Fe.

THREE STONES
COLLAGE/CANVAS
48 X 36 INCHES
Private Collection

NANCY ORTENSTONE

Look, and look again. And again. Each time there is something more, something different, something deeper. The view from one's own front door changes continually with the seasons, the light, the weather, the time of day, and the movement of passersby. A neighboring hillside, seen every day, slowly becomes familiar. After a year or so, the most minute deviations are immediately perceptible. One can spot the lightning-struck tree, the dislodged boulder, the progress of new growth.

In the same way, one's viewpoint expands when regarding an abstract work of art. The image is clear enough to be registered in an instant, yet a lifetime is not enough to absorb every subtle and secret passage. This is amazing, especially considering that a painting never changes. Not one brush stroke moves. In order to keep unfolding, the wily image must offer successively more literate interfaces, must yield its secrets slowly, must wait around every corner for the unfolding of the mind that comes before it each day.

Nancy Ortenstone is able to project endlessly complex and subtle shifts in consciousness because she has chosen to concentrate on the light of northern New Mexico as her creative vehicle. When she arrived from San Miguel de Allende in 1986, she was so stunned by the quality of the light on the land that she immediately began to paint full time. "It was like coming home to the right world and the right medium," she says. "I had come home to myself. It had to do with the wealth of art and artists in the area, with living every day in this incredible light. Everything changed when I came to New Mexico."

Ortenstone is thoroughly grounded in her own mind and skin as well as in her environment. She has an acute sense of place, not only of her lyrical surroundings in the quiet mountain village where she lives and works, but of the swift and dizzy spinout of the larger world. Transition has become a way of life for her. "I need for my paintings to be more spacious right now," she says. "I hope they are evolving from a deeper place."

She paints, observes, paints, and observes some more. The image changes, and changes again. And again. "I think I've become more trusting," says Nancy Ortenstone. "It's not that my paintings are easier to paint now, it's that I've learned how to trust the whole process of transformation."

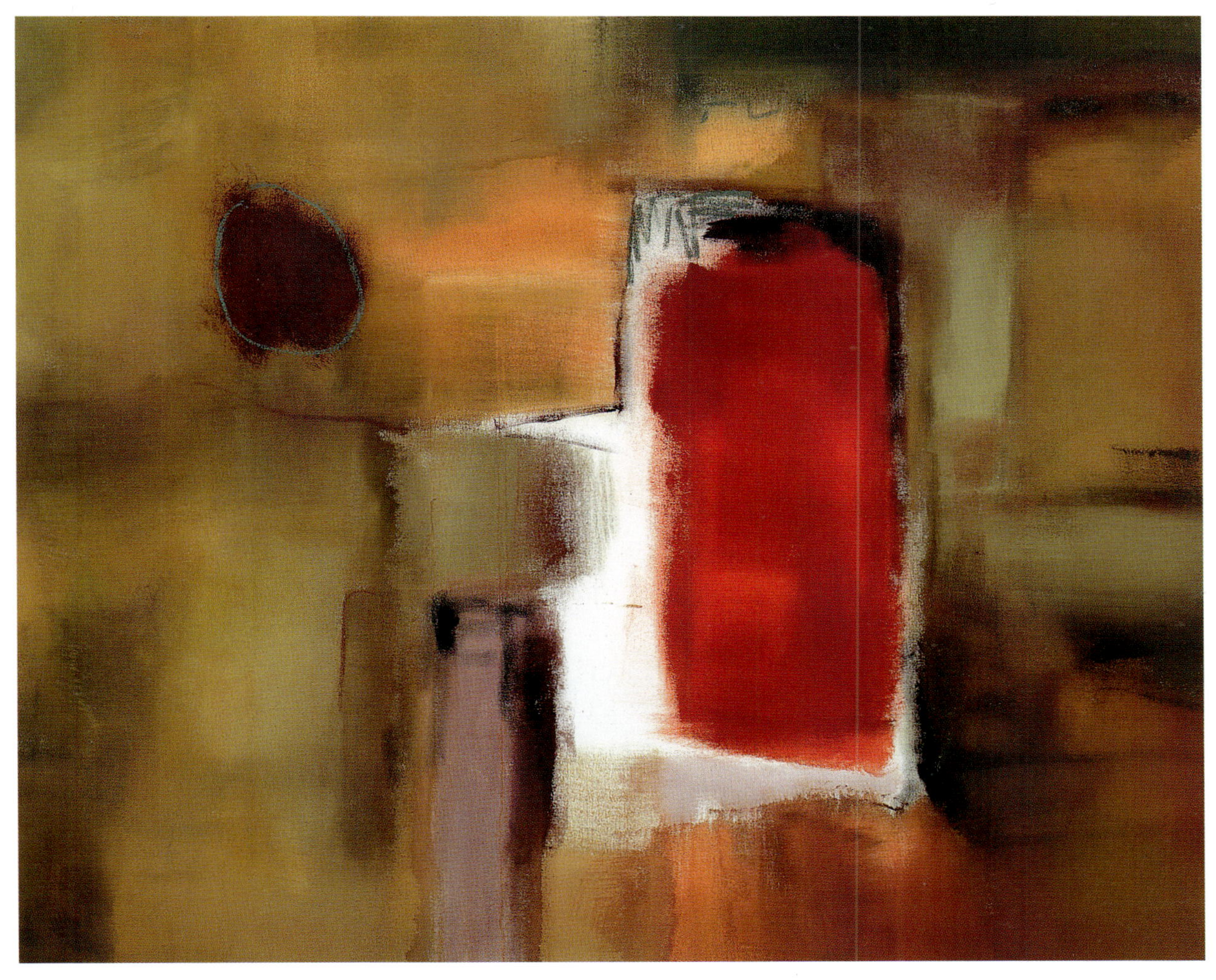

IN HARMONY, 1999
ACRYLIC
46 X 58 INCHES

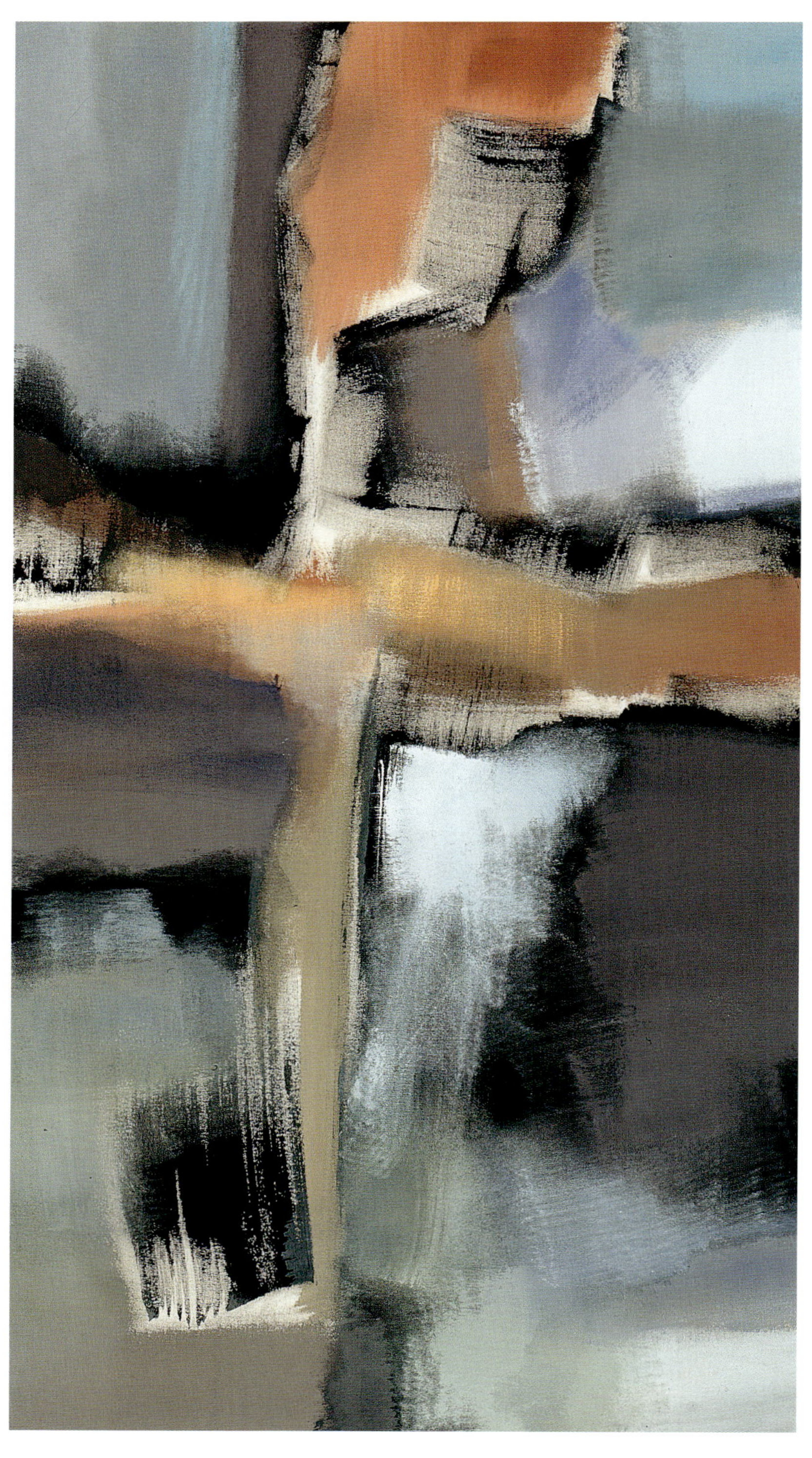

STILLPOINT TURNING, 2001
ACRYLIC
46 X 26 INCHES

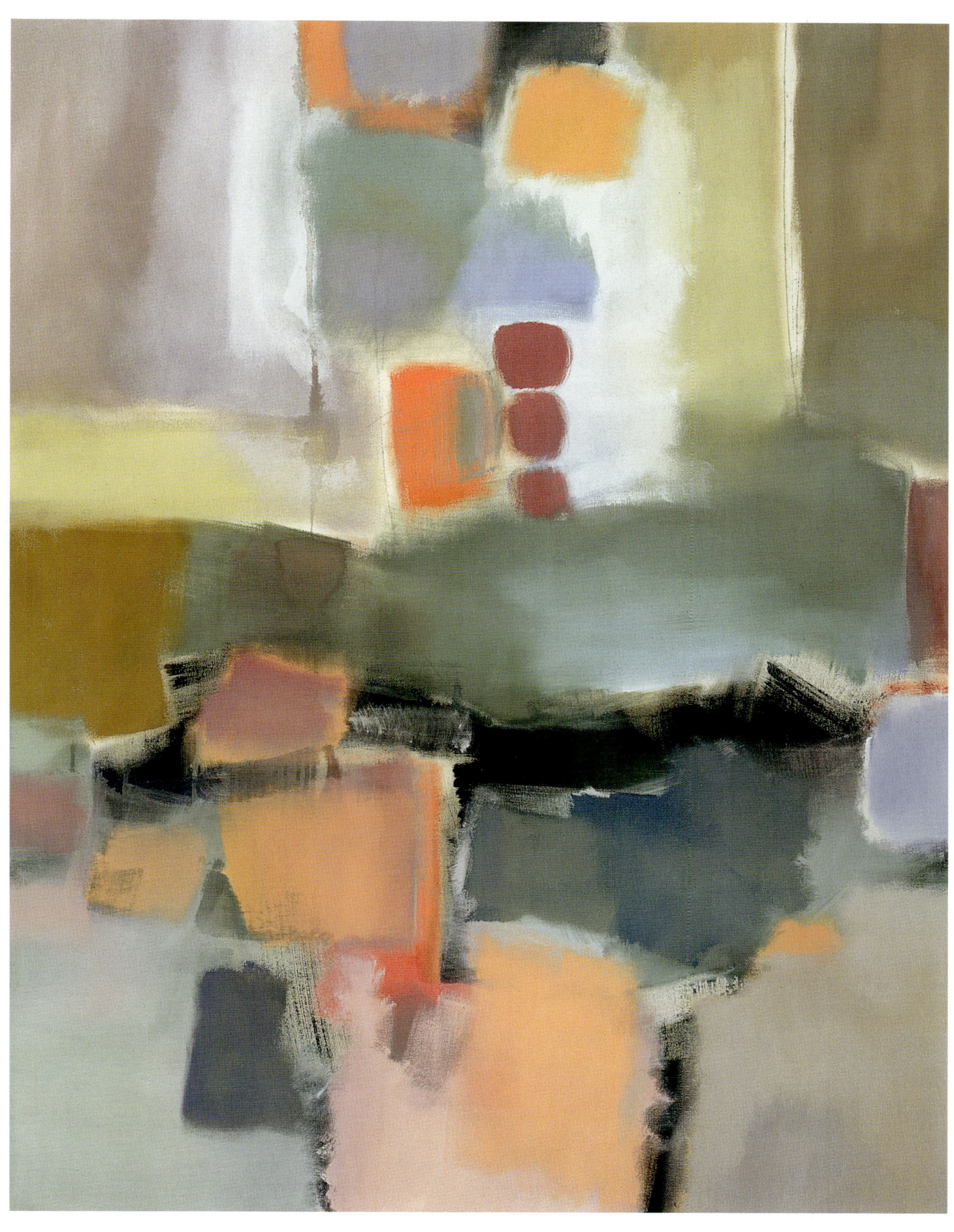

MELODY FOR THE MUSE, 2001
ACRYLIC
58 X 46 INCHES

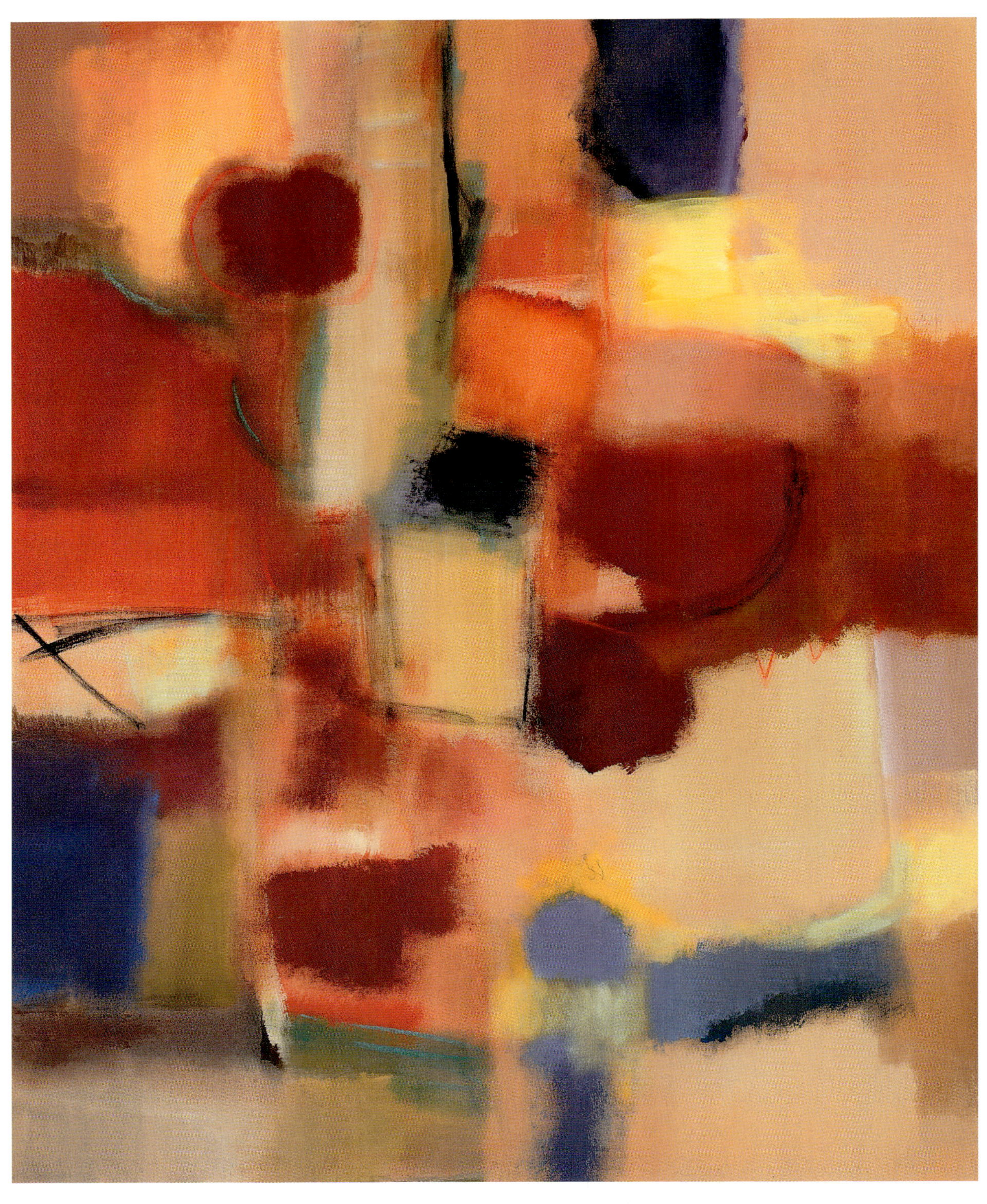

FLOWERING, 2001
ACRYLIC
48 X 40 INCHES

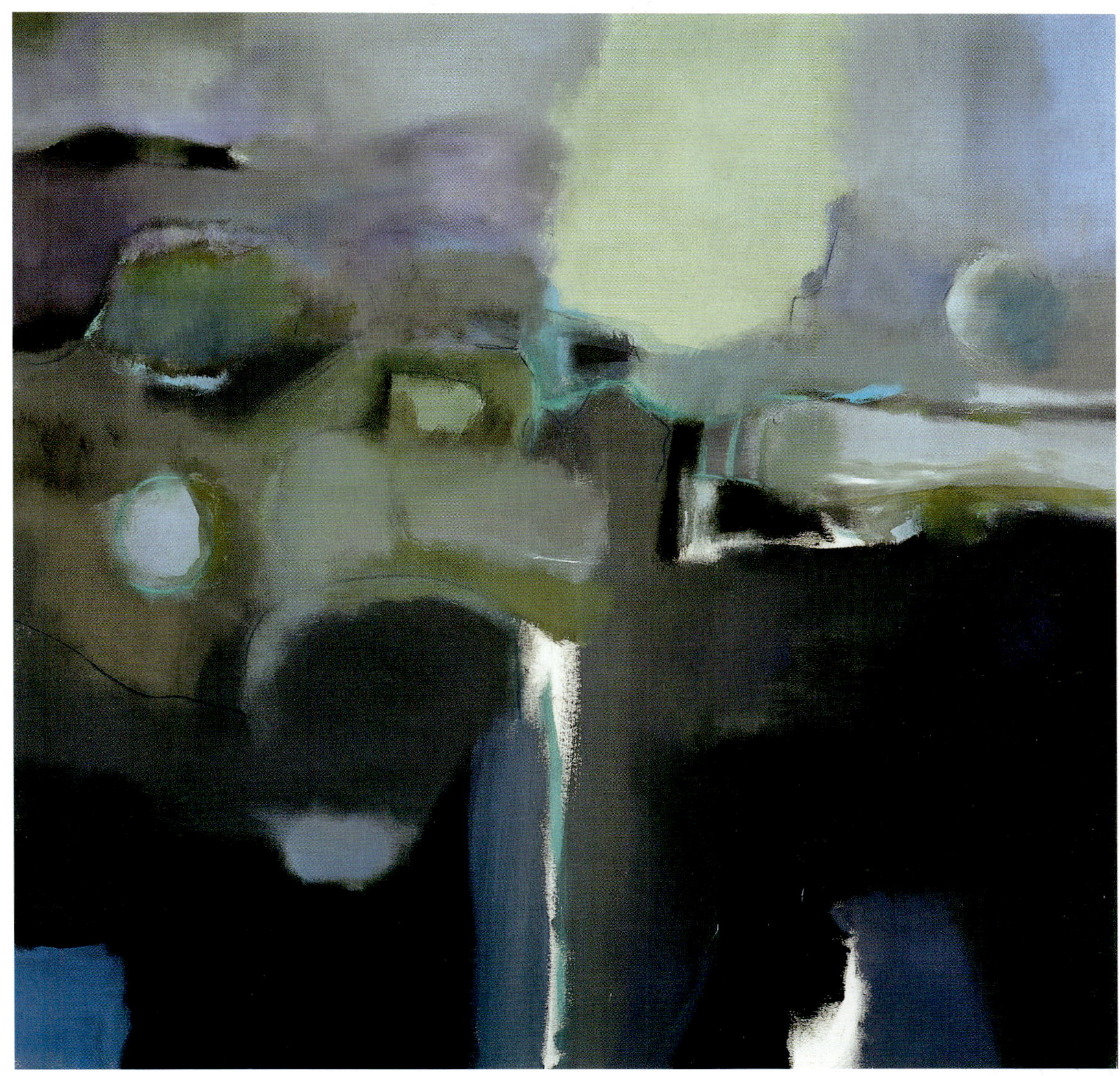

NANCY ORTENSTONE b. 1944 Minneapolis MN. Ed: MFA Universidad de Guanajuato, Mexico; Santa Fe Institute of Fine Arts. Coll: Millennia, Boston; Terra Nova Pictures, Los Angeles; Macy's, NYC; Blue Cross, Blue Shield, MA; etal. Representation: Expressions in Fine Art, Santa Fe; Jack Meier Gallery, Houston TX; Hopkins Fine Art, Scottsdale AZ; Blue Gallery, Kansas City MO; Bruce McGaw Graphics, West Nyack NY.

DISTANCE TO DAWN, 2003
ACRYLIC
46 X 48 INCHES

FRANK ETTENBERG

Somebody's got to have a conscience. Particularly in the art world - where fifteen minutes of fame is just not enough, where even the best of artists sometimes fall prey to the artificial urgency of the market and the snooty posturing of academe - somebody has got to ask the right question.

It helps a lot if that person is a very fine artist, a decent and respected person, and has the ability to spot a hole in an argument and drive a truck through it. Such an individual may be a little slow to accept the unacceptable, and may be a shade too idealistic, but that beats chasing after every trend until one no longer knows one's own mind. At the very least, the artist with a conscience can define the parameters of conflict and resolution, and provide comfort to exhausted refugees from an overheated art scene.

The art of Frank Ettenberg begins with dissonance and ends with asymmetrical harmony. He calls it "unobserved painted images neither preconceived nor copied from nature." The artist is not afraid to get in there and mix it up with a thorny issue, then bring it to a point of clarity. He takes the high road, always. Facile solutions are not a part of his visual vocabulary.

Ettenberg started out painting in oil but shifted to acrylic in the mid-nineties. He begins each piece with a chaotic burst of marks, then works with them until they resolve their interrelationships. He has a special knack for creating a sense of grand scale regardless of the actual dimensions of the piece, which may in actuality be rather small. He is able to contrast the darkest colors and the most opaque passages with an inner illumination that permits the transmission of light through layers of brushwork.

Since he began painting in acrylics, the paintings have gotten more loose and expressionistic, harking back to his original grounding in the tactile, deliberately imperfect mode of the New York school of Abstract Expressionism. His return to a more forceful style is partly the result of giving up the formal practice of meditation, and partly due to repeated painting vacations in Austria, where he developed a sympathy for gritty European abstract expressionism.

"I find that this place permits human error in art and relationships more in than America, where people hide behind propriety," he says. "I like that. Farmers and bankers and car dealers and collectors have the courage to get in your face. It's a juicy climate for me, and this has gotten into my work."

Back in the United States, Frank Ettenberg continues to anchor the Santa Fe art community as he has for more than thirty years. A contemplative artist and a conscientious friend, he brings a newly robust energy to his role in the ongoing and passionate conversation among artists about art.

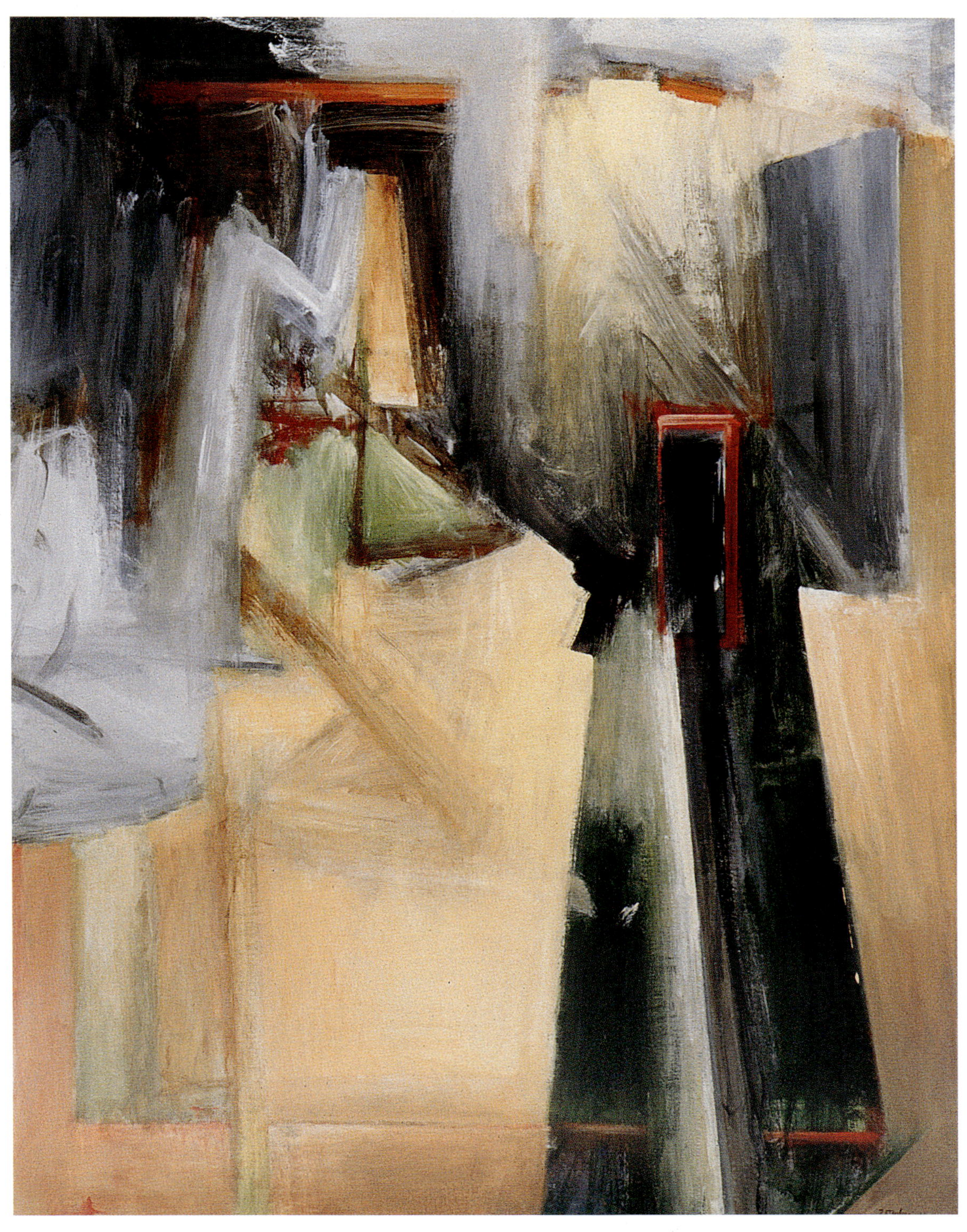

NORA'S VERSION, 1998-2001
ACRYLIC ON CANVAS
58 X 46 INCHES

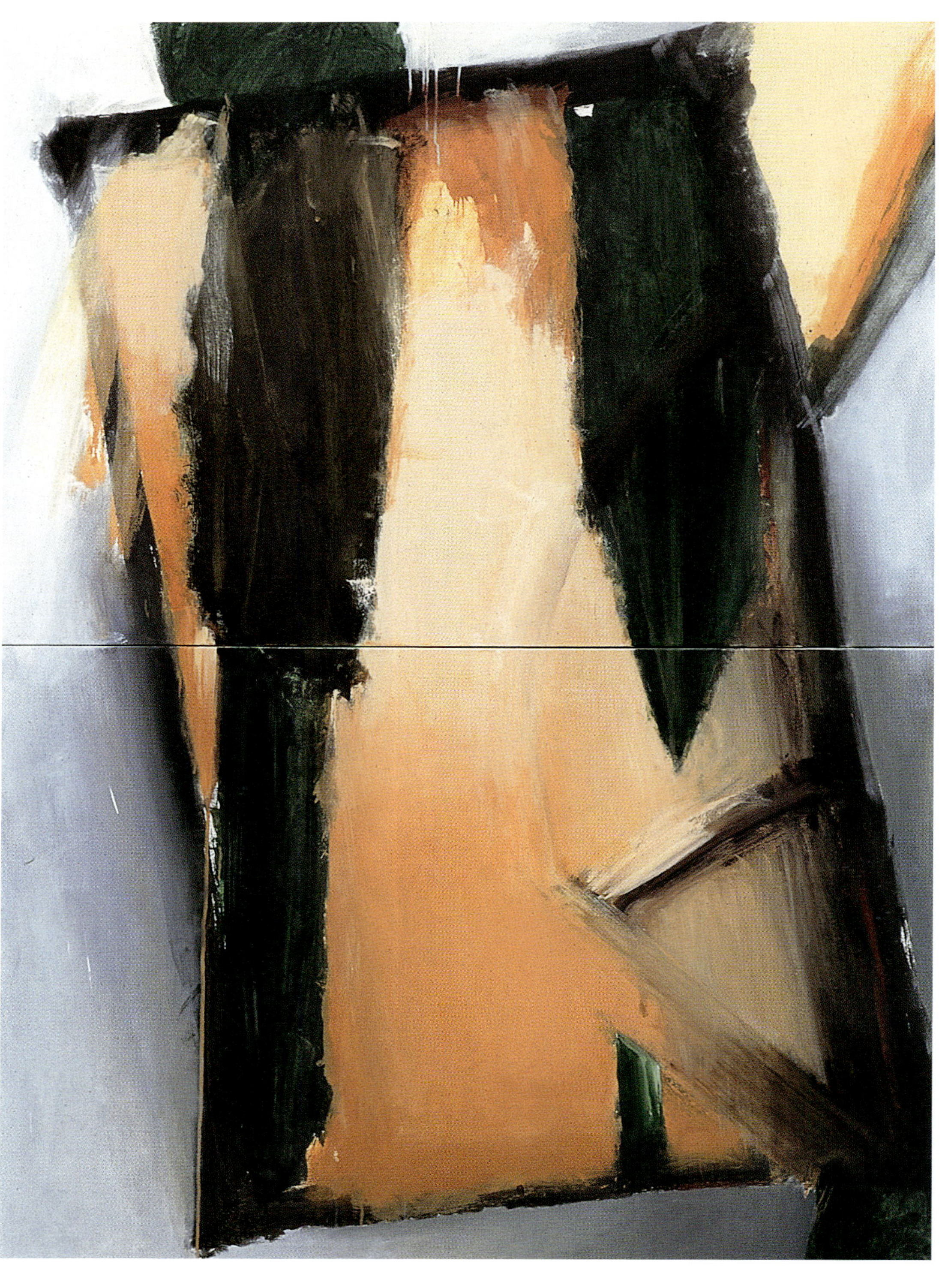

JUMPING THE FRAME, 2001,
ACRYLIC ON CANVAS, DIPTYCH
84 X 64 INCHES

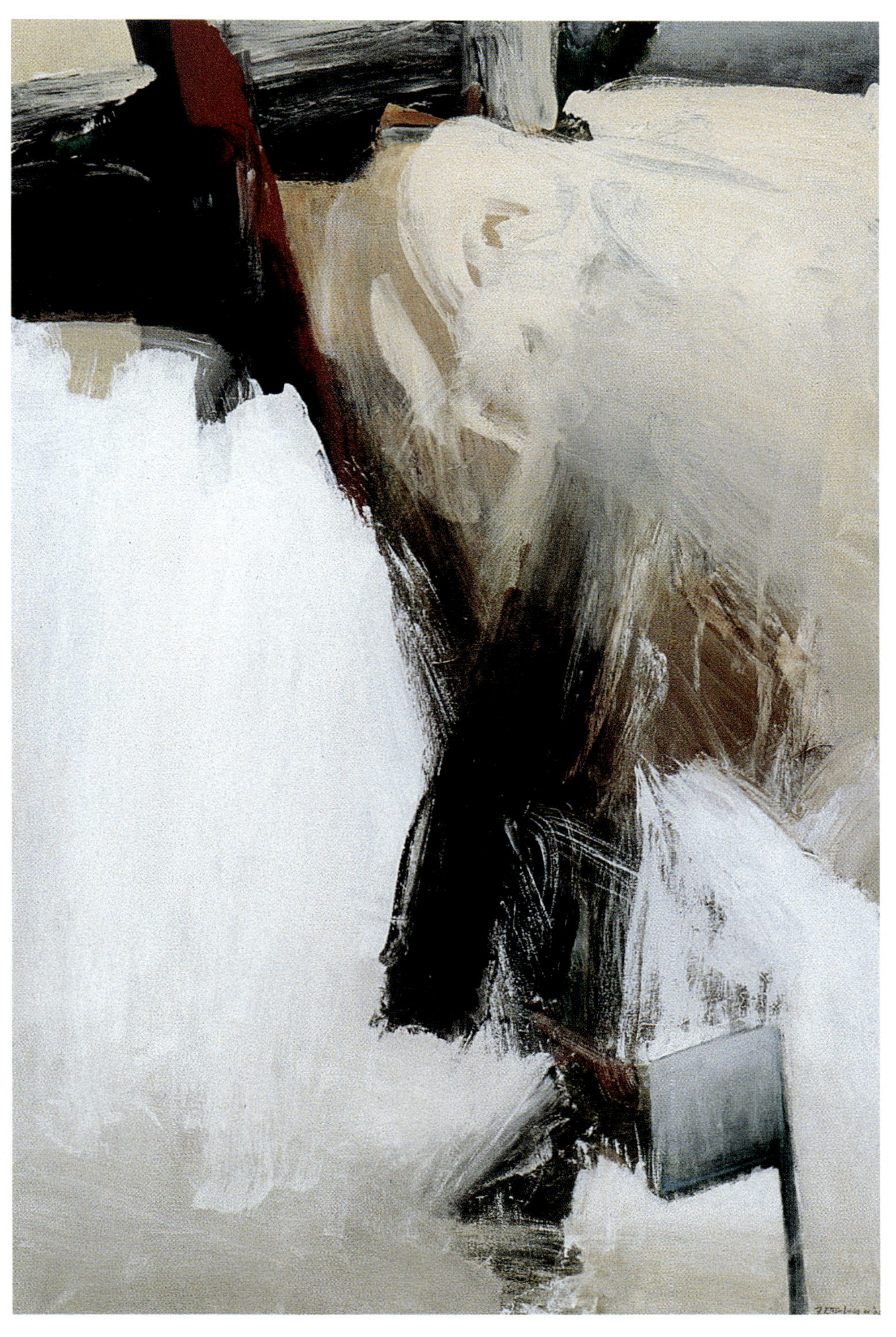

CAVEAT, 2001-2002
ACRYLIC ON CANVAS
56 X 38 INCHES

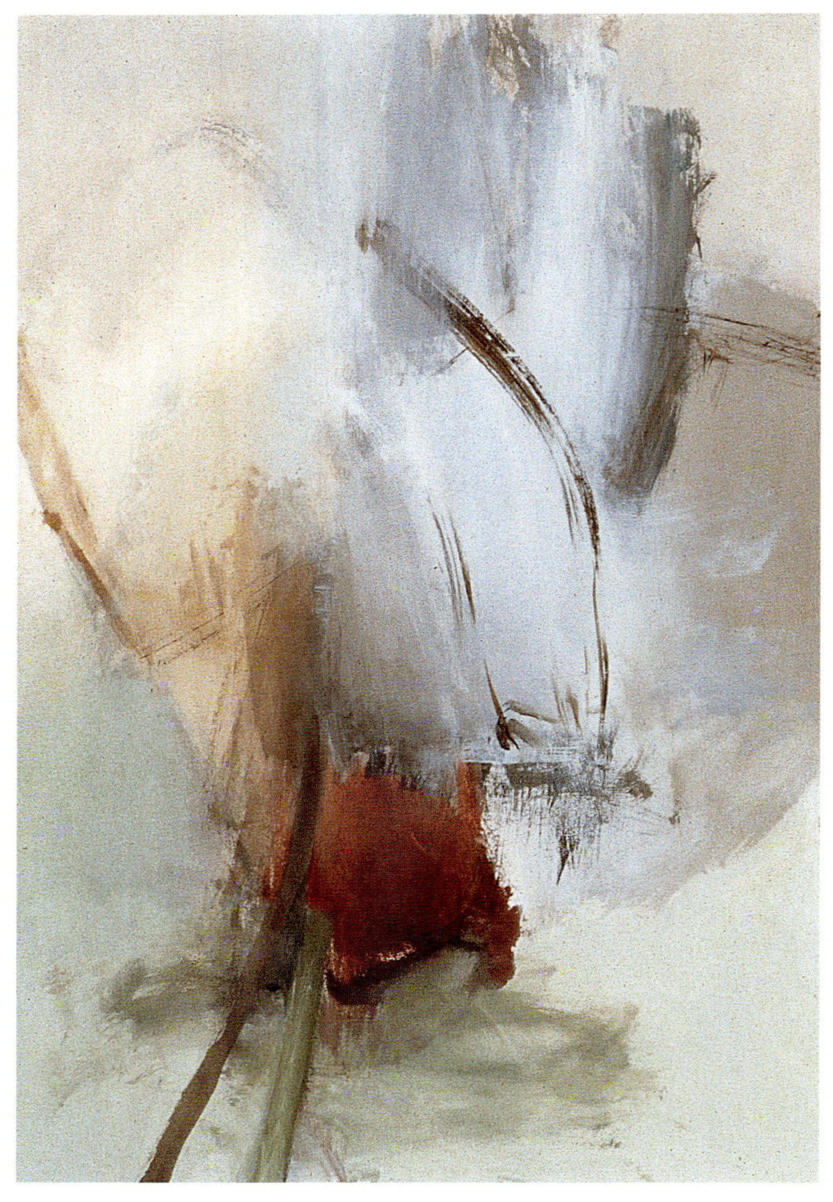

COOL OF SPRING
ACRYLIC ON CANVAS, DIPTYCH
58 X 80 INCHES

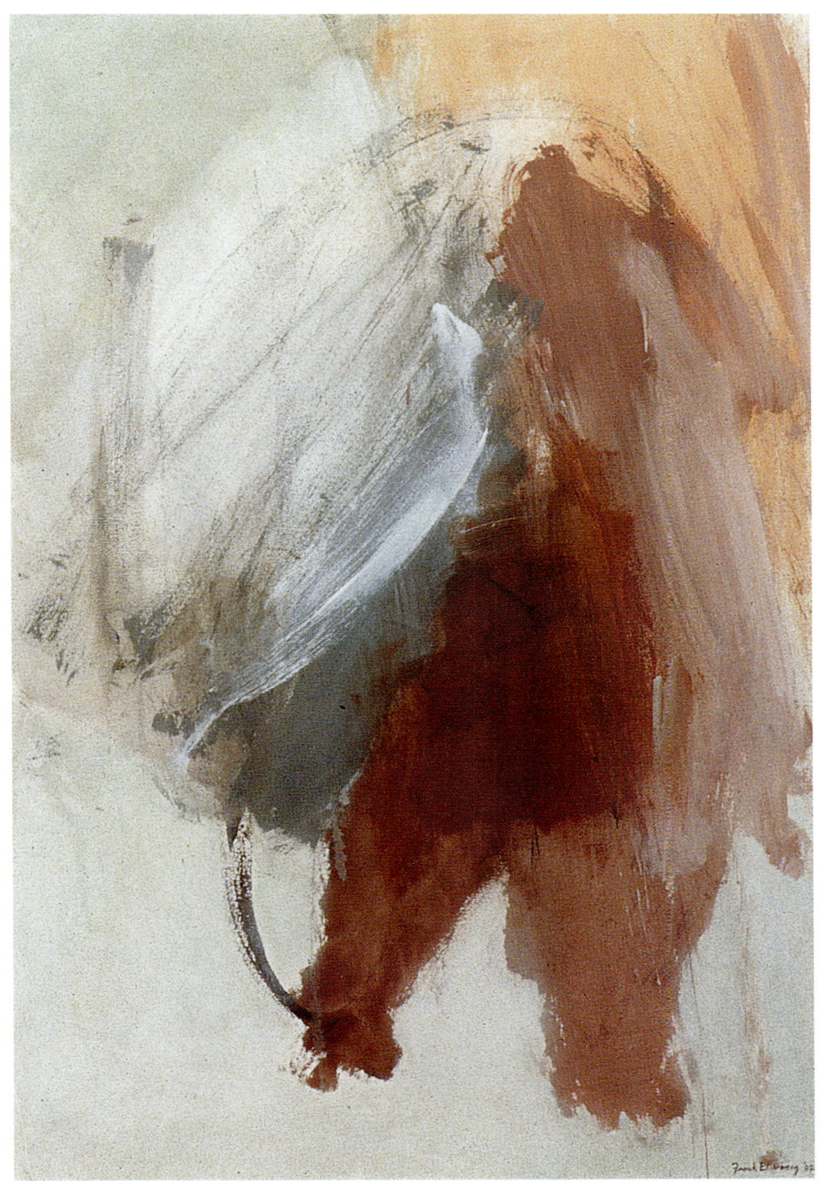

FRANK ETTENBERG b. 1945 Brooklyn NY. Ed: MA Univ. New Mexico; BS Univ. Michigan. Honors: Tamarind Institute Fellowship; merit award, Museum of Fine Arts biennial, Santa Fe. Coll: Minnesota Museum of Art; Detroit Institute of Art; Albuquerque Museum; BankAustria, Vienna; Citicorp; Exxon; etal. Representation: Eldridge McCarthy Gallery, Santa Fe.

COOL OF SPRING
ACRYLIC ON CANVAS, DIPTYCH
58 X 80 INCHES

ROBERT KELLY

A mantra is designed to penetrate the surface of thought and bring up non-intellectual information stored in the subconscious. A visual mantra is designed to organize and balance intuition, filling in the gaps, supplying details, and bringing every tangent back around to its origin. Where a mantra leaves off is where consciousness begins. Vision burns phoenix-like through the ashes of the status quo. Light penetrates the glaze of familiarity and affords perception of the wisdom beneath.

Robert Kelly's art projects a sense of Zen-like reduction. His process is vigorous yet meditative, as he applies paint, scrapes it away, glazes it, and repeats the process until he achieves the texture for which he is justly famous. The spirit of time lingers in the finished painting, invoking weathered manuscripts and age-darkened amber. "I have a great reverence for history, for what time and civilization do to the surface of things," says Kelly. "I am interested in the barely discernible meaning found in weathered surfaces."

Kelly is one of the few abstract painters in Santa Fe who can lay claim to having been born in the old city. Having secured his education and his international reputation in the metropolitan Northeast, he was in the fortunate position of being able to return to his birthplace on his own terms when Santa Fe developed into a major art center.

Kelly resides in both New Mexico and New York. He was at work the day the World Trade Center fell, just three blocks from his studio. With no thought for his own safety, he grabbed a camera and began chronicling what he saw and felt as the structures gave way and the smoke and dust blotted out the sun. One week later, his studio still off limits in the Red Zone, he was able with official help to go in and hand carry his paintings two blocks to a waiting truck parked outside the fences. He got them to New Mexico barely in time for his exhibit in Galisteo.

Kelly's longtime fascination with the buried history of mark making was sharpened during that period. Objects, architecture, and surfaces change with time as they are washed with color or covered with marks, then wiped clean. Marginal notations are made and removed. The few remaining traces fascinate the eye with their suggestion of what might still be there.

With his new work becoming more formal and less referential, Robert Kelly seems more interested in the play of edges that create a tonal and atonal concerto of lines. As he cuts and realigns blocks of color into configurations like musical scores, calligraphic notations, or quilted puzzles, ancient information rises to the surface and becomes almost visible.

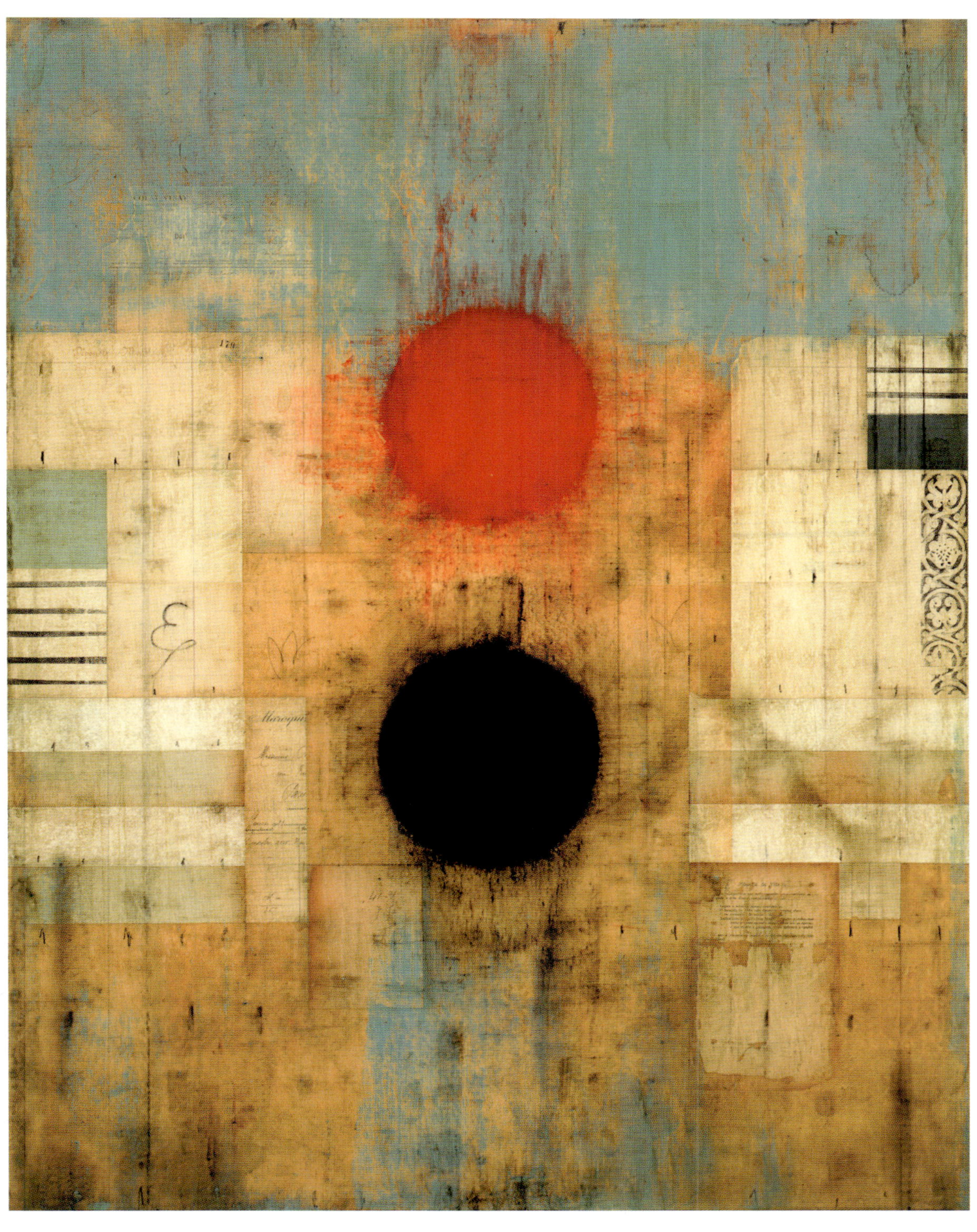

SHEBIA RUZ XI, 1998
OIL AND MIXED MEDIA ON CANVAS
45 X 36½ INCHES

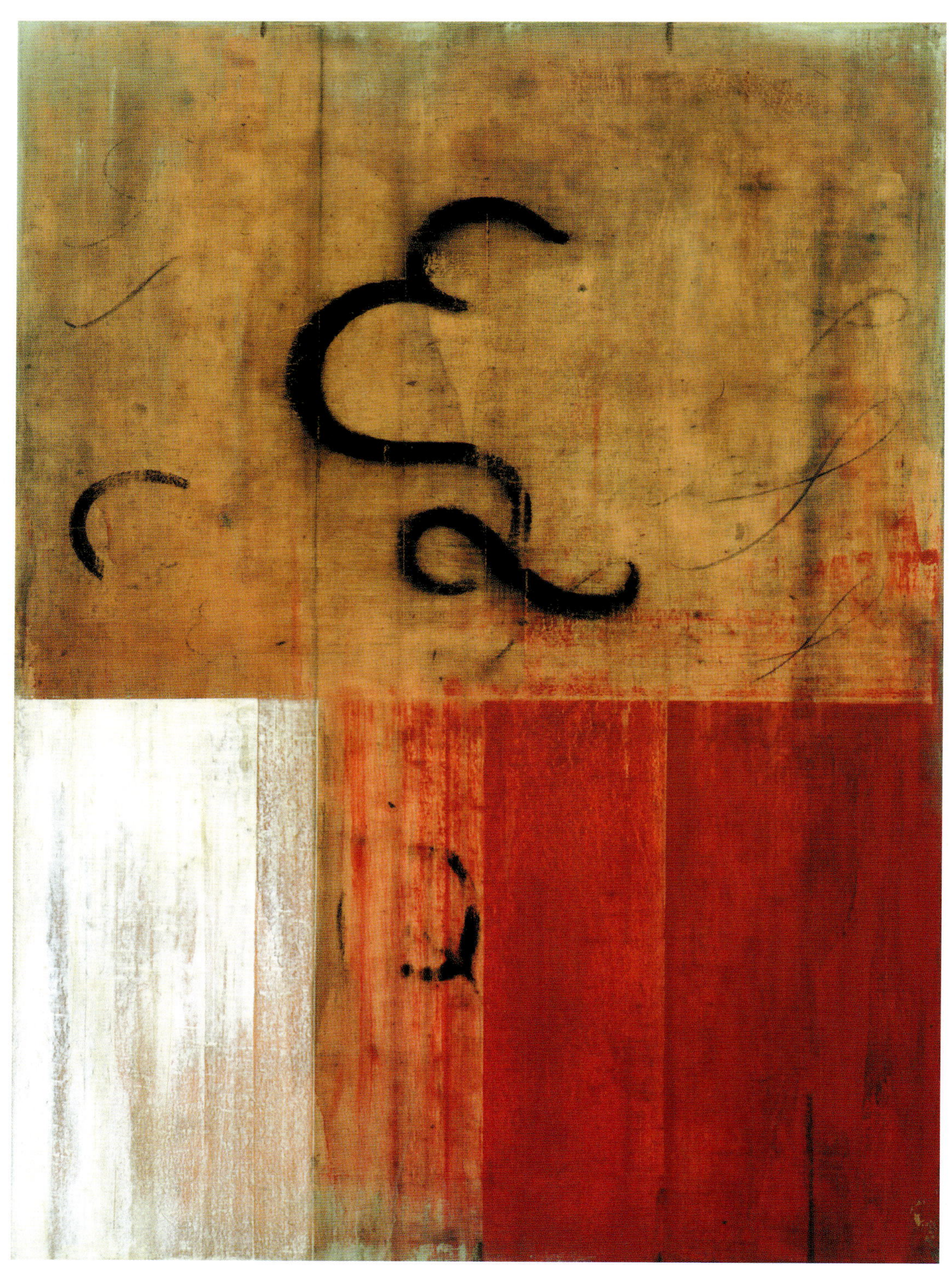

VOTING DAY IN NEPAL X, 1999
OIL AND MIXED MEDIA ON CANVAS
40 X 36 INCHES

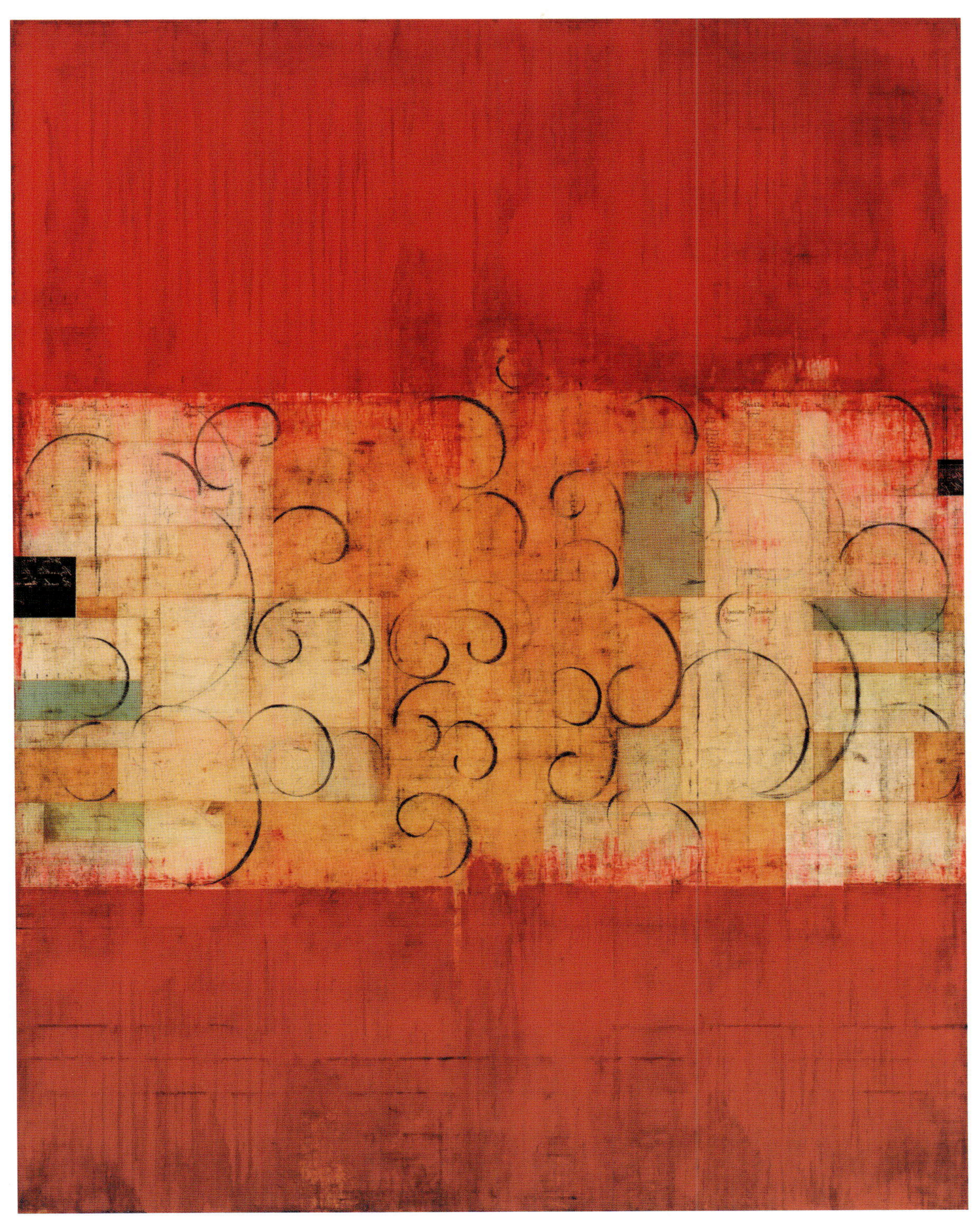

GUARDIANS OF THE GATE XXXVI
OIL AND MIXED MEDIA ON CANVAS
80 X 64 INCHES

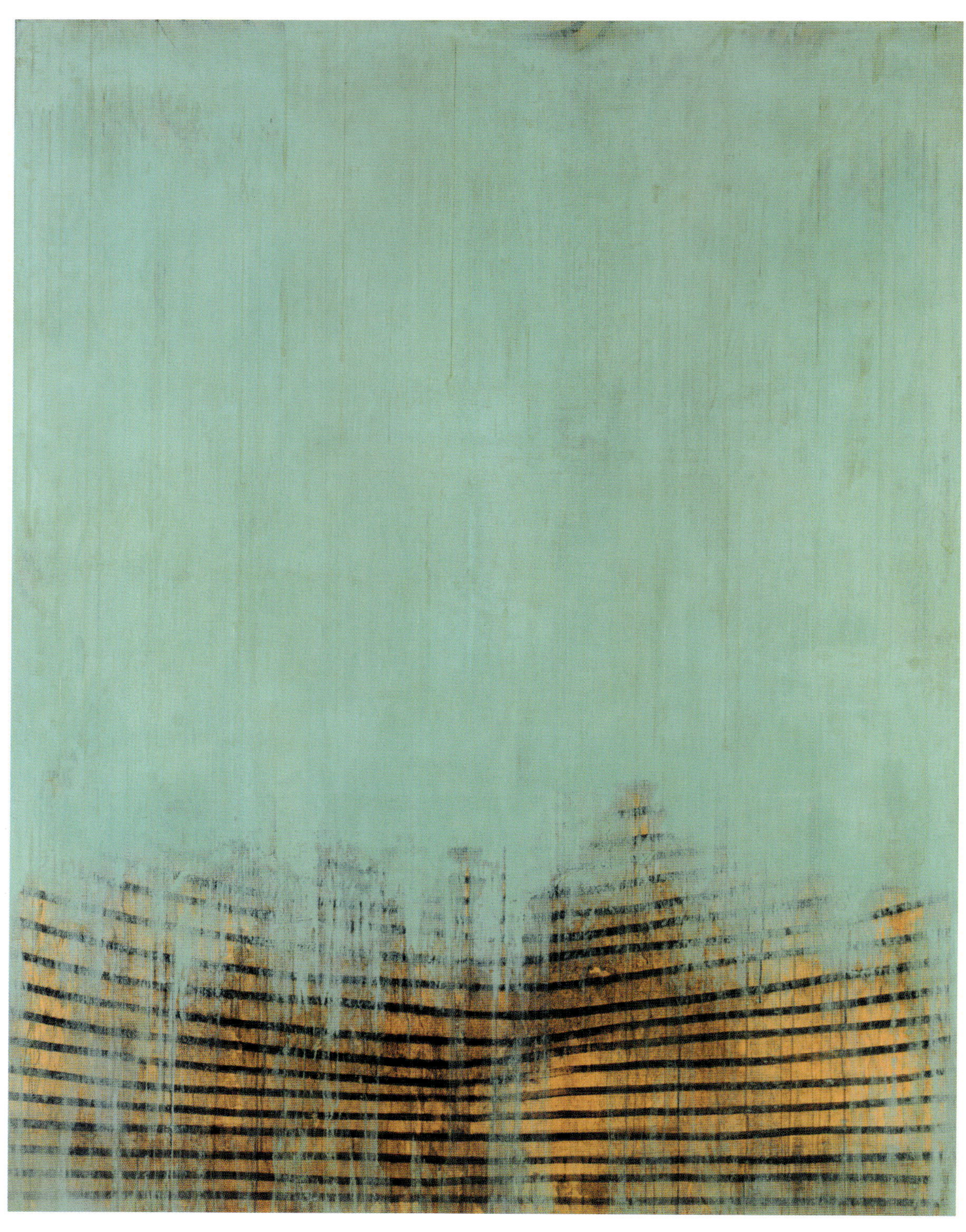

ARBOR VITAE IX, 2000
OIL AND MIXED MEDIA ON CANVAS
80 X 64 INCHES

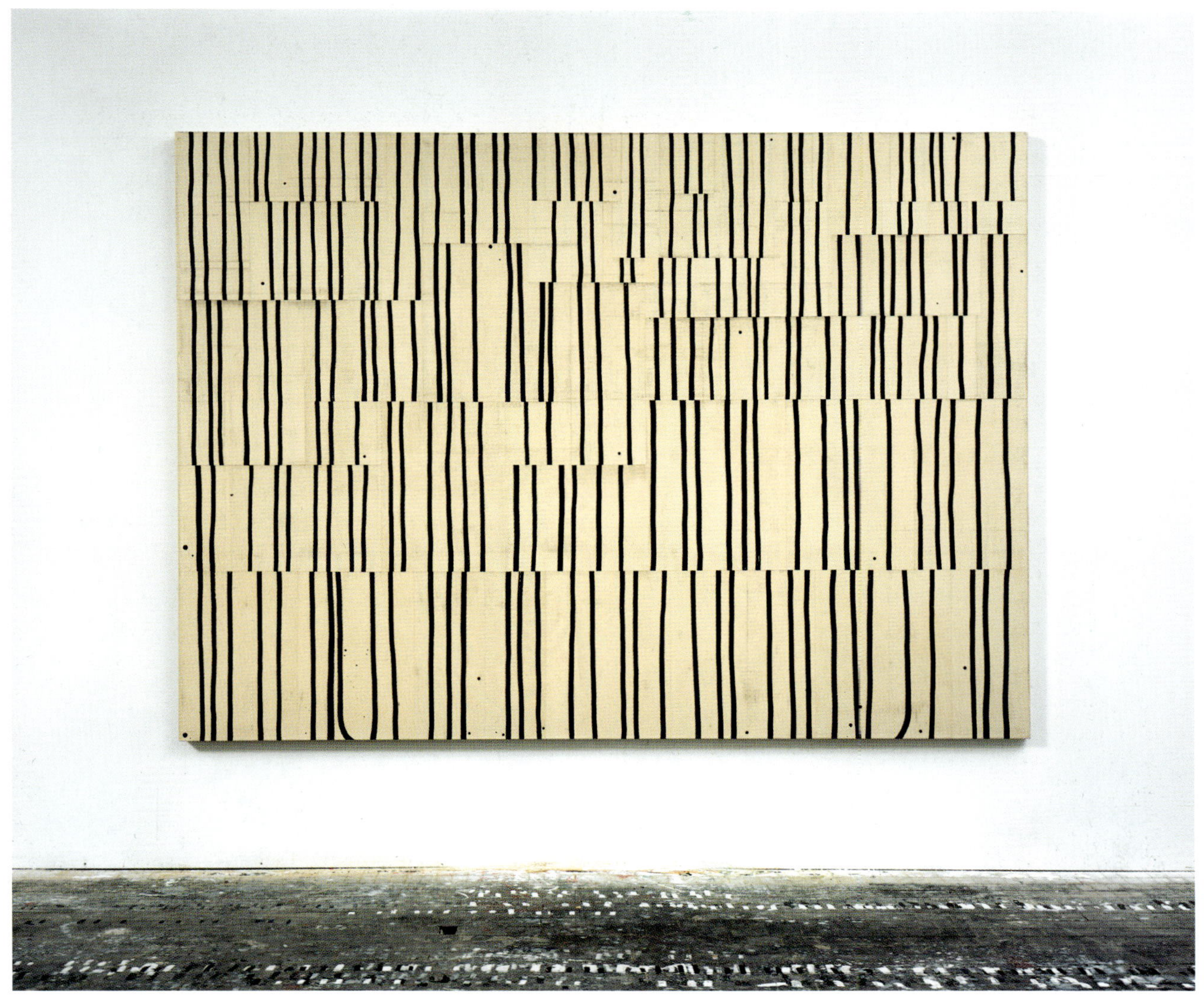

ROBERT KELLY b. 1956 Santa Fe NM. Ed: BA Harvard. Exhib: SITE Santa Fe; Museum of Fine Arts, Santa Fe. Coll: Brooklyn Museum; Fogg Museum MA; Milwaukee Art Museum WI; Montgomery Museum of Fine Arts AL; McNay Museum TX; Smith College MA; AT&T; Dupont; IBM; Mitsubishi; etal. Representation: Linda Durham Contemporary, Galisteo NM and New York; John Berggruen Gallery, San Francisco; Senior and Shopmaker Gallery, New York; Bentley Gallery, Scottsdale; Anne Reed Gallery, Ketchum ID; Barbara Davis Gallery, Houston; Doug Udell Gallery, Vancouver and Edmonton, Canada.

THICKET LXV, 2002
OIL AND MIXED MEDIA ON CANVAS
80 X 114 INCHES

RICARDO MAZAL

Time rushes by; art stands still. The eye rivets itself on an unfamiliar detail, a moment of pure perception, a certain face, and for an instant it stops as all else passes in a blur of speed. Veils cascade downward like walking rain, revealing staccato glimpses of a deep and slumbering landscape. Indistinct shapes rise to the surface of thought, becoming clear for an instant before disappearing down the avalanche of too much information. Life rushes by, but in one moment of transcendence, time stands still.

The work of Ricardo Mazal articulates these sensations in the form of importantly scaled paintings that crackle with energy. "The act of painting is like my own language that I can communicate as easily as speaking," says the artist. Mazal sets the tone of the communication carefully. He treats each exhibition as a complete conversation, working with the available space in advance and making digital sketches to create a site specific installation of individual paintings. Once the plan is in place, the computer is turned off and the real work begins. Each painting is separate and distinct, yet related; the atmosphere is one of unity.

Mazal began his present career as a painter by moving from Mexico to Barcelona in the mid-1980s. He spent the next eight years painting and establishing the direction his art would take, then moved to New York City. There, he has developed an art career that includes exhibitions in major North American cities as well as the Spanish-speaking art worlds of Mexico and Spain.

In 2001 he established a second residence and studio in Santa Fe, one of the oldest European settlements in the United States. Santa Fe was the northern capital of New Spain in the 16th, 17th, and 18th centuries, and still retains a strong Hispanic flavor. It has proved a good fit for Mazal, as the international art scene has established a firm presence in the formerly provincial area. Mazal and his wife, who is also Mexican, love the culture and the landscape. They describe the old city as being "halfway between New York and Mexico," both figuratively and literally.

The highlight of Mazal's career to date was a recent ten-year retrospective exhibition at Museo de Arte Contemporáneo de Monterrey, arguably the most important museum in Latin America. The show was a tremendous success. Most importantly, it afforded him recognition by his own country as one of the leading abstract artists from Mexico.

The retrospective showed clearly that the art of Ricardo Mazal does not stand still but moves at the pace of contemporary life, blurring international boundaries, stopping to focus on a crucial moment, then racing again toward the future.

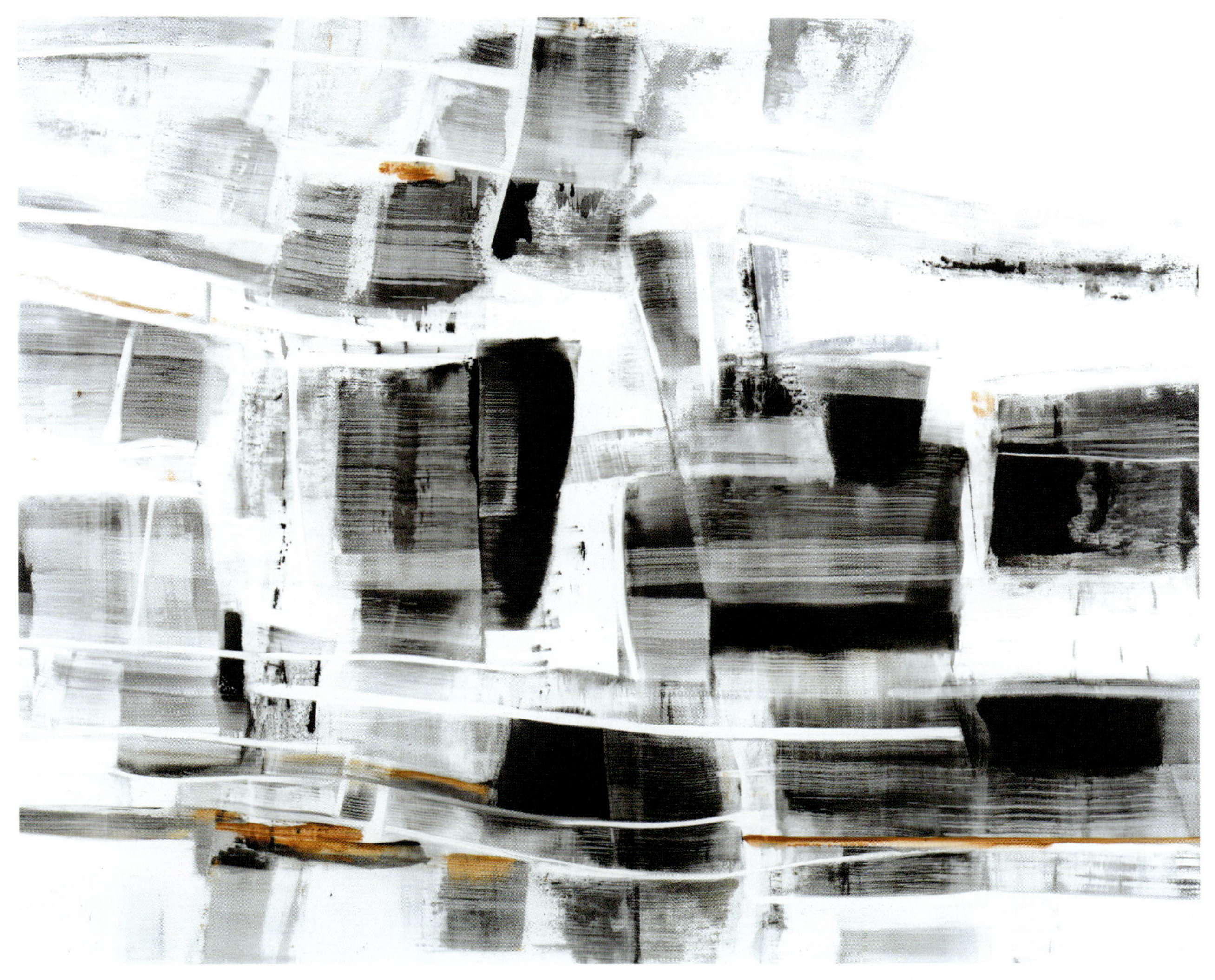

ABRIL 2, 2002
OIL ON LINEN
96 X 120 INCHES

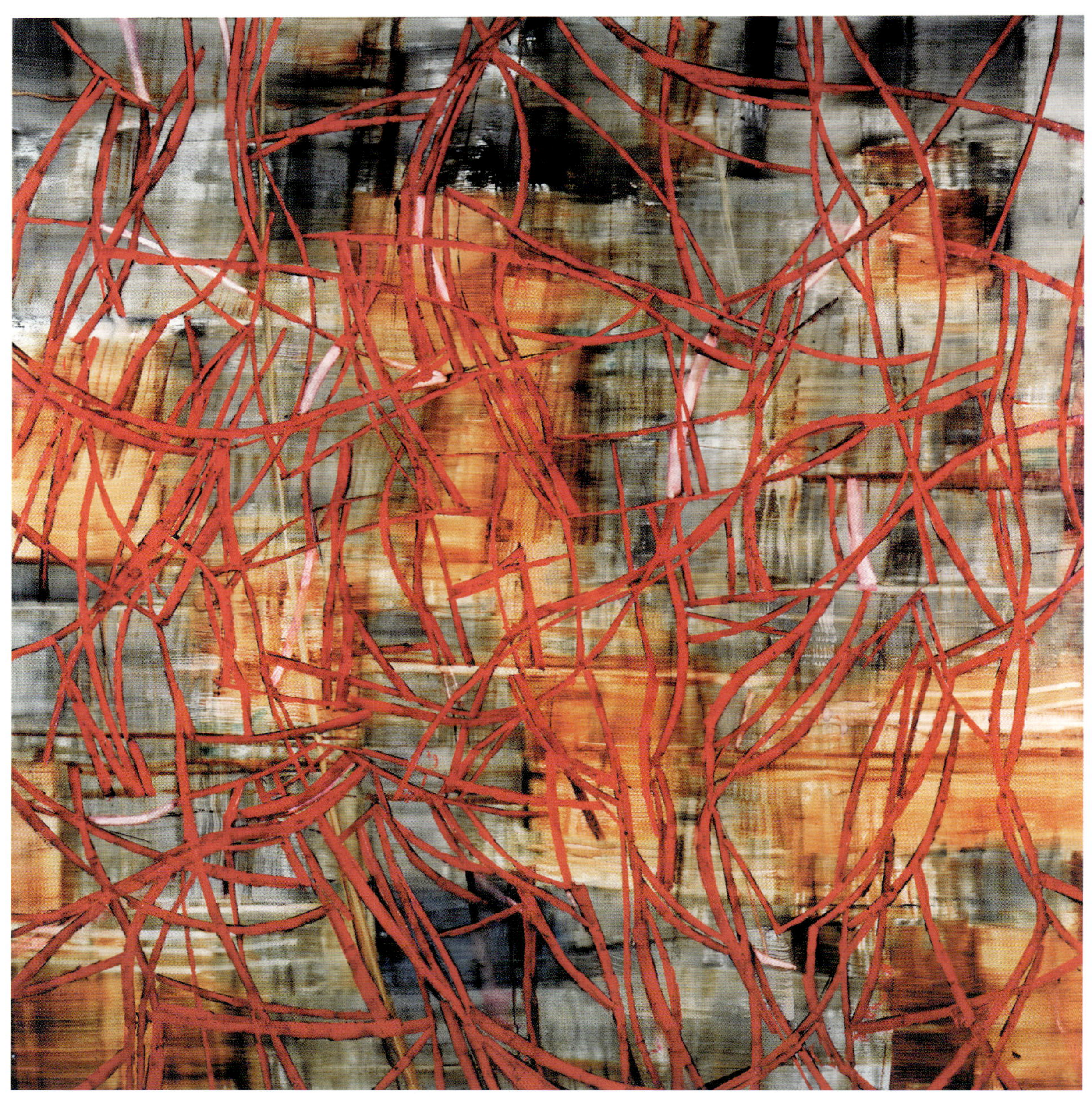

FRAGMENTS IN RED 2, 2001
OIL ON LINEN
80 X 80 INCHES

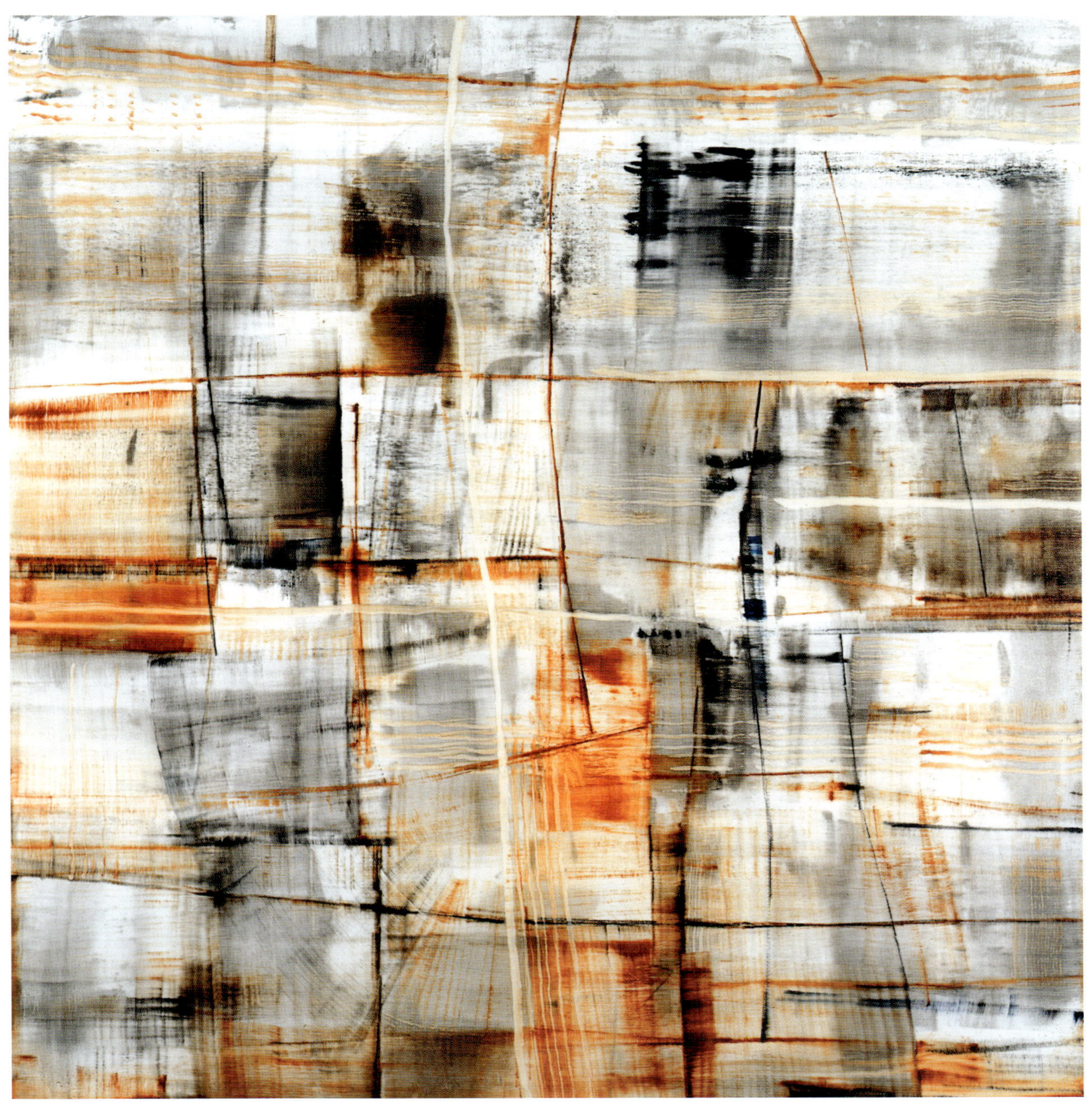

ONE INCH ABOVE 2, 2001
OIL ON LINEN
80 X 80 INCHES

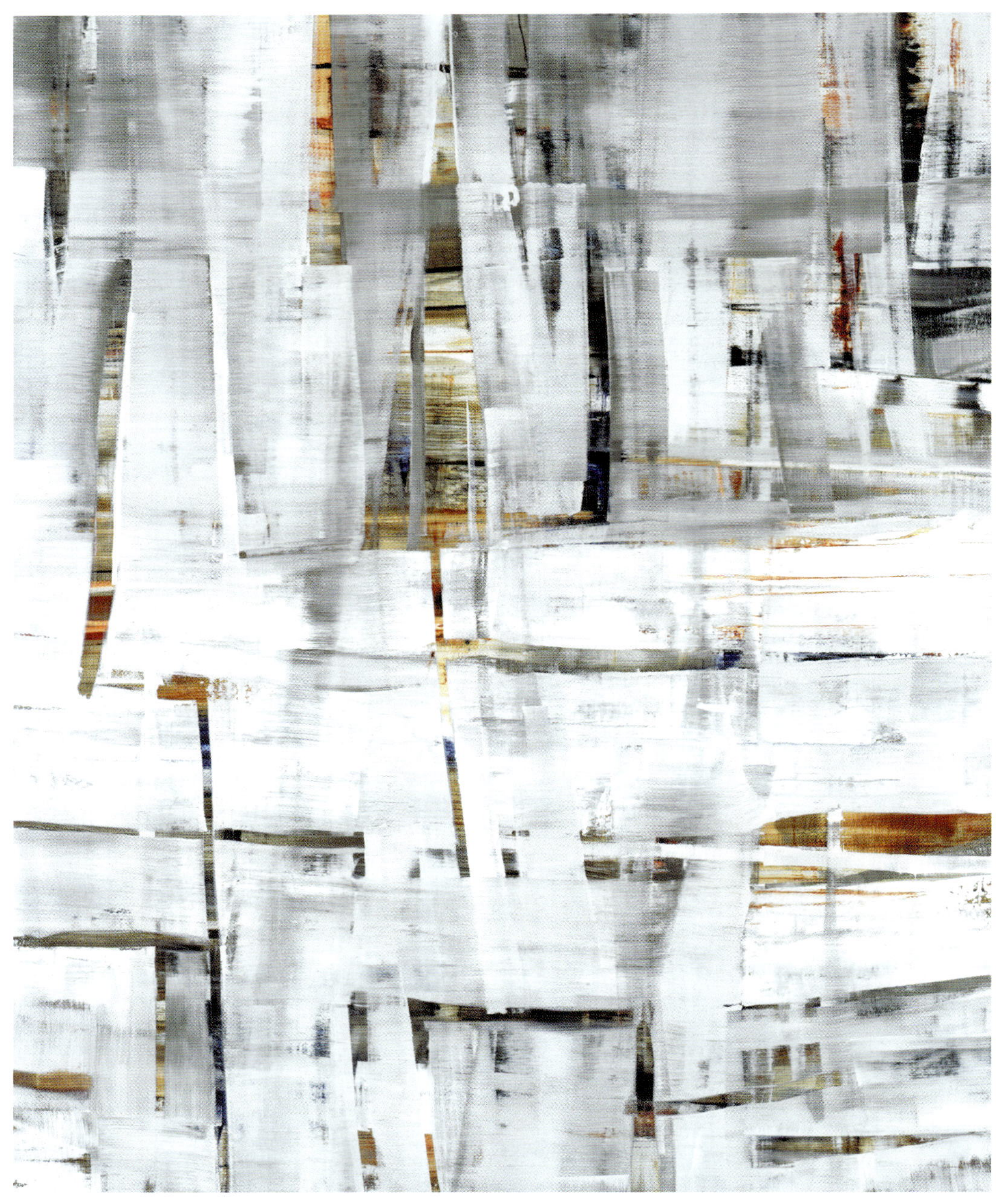

MARZO 20, 2002
OIL ON LINEN
78 X 66 INCHES

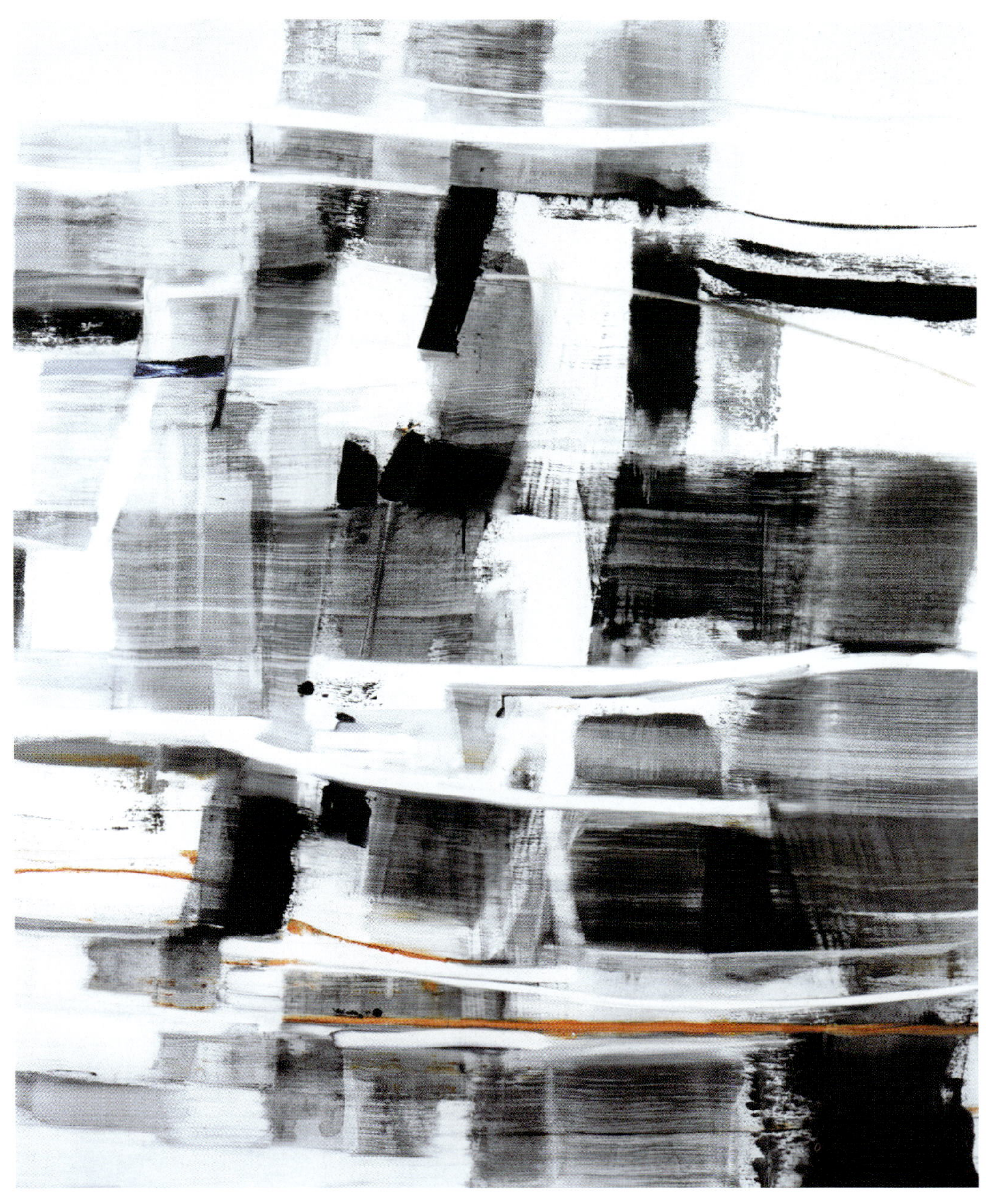

RICARDO MAZAL b. 1950 Mexico. Ed: Universidad Ibero Americano; Univ. Illinois. Solo exhibitions: NYC etal, USA; Europe; Mexico. Coll: Museo de Arte Contemporaneo de Monterrey (MARCO), Mexico; Museo de Arte Abstracto, Zacatecas, Mexico; Scottsdale Museum of Art AZ; etal. Representaticn: Chiaroscuro Gallery, Santa Fe.

MARZO 1, 2002
OIL ON LINEN
78 X 66 INCHES

LINDA J GING

An abstract work of art is an open secret. Its openness derives from its emotional engagement. Its mystery derives from its deliberate departure from representation, its withholding of text and diagram and reference, its ability to relate to each viewer in a different way based on that person's mindset.

Linda Ging's work does not yield up its secrets lightly, but its content is readily accessible to anyone who lives with open eyes in the world of light, weather, and thought. She is able, through color gradation and carefully orchestrated proportion, to capture the emotional experience of being alive. One's heart beats a little faster in recognition; one's mind recognizes without fully understanding.

Ging is an artist's artist. She has been living in Santa Fe for over two decades, doing a tremendous amount of work that has produced a radiant succession of canvases. "One of the glories of Santa Fe is the respect accorded to artists," she says. "My friends and collectors know that it is my choice to be in the studio, to work. My collectors have come by way of studio visits, galleries, and word of mouth."

Ging finds her own work mysterious. "I look at it and wonder where it comes from," she says. "I have to stay open to the twists and turns, and trust stepping into the abyss. When it stops feeling like terror, I know the work has started to shift. It happens every time. When you cross over into being an artist, you're looking at everything in a different way. Your vision has changed dramatically. Every once in awhile my eye will fall on something, and all I can see is color and texture. I study it for a while, and finally realize I'm looking at something completely familiar, like the end of a paintbrush. It's an extraordinary way to live your life."

Linda Ging's secret is her clarity about her work. "I speak in colors," she says. "My voice finds its cadence in pigment and canvas. Joy erupts. And underneath its raucous shouts, grief, reclusive and tenacious, peers out from those two-dimensional points of convergence, obscured in the nuances of form and hue."

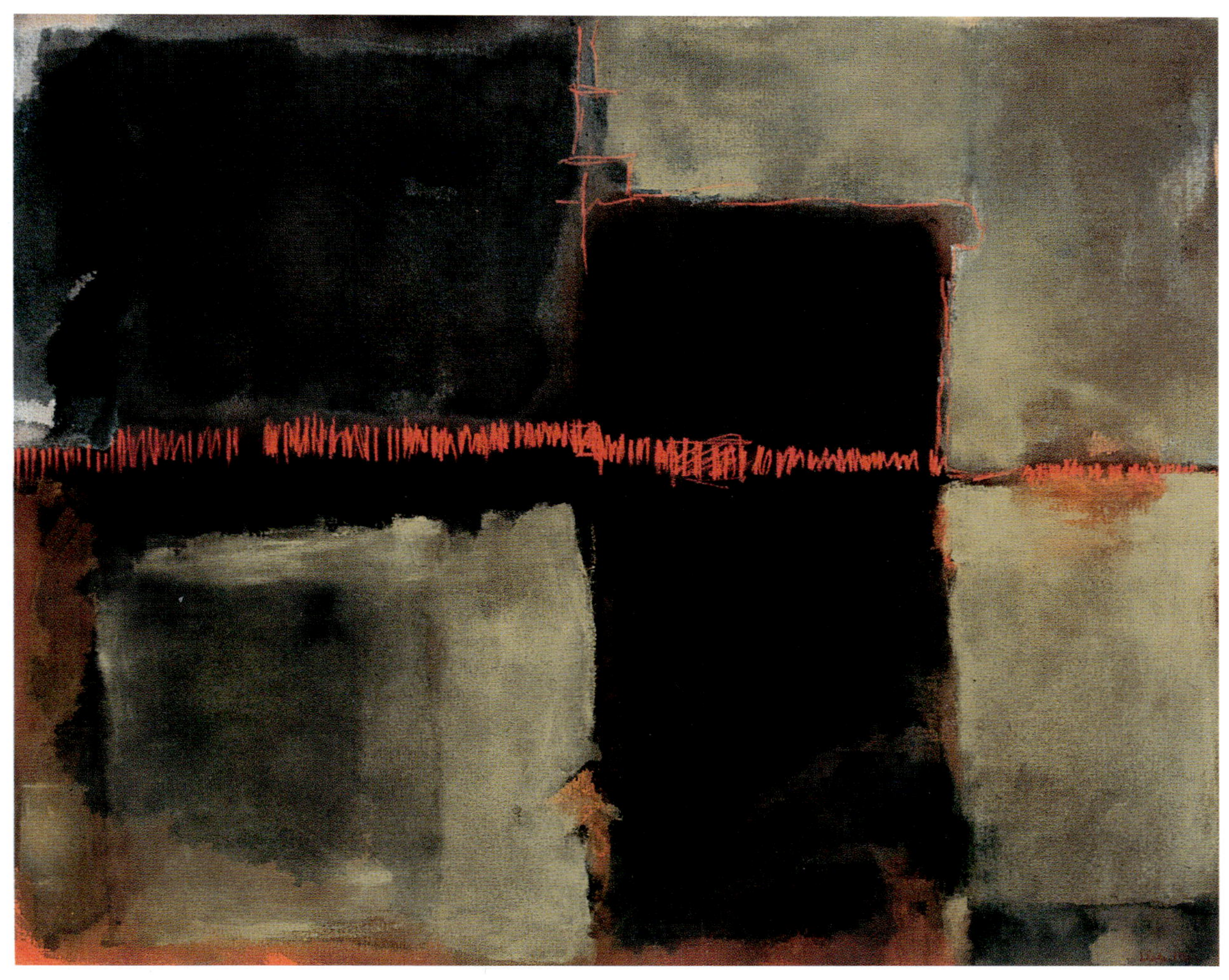

CONTROLLED BURN
ACRYLIC ON CANVAS
37 X 47 INCHES

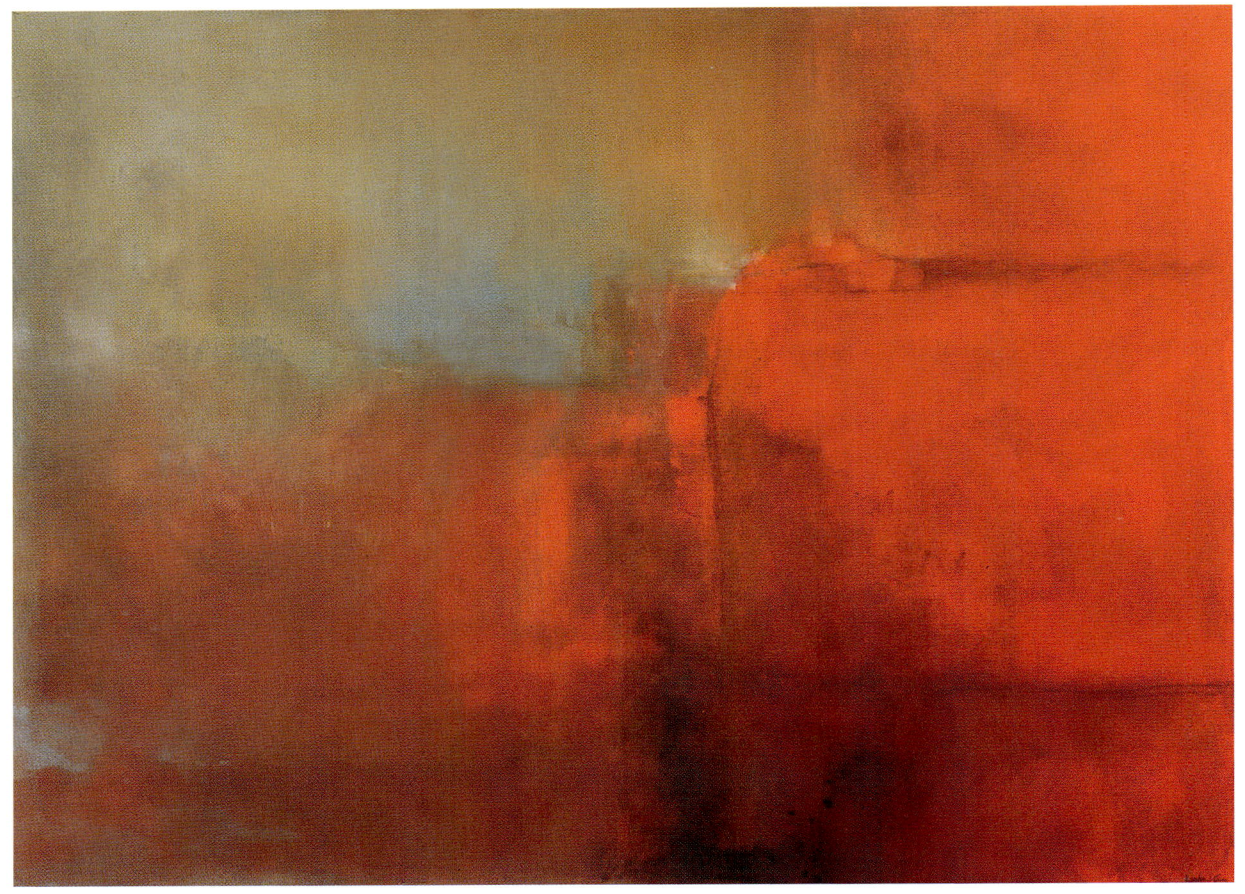

XANADU XVII
ACRYLIC ON CANVAS
46 X 64 INCHES

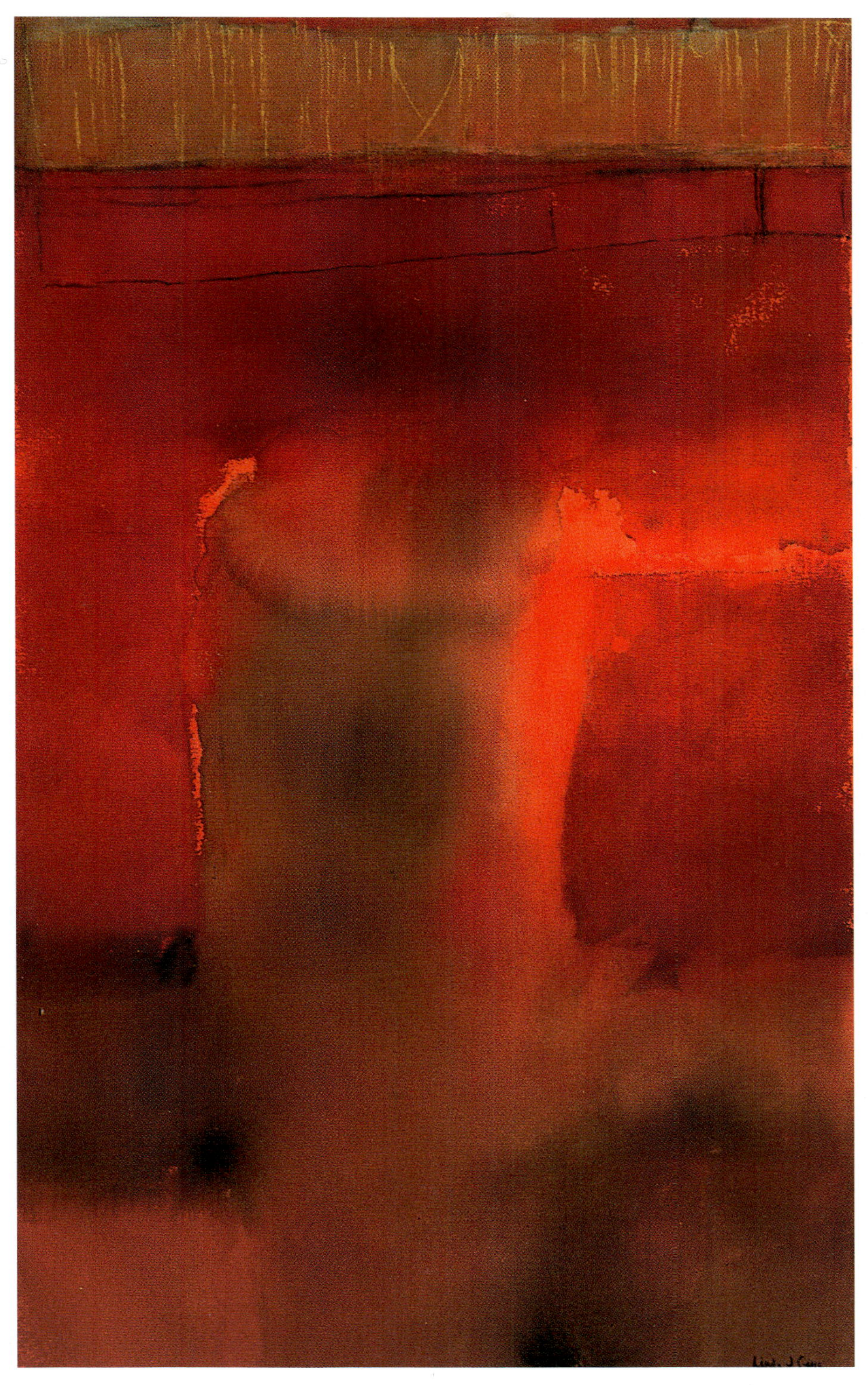

EVERY ANGEL IS TERRIFYING II (RILKE)
ACRYLIC ON CANVAS
48 X 31 INCHES

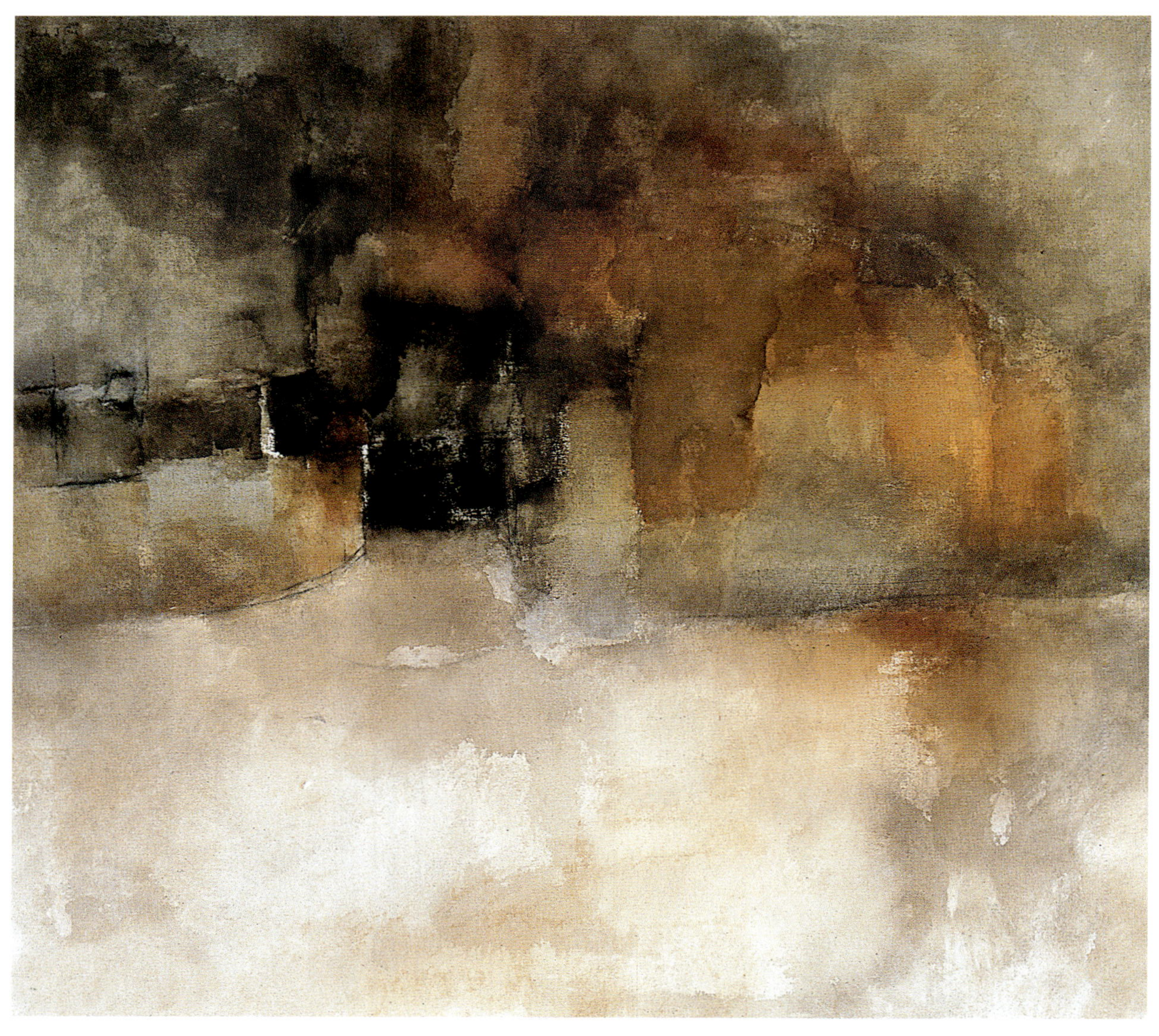

VISITING THE DRAGON
ACRYLIC ON CANVAS
58 X 66 INCHES

LINDA J GING b. 1941 Hutchinson KS. Ed: BA Studio Arts, Bethany College, Lindsborg KS. Exhib: Kansas 7, Washburn Univ., Topeka; WomanArt 8, Wichita KS; Representation: Linda Ging Studio, Santa Fe NM.

SURFING THE COSMOS II
ACRYLIC ON CANVAS
54 X 64 INCHES

TIM KLABUNDE

The spark of life is struck in the synapse between the fixed and the mutable, between stasis and involuntary motion, between contemplation and action. There is no balance without unbalance. In the Kanji characters of Asian writing, in dance, in nature itself, the constant dynamic interplay of symmetry and asymmetry animates even the simplest of forms.

Tim Klabunde's art, as well as his personal trajectory, reflects this vital balance. As a young man, he moved from college into the arena of hands-on work with railroad and bridge construction. It was during this robust period that he developed his lifelong love of steel. His art rose naturally and spontaneously from his desire to apply his ideas to the materials and techniques that were familiar to him.

"I've always been around steel," says Klabunde. "I'm drawn to the power of it. Steel is a hard, heavy, dirty material to work with, but because of its strength you can do a lot of structural things that you can't do with other materials. You can bend it, shape it, make it graceful and flowing."

Klabunde begins each piece by working directly with the steel. There are no sketches, although he does make models and draw on the metal with soapstone. He is careful with the angles so that when the viewer walks around a finished piece there is an experience of change. Forms tilt this way and that; they float or plunge through openings; they thrust upward toward the sky. Rusty patinas contrast with polished stainless steel. "There has to be movement," he says. "I'll study the piece for hours or days, getting the lyricism and feeling in there."

Klabunde was a talented amateur when he moved to Santa Fe in 1980. The ensuing decade is remembered fondly by all as a rowdy, funny, freewheeling, profoundly generative era in the local art world. Klabunde caught the wave and began to produce heartfelt, importantly scaled sculpture that found ready acceptance in a community that was itself on the verge of greatness.

Then a motorcycle accident in the early 1990s sidelined him for four years. In typical self-contained fashion, he took charge of his own recovery and returned to his art a more serious professional than ever. He resumed production of monumental steel sculpture with a new depth of feeling, a changed attitude toward the business of art, and a renewed dedication to abstract art.

"My early work was figurative," he says, "but it didn't express the feelings I have about certain things. It didn't have the essence, the feeling, the movement. Abstract works for me."

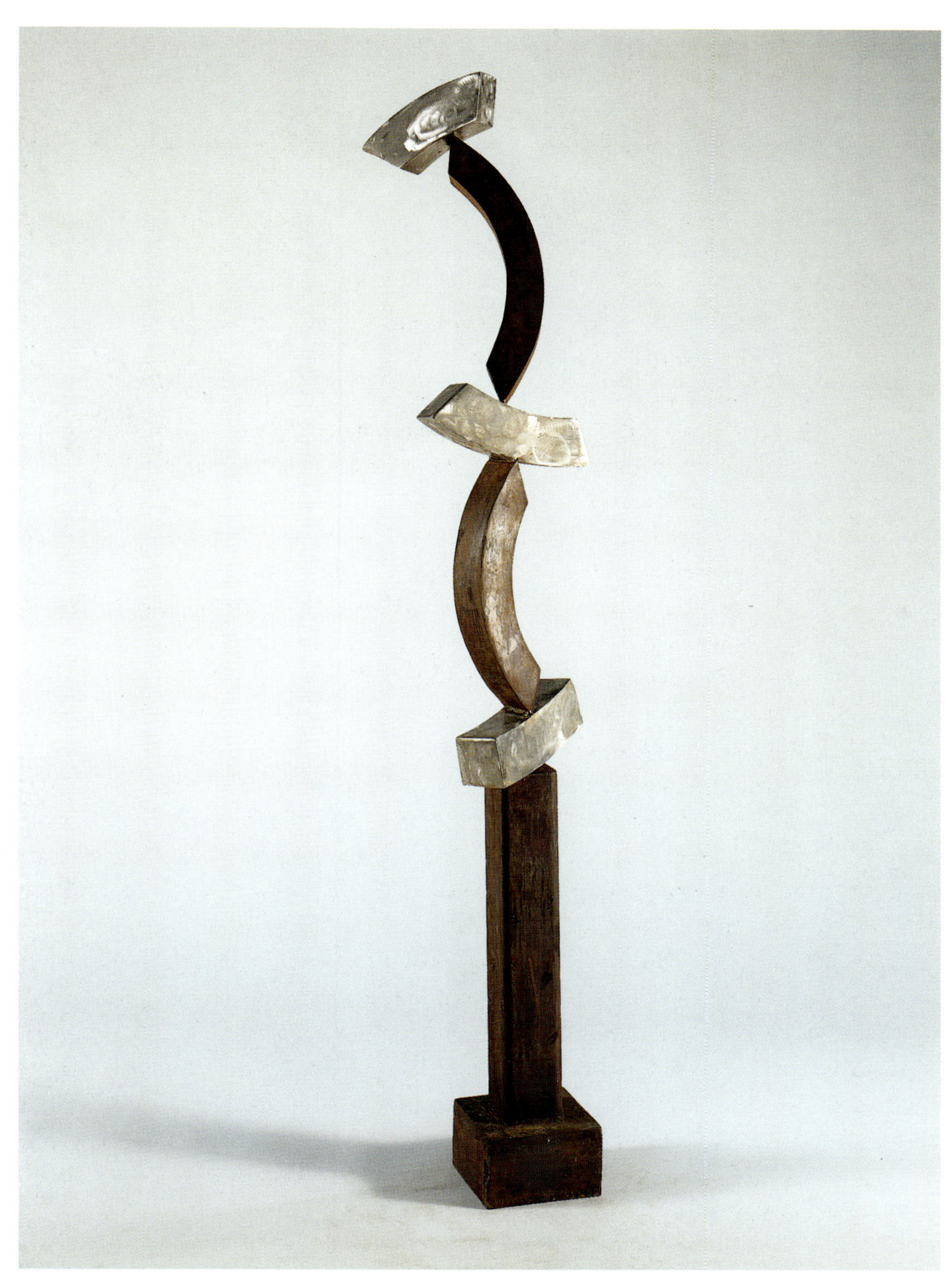

UNTITLED 1
COR-TEN™ STEEL AND STAINLESS STEEL
6 FEET

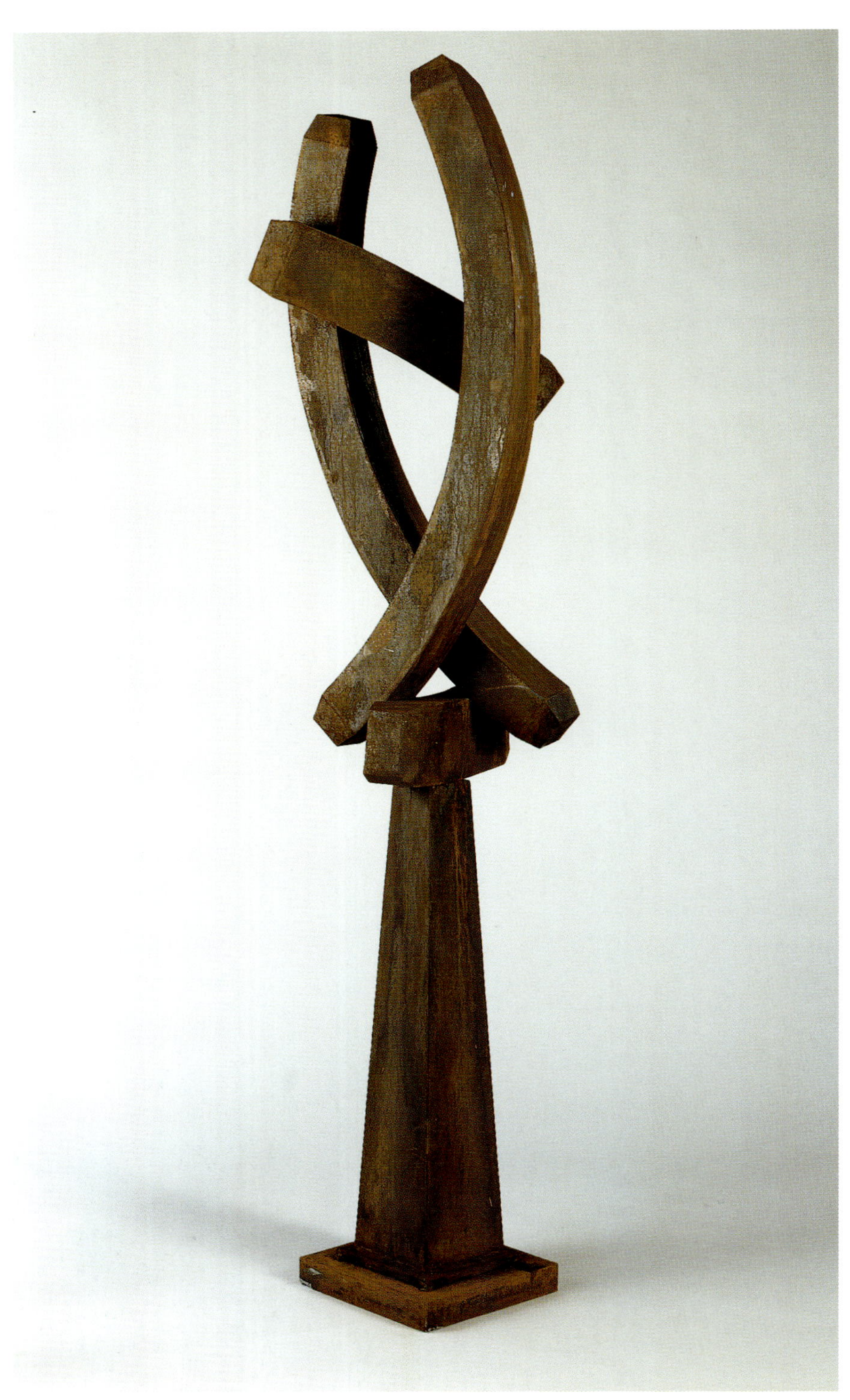

UNTITLED
STEEL
8 FEET

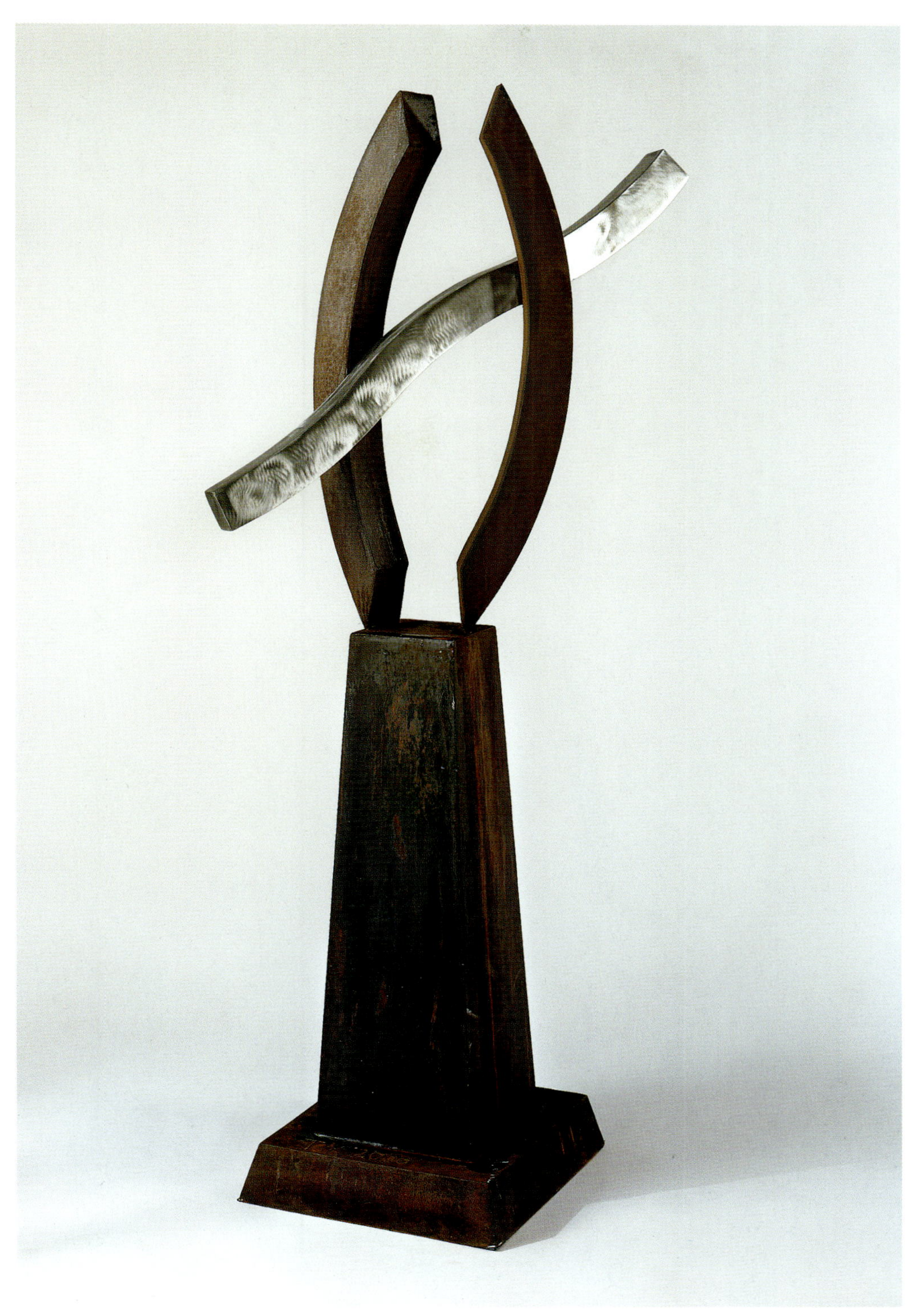

RIO GRANDE
COR-TEN™ STEEL AND STAINLESS STEEL
7 FEET

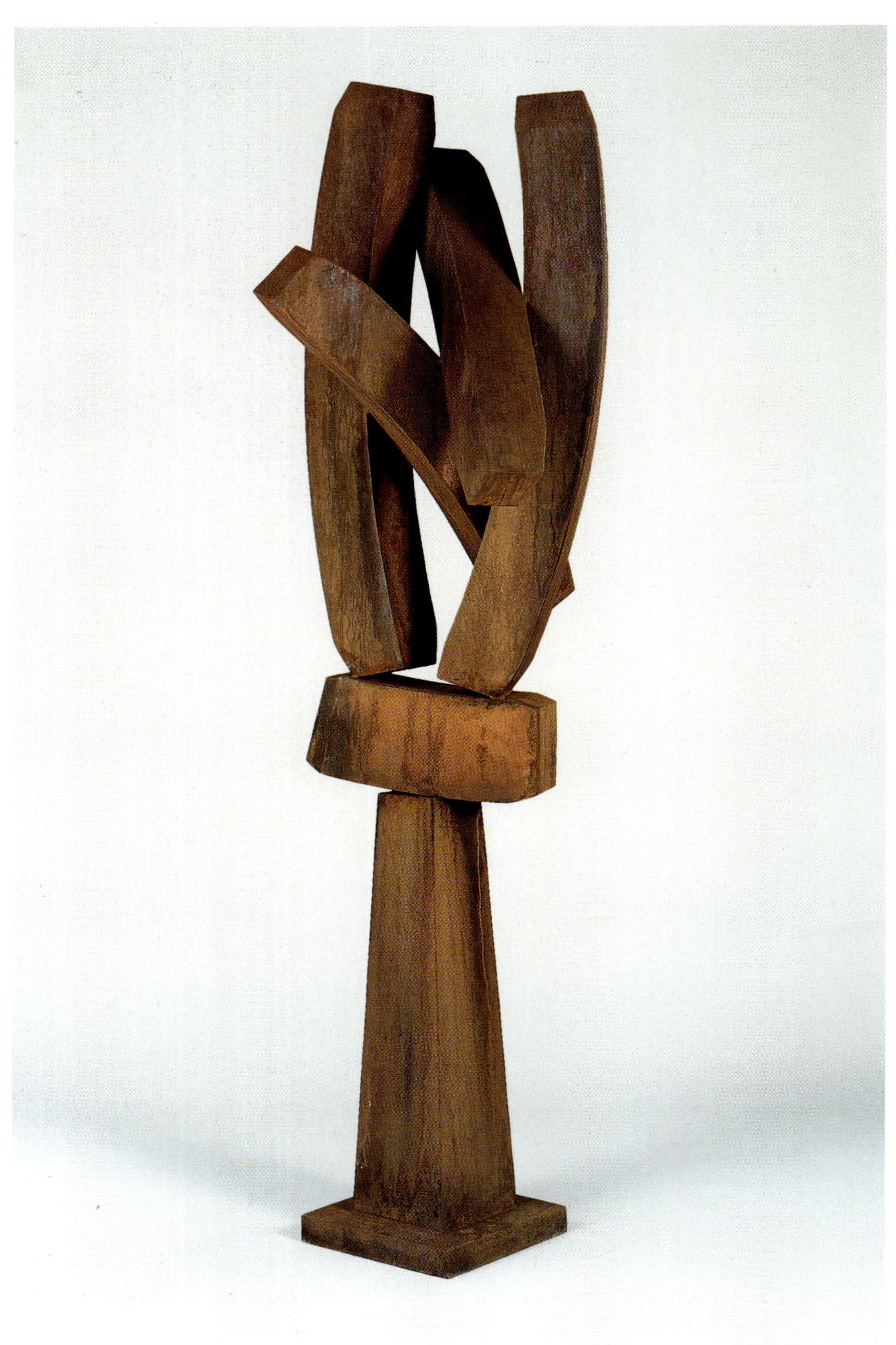

GARDEN OF THE GODS II
STEEL
8 FEET

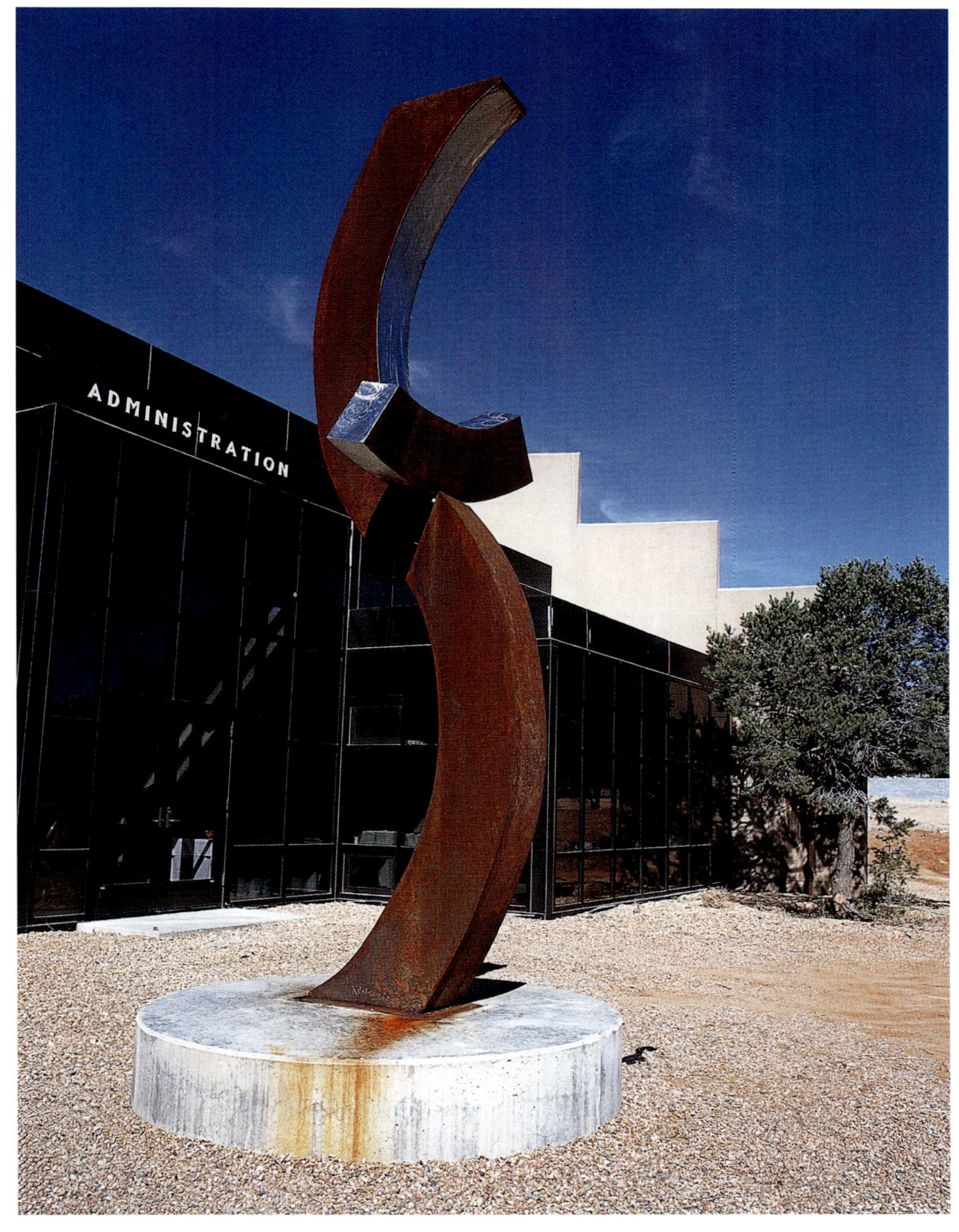

TIM KLABUNDE b. 1947 Aberdeen WA. Ed: Univ. Minnesota. Installations: New Mexico Academy; Armory for the Arts, Santa Fe NM. Exhib: College of Santa Fe Sculpture Project; Governor's Gallery NM; North American Sculpture Exhibition, Denver CO. Awards: Santa Fe Festival of the Arts.

MOTHER AND CHILD
COR-TEN™ STEEL AND STAINLESS STEEL
18 FEET

STAN BERNING

The voluptuous elegance of the New Mexico landscape mirrors the hills and valleys of the recumbent human figure, a fact that has long been noticed and exploited by all manner of representational painters. The shops are full of semi-erotic, dreamy, impressionistic references to this phenomenon.

It takes a particular kind of artist, however, to vault over the obvious, to embrace the sun-ripped mineral brilliance of the desert, to fuse the sensuous texture of cloud and canyon with the austere poetry of the body. Abstraction affords an emotional connection that is not inconsistent with intellectual distance.

Stan Berning's art fuses the physical with the terrestrial by means of line and color His affinity for line informed even his earliest work. Color became a catalyst after he became interested in fine print media. He participated in several workshops in Santa Fe, and also became an assistant printer at Graphics Workshop, one of the top printmaking ateliers of its time.

Berning was especially drawn to the monotype process, which produces a print that has an edition of one. Dampened paper is placed over a flat inked plate with nothing etched into it, and both are run through a printing press. "In the monotype," he says, "I rediscovered the flexibility of the sketchbook, while the medium yielded finished pieces of art."

He also rediscovered his abstract roots, and his work became progressively purer. However, he retains his appreciation for realism, finding it to be a rejuvenating influence even in his most rigorous abstract pieces.

During those generative early years of printing, Berning began to study color in earnest by devising various experiments. One weekend, he decided to lay various colors alongside each other in varied hues and proportions, just to see what might happen. "After three twelve hour days," he says, "when I had pulled dozens upon dozens of these quick experimental prints, I remember locking the studio door behind me and turning to find a world transformed. It was late night and a yellow fire hydrant down the street leaped out at me. The deepest shadows radiated a purple glow. Some huge yet subtle shift had occurred in my brain. For the first time in my life I was seeing color as it is rather than as I had been taught to see it. 'This will be gone in the morning,' I thought. But it never left me."

Within the past year Stan Berning has begun a new series of paintings and prints which opens up an entirely new range of possibilities. These graphically sophisticated images function as wholly abstract meditations on form. They may also allude to anything the viewer wants to read into them. Life moves in ecstatic moments and geological epochs. Landscape becomes figure becomes landscape. Nature shows itself to be a single organic reality.

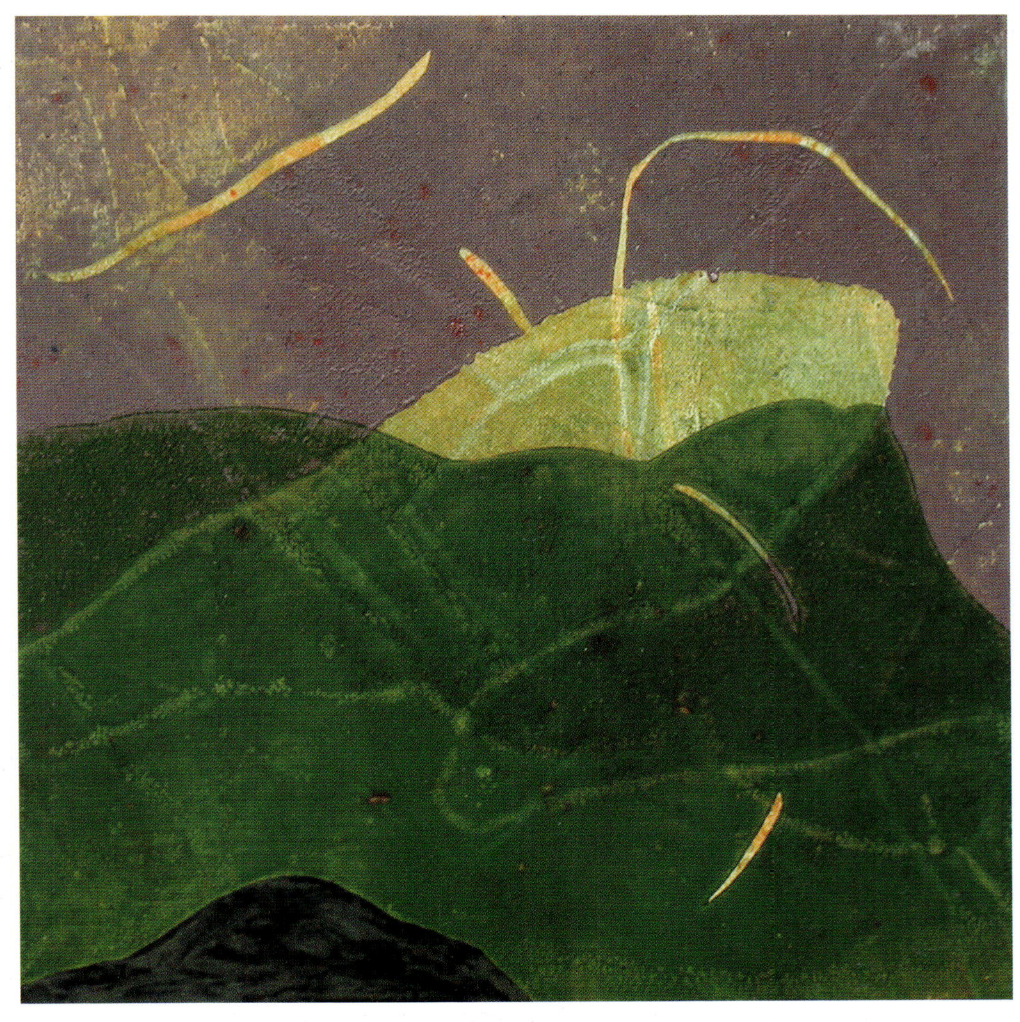

PASTORALE #19, 2002
MONOPRINT
9 X 9 INCHES

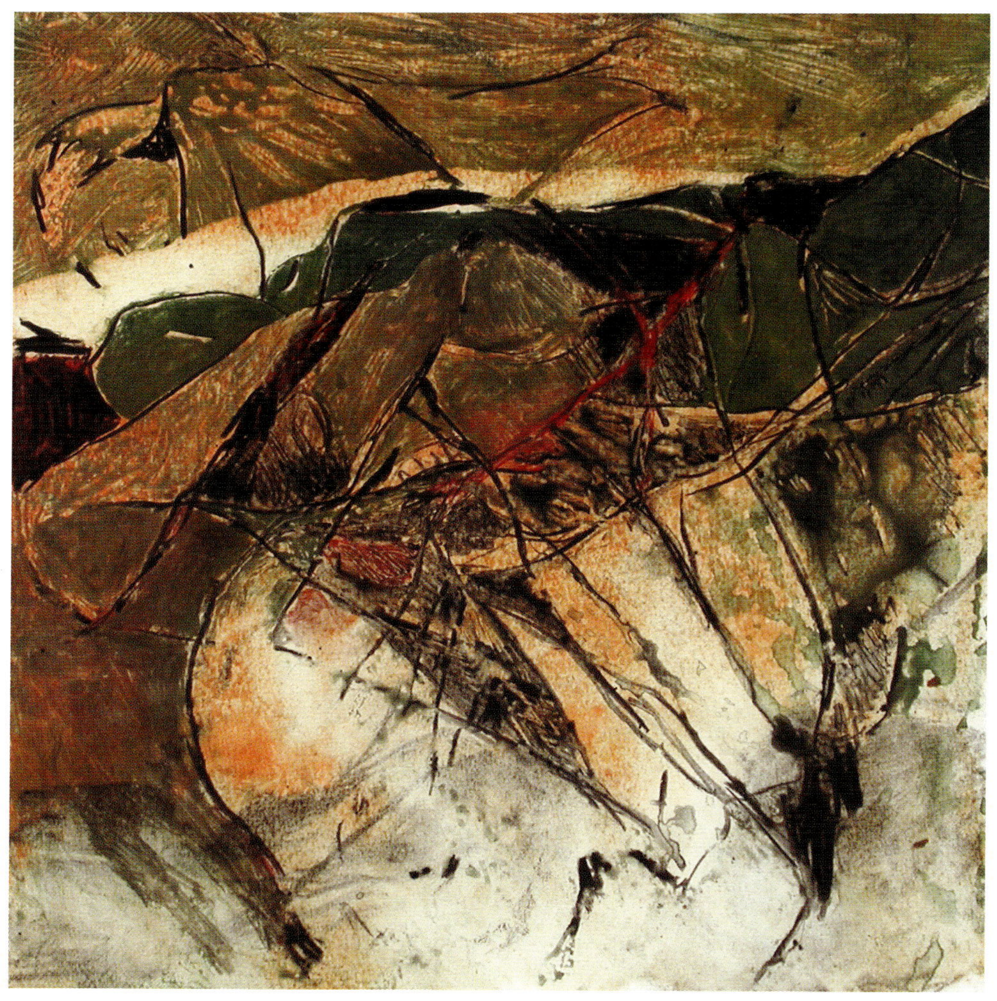

POWER STUDY PART TWO #1, 2003
MONOTYPE
12 X 12 INCHES

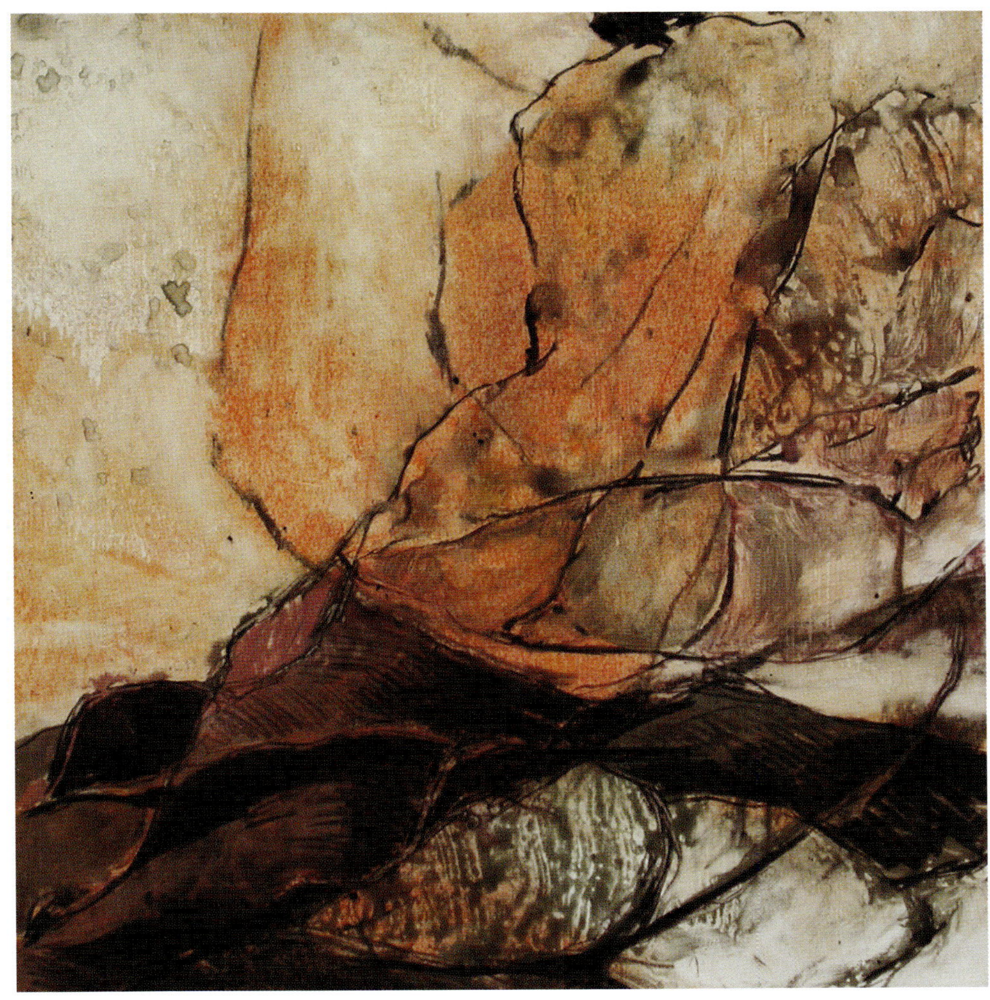

POWER STUDY PART TWO #2, 2003
MONOTYPE
12 X 12 INCHES

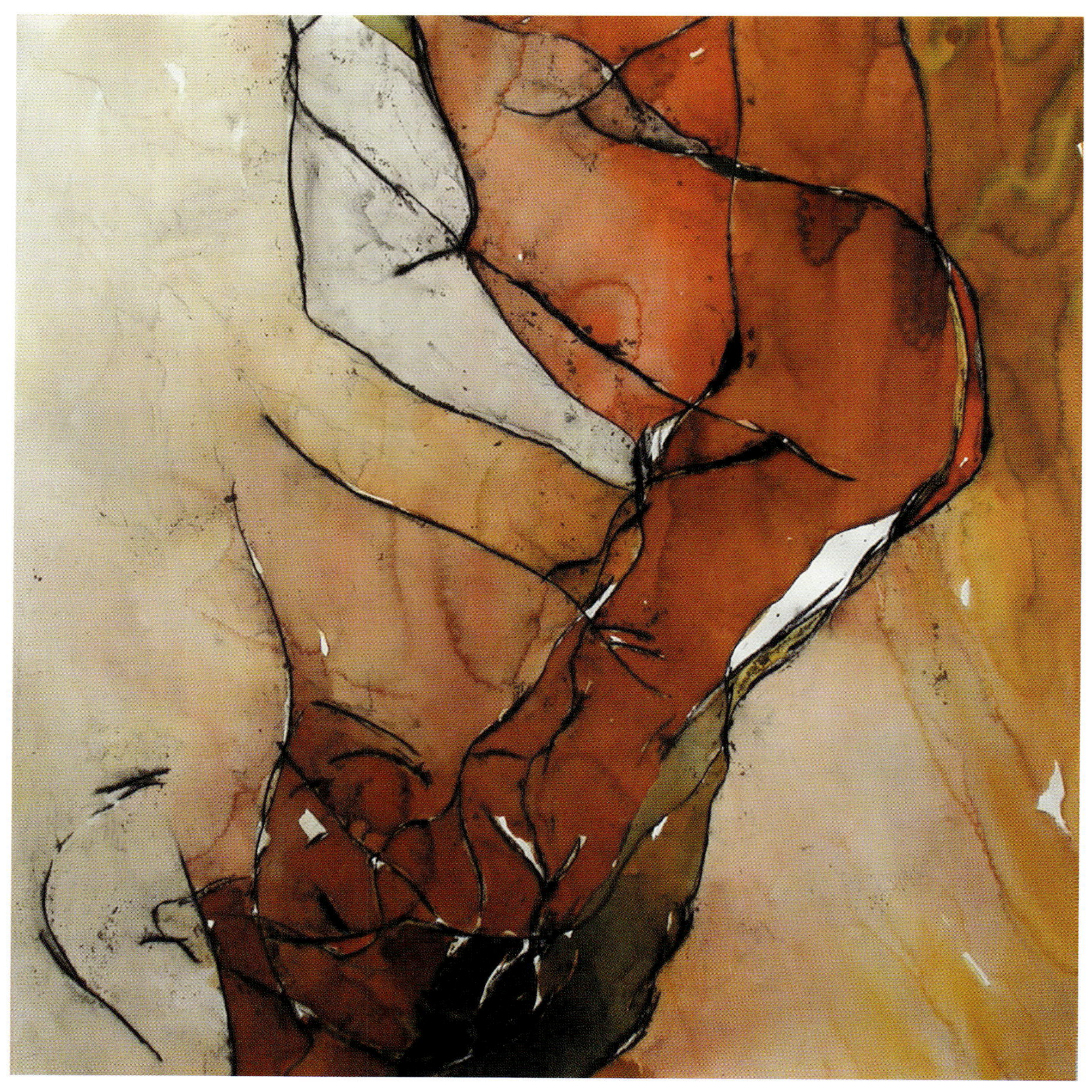

A NATURAL HISTORY PART TWO #10, 2003
CHARCOAL AND WATERCOLOR
40 X 40 INCHES

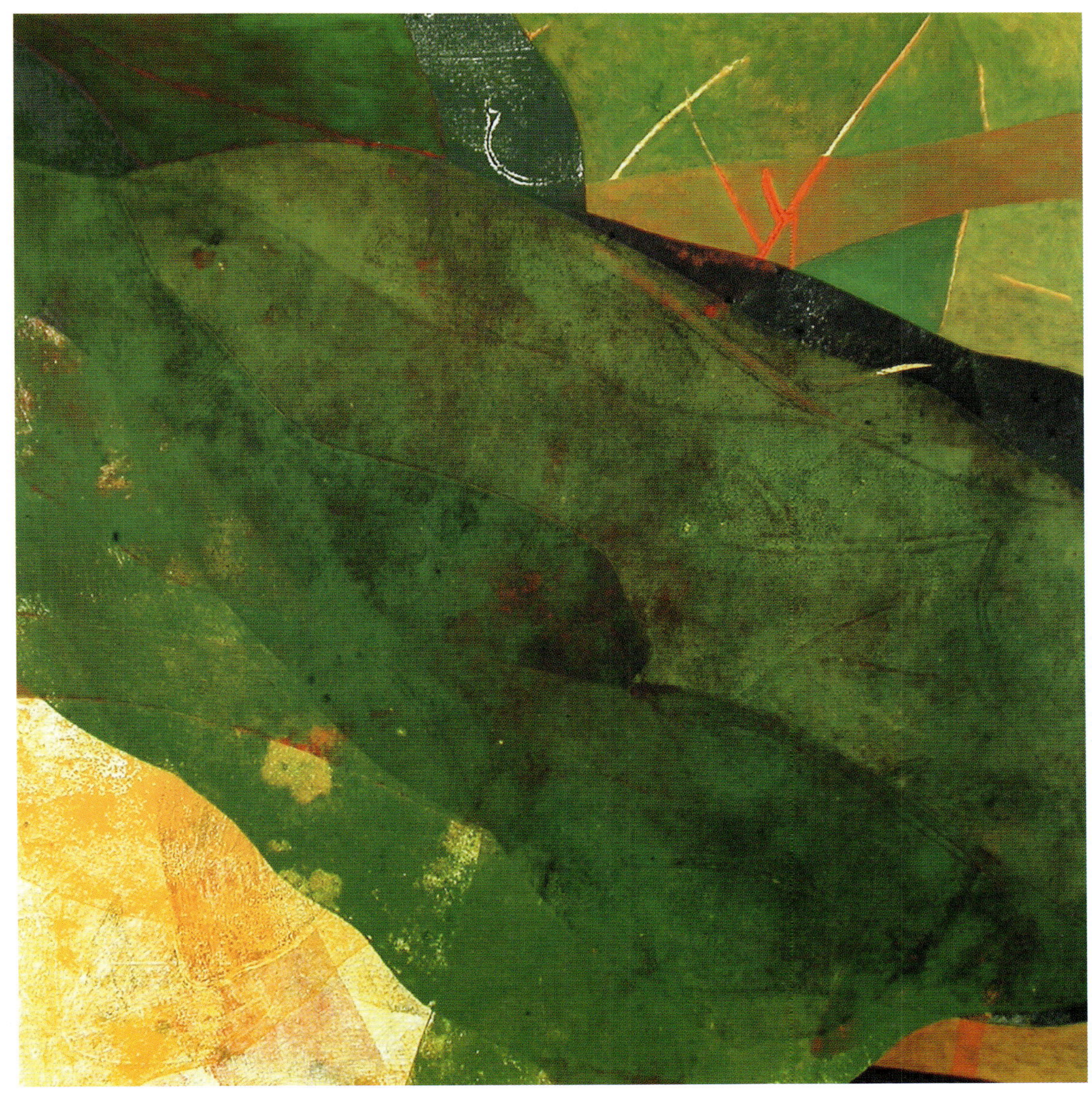

STAN BERNING b. 1951 New Bremen OH. Ed: Oberlin College OH; Earlham College IN. Invitational exhib: Foothills Art Center, Colorado Springs CO; Faber Birren National Color Awards Show CT. Coll: Merrill Lynch; Bank of Tokyo; Hallmark; Volvo; Compaq; etal. Representation: Marie Park, Dallas; Dremillion and Co., Houston; Joseph Gierek Fine Art, Tulsa; Elins Eagle-Smith Gallery, San Francisco.

OVERTURE #13, 2002
MONOPRINT
30 X 30 INCHES

STEPHANIE DRAGON

The slow disintegration of unknowing allows us to know; our knowledge of the infinite depends upon our piercing the veil of the finite. At birth, we begin to be bombarded by opaque sensory stimuli that conceal content behind appearance. Our entire environment seems to be a mirror that reflects our being, and we believe that what we see on the surface is what the world is like.

If we can learn to pay attention, however, this mirror of ourselves gradually becomes a window to the other. The perceived surface gives way to the meaning that lies beneath it. Sensory impression gives way to understanding. To the extent that we can control our access to the unconscious, we become conscious.

The art of Stephanie Dragon touches on this phenomenon in a conceptual rather than a literal way. In some of her works, light forces its way out from behind the cracks in a dark surface; in other pieces, the light falls on a flat plane whose fissures reveal the depths beneath. In either case, the careful manipulation of paint sets up a magnetic pull that involves the viewer in the process.

Dragon works with the pull of gravity to get her surfaces to crack and f ow. The process is very controlled right up to the point where she lets go and allows the painting to take over. "I start at the top and work down," she says, "building up many layers as I go. Sometimes the movement of the paint happens fas-, or sometimes nothing happens for twenty minutes and then it will come together. It's the sitting back after all the work and watching it happen that is so magical."

Dragon worked as a studio assistant for Kenneth Noland for several years in the late 1980s. During that time, she learned a great deal about methods, materials, and approach, and became especially interested in the properties of paint. "There are many variables," she says. "Humidity, different colors and mediums, thickness and thinness, gloss and matte all affect the outcome."

By 1992, she was ready to move to Santa Fe and to concentrate on her own swiftly evolving art. Her distinctive style of today is the result of a creative inci- dent. "I was playing with layers and transparencies," she recalls, "trying to get a reaction to repeat itself. At one point I covered the whole thing with white, then went out for an hour. When I came back, the paint had settled, and there was the image I had been working toward."

Stephanie Dragon continues to push the boundaries between the seen and the sensed, stretching the picture plane toward infinity. "I've always been driven," she says. "I feel an inner call to do this work."

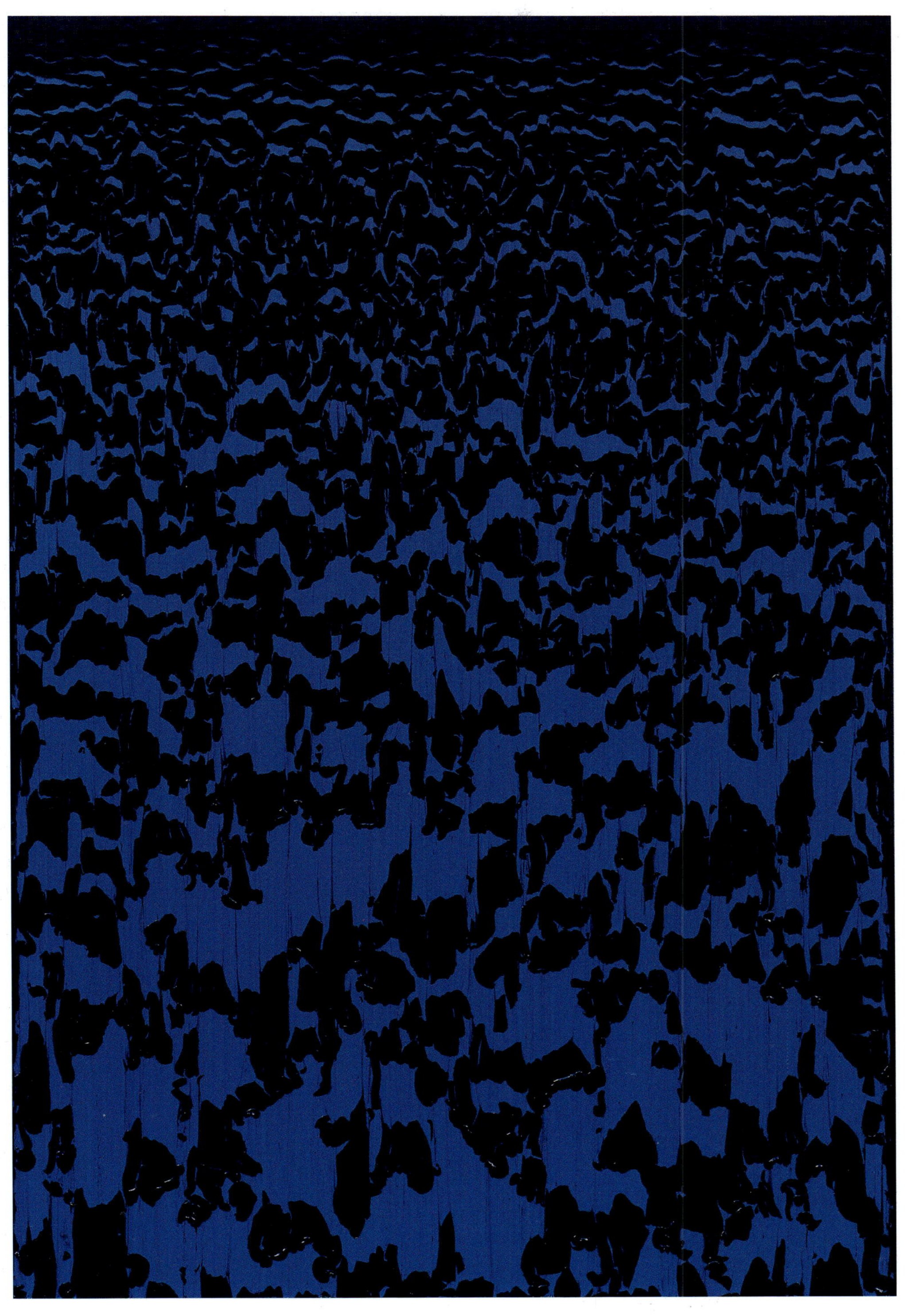

20203
ACRYLIC ON CANVAS
60 X 40 INCHES

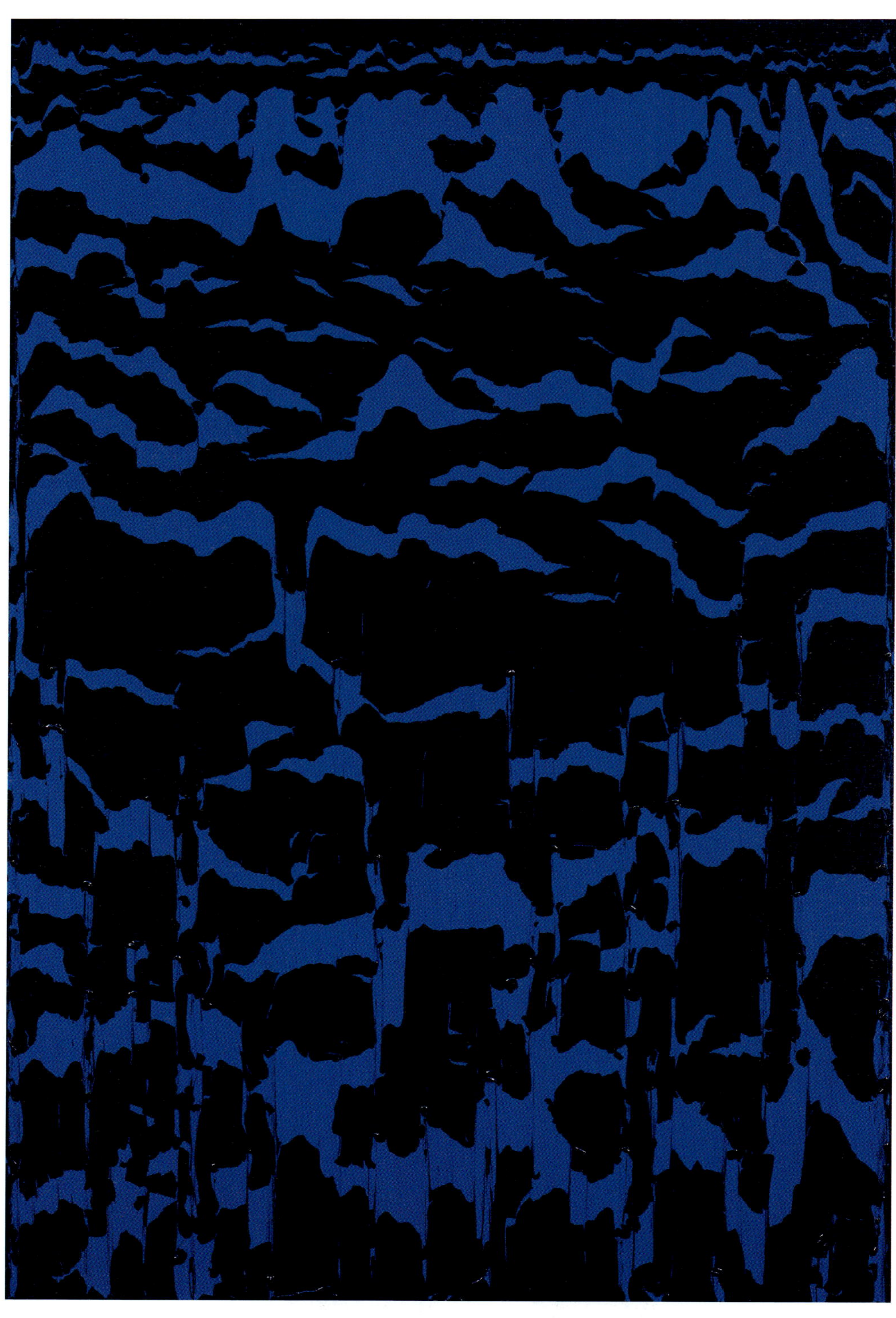

52402 SHADES OF BLUE
ACRYLIC ON CANVAS
64 X 24 INCHES

STEPHANIE DRAGON

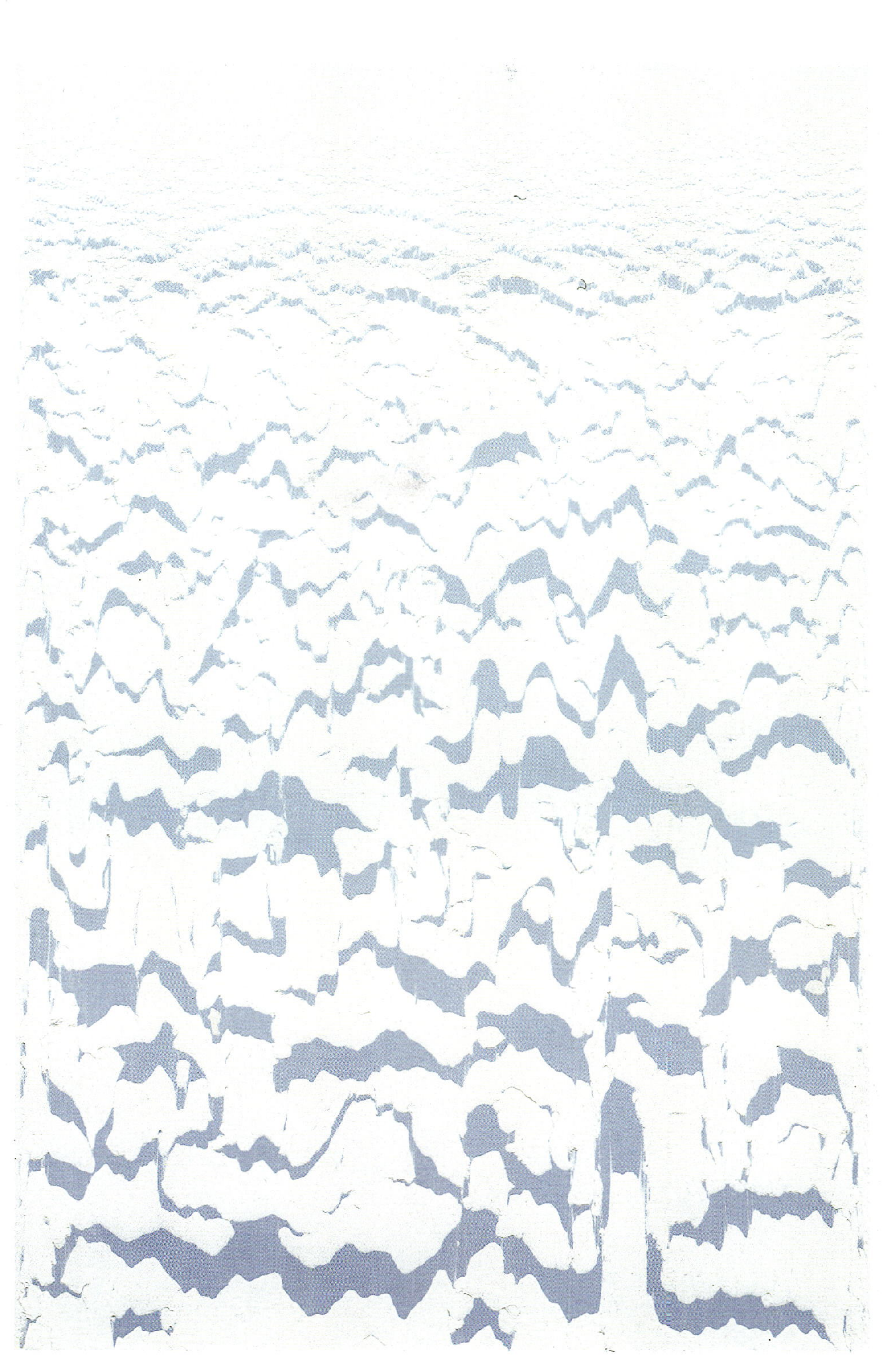

60602 SHADES OF BLUE
ACRYLIC ON CANVAS
36 X 24 INCHES

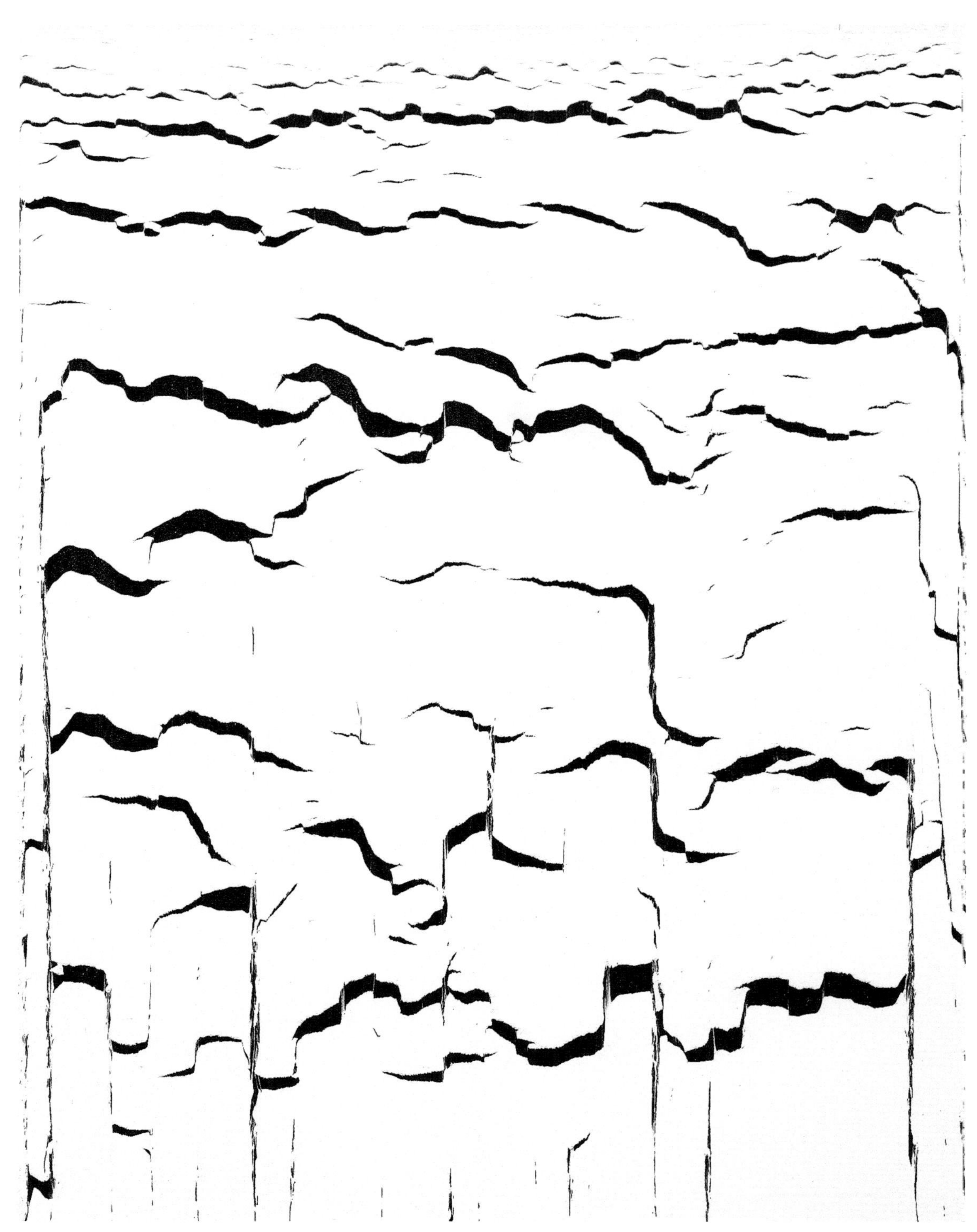

41402 SHADES OF BLUE
ACRYLIC ON CANVAS
30 X 24 INCHES

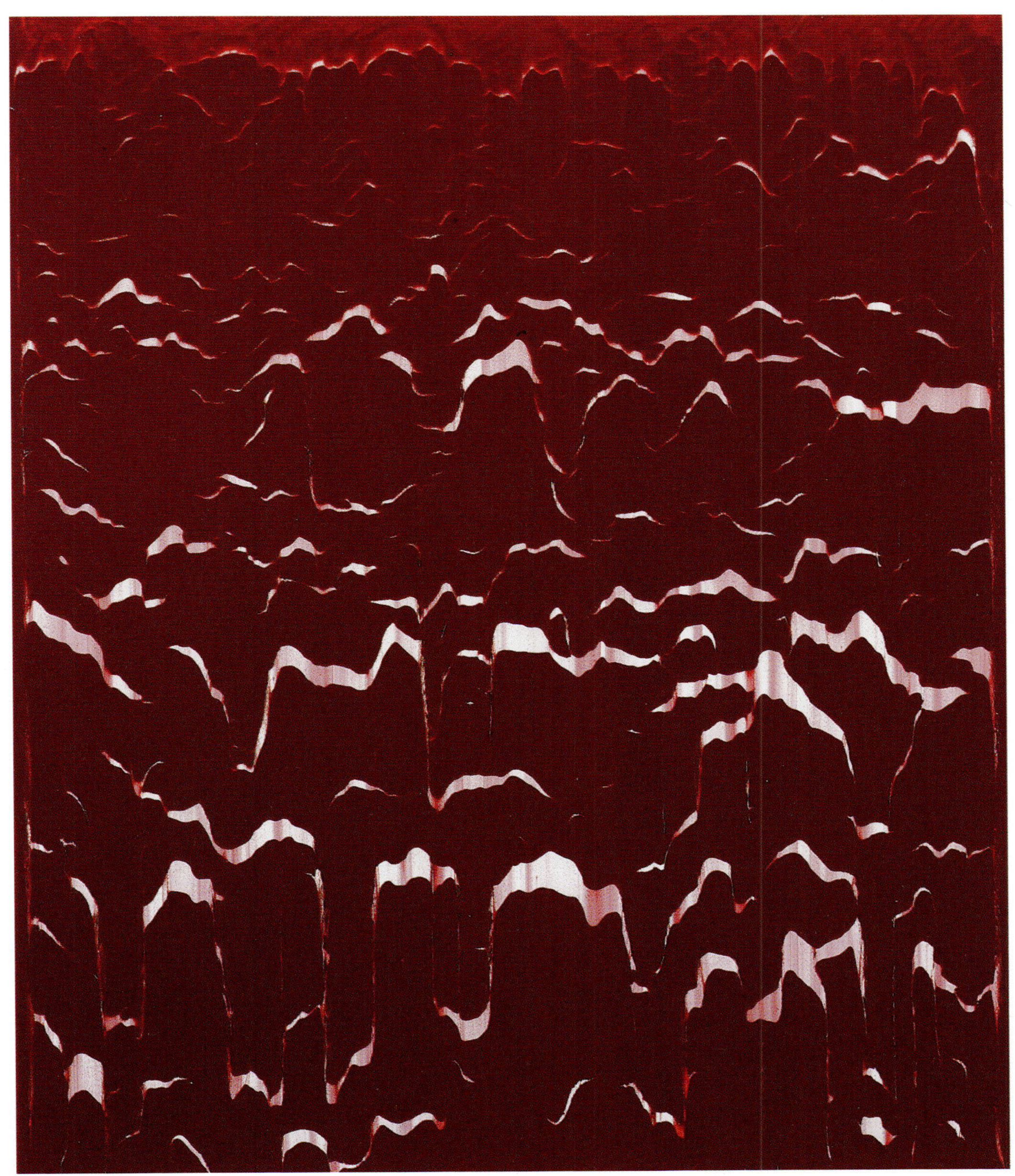

STEPHANIE DRAGON b. 1943 Los Angeles. Ed: Honors graduate, Santa Barbara Art Institute; worked and studied with Kenneth Noland. Group shows: Friends of Contemporary Art Annual Exhibitions, Santa Fe. Representation: EVO Gallery, Santa Fe.

42101
ACRYLIC ON CANVAS
28 X 24 INCHES

DERUSHA

Our culture screens out many experiences, both good and bad ones, by means of our social structure and the media. We ourselves screen out many of our own perceptions, usually as a matter of comfort. We simply are not strong enough to do everything and know everything.

The strongest events and ideas push through our screens, demanding to be acknowledged. They present themselves to us first as random dots of knowledge. Then they begin to line up and make sense, then evolve into pure abstractions. Finally they become part of our personal framework.

Derusha is an artist who has set out to get behind the filters and seek elemental experience. Before moving to Santa Fe, she painted in Australia for fourteen years, including eight years in the desert. During one outing, she was approached by an Aborigine who carried a digging stick and introduced himself as artist Johnny Warangkula. He encouraged her to paint with him, and through him she met other artists and learned much about their culture.

"These artists taught me a lot about life and spirit," she says. "I believe at this time my inspiration and life changed dramatically." The connection led to a series of figurative and abstract paintings that were shown in various Australian and American venues.

It was in Australia in 1997 that Derusha started using Bubblewrap™ as an overdotting method. Some of her paintings were packaged in the wrap, and she noticed the transparency of dots laid over dots. It reminded her of the work of Johnny Warangkula, who achieved atmospheric effects using layers of dots in different sizes, shapes, colors, and directions, all adding to the movement and space of his composition.

Derusha began using wrap as an actual medium, painting on both the front and the back and also printing it directly onto Belgium linen canvas. Sometimes the dots appear as negative spaces, suggesting a mesh screen. Often they are raised, conjuring up not only aboriginal Dreamtime paintings but the Ben-Day dots of Pop Art or the pixels of early photo-reproduction. These passages contrast with painterly areas that reveal what she calls "the movement of the human natural hand against the repetitive machine-made dots."

Sometimes she glues wrap to the canvas. "These surfaces are fragile to the human touch," she says, "but they last a long time because the wrap is pure plastic and not the disintegrating type made from corn. In this way, they're like whole cultures. If we go into them without great care, our impact can destroy them."

Derusha's ideas migrate across the vastness of her canvases. They drift into irregular patterns like the rise and fall of current topics. They reveal more than they conceal. Their surfaces are, she says, "like my own skin, weathered and alive."

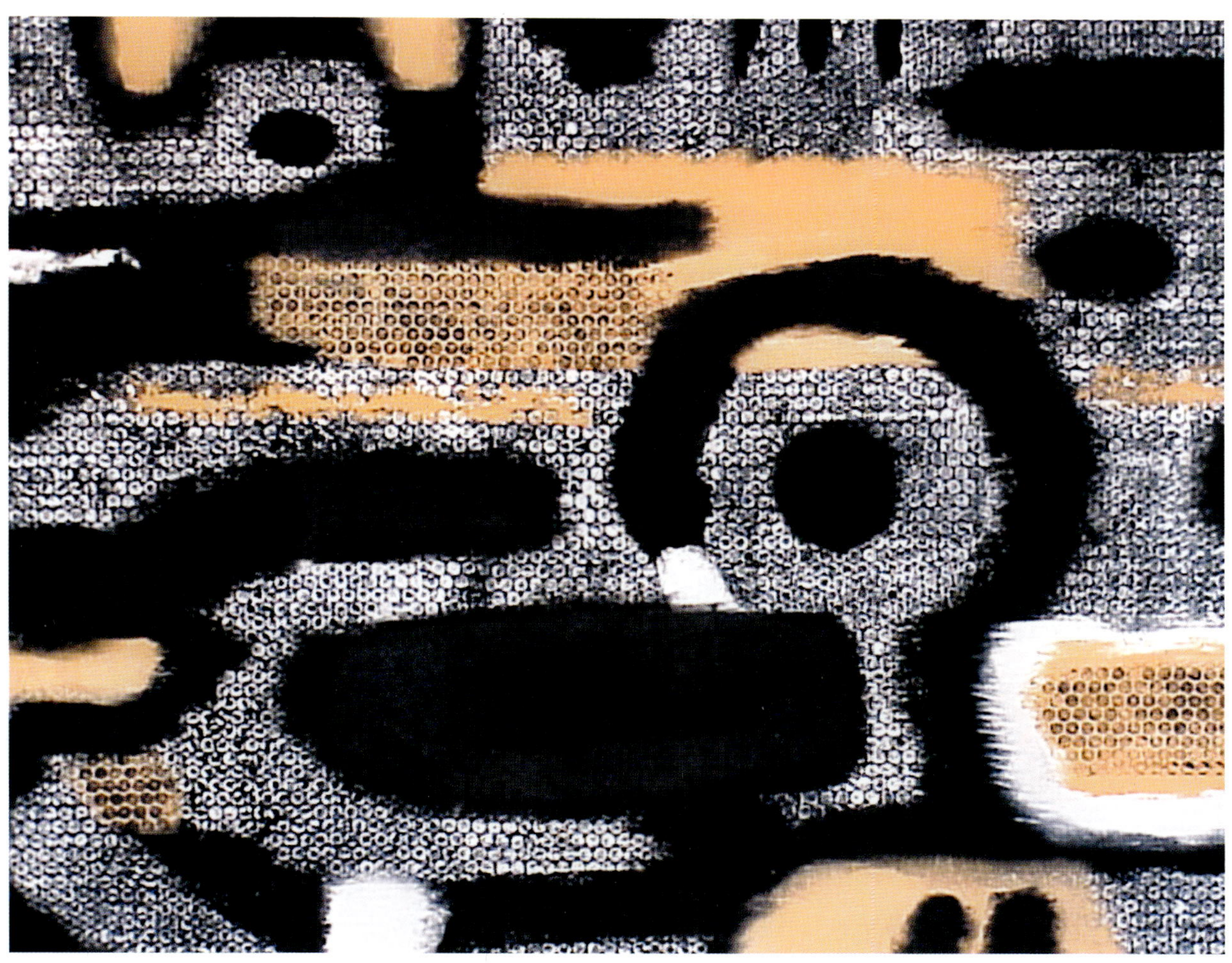

CITY OF SILENCE
SYNTHETIC POLYMER ON BELGIUM LINEN
28 X 36 INCHES

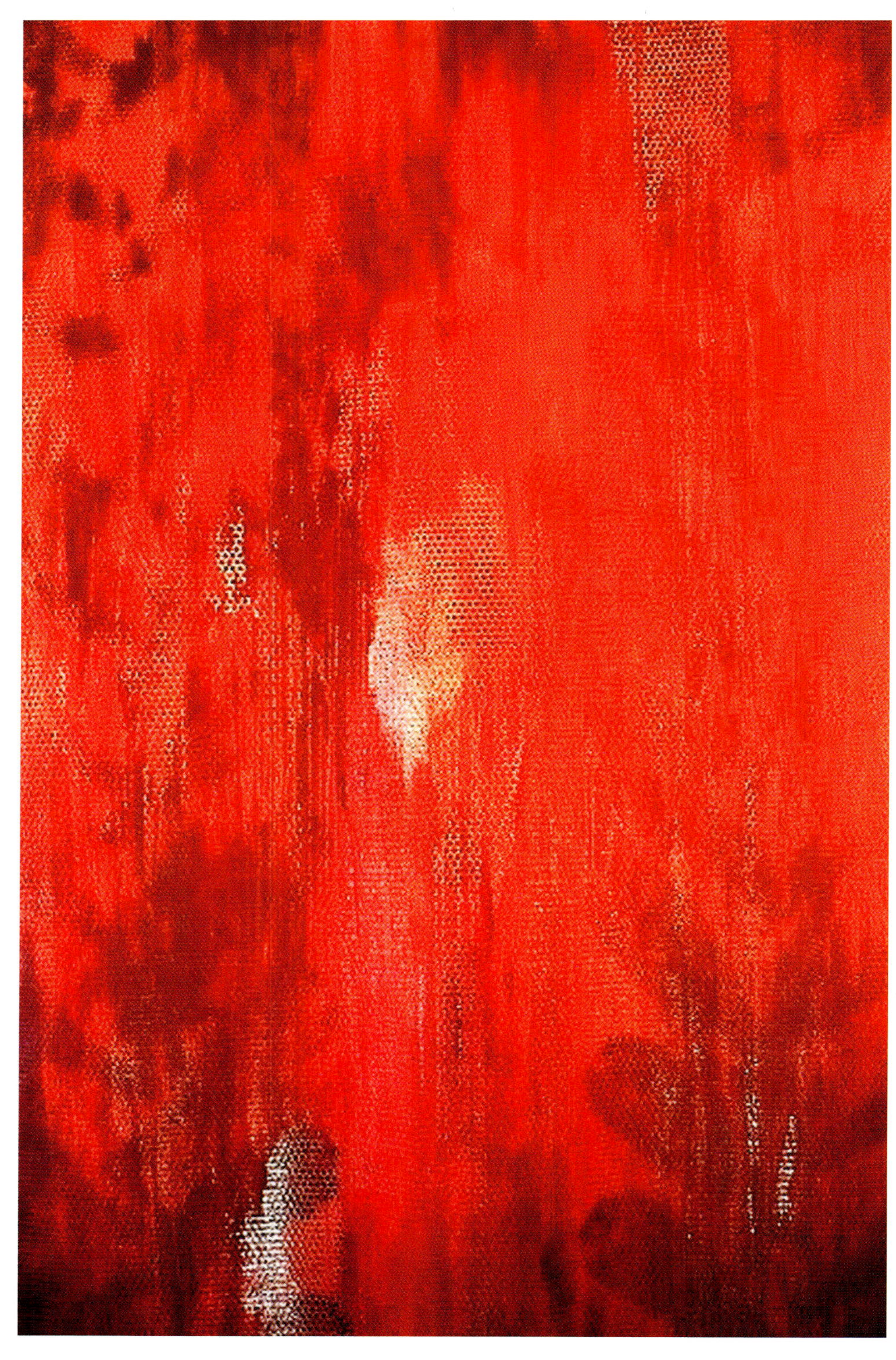

DEAR ALICE
SYNTHETIC POLYMER ON SYNTHETIC POLYMER
108 X 48 INCHES

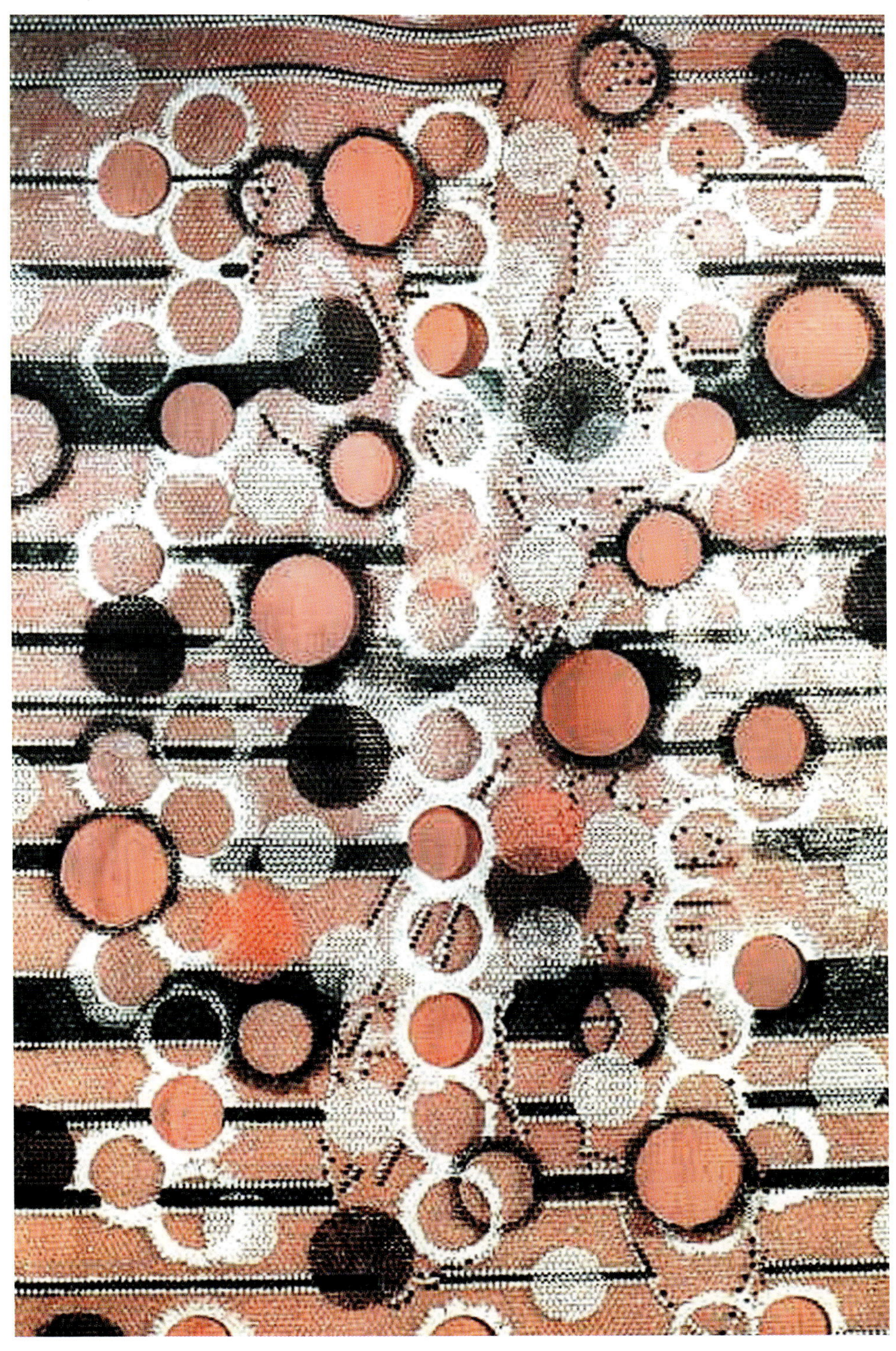

BAR CODE
SYNTHETIC POLYMER ON SYNTHETIC POLYMER
108 X 48 INCHES

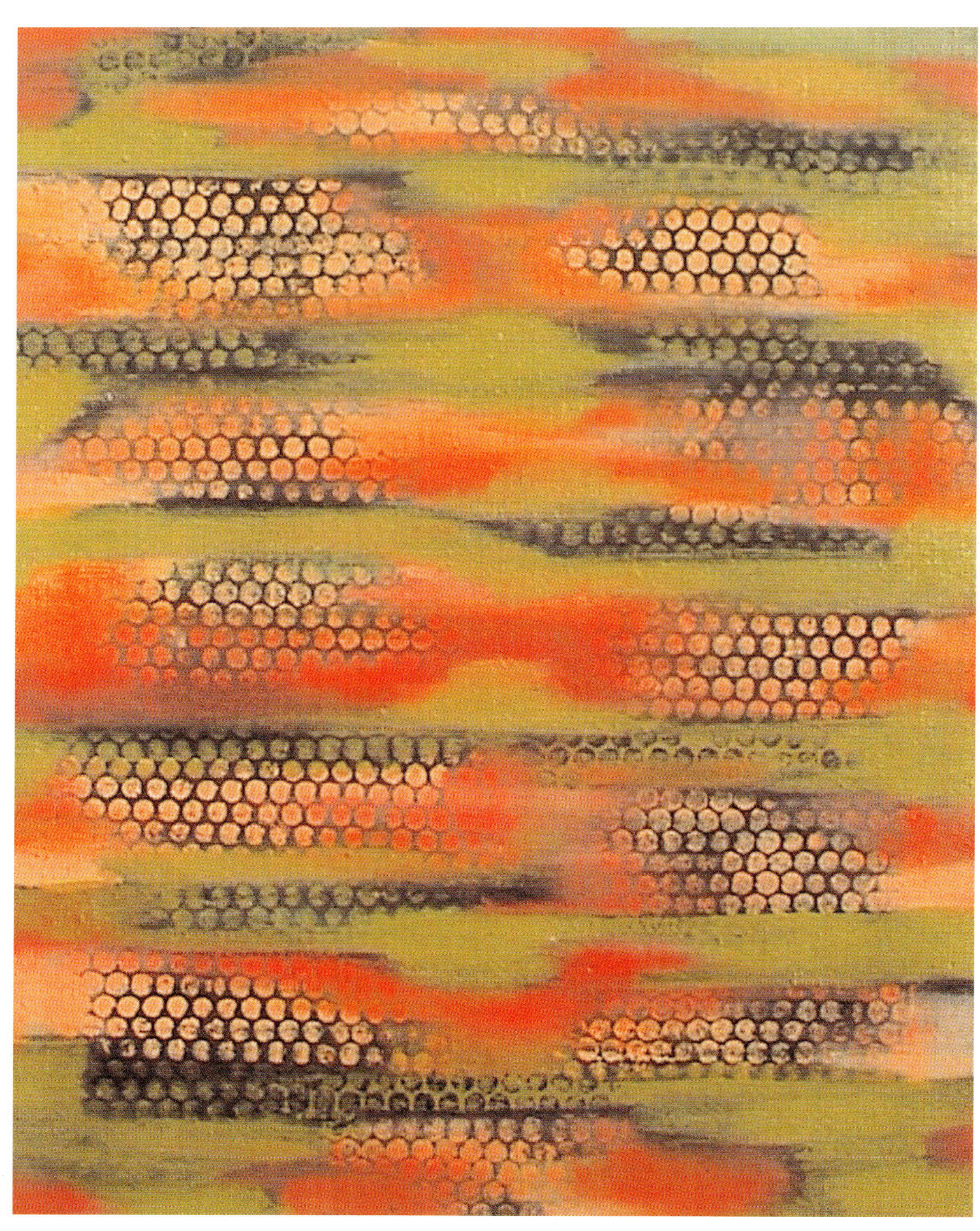

CATERPILLARS AT SUNSET
SYNTHETIC POLYMER ON BELGIUM LINEN
22 X 18 INCHES

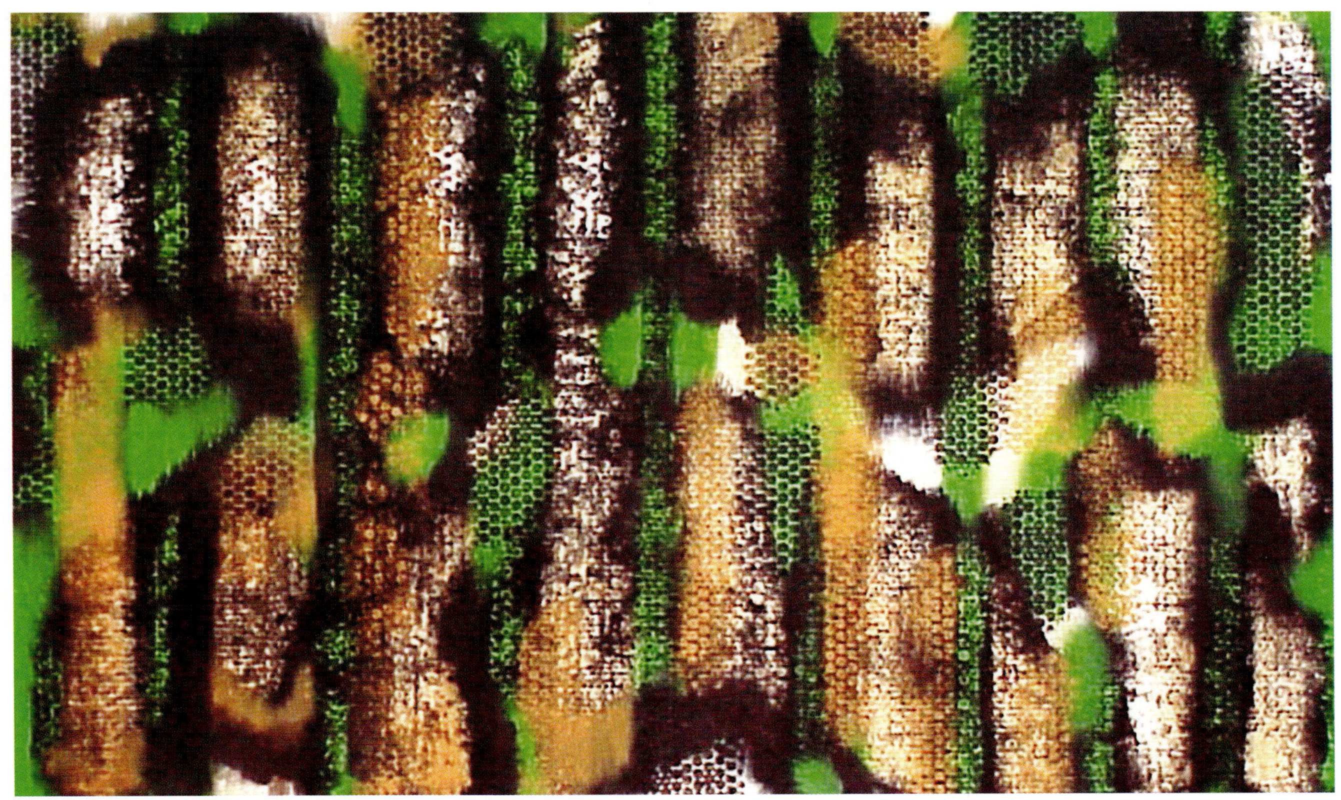

DERUSHA b. 1958 Menominee MI. Ed: BS Univ. Wisconsin; Art Center College of Design, Pasadena CA. Exhib: Univ. Wisconsin; Big Horn Center for Arts and Humanities WY; Araluen Arts Museum, Alice Springs, Australia; etal. Lectures: Fairfield Art Museum WI; Australia; etal. Representation: Derusha Studio, Santa Fe; Watch This Space, Alice Springs NT, Australia.

GREEN CATERPILLARS
SYNTHETIC POLYMER ON BELGIUM LINEN
60 X 28 INCHES

PETER SARKISIAN

When the human figure is put to the service of expressing an abstract idea, it ceases being figurative and becomes an abstraction in itself. It embodies experience; it interprets emotion; it is medium rather than subject.

When a filmmaker becomes a sculptor and creates installations, the projection screen comes off the wall and becomes part of the image. The viewer is forcibly separated from the usual experience of passive observation. Instead, he or she becomes actively engaged with the piece by occupying the same physical space as the art, and by participating in the passage of time.

Peter Sarkisian is in the forefront of a small number of contemporary artists who deal with these concepts using the latest technology. With installations on exhibit all over the world, he is gaining an international reputation. He makes powerful statements about a wide range of subjects and ideas.

Several of his best known pieces have involved the human figure as image, instrument, and metaphor. Utilizing video projected on the planar surfaces of geometric solids, Sarkisian creates impossibly complex environments that evoke memories of events not yet imagined. Ambient whispers emerge from darkness to underscore the isolation of normal experience. In a pair of conjoined cones, bodies are drawn into and expelled from the vortex. In a rectangular cube, a man and a woman jostle for space as they experience its confines. In another cube, a woman and her infant child explore the process by which one person becomes two. Sarkisian also makes use of ordinary objects such as suitcases and newspapers to imprint experience. The suitcases conceal personal artifacts and records of the journey, as the lights and noises of passing traffic isolate them in time. Newspapers, the most ephemeral of reading matter, are given gravity and drag by the mechanical sound of repetition that underscores the lockstep turning of their pages.

Sarkisian grew up in New Mexico as the son of two working artists. Giving form to ideas was a natural part of life, in no way exceptional to the daily round of activities. He experimented freely as a child, and as an adult sought further education in schools that could provide him with the resources he needed. At one point he was awarded a six-month residency in Antibes, France, sponsored by the Picasso Museum.

"I always begin with ideas that excite me and then find ways to work them out using technology," says Sarkisian. "But video as a tool has never triggered an idea for me. The technology alone doesn't interest me." Peter Sarkisian's art involves a mixture of ideas found in life and science, specifically quantum physics. "What does interest me," he says, "Is how the balance of opposites that we find in physics fits so perfectly with life's basic truths, such as the equal and opposite relationship between clarity and obscurity, growth and decay, life and death."

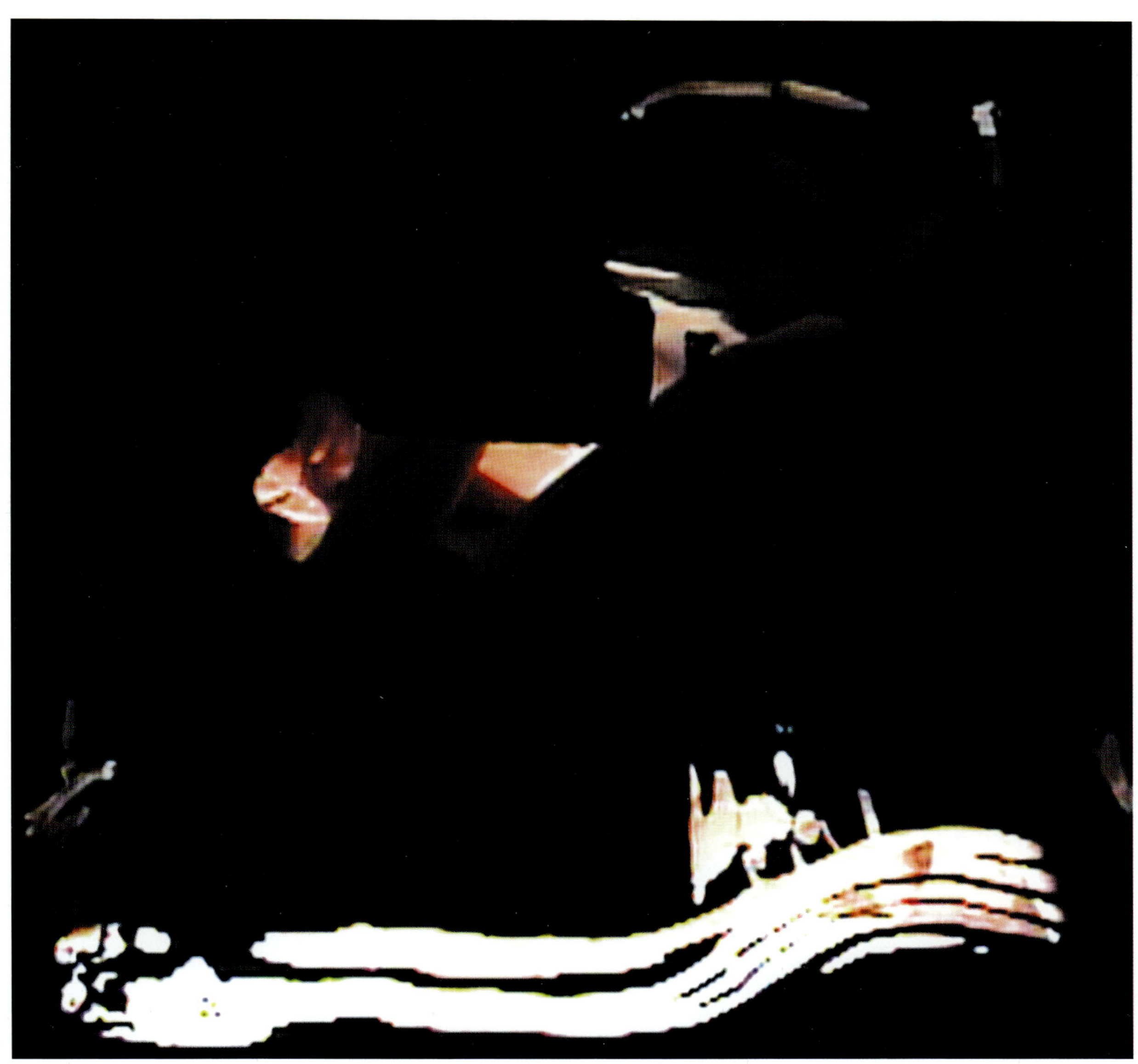

DUSTED
VIDEO STILL I FROM INSTALLATION

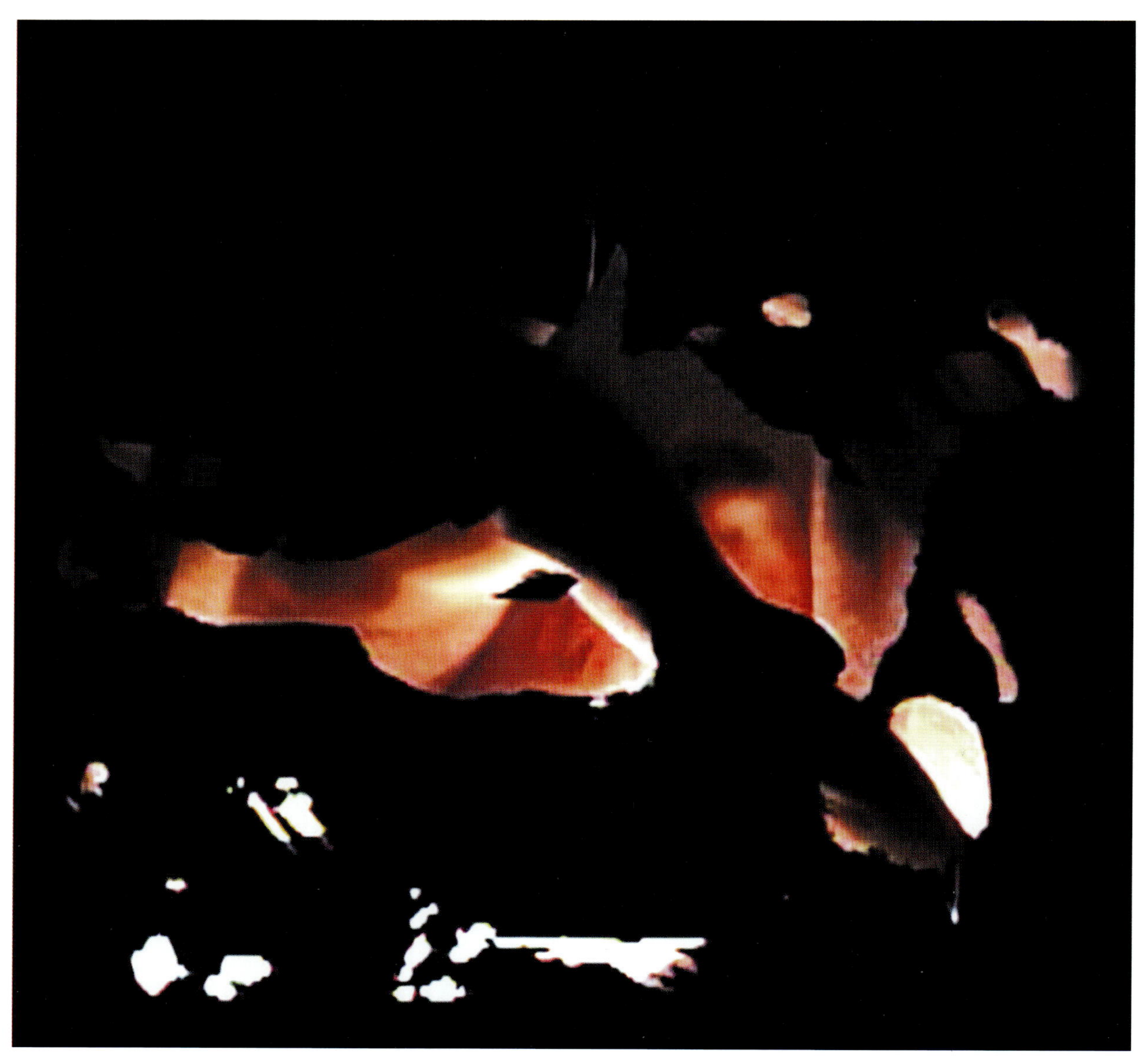

DUSTED
VIDEO STILL 2 FROM INSTALLATION

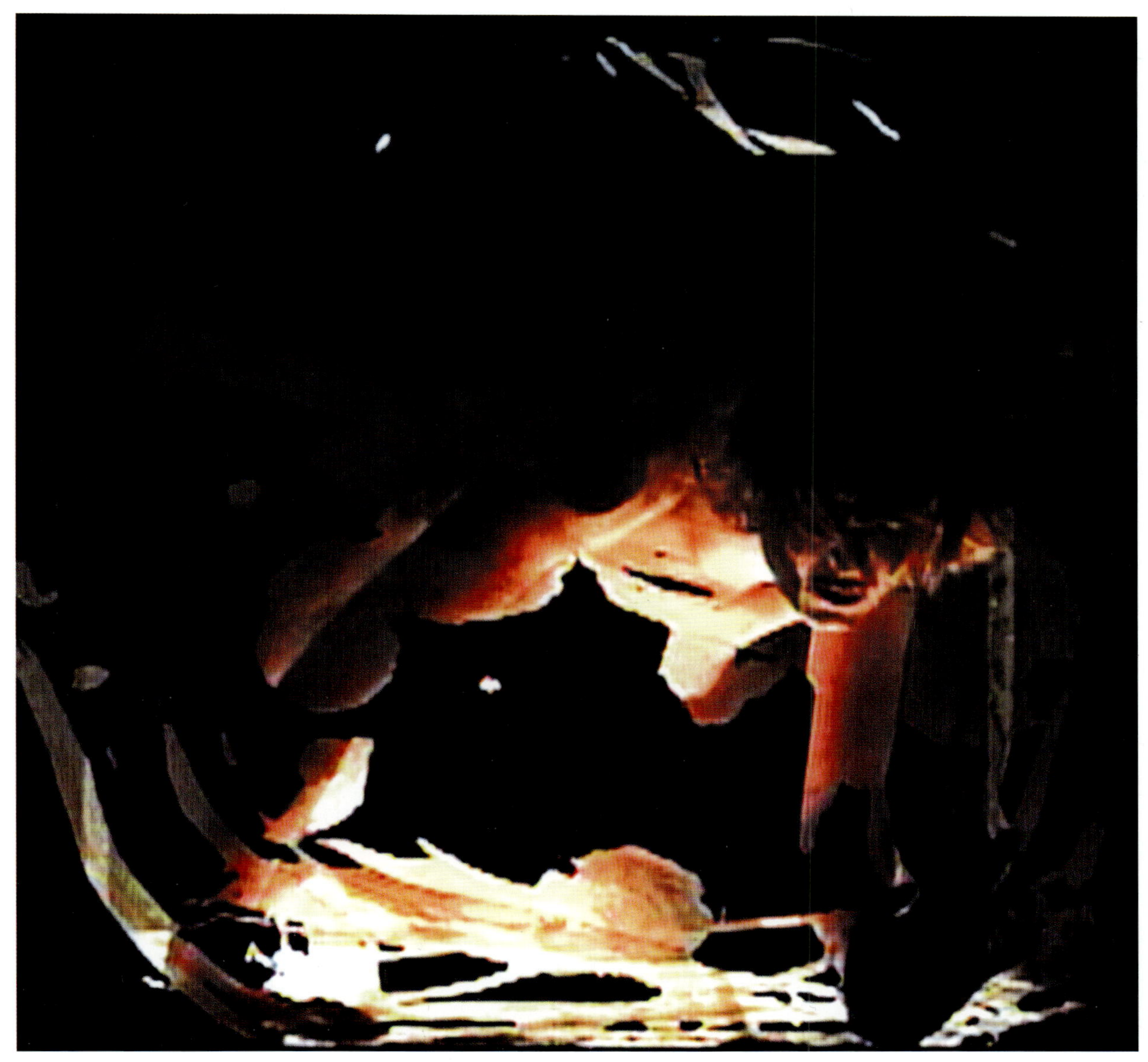

DUSTED
VIDEO STILL 3 FROM INSTALLATION

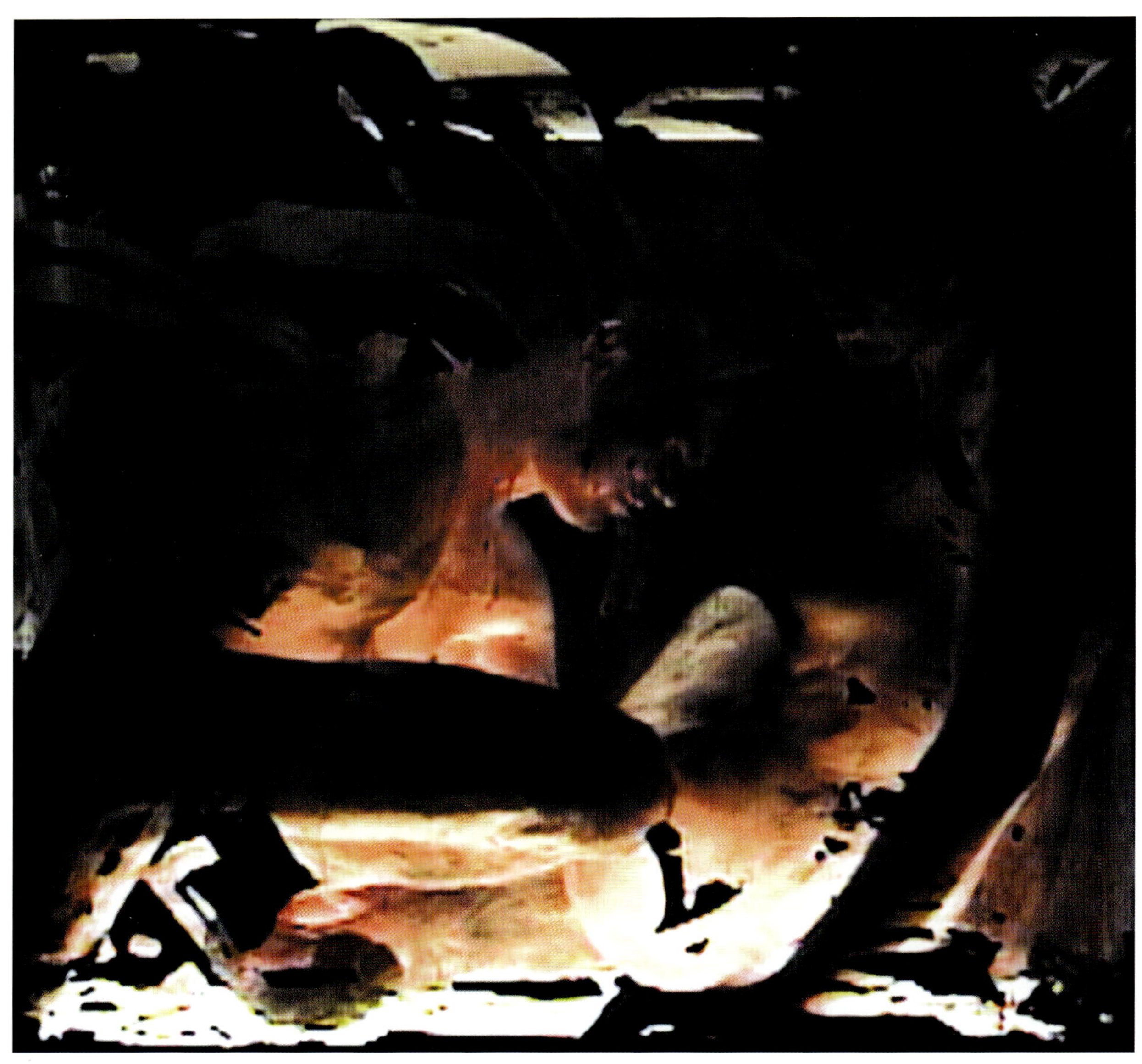

DUSTED
VIDEO STILL 4 FROM INSTALLATION

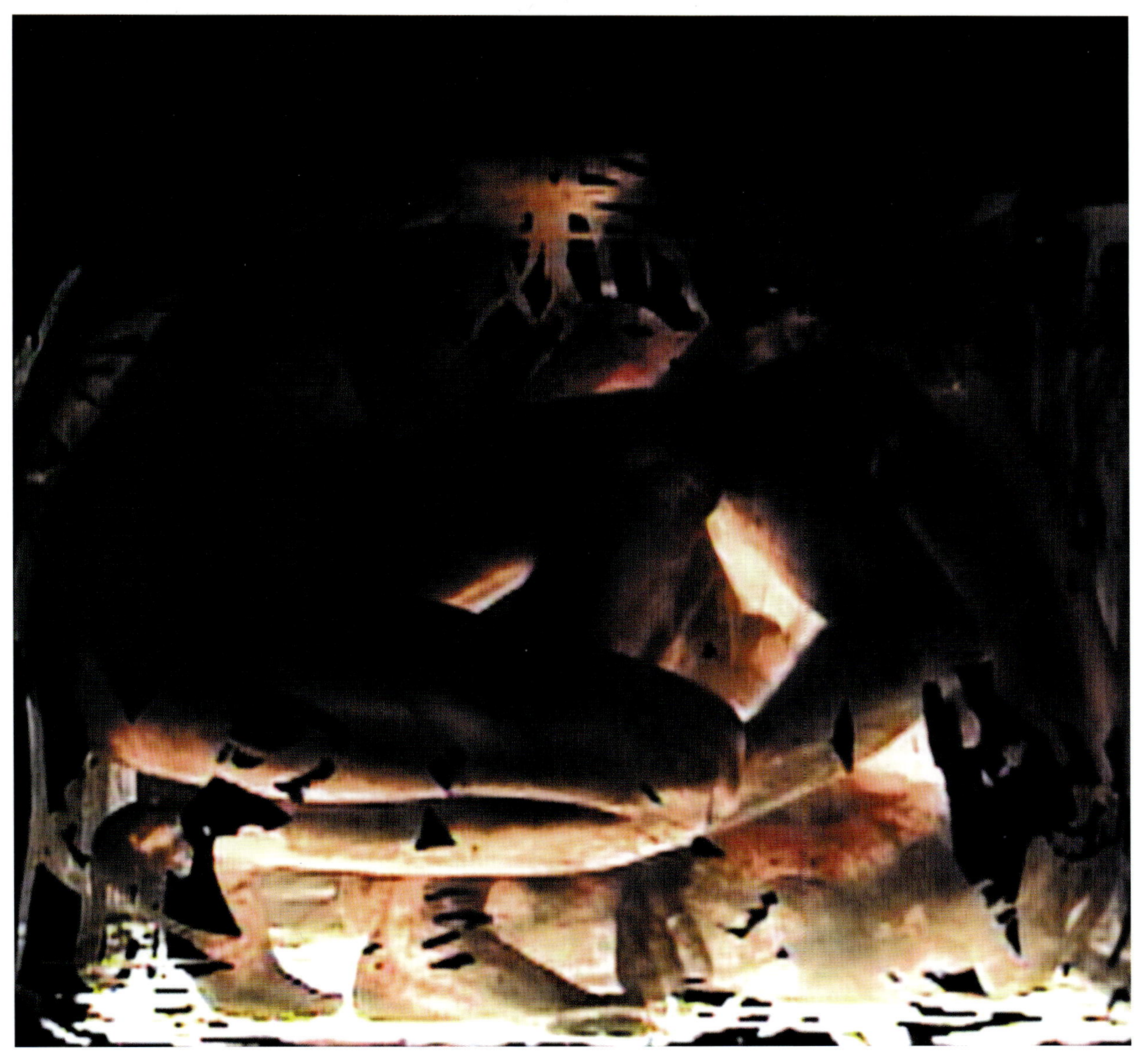

PETER SARKISIAN b. 1965 Glendale CA. Ed: Cal Arts, American Film Institute CA. Solo exhib: Museé Picasso, Antibes France; Edinburgh College of Art, Scotland; Houston Museum of Fine Arts TX; SITE Santa Fe NM. Coll: Whitney Museum of American Art NY; San Francisco Museum of Modern Art CA; Kumamoto Museum of Contemporary Art, Japan. Representation: Linda Durham Contemporary Art, Galisteo NM and New York.

DUSTED
VIDEO STILL 5 FROM INSTALLATION

INDEX

Valdez Abeyta y Valdez
Anderson Contemporary Art, Santa Fe
www.anderson-contemporary.com

Sally Anderson
Anderson Contemporary Art, Santa Fe
www.anderson-contemporary.com

Seth Anderson
Anderson Contemporary Art, Santa Fe
www.anderson-contemporary.com

Garo Antreasian
Cline Fine Art, Santa Fe/Scottsdale
Fenix Gallery, Taos
www.clinefineart.com
www.fenixgallery.com

Bill Barrett
Kouros Gallery, New York
Thomas McCormick Gallery, Chicago
Shidoni Sculpture Gallery, Santa Fe
www.kourosgallery.com
www.thomasmccormick.com
www.shidoni.com

Larry Bell
Larry Bell Studio Annex, Taos
www.larrybell.com

Stan Berning
www.stanberning.com

Derusha
Derusha Studio, Santa Fe
www.trueartist.net

Stephanie Dragon
EVO Gallery, Santa Fe
www.evogallery.org

Frank Ettenberg
Eldridge McCarthy Gallery, Santa Fe
www.eldridgemccarthy.com
www.frankettenberg.com

Linda J Ging
Linda J Ging Studio, Santa Fe
gingworks@comcast.net

Frederick Hammersley
Richard Levy Gallery, Albuquerque
Charlotte Jackson Fine Art, Santa Fe
www.levygallery.com
www.charlottejackson.com

Richard Hogan
Linda Durham Contemporary Art
Galisteo, NM and New York City
www.lindadurham.com

Robert Kelly
Linda Durham Contemporary Art
Galisteo, NM and New York City
John Berggruen Gallery, San Francisco
Senior and Shopmaker Gallery, NYC
Bentley Gallery, Scottsdale
Anne Reed Gallery, Ketchum, ID
Barbara Davis Gallery, Houston
Doug Udell Gallery, Vancouver
and Edmonton, Canada
www.lindadurham.com

Tim Klabunde
Tim Klabunde Studio, Santa Fe
505 473-3880

Nancy Kozikowski
Dartmouth Street Gallery, Albuquerque
www.dsg-art.com

Janet Lippincott
Karan Ruhlen Gallery, Santa Fe
www.karanruhlen.com

Mercedes Little Crow Velarde
Little Crow Gallery, Santa Fe
505 986-8056

Helmut Löhr
EVO Gallery, Santa Fe
www.evogallery.org

Ricardo Mazal
Chiaroscuro Gallery, Santa Fe
www.chiaroscurosantafe.com

Connie Mississippi
Anderson Contemporary Art, Santa Fe
www.anderson-contemporary.com
www.conniemississippi.com

Eugene Newman
Linda Durham Contemporary Art
Galisteo, NM and New York City
www.lindadurham.com

Nancy Ortenstone
Expressions in Fine Art, Santa Fe
Jack Meier Gallery, Houston
Hopkins Fine Art, Scottsdale
Blue Gallery, Kansas City, MO
Bruce McGaw Graphics, W.Nyack, NY
www.expressionsinfinearts.com

Pascal
Seven-O-Seven Contemporary Art
Santa Fe
www.seven-o-seven.com
www.pascalstudio.com

Florence Pierce
Charlotte Jackson Fine Art, Santa Fe
www.charlottejackson.com

Ken Price
Fenix Gallery, Taos
Franklin Parrasch Gallery, NY
L.A. Louver, Venice, CA
www.fenixgallery.com
www.franklinparraschgallery.com
www.kenprice.com

Zacariah Rieke
EVO Gallery, Santa Fe
www.evogallery.org

Alan Paine Radebaugh
Coleman Gallery Contemporary Art
Albuquerque
www.colemancontemporary.com
www.radebaughfineart.com

Johnnie Winona Ross
James Kelly Contemporary, Santa Fe
Richard Levy Gallery, Albuquerque
www.jameskelly.com
www.levygallery.com

Peter Sarkisian
Linda Durham Contemporary Art
Galisteo, NM and New York City
www.lindadurham.com

Sam Scott
Wiford & Vogt Fine Art, Santa Fe
Parks Gallery, Taos
Robischon Gallery, Denver
samscott@taosmesa.com

Richard C Smith
Linda Durham Contemporary Art
Galisteo, NM and New York City
Richard C. Smith Studio, Santa Fe
www.lindadurham.com

Earl Stroh
Fenix Gallery, Taos
www.fenixgallery.com

Kevin Tolman
Karan Ruhlen Gallery, Santa Fe
www.karanruhlen.com

Emmi Whitehorse
LewAllen Contemporary, Santa Fe
www.lewallenart.com

Ernest Wilmeth
Ernest Wilmeth Studio, Albuquerque
Shidoni Gallery
www.shidoni.com
www.ernestwilmeth.com

Michael Wright
Anderson Contemporary Art, Santa Fe
www.anderson-contemporcry.com
www.michaelwrightart.com

Karen Yank
Munson Gallery, Santa Fe
www.munsongallery.com

PHOTOGRAPHY: CREDITS

51: David Nufer
19:52-55: Damian Andrus
67,129: David Marlow
69-73,153-157: Denny Welker/
Image Resources, Inc.
81: Pat Pollard